Africa and Africans
in Antiquity

Africa and Africans
in Antiquity

EDITED BY

EDWIN M. YAMAUCHI

MICHIGAN STATE UNIVERSITY PRESS

EAST LANSING

Michigan State University Press
East Lansing, Michigan 48823-5202

Printed and bound in the United States of America
04 03 02 01   1 2 3 4 5 6

Library of Congress Cataloging-in-Publication Data

Africa and Africans in antiquity / edited by Edwin M. Yamauchi.
    p. cm.
Revision of papers orignally presented at a conference on "Africa and
Africans in Antiquity" on Mar. 1–2, 1991, at Miami University, Oxford,
Ohio.
Includes bibliographical references and index.
    ISBN 0-87013-507-4 (alk. paper)
1. Africa—History—To 1498—Congresses. 2. Africa,
North—History—To 647—Congresses. 3. Africa—Antiquities—Congresses.
4. Africa, North—Antiquities—Congresses. I. Yamauchi, Edwin M.
DT24 .A38 2001
960.1—dc21   2001001603

Cover design by Nicolette Rose
Book design by Bookcomp, Inc.

Cover photo: Herm with the head of a Negro (Front) from the Baths
of Antoninus Pius, Carthage. Courtesy, Musée National du Bardo, Tunis.

Visit Michigan State University Press on the World Wide Web at:
www.msupress.msu.edu

Dedicated to Our Colleague
A True Gentleman and Scholar

MAYNARD W. SWANSON

1929–95

Contents

Abbreviations

AEL I	Miriam Lichtheim, *Ancient Egyptian Literature I* (1975)
AEL II	Miriam Lichtheim, *Ancient Egyptian Literature II* (1976)
AfrIt	*Africa Italiana*
AHR	*American Historical Review*
AHS	*African Historical Studies*
AJA	*American Journal of Archaeology*
AJP	*American Journal of Philology*
ANRW	*Aufstieg und Niedergang der römischen Welt*
ASAE	*Annales du Service des Antiquités de l'Égypt*
BAR	*British Archaeological Reports*
BIFAO	*Bulletin de l'Institut Français d'Archéologie Orientale*
BSA	*Annual, British School at Athens*
BSR	*Papers of the British School at Rome*
CP	*Classical Philology*
CR	*Classical Review*
CRAI	*Comptes-rendus des séances de l'Académie des Inscriptions et Belles Lettres*
CRIPEL	*Cahiers de Recherches de l'Institut de Papyrologie et d'Égyptologie de Lille*
GJ	*Geographical Journal*
HAS	*Harvard African Studies*
HTR	*Harvard Theological Review*
IFAO	*Institut Français d'Archéologie Orientale*
IJAHS	*International Journal of African Historical Studies*
JAA	*Journal of Anthropological Archaeology*
JAH	*Journal of African History*
JARCE	*Journal of the American Research Center in Egypt*
JEA	*Journal of Egyptian Archaeology*
JES	*Journal of Ethiopian Studies*

JFA	*Journal of Field Archaeology*
JHS	*Journal of Hellenic Studies*
JMA	*Journal of Mediterranean Anthropology and Archaeology*
JNES	*Journal of Near Eastern Studies*
JRS	*Journal of Roman Studies*
JSSEA	*Journal of the Society for the Study of Egyptian Antiquities*
JWP	*Journal of World Prehistory*
LA	W. Helck et al., eds., *Lexicon der Ägyptologie* (1972–86)
MDAIK	*Mitteilungen der deutschen Archäologischen Instituts, Abteilung Kairo*
MIFAO	*Mémoires de l'Institut Français d'Archéologie Orientale*
QAL	*Quaderni di Archeologia della Libia*
RdE	*Revue d'Égyptologie*
REL	*Revue des Études Latines*
RSO	*Rivista degli Studi Orientali*
SLS	*Annual Report of the Society for Libyan Studies*
ZÄS	*Zeitschrift für ägyptische Sprache und Altertumskunde*
ZPE	*Zeitschrift für Papyrologie und Epigraphik*

Figures

Acknowledgments

❈

A panel of distinguished scholars participated in a conference on "Africa and Africans in Antiquity" on 1–2 March 1991, at Miami University, Oxford, Ohio. This was made possible by the E. E. McClellan Lecture Fund and by the assistance of the Departments of Art, Classics, Geography, Sociology and Anthropology, the Department of Affirmative Action, the Provost's Office, the College of Arts and Sciences, and the Graduate School. I would like to record my thanks to my colleagues, Professors Sherman Jackson and Maynard W. Swanson for their assistance in convening the conference.

I am especially grateful for the contributions of the nine scholars, each distinguished in his or her specialty, who participated in the conference and who revised their papers for this volume. I am also pleased to include the essay of Professors Bard and Fattovich, who were not participants at this conference. It was gratifying to learn of the keen interest in the subject from both those who attended and those who corresponded with us about the conference.

The support and the patience of Professor Harold G. Marcus, Editor of the Africa Series, Michigan State University, and of Dr. Frederic Bohm, Director of the Michigan State University Press, have been warmly appreciated. I am also grateful to Annette K. Tanner, who supervised the production of the book.

I am especially grateful to our secretary, Liz Smith, who did most of the retyping, and to my wife, Kimie, who also did some of the typing. Michael Lucas, a graduate student in the Geography Department prepared many of the maps. Funds for photos were provided by the History Department, the Classics Department, the Art Department, and the College of Arts and Sciences.

Introduction

EDWIN M. YAMAUCHI

❋

In the past European and American historians have treated much of the African past with condescension, which today would be recognized as racism (see especially the essays by S. Burstein and M. W. Swanson). On the other hand, in recent years Afrocentric scholars, in seeking to reclaim the achievements of the continent for African Americans, have gone to the other extreme in claiming that they are the rightful heirs to the glories of Egypt, as though the Egyptians were black Africans.[1] This is rather ironic in that the Egyptians were among the most ethnocentric of all peoples, and generally regarded black Africans of Nubia, as well as all other non-Egyptians, with contempt.

This volume re-examines northeast Africa, as this is the area which is best documented for antiquity by texts, monuments, and archaeological excavations. We must recognize that this was a multi-ethnic and multi-cultural region, which included Phoenicians and Berbers in Carthage, Greeks in Cyrene, as well as Egyptians and Nubians. Though the outstanding culture was indeed that of Egypt, the Nubians south of Egypt did make their own contributions, and established the little known but remarkable kingdom of Meroe, which endured for nearly a millennium.

Linguist Carleton T. Hodge examines the linguistic relations of this region in his essay *"Afroasiatic."* He reviews the history of research in these languages, noting that the term "Afroasiatic" was first coined by Joseph Greenberg in 1950. He then examines how far back in time each of these languages is attested in writing. Egyptian has the longest history, stretching well over three millennia, with Semitic dialects also well attested. Berber is attested only from the second century B.C. The other languages are known only from recent times. Hodge also lists the linguistic and lexical references which are available for some of these languages.

He notes in chart form the well-documented relationships between

1

Egyptian and Semitic languages. The proto-language of these two branches, which was formerly known as Hamito-Semitic, but which is now called Afroasiatic, includes four other language groups: 1) Berber in North Africa; 2) Chadic in west central Africa; 3) Omotic and 4) Cushitic which are both spoken in the Horn of East Africa. He notes that languages included under this rubric form two west-to-east tiers: 1) a northern tier (Berber, Egyptian, Semitic), and 2) a southern tier (Chadic, Omotic, Cushitic). After summarizing the comparative studies of the last 20 years, he gives many specific examples to illustrate their relationships. He also sets forth their putative sound correspondences. Hodge points out some interesting phonological similarities between Semitic, Egyptian, and Hausa, a language spoken in Nigeria.

Egyptologist Frank J. Yurco in "*Egypt and Nubia: Old, Middle, and New Kingdom Eras,*" summarizes the relationship between Egypt and its southern neighbor (now mainly in the Sudan) over a period of two millennia. An abundance of archaeological evidence has been provided by the surveys and salvage excavations, which were undertaken before Lake Nasser, which was created by the High Aswan Dam, inundated the area. Following the lead of Bruce Williams, Yurco claims that the antecedents for pharaonic Egypt came from Qustul, a site in Nubia, which had a royal cemetery dated c. 3300 B.C. Yurco suggests that the wealth of the Qustul monarchy was due to mineral resources and the control of trade. As early as the First Dynasty pharaohs such as Aha sent expeditions to Nubia. During the Old Kingdom (Dynasties III–VI) the Egyptians periodically raided Nubia, bringing back numerous captives who were integrated into Egyptian society. From the Sixth Dynasty, we have the informative autobiographies of such officials as Weni and Harkhuf, who conducted expeditions deep into Nubia.

In contrast with earlier scholars, Yurco emphasizes the continuity between the so-called "A-Group" and the later "C-Group" of Nubians. After the Egyptians, during the Old Kingdom, virtually eliminated the A-Group, the related C-Group moved into Nubia. During Egypt's weakness in the First Intermediate Period (Dynasties VII–X), Nubia flourished. The founder of the Twelfth Theban Dynasty (Middle Kingdom) may have had some Nubian blood in his ancestry. The pharaohs of this dynasty, such as Senwosret I and Senwosret III, built numerous forts near the second cataract, the remains of which are among those inundated under Lake Nasser. Among measures designed to control the Nubians were magical execration texts.

When Lower Egypt was invaded by the Hyksos during the Second

Intermediate Period, a strong Kushite center developed at Kerma in Nubia. Archaeological and textual evidences indicate that the Hyksos maintained friendly contacts with the Kushites against their common enemy in Upper Egypt. Scholars are divided as to what happened to the Egyptian garrisons in Nubia at this time. Yurco suggests that some of the Egyptians became subject to the Kushite king, and that others may have joined forces with the C-Group.

The expulsion of the Hyksos from Egypt by the Eighteenth Theban Dynasty once again saw the dominance of Egypt in Nubia. Thutmose I invaded Kush, slaying its king and penetrating as far south as the fourth cataract. The famous female pharaoh, Hatshepsut, launched three campaigns deep into Nubia. Her successor, Thutmose III, established the key site of Napata by the sacred mountain, Gebel Barkal.

Despite the pejorative rhetoric of the Egyptians, who referred customarily to the Kushites as "vile" or "wretched," individual Nubians did find places in the royal harem and in the Egyptian nobility. Egyptianized Nubians, especially the Medja, played a major role in the army and police forces. Some Nubian gods were also honored.

Art historian Edna R. Russmann in "*Egypt and the Kushites: Dynasty XXV*," reviews the remarkable ascendance of the Kushites in the south (i.e. in the area of modern Sudan) to dominance over Egypt for a half-century (716–656 B.C.). She notes that classical writers called these people "Ethiopians" (from the Greek *aithiops* "sun-burned face"), and that modern writers refer to them as Nubians. Although deeply indebted to the Egyptians in language and religion, the Kushites manifested many indigenous traits such as their system of royal succession and bed burial under a tumulus.

As noted in Yurco's essay, a great kingdom developed at Kerma during the eighteenth-sixteenth centuries B.C. After the long domination of this area during the Egyptian New Kingdom, a powerful new state was developed by the Kushites during the so-called Third Intermediate or Post-Empire period of Egyptian history.

Kashta, i.e. "The Kushite," was the first to claim the right to rule over Egypt but he may not have penetrated north of Nubia. His son Piankhy invaded Egypt c. 730 and succeeded in capturing Memphis in Lower, i.e. northern, Egypt. Russmann considers Shabako, who remained in Egypt, as the "true founder" of the Twenty-Fifth Dynasty. Traces of his building activities may be found throughout Egypt. Shebitku was emboldened to intervene in Palestine against the expanding Assyrian power. His nephew, the famous Taharqa, left many buildings, most notably at Thebes and also

at Gebel Barkal, the sacred mountain of Nubia. It was in Taharqa's reign
that the Assyrians under Esarhaddon and Ashurbanipal, invaded expelling
the Kushites from Egypt. Tanwetamani launched a counter-attack, but the
Assyrians responded by penetrating as far south as Thebes, forcing the
Nubians back to their ancestral homeland in the area of Napata. Psamtik
II of the Twenty-Sixth or Saite Dynasty, which was now free of Assyrian
control, attacked Kushite territory, prompting the Kushites to move their
center further south to Meroe.

Russmann reviews the recent findings of Timothy Kendall at the site
of Gebel Barkal, which is a spectacular plateau rising dramatically from the
plain. His insights help us to understand the Kushite crown with the double uraeus (cobra) emblem. Russmann discusses the evidence of the small
pyramid tombs of the Kushite kings and queens in the cemeteries near
Gebel Barkal. Important remains of the Kushite rulers were also found at
Thebes, the capital of Upper Egypt, and at Memphis, the capital of Lower
Egypt, including the famous Shabako stone, which contains an account of
the so-called "Memphite Theology" of Ptah. Russmann concludes that
the Kushite statues successfully emulated the Old Kingdom models.

Historian Stanley M. Burstein describes the fascinating story of *"The
Kingdom of Meroe,"* which, though it was well known to the Greeks and
Romans, has until recently been neglected. Meroe, which was one of the
southernmost cities known to the Greeks, was located 600 miles south of
Aswan just below the juncture of the Atbara and Nile Rivers (in the
Sudan). One of the problems which has hindered progress is the incom-
plete decipherment of the Meroitic language, which was written in a script
derived from Egyptian. Another problem was its isolation, making contact with Greeks and Romans episodic.

The site was first rediscovered by James Bruce in 1772. Many subsequent travelers left important descriptions of monumental ruins, which in
some cases have disappeared. Burstein reviews the attempts to excavate
Meroitic sites, including the rather unsatisfactory efforts of E. A. W.
Budge and John Garstang, which were destructive and poorly published.
He highlights especially the efforts of George Reisner early in the twentieth century. Though Reisner laid the foundations for all subsequent studies in establishing a chronological framework by his study of the royal pyramids, his views stressed the Egyptian contribution to the slighting of
indigenous elements.

The area of Meroe far to the south of Lake Nasser has not profited
from the flurry of salvage excavations and surveys to the north, but those
efforts have indirectly stimulated the field of Meroitic studies, which has

been invigorated by scholars from a variety of disciplines. These new studies have forced a revision of earlier views of Meroitic history, underlining the independent policies of Meroe in the face of Ptolemaic influence. Instead of the decline during the Roman period postulated by Reisner, recent scholars have viewed this period as a time of prosperity.

Anthropologist William Y. Adams relates recent archaeological discoveries to illuminate *"The Ballaña Kingdom and Culture: Twilight of Classical Nubia."* The Ballaña Kingdom developed between the first and the third cataracts of the Nile from a blending of Byzantine and Egyptian influences with the local culture. Though their own writing consists of only a handful of inscriptions in a kind of "pidgin Greek," this area was noted by classical and Christian writers. These notices spoke of warlike peoples called the Blemmye and the Nobatae (Nobadae), who fought both the Romans and each other. Both groups, however, were united in their worship of the Egyptian goddess Isis. What eventually emerged was a pseudo-Byzantine state rather than a Kushite successor state.

Important new archaeological data on this kingdom have been provided by surveys and excavations of the twentieth century, particularly from the last twenty years. The earliest surveys were conducted by George Reisner when the Aswan Low Dam was constructed. Reisner labeled the four indigenous cultures which he discovered the A, B, C, and X Groups. While the first three were contemporary with the great Egyptian Kingdoms, the last formed the link between the Kushite and the Medieval eras. It appears that the rulers of the latter may have resided in the fortress of Qasr Ibrim, and may have been buried in the graves of Ballaña and Qustul. Reisner excavated 418 graves in 28 cemeteries with remains of the X-Group, but did not excavate any townsites.

C. L. Woolley, excavating for the University of Pennsylvania, did uncover a townsite at Karanòg, but this was not at first associated with the X-Group because of an error in dating the finds. When the Aswan Dam was raised a second time, new surveys were conducted between 1929 and 1934. The most spectacular results came from the uncovering of huge tumuli at Ballaña and Qustul near the Sudanese border. The excavator, W. B. Emery, identified these finds with the Blemmyes mentioned in the texts, though these sites were farther south than the territories mentioned in the literature.

More recent discoveries have revealed that the X-Group, now called the Ballaña culture, extended from Aswan to Sai Island or over 300 miles. The numerous surveys carried out prior to the completion of the new High Dam at Aswan have now yielded more than 100 new Ballaña sites including the stratified mound of Meinarti. These new data have now shown that the X-Group was not a mysterious outside population but a continuation of earlier indigenous groups.

Excavations by the Czechs of two large cemeteries near Kalabasha, which has been identified as the Blemmyan capital, have revealed a culture, which was different from the X-Group assemblage. This led Eugen Strouhal to suggest that the X-Group should be identified with the Nobadae. One of the most dramatic sites, which is still elevated above the waters of Lake Nasser, is the fortified bluff of Qasr Ibrim. Here the Ballaña levels have yielded a wealth of materials, including basketry and textiles. The latter indicates that the new cultivation of cotton may have been a key to the site's prosperity. Important religious structures indicate the worship of the Greco-Roman Isis. Here alone in Nubia Byzantine coins have been found. Most significant is a letter in "pidgin Greek" from a Blemmyan king Phonen responding to an offer of peace by a Nobadian king Abourni. This may indicate that Qasr Ibrim was the Nobadian capital, though alternative sites are now underwater.

The current situation leaves us with substantial textual information on the Blemmyes, and rich archaeological data for the Nobadae. Though the classical texts indicate that both groups were newcomers, the graves of the commoners reveal strong elements of continuity with the earlier Kushites. On the other hand, the Nobadae used an East Sudanic language. Adams proposes that the Nobadae were already present in the Nile Valley during late Kushite times, but adopted Meroitic as their official language. He also suggests that the Blemmyes, who were never very numerous, moved into territory evacuated by the Romans and established hegemony over Nobadae. Archaeological evidence confirms the rapid Christianization of the Nobadae in the sixth century A.D. By this time the Blemmyes were pushed out into the Red Sea Hills, where they also were evangelized.

Geologist and archaeologist Reuben Bullard examines "*The Berbers of the Maghreb and Ancient Carthage.*" He first describes the geological formations of the Maghreb, i.e. western North Africa, including Morocco, Algeria, Tunisia and Libya, as well as the region's climate and vegetation. He then introduces us to the history of modern excavations of ancient Carthage in present-day Tunisia. Carthage was the great Phoenician colony, founded according to tradition in the late ninth century B.C. The expansion of the modern city of Tunis has encroached upon the ancient ruins. Since the appeal of the Tunisian Institute of Art and Archaeology to UNESCO in 1972, a concerted international effort has been undertaken to survey and excavate these ruins.

The Carthaginians, and thereafter the Romans and other colonizers, encountered an indigenous people, the Berbers, whose customs and culture have changed little over the centuries. The name "Berber" is derived from the Greek *barbaros* "strange," hence the related word "barbarian." The Berbers appear to have been indigenous to the area of North Africa since antiquity. Since we have no texts of the ancient Berbers themselves, Bullard uses the insights of "ethno-archaeology," that is the observations of modern Berbers, to elucidate the traits of the ancient indigenous peoples.

After describing the arrival of the Phoenicians and the beginning of Carthage, he examines in detail the excavations of the harbor areas, and comments in particular on the variety of stones used and their quarries. No doubt the most striking discoveries are those of the cremated remains of the sacrifices of children from the Tophet area, which confirm Roman descriptions of this practice.[2]

Bullard relates the history of three major Berber kingdoms: 1) the Moors in Mauritania (Morocco), 2) the Massaesylins in the area east of the Moulouga River to Numidia, and 3) the Massylins in Numidia proper. He reviews the extraordinary careers of the ancient Berber chiefs, Masinissa and Jugurtha, whom the Romans encountered in Numidia in the hinterland of Carthage. He then summarizes the transition from Punic to Roman dominance in North Africa, also noting the importance of Christian leaders and movements arising out of the Berbers. He finally comments on the outstanding mosaics, ceramic products, and the use of stones by the Romans in the area of Carthage.

Archaeologist Donald White presents *"An Archaeological Survey of the Cyrenaican and Marmarican Regions of Northeast Africa."* These are the little known coastal regions of eastern Libya (Cyrenaica) and western Egypt (Marmarica). Because of the area's isolation and the ferocity of the Bedouins, few European travelers ventured into the area until the eighteenth century. Travelers in the next century left invaluable accounts, much more so of Cyrenaica than of Marmarica.

Cyrenaica was dominated by the Greek colony of Cyrene, founded in 631 B.C., at the base of a 2000-foot high mountain, the Gebel Akhdar "Green Mountain." Blessed with perennial springs and sufficient rainfall, Cyrene prospered along with the four other cities of its Pentapolis—its port Apollonia, Barcaia, Tauchira, and Euesperides. Much of the territory to the east was sparsely habited, though inland was the famed oasis of Siwa with its oracle temple of Zeus Ammon that was visited by Alexander the Great in 331 B.C.

Egyptian sources provide abundant information on the Libyan tribes of the area of Mamarica, who eventually invaded Egypt, settled in the western Delta, and even provided a number of late dynasties which ruled Egypt. Much later, Herodotus also included some valuable observations about the Libyans.

Since 1985, White has been excavating a settlement at the end of a lagoon east of Marsa Matruh, which has provided the first assemblage of Libyan cultural objects from an occupation site, though it was not itself a Libyan settlement but a way-station maintained possibly by Cypriote mariners. This was the only usable natural harbor between Cyrenaica and Alexandria.

Cyrene, where White has also excavated, has provided an abundance of Greek and Roman monuments. In 1966, White found, just outside the city walls, a rich deposit of votive dedications from the Archaic Era (631–500 B.C.), including a *kouros* torso and two *korai*. Bronze sheets, which once adorned a building, depict wrestlers. These materials were evidently buried after the Persian expedition of 515 B.C. had destroyed the building. Whereas earlier archaeologists concentrated on recovering monumental statuary, more recent American, British, and Italian expeditions have paid attention to more mundane objects like pottery.

Cyrene, during the Classical and Hellenistic Eras (500–100 B.C.), produced outstanding sculptural and architectural monuments, including the enormous Temple of Zeus, which was longer than the Parthenon. The copy of the colossal statue of Zeus by Phidias was destroyed by the Christians except for its fingers and toes.

Though partially submerged, the port of Apollonia has yielded important remains to Italian, American, and French excavators. These include a largely intact Hellenistic wall, and three splendid Byzantine churches. The city of Ptolemais, refounded by Ptolemy III (246–221 B.C.), was a large city that has only been partially excavated. One structure is a magnificent villa, the so-called *Palazzo delle colonne*.

The Romans absorbed the Pentapolis in 96 B.C. The emperors, from Augustus on, made important dedications, especially at Cyrene. The major revolt of Jews under Trajan wreaked havoc at Cyrene in 115. Hadrian established a new city called Hadrianapolis between Berenice and Tauchira. Excavations by the Libyans have been conducted in the city of Benghazi, which lies over the remains of ancient Berenice. In the countryside there is evidence that Roman techniques contributed to agricultural prosperity during the second century A.D. One negative development was the disappearance of the valuable silphium plant due to unrestricted grazing.

For the Byzantine Era our richest resource is the writing of Synesios, the famous bishop of Cyrene. His letters reveal a situation of privation and insecurity caused by the raids of tribal peoples. Archaeological remains from this period include numerous churches with splendid mosaics, such as the church at Gasr el-Lebia.

Classicist Frank M. Snowden, Jr. discusses *"Attitudes toward Blacks in the Greek and Roman World: Misinterpretations of the Evidence."* He begins by defining several terms. The word "Ethiopian," derived from the Greek *Aethiops,* originally meant "sun-burnt face," and was used by Greeks and Romans when referring to dark- and black-skinned people south of Egypt. Ancient literary and artistic representations included not only skin color, but also wooly hair, broad noses, and thick lips as typical of such peoples.

Snowden reviews past treatments of this subject including G. H. Beardsley's *The Negro in Greek and Roman Civilization* (1929), which he faults for several failings, including a tendency to read back into the texts modern ideas of color prejudice. This was also the general trend in works prior to Snowden's own comprehensive studies (*Blacks in Antiquity* [1970]; *Before Color Prejudice* [1983], though earlier a few perceptive scholars realized the difference between ancient and modern attitudes.

Snowden then responds to critics of his thesis, who cite the so-called ugliness of artistic representation of negroes, black-white symbolism, and certain beliefs about physiognomy. He argues that ancient depictions are not distortions but are accurate portrayals, which were not intended as denigrating. He notes that ancient theories as well as Janiform jars (two-faced jars) used blacks as typifying southern extremes just as white Scythians typified the northern extremes. He concludes that the Greeks and Romans regarded black and white skin as accidents without any necessary stigma attached to them.

He also discusses various views of beauty, some of which included a preference for women with dark or black skin. He takes issue with L.A. Thompson's view of a famous description of a black woman as an example of mockery, as well as some scholarly interpretations of passages in Juvenal and Seneca. In spite of the widespread association of white with good and black with evil, Snowden contends that in view of the overall favorable attitude towards blacks in the Greek and Roman world, it is not likely that such symbolic associations had an adverse affect on day to day relations.

Snowden finally examines references to blacks among early Christian writers such as Augustine. While it is true that blackness or Ethiopians were often associated with demons, this did not affect the status of blacks in the Church. On the other hand, Ethiopians also represented the universality of the Gospel as seen in the exegesis of Origen and Augustine. One of the outstanding monks of Egypt was the black Moses, who left behind seventy disciples. Snowden concludes that there is no evidence that the classical or Christian use of black as a symbol for evil meant the rationalization of black people as inferiors.

Archaeologists Kathryn A. Bard and Rodolfo Fattovich compare parallel developments of "state formation" in ancient Egypt and Ethiopia, based in part on their fieldwork at Aksum, Ethiopia, since 1993. The geographies of these regions were different, with Egypt dominated by the Nile River and Ethiopia located in mountainous terrain. Whereas the former region was well suited to large scale irrigation, the latter area was better suited to pastoralism. State formation had already occurred in Egypt in the 4th millennium B.C., but did not develop until the first millennium B.C. in Ethiopia.

Despite these differences, Bard and Fattovich note some parallels. In both areas the rise of complex societies occurred only *after* the introduction of domesticated cereals and agricultural technology. Food surplus that could support specialists was a prerequisite for complex societies. Both states developed as a result of complex economic interactions and the spread of the ideas of hierarchical control and organization. These processes culminated in unitarian states with strongly institutionalized kingships.

Scholars have determined that an early state arose in Upper Egypt in the late fourth millennium B.C. and quickly expanded to the Delta. Early in the fourth millennium the Badarian graves reveal evidence of trade with Palestine and the Red Sea region. During Nagada I (3800–3600 B.C.), there is yet no evidence for a highly differentiated society. By Nagada II (3600–3300 B.C.), there is increased evidence of trade even with Mesopotamia and Ethiopia. Such trade probably represents the greater control of the economy by the elites and a developing bureaucracy. At this period there is increased evidence of social differentiation in the cemeteries. An ideology, which stressed participation in a mortuary cult, also emerged.

In Nagada III (3300–3100 B.C.), commercial expansion increased. The eastern Nile Delta was colonized by peoples from Upper Egypt. At the end of this period an early state with an elaborate royal ideology appeared in Upper Egypt, the so-called Dynasty 0. Maadi, in Lower Egypt, was an important link in trade with Syria-Palestine. Buto, in the northern Delta, provides possible evidence for contacts with the Uruk culture of Mesopotamia. Southern kings then unified Upper and Lower Egypt at the end of the fourth millennium B.C.

State formation in Ethiopia has been studied mainly by historians and linguists. New archaeological evidence suggests that the earliest complex societies arose at Kassala in the lowlands of eastern Sudan and possibly in

Eritrea. The Gash Group at Kassala (c. 2500–1500 B.C.) served as the intermediary between Kerma in Egypt, the Ethiopian plateau, and the Red Sea. Burials associated with stelae from Kassala (c. 2300–1800 B.C.) and mud-brick buildings with magazines (c. 1800–1500 B.C.) are evidence of hierarchical settlements.

After the collapse of New Kingdom Egypt (c. 1085 B.C.), strong trade contacts developed between South Arabia and the Tigrean plateau, leading to the rise of the earliest Ethiopian state, the kingdom of Daamat. Plow agriculture and simple irrigation may have been introduced into the highlands at this time. South Arabian wares have been found at Yeha, a major center of this kingdom. Pre-Aksumite sherds at Kassala indicate that commercial links connected the eastern Sudan, northern Ethiopia, and the west Arabian coast.

Inscriptions of the Daamat kingdom (c. 700–300 B.C.) were written in South Arabian script. From South Arabia also came the cult of the sun and moon gods who were housed in stone temples. All of the South Arabian elements in northern Eritrea and Ethiopia are connected with elite centers. Whereas Conti Rossini (1928) proposed that Daamat was established by South Arabian migrants, it is more probable that local chiefs adopted the South Arabian model of a state.

Another complex society arose in western Tigray in the late first millennium B.C., as evidenced by a field of stelae the authors have excavated northwest of Aksum. The pottery evidence includes "Proto-Aksumite" ware, which is earlier than those found in the Early Aksumite burials. This may push back the beginning of Aksum by one to two centuries into the late first millennium B.C.

Aksum prospered in the first-second centuries A.D., and gained control of the Tigrean plateau in the second to third centuries A.D. as indicated by a Greek inscription recorded by Cosmas Indicopleustes. By the third century A.D. Aksum had expanded its influence west as far as Meroe and to South Arabia. Aksum became a very important trading partner, first of the Ptolemies, and then later of the Romans. Aksum's strategic location gave it access to sources of ivory and gold. Aksum also had highly fertile land that could produce the agricultural yield necessary to support a population of rulers, elites, and specialists.

In both Egypt and Ethiopia internal processes of state formation were also affected by external forces such as long-distance trade. Aksum developed a powerful kingship that must have exercised a monopoly on the lucrative trade. Further archaeological evidence may illuminate how this trade was organized.

Historian Maynard W. Swanson discusses the many attempts, some quite racist, to explain some extraordinary monuments in his essay, *"Colonizing the Past: Origin Myths of the Great Zimbabwe Ruins."* Zimbabwe, which in the Shona language means "venerated house," is today the name of the former British colony of Southern Rhodesia. The Great Zimbabwe is a set of massive and mysterious stone structures situated on the edge of a plateau with fourteen-feet-thick walls up to thirty feet high. A monumental tower rises fifty-six feet. The structures were made of granite stones set without mortar.

A variety of explanations have been set forth as to the builders of these structures. The German geologist, Karl Mauch, who saw the ruins in 1871, was the first to set forth the Semitic myth that the builder was Solomon. Cecil Rhodes, who seized the area in 1890, also favored this explanation. The first scientific explorer was James Theodore Bent, sponsored by the Royal Geographical Society. He rejected the Solomonic explanation in favor of either the Arabs or Phoenicians. Much damage and looting was conducted by Rhodes and company. Rhodes appointed Richard Nicklin Hall, a journalist, to reinforce the Semitic myth. Such Europeans were imbued with a colonialist ethos, which could not conceive that the indigenous peoples could be capable of erecting such magnificent structures.

The first challenge to the prevailing "diffusionist" view came with the investigations of David Randall-MacIver, a protégé of the famous Egyptologist, Flinders Petrie. His publication, *Medieval Rhodesia*, argued that these ruins were the achievements of the indigenous peoples. This was to touch off a bitter controversy for the next seventy-five years between the "diffusionist" school and the "indigenous" school. Randall-MacIver's conclusions were supported by the work of another archaeologist, Gertrude Caton-Thompson, who investigated the site in 1929.

Swanson reviews the development of "The Hamitic Hypothesis," which interpreted the biblical curse on Ham as a means of expressing the inferiority of African peoples. Such views were given scholarly exposition in works such as C. G. Seligman's *Races of Africa* (1930). Another diffusionist hypothesis advocated by the German anthropologist, Leo Frobenius, suggested that outstanding achievements in Zimbabwe were due to diffusion from across the Indian Ocean. Even among the "indigenist" school, there are differences between those who would ascribe the structures to an autochthonous Shona people, and those who would ascribe them to a Nilotic incursion southward by the Bantu.

Archaeology has confirmed the "indigenist" theory, and radio-carbon dates have established dates between the tenth and fifteenth centuries for the construction of the buildings. Studies have also linked the functions of the Great Zimbabwe with the institutions of the Shona people.

A leading authority, Roger Summers, has explained the site as a sacred place for kings, serving as the center of a confederacy, which prospered as a trading center. Even after its decline about 1500, the Great Zimbabwe served as a center of Shona religion until the nineteenth century.

The politics of the struggle between the colonists and the nationalist impulse for independence embroiled scholars and writers in the interpretation of the Great Zimbabwe, so that there was a revival of diffusionist mythology in the 1970s. For example Lord Robert Gayre in a work published in 1972, asserted that the monuments had been built by "Judaized" Sabaean gold seekers rather than by the Bantu. As recently as 1981 Cyril Hromnik revived the old Erythrean theory of an influence from the area of India.

Both the "diffusionists" and the "indigenists" assumed that change was the result of new migrations of people either from outside Africa in the former case, or from northern Africa in the latter case. But the best recent explanation offered by Peter Garlake argues for a purely autochthonous development on the basis of a shift from a matrilineal agricultural society to a patrilineal trading society.

Even after the independence of Zimbabwe, new solutions were offered as, for example, by Wilfred Mallows in his *The Mystery of the Great Zimbabwe* (1984). He analysed the structures from an architect's point of view as primarily a treasure house and assembly point for a massive slave trade. In contrast, Thomas Huffman's *Symbols in Stone* (1987) elucidated the buildings in terms of Shona symbolism, an interpretation which seems most persuasive to Swanson.

The essays included in this volume by a number of distinguished scholars in a variety of fields have sought to review and summarize both new data and new interpretations of areas in northeastern Africa such as Carthage, Cyrene, and Nubia/Meroe, whose ancient cultures and histories deserve to be better known both to specialists and to a general audience.

NOTES

1. This was a view advocated by the Senegalese scholar Anta Cheikh Diop, *Nations Nègres et Cultures: de l'Antiquité Négro-Egyptienne aux problèmes culturels d'Afrique Noire d'Aujourd'hui* (Paris: Présence Africaine, 1955); idem, *The African Origin of Civilization: Myth or Reality* (Westport, Conn.: Lawrence Hill and Co., 1974); idem, "Origin of the Ancient Egyptians," in *General History of*

Africa, ed. G. Mokhtar (London: J. Currey Publishers; Berkeley: University of California Press; Paris: UNESCO, 1990). This thesis has been warmly embraced by American Afro-Centrists. For a bibliography see L. A. Hoskins, ed., *Afrocentrism vs. Eurocentrism: The National Debate* (Kent, Ohio: The Institute for African American Affairs, Kent State University, 1991), 61–63. For a critique, see Mary Lefkowitz, *Not Out of Africa: How Afrocentrism Became an Excuse to Teach Myth as History* (New York: Basic Books, 1996).

2. See L. E. Stager and S. Wolff, "Child Sacrifice at Carthage—Religious Rite or Population Control," *Biblical Archaeology Review* 10, no. 1 (1984): 30–51; S. Brown, *Late Carthaginian Child Sacrifice and Sacrificial Monuments in Their Mediterranean Context* (Sheffield, England: Sheffield Academic Press, 1991).

1

Afroasiatic

CARLETON T. HODGE

❋

A connection of Semitic with some of the languages of Africa is implied in the Table of Nations of Genesis 10, but the modern investigation of this possibility began in the 1830s.[1] By the end of the nineteenth century, Semitic, Egyptian, Berber, Cushitic (which then included Omotic) and the Chadic language Hausa were all seen as possibly or probably related to each other. The term "Afroasiatic" was coined by Joseph Greenberg in 1950 to designate this group of languages, including Chadic, which stretches from Africa into Asia.[2] It replaced the term Hamito-Semitic, which implied a division between the African (Hamitic) and Asian (Semitic) parts of the phylum. This was a false dichotomy, as had been recognized by Cohen many years before.[3] For overviews and bibliography on the history of Afroasiatic studies see Cohen,[4] Hodge,[5] and Petráček.[6] For a general treatment stressing morphology more than lexical comparison see Diakonoff.[7]

Geographically these languages roughly form two East-to-West tiers, a northern one (Berber, Egyptian, Semitic) and a southern one (Chadic, Omotic, Cushitic). (See fig. 1.1.) The Semitic group has also gone south into the Arabian peninsula (Arabic, South Arabian) and back into Africa (Ethiopic Semitic). It is not known with any precision how many languages are included in the phylum as a whole. Approximate figures are: Egyptian 1, Semitic 70,[8] Berber 24,[9] Chadic 150 (a frequently used estimate; Voegelin-Voegelin list 108), Omotic 22,[10] and Cushitic over 40.[11]

In 1977 P. Munson, an archaeologist, pointed out that there was on the Upper Nile about 20,000 years ago a culture characterized by

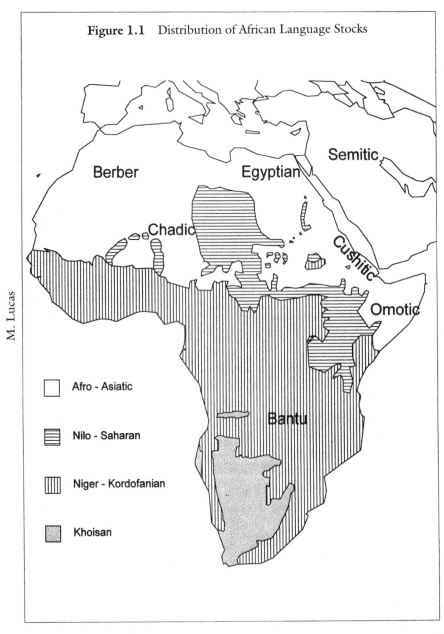

Figure 1.1   Distribution of African Language Stocks

M. Lucas

microlithic flints. This prehistoric culture can be traced as it later moved into northwest Africa (Berber country), west central Africa (Chadic country) and into the Horn of East Africa (Cushitic and Omotic country). It also went down the Nile and into the area of Palestine, thus including Egyptian and Semitic. It is always hazardous to connect prehistoric remains with any language, which by definition is not found with it. Nevertheless, the fit of the prehistoric remains with the historical position of peoples is too good for it to be a matter of accident. Munson made the connection with Afroasiatic and I feel that he was justified in doing so. If we can establish the relatedness of these languages, we will be reconstructing relatively reliable proto-forms at a time-depth not usually considered attainable.

There are three groups as far as attestation is concerned: 1) Egyptian and Semitic, with a wealth of inscriptional and literary materials and both having histories going back beyond those of any other language families. 2) Berber, with scattered inscriptional material, some as early as the second century B.C. 3) Languages in which we have little or nothing in the way of older material. Egyptian and Semitic have also received far more scholarly attention than the rest of Afroasiatic, though this has been changing rapidly.

Before taking up the problems of comparison, a brief statement on the lexical sources available is appropriate. For Egyptian we have dictionaries covering the older language,[12] one on Late Egyptian in progress,[13] Demotic,[14] and Coptic.[15] For Semitic we have two long lists of reconstructed forms by P. Fronzaroli,[16] and W. S. Lasor.[17] Very useful lists of related forms are given under numerous entries in W. Leslau's comparative dictionary of Geez.[18] An extensive set of reconstructions is scattered through the three volumes of K. G. Prasse's Tuareg grammar.[19] These are called proto-Tuareg, but he means them to be taken as proto-Berber (personal communication). There is an older list of Berber roots in A. Renisio's study.[20]

There are three branches of Chadic: West, Central and East. Most materials deal with West and Central Chadic, but we are now getting some reliable data on East Chadic. The two main lists of reconstructed forms are by P. Newman,[21] and by H. Jungraithmayr and K. Shimizu.[22] For West Chadic see also O. V. Stolbova,[23] N. Skinner,[24] and R. G. Schuh (verbs only).[25] M. O. Rossing reconstructs some Central Chadic.[26] The Omotic group was recognized as a family separate from Cushitic by Fleming, who has given us several valuable surveys, with some reconstructions.[27] More recently, Bender has contributed over one hundred reconstructions.[28] As late as 1970 Zaborski referred to Cushitic as "an unexplored subcontinent,"[29] but there has since been a flurry of activity, with reconstructions in proto-Sam,[30] proto-East Cushitic,[31] proto-South Cushitic,[32] as well as Cushitic as a whole.[33] The last is the most comprehensive. A. B. Dolgopolsky's earlier Cushitic reconstructions are still very useful.[34] One must keep in mind that all of our reconstructions are tentative and subject to constant reworking.

Compared to the rest of Afroasiatic, the Semitic languages are fairly close to each other. There is a great deal of common vocabulary, and one can usually predict which consonant in one language will correspond to which consonant in another language. If we take typical examples in representative languages,[35] we have sets such as:

Akkadian	Arabic	Hebrew	Aramaic/ Syriac	Geez
dāmu	damun	dam	dəmā	dam
blood	blood	blood	blood	blood
barru	barrara	bārer	bərar	barra
pure	consider pure	purify	purify	purify
gabru	ğabrun	gibbōr	gabber	gabra
strong	powerful man	manly	prevail	act, work
batālu	batala	baāṭal	bəṭel	baṭala
stop, cease	be useless	stop working	be void	be useless
šūru	θawrun	šōr	tōrā/tawrā	sor
bull, ox	bull, ox	bull, ox	bull, ox	bull, ox
ʾelū	ᶜalā	ᶜalā	ᶜalā	laᶜala
go up	go up	go up	go up	be high

All of the languages have **b, d, ṭ, r, 1, m** in common, and one can reconstruct all of these for proto-Semitic forms. A Semitic root is usually a set of consonants to which different vowel patterns may be added, so that there is vowel variation in the above examples. For "pure" the root is ***b-r-r**. This is clearly ***b-r** with reduplication, so we can expect roots of only two consonants, such as ***d-m**, as well as the more common three consonant ones, such as ***g-b-r**.

In several of the examples different consonants occur but in a regular (predictable) manner. Where the other languages have **g,** (Classical) Arabic has **ğ.** (Some colloquial Arabic has **g.**) Where (Classical) Arabic has θ, Akkadian and Hebrew have **š,** Aramaic (including Syriac) has **t,** and Geez has **s.** We reconstruct ***θawr-** "ox," and the various shapes are predictable. In "go up" the pharyngeal **ᶜayin** has in Akkadian changed the vowel from **a** to **e** and has itself been replaced by **ʾ**.

On the basis of such comparative vocabulary, a quite regular set of sound correspondences has been established.[36] There are, however, a number of cases where these do not hold. For example, Ar. **batala** "to separate" but G. **batana** "to disperse," G. **dabr** "territory" but Tigrigna **dämbar.** Such variation often occurs in the same language. In Arabic we find **θalaba** and **θalama** "to slander," **ṣarafa** "to send away" and **ṣarama** "to forsake," **watada** "to fix firmly" and **waṭada** "to make firm." These show alternations between labials (**b~mb, b~m, f~m**), dentals (**t~ṭ**), and between **l** and **n.** The words seem too close in form and meaning not to be related, but they do not follow the rules. Leslau has used the phrase "related to" to identify such combinations.[37] The relationship is claimed but is not defined in terms of regular sound correspondences.

When one compares Semitic with Egyptian and the other branches of Afroasiatic, the same situation is found, except that the apparent irregularities are far more frequent. For example,

Egyptian	Semitic	Berber	Chadic	Omotic	Cushitic
m who, what?	***mā** what?	***mā** what?	***mi /*mə** what? (how) many	***amb** what?	***mA-**
m-w-t to die	***mawt-** to die	***(h-)m-t** to die	***m-w-t** to die		***mUt** to die
b-3-'-w damp	***wabl-** stream		***bələ** wet		***bAl-** blood (color)
			*b-n rain		Or.(dā)mbal flood plain
			*ᵐb-l /*m-l water		
s-n they	Akk. -**šunu** they (m.)	***-san** they (m.)	***sun** they		
s-n to smell	*** θ-w-n** give off odor	***s-n** to know	***sunə** to smell	***sint'-** nose	EC ***san-** nose
			*-t-n nose		

These show great regularity, along with variants which call for explanation. Proto-Semitic ***θ** corresponds to **s** and **t** in the other languages, as it does within Semitic. The fact that Chadic has both **s** and **t** is due to dialect variation as yet unexplained. Omotic has in the first example **mb** corresponding to **m** elsewhere. In the "wet" example, Chadic has variants **b~ᵐ**, **b~m** and **l~n**. We are meeting the same kinds of alternations which we found in Semitic. Some further examples are:

Egyptian	Semitic	Berber	Chadic	Omotic	Cushitic
t-k-3	*-qluw-		*k-l /*k-r / *k-n		*kal-
flame	to roast		to burn		to burn
n-s, Co las	*lišān	Tou. îləs	*l-s$_3$		
tongue	tongue	tongue	tongue		
b-3-q	*baraq-		WCh *b[H]-l	*b-r-k'	*bark'-
bright	lightning		to burn	lightning	to flash
d-q-r	*-dkuku- / *dquq-		*d-k		
flour	to pound		to beat		
n-g-b	G. gabbaba			*gub'	Afar ǧūb
turn aside	be bent			knee	be bent

"Tongue" has the alternation l~n, "lightning" has l~r and "burn" l~r~n. The last shows that we have a threefold pattern of variation, of which l~n and l~r are just a part. We also see that k may alternate with the back velar q. In Geez this is glottalized k', as is also the case in Omotic and Cushitic, as seen in the word for "lightning." Plain b varies with glottalized b' in "bend."

Linguists have found that a meaningful distinction may be made between speech sounds made in the mouth (oral), those made in the throat (glottal, pharyngeal) and ones made in the mouth but combined with articulation in the throat. In Afroasiatic, typical oral sounds are p t k b d g, while throat sounds are ' and h (glottal), voiceless ḥ and voiced ᶜ (pharyngeal). The latter two, made by constricting the pharynx, are found in many Afroasiatic languages. Whether others had them and lost them or never had them cannot yet be determined. They occurred in proto-Indo-European according to some versions of the laryngeal hypothesis,[38] but no present Indo-European language has them.

In Afroasiatic oral sounds (p t k, etc.) may be combined with glottals (', h) with pharyngeal constriction. For example, in Hausa (Chadic) we have glottal combinations: b', d', k'. In Ethiopic Semitic we also have glottalized consonants: p', t', k.' In Arabic there are several pharyngeal-ized ones: ṭ, ḍ, ṣ, ẓ.[39] Classical Arabic q is a k made farther back, that is, toward the pharynx, but it is not pharyngealized or glottalized. Some Arabic dialects appear to have had a glottalized k', as q is replaced by a glottal stop (') in the Arabic of Cairo.

Combinations with h, such as ph, bh, dh, gh, are not common in Afroasiatic but are in Indo-European. Greek phérō carry" was pronounced with a strongly aspirated **ph**. This later became **f**, Modern Greek **féro**. Older Egyptian **f** was such a strongly aspirated sound, **ph** or **bh**, and it also became **f**, which is its pronunciation in Coptic. The spelling **f** for Egyptian is from the Coptic pronunciation and does not represent the older phonetic value. Compare our pronunciation of ancient Greek **phérō** as **féro**.

A number of the alternations that we have been discussing are, then, differences between plain oral consonants and oral consonants combined with a glottal or pharyngeal component. Another group of alternations involves non-nasal consonants, such as **b**, and the corresponding nasal, such as **m**. It is a basic principle of comparative linguistics that one must posit as many proto-phonemes as are necessary to produce the forms found in the extant languages. If one were to reconstruct a separate proto-form for each of the above sets in which one of our alternations occurs, one would have a highly complex proto-phonemic system, with many phonemes which would account for only a single word each. There should be a more reasonable explanation.

The clue to how this problem may be solved is found on examining the stop phonemes that have been reconstructed for proto-Chadic:[40]

p	b	b'	^{m}b
t	d	d'	^{n}d
k	g	k'	^{n}g

Illič-Svityč suggested that the nasal of *^{m}b was an affix, and he writes *mb.[41] Following his lead and expanding it to the last two columns above, we formulate the hypothesis that the glottalized series is derived from the plain series (either column) by the addition of a glottal or pharyngeal affix (which we symbolize by **H**), and the nasal series likewise formed by adding a nasal affix (**N**). The **H** affix may be **'**, **h** or pharyngeal constriction, as noted above. The **N** was **m** before **p** or **b**, **n** before **t**, or **d**, and **ŋ** before **k** or **g** (simple assimilation). That this is a correct approach is seen by the following examples taken from Jungraithmayr and Shimizu's list of proto-Chadic reconstructed roots (referred to in n. 40):

Plain	plus H	plus N	meaning
*k-b	*k-b'		to close
*d	*d'	*^{n}d-r	to do
*k-d	*k-d'-r	*k-^{n}d-r	fat

There must have been differences of meaning between the various forms of the same root, but these are not yet determined. That is, we do not know what meaning **H** and **N** had. We do know that such alternations, which can be accounted for by the addition of **H** and **N**, occur throughout Afroasiatic (and Indo-European). This type of alternation has been called "consonant ablaut."[42]

We next inquire as to whether we can fit **l~r~n** into this pattern. Attested **r**'s in the Afroasiatic languages are usually tongue tip trills or flaps. If we are to consider **r** to be from *****lH**, we need some evidence of a back quality for proto *****r**. Moscati remarks that "**r** is pronounced as a uvular . . . [r]" in certain spheres of the traditional pronunciation of Hebrew and shares several of the characteristics peculiar to pharyngeals and laryngeals—thus pointing to a uvular articulation."[43] There was widespread secondary pharyngealization in Arabic, and both ṛ and ḷ are reported.[44] Much earlier evidence for a back quality to **r** is found in Indo-European. In Sanskrit **r** retroflexes a following **n**: **rn>ṛṇ** (See below for the relationship of Afroasiatic to Indo-European.) It is therefore reasonable to consider the **l~r~n** alternation as derived from **l~lH~Nl** respectively.

The proto-Chadic phonemic set also shows that either *****p** or *****b** plus **H** results in **b'** and that **N** plus either *****p** or *****b** results in *****mb**. The reconstructed pattern of stops and **l** is as follows:

Plain		p	b	t	d	k	g	l
Plus	**H**		bH		dH		gH	lH
Plus	**N**		Nb		Nd		Ng	Nl

The combinations with **N** are usually, but not always, reduced to a simple nasal in the extant languages, **m** from *****Nb**, **n** from *****Nl**, etc.

The following selection from the examples given above illustrates how the differences between forms may be due to different consonant ablaut in the proto-language: [Note: The following language abbreviations are used: AAs=Afroasiatic, Akk.=Akkadian, Ar.=Arabic, Ch.=Chadic, Co.=Coptic, ECu.=East Cushitic, Eg.=Egyptian, Eng.=English, G.=Geez, Ha=Hausa, IE=Indo-European, Om.=Omotic, Or.=Oromo, Sem.=Semitic, Tna.= Tigrigna.]

Proto	Proto				
Ar.	batala	*1	G.	batana	*Nl
G.	dabr	*b	Tna.	dämbar	*Nb
Ar.	θalaba	*b	Ar.	θalama	*Nb
Ar.	ṣarafa	*p	Ar.	ṣarama	*Nb
Ar.	watada	*t	Ar.	waṭada	*dH
Ch.	*bələ	*1	Ch.	*b-n	*Nl
			Ch.	*ᵐb-1 /*m-1	*Nb
Ch.	*k-1	*1	Ch.	*k-r	*lH
			Ch.	*k-n	*Nl
Eg.	(t-)k-3	*k	Sem.	*-qluw-	*gH
Sem.	*-dkuk-	*k	Sem.	*-dquq-	*gH
Eg.	(n-)g-b	*b	Om.	*gub'	*bH

As such an analysis reconciles many apparent discrepancies between forms of the same basic vocabulary item, it helps us to establish without question that Egyptian, Semitic, Berber, Chadic, Omotic and Cushitic are all related languages, derived from a common proto-language which we have labeled Afroasiatic. By attributing a large number of differences to two proto-affixes, **H** and **N**, we have avoided the reconstruction of numerous different phonemes. Proto-Afroasiatic had a much simpler phonemic system than is reconstructed for any of the branches.

This is not to say that we have solved the problems of reconstructing Afroasiatic. There are irregularities still unexplained, both in Semitic and the other languages. Despite the work of many scholars over the last 150 years, the study of Afroasiatic as a whole is still in its infancy. The relationship of the various branches has been proven, but the detailed establishment will require much further research. Many of the languages are as yet little known, and each branch of the family needs additional work before we have a truly reliable set of reconstructed proto-forms for each.

Consonant ablaut also plays an important role in Indo-European etymological relations,[45] and in connecting Indo-European with Afroasiatic.[46] A great many, if not most, Afroasiatic roots have Indo-European cognates. An important sound correspondence is AAS **b**, IE **w**. For example, AAS *b-s is a root meaning "on." This gives us Ha. **bisà** "on," Eg. ḥ-b-s "to clothe" and Sem. *1-b-s "to clothe." (Note that ḥ and 1 are affixes, not part of the Afroasiatic root.) Sem. *ḥ-b-s has the specialized meaning "to make prisoner" from "to put on" ropes or other restraints. The corresponding IE *wes-, with **w** from *b, also means "to clothe" (as in Eng, **vestment**, from Latin). AAS *b-1 "to carry" gives Eg. n-b-3 "carrying-pole" and Akk. **wabālu** "carry." The ablaut form *bH-1 becomes Eg. f-3-' "to lift up," while *bH-lH yields IE *bher- "carry" (Eng. **bear**, with **b** from *****bh**). Numerous such examples are to be found in the literature. Both Afroasiatic and Indo-European are vital parts of a large phylum of languages, most of which are still spoken in Africa. [NOTE: In the transcriptions, forms preceded by an asterisk (*****) are reconstructed and are meant to represent a prehistoric stage of the language. A hyphen is used between consonants where no vowels are given in the transcription. This is a convenient spacing device to facilitate reading and has no meaning.]

In Egyptian we can only deduce the consonants from the hieroglyphic script (and derivations thereof). Coptic used mostly Greek letters, and so has vowels. The letters used here for Egyptian differ somewhat from traditional usage, which is typographically inconvenient.

The Semitic root was generally three consonants. Fronzaroli reconstructed vowels for most of his proto-Semitic forms. LaSor and most others do not.

Renisio reconstructs only consonants for proto-Berber. Prasse usually has vowels. For proto-Chadic, Newman and Stolbova reconstruct vowels; Jungraithmayr and Shimizu do not. Illič-Svityč use ə for the vowels, as an indeterminate symbol. Bender and Fleming reconstruct vowels for most proto-Omotic forms. Dolgopolski considered his vowel reconstructions for proto-Cushitic as mere approximations and used capital letters for them. Ehret, Heine and Sasse reconstruct vowels. Vowels are reconstructed for Indo-European.

It is probable that the proto-language had roots made up of consonants (generally two), to which vowel patterns and other affixes were added.

For Further Reading

Basset, André. *La langue berbère*. Handbook of African Languages, pt. 1. London: Oxford University Press, 1952.

Bergstrasser, G., and Daniels, P. T. *Introduction to the Semitic Languages*. Winona Lake, Indiana: Eisenbrauns, 1983.

Comrie, Bernard, ed. *The World's Major Languages*, 645–723. New York: Oxford University Press, 1987.

Hodge, Carleton T. "Touching the Bases." In *The Fifteenth LACUS Forum 1988*, 5–21. Ed. R. M. Brend and D. G. Lockwood. Lake Bluff: LACUS, 1989.

———. "The Role of Egyptian within Afroasiatic (/Lislakh)." In *Linguistic Change and Reconstruction Methodology*, 639–59. Ed. P. Baldi. Trends in Linguistics, Studies and Monographs 45. Berlin/New York: Mouton de Gruyter, 1990.

Notes

1. See R. Lepsius, *Über den Ursprung und die Verwandtschaft der Zahlwörter in der Indogermanischen, Semitischen und der Koptischen Sprache* (Berlin: Ferdinand Dümler, 1836).

2. J. H. Greenberg, *Studies in African Linguistic Classification* (New Haven: Compass, 1955).

3. This observation was made originally in 1934. See M. Cohen, *Cinquante années de recherches* (Paris: C. Klincksieck, 1955).

4. M. Cohen, *Essai comparatif sur le vocabulaire et la phonétique du chamito-sémitique*, Bibliothèque de l'École des Hautes Études 291 (Paris: Honoré Champion, 1947).

5. C. T. Hodge, "Afroasiatic: An Overview," in *Afroasiatic: A Survey*, Janua Linguarum, SP 163 (The Hague: Mouton, 1971); idem, "Lisramic (Afroasiatic): An Overview," in *The Non-Semitic Languages of Ethiopia*, ed. M. L. Bender, Committee on Ethiopian Studies, OP 5 (East Lansing: African Studies Center, Michigan State University, 1976), 43–65; idem, "Afroasiatic: The Horizon and Beyond," *Jewish Quarterly Review* 74 (1983): 137–58.

6. K. Petráček, *Altägyptisch, Hamitosemitisch und ihre Beziehungen zu einigen Sprachfamilien in Afrika und Asien*, Acta Universitatis Carolinae Philologica 90 (Prague: Univerzita Karlova, 1988).

7. I. M. Diakonoff, *Afrasian Languages*, Languages of Asia and Africa (Moscow: Nauka, Central Department of Oriental Literature, 1988).

8. C. Rabin, *The Scope of Semitic*, Institute of Semitic Studies, OP 1 (Princeton: Institute of Semitic Studies, 1986).

9. C. F.Voegelin and F. M. Voegelin, *Classification and Index of the World's Languages* (New York: Elsevier, 1977).

10. M. L. Bender, "Proto-Omotic Phonology and Lexicon," in *Cushitic-Omotic: Papers from the International Symposium on Cushitic and Omotic Languages*, ed. M. Bechhaus-Gerst and F. Serzisko (Hamburg: Helmut Buske, 1988), 121–59. *Cf.* H. C. Fleming, "Omotic Overview," in *The Non-Semitic Languages of Ethiopia* (no. 5), 299–323.

11. A. Zaborski, "Cushitic Overview," in *The Non-Semitic Languages of Ethiopia*, 67–84.

12. A. Erman and H. Grapow, *Wörterbuch der ägyptischen Sprache*, 6 vols. (Berlin: Akademie-Verlag, 1926–57); R. C. Faulkner, *A Concise Dictionary of Middle Egyptian* (Oxford: Clarendon Press, 1962).

13. L. H. Lesko and B. S. Lesko, eds., *A Dictionary of Late Egyptian*, vol. 1 (Berkeley: B. C. Scribe Publications, 1982).

14. W. Erichsen, *Demotisches Glossar* (Copenhagen: Ejnar Munksgaard, 1954). A new lexicon is being compiled.

15. W. E. Crum, *A Coptic Dictionary* (Oxford: Clarendon Press, 1939); W. Vycichl, *Dictionnaire étymologique de la langue copte* (Leuven: Peeters, 1983).

16. P. Fronzaroli, "Studi sul lessico comune semitico I-VII," *Rendicoti dell 'Accademia Nazionale dei Lincei, Classe di scienze morali, storiche e filologiche,* series 8 (1964–71), 19.155–72, 243–80; 20.135–50, 246–69; 23.267–303; 24.285–320; 26.603–42.

17. W. S. LaSor, "Proto-Semitic: Is the Concept no Longer Valid?" *Maarav* 5–6 (1990): 189–205.

18. W. Leslau, *Comparative Dictionary of Ge'ez (Classical Ethiopic)* (Wiesbaden: Otto Harrassowitz, 1987).

19. K. G. Prasse, *Manuel de grammaire touarègue* vol. 2 (Copenhagen: Akademisk Forlag, 1972–74).

20. A. Renisio, *Étude sur les dialectes berbères des beni Iznassen, du Rif et des Senhaja de Sraïr,* PIHEM 22 (Paris: Ernest Leroux, 1932).

21. P. Newman, "Chadic Classification and Reconstruction," *Afroasiatic Linguistics* 5, no. 1 (1977): 1–42.

22. H. Jungraithmayr and K. Shimizu, *Chad Lexical Roots II,* Marburger Studien, Serie A, Afrika 26 (Berlin: Dietrich Reimer, 1981).

23. O. V. Stolbova, "Sravniteljno-istoričeskaja fonetika i slovarj zapadnočadskix jazykov," in *Afrikanskoe Istoričeskoe Jazykoznanie,* ed. V. J. Porxomovskij (Moscow: Nauka, 1987).

24. N. Skinner, "North Bauchi Chadic Languages: Common Roots," *Afroasiatic Linguistics* 4, no. 1 (1977): 1–49.

25. R. G. Schuh, "West Chadic Verb Classes," in *Papers in Chadic Linguistics,* ed. P. and R. M. Newman (Leiden: Afrika-Studiecentrum, 1977), 143–66.

26. M. O. Rossing, *Mafa-Mada: A Comparative Study of Chadic Languages in North Cameroun,* Ph.D. diss., University of Wisconsin (Ann Arbor, Mich.: University Microfilms, 1978).

27. H. C. Fleming, "Omotic as an Afroasiatic Family," *Studies in African Linguistics* 5 (supplement 1974): 81–94. *Cf.* idem, "Omotic Overview" (n. 10).

28. M. L. Bender, "First Steps toward Proto-Omotic," in *Proceedings of the 16th Conference on African Linguistics,* ed. D. Otten, Current Approaches to African Linguistics 4 (Dordrecht: Foris, 1987), 21–35; and, "Proto-Omotic Phonology and Lexicon" (n. 10).

29. A. Zaborski, "Cushitic Languages–An Unexplored Subcontinent," *Bulletin of the International Committee on Urgent Anthropological and Ethnological Research* 12 (1970): 119–28.

30. B. Heine, "The Sam Languages; A History of Rendille, Boni and Somali," *Afroasiatic Linguistics* 6, no. 2 (1978): 23–115.

31. H. J. Sasse, "The Consonant Phonemes of Proto-East-Cushitic (PEC): A First Approximation," *Afroasiatic Linguistics* 7, no. 1 (1979): 1–67. See also G. Hudson, *Highland East Cushitic Dictionary,* Cushitic Language Studies 7 (Hamburg: Helmut Buske, 1989).

32. C. Ehret, *The Historical Reconstruction of Southern Cushitic Phonology and Vocabulary,* Kölner Beiträge zur Afrikanistik 5 (Berlin: Dietrich Reimer, 1980).

33. C. Ehret, "Proto-Cushitic Reconstruction," *Sprache und Geschichte in Afrika* 8 (1987): 7–180.

34. A. B. Dolgopolsky, *Sravniteljno-istoričeskaja Fonetika Kušitskix Jazykov* (Moscow: Nauka, 1973).

35. The examples are taken from Leslau (n. 18).

36. Leslau, xxvii.

37. Leslau, xxii.

38. *Cf.* C. T. Hodge, "The Multivalence of Hittite *H*," in *The Seventeenth LACUS Forum 1990*, ed. A. Della Volpe (Lake Bluff: LACUS, 1991): 368–74.

39. S. H. al-Ani, *Arabic Phonology,* Janua Linguarum, S. P. 61 (The Hague: Mouton, 1970), 44, traditionally called "emphatic."

40. H. Jungraithmayr and K. Shimizu, *Chadic Lexical Roots II,* Marburger Studies, Serie A, Afrika 26 (Berlin: Dietrich Reimer, 1981), 19–20.

41. V. M. Illič-Svityč "Iz istorii čadskogo konsonantizma: labijaljnye smyčnye," in *Yazyki Afriki,* ed. B. A. Uspenski (Moscow: NAUKA, 1966), 17.

42. C. T. Hodge, "Consonant Ablaut in Lislakh," in *FUCUS, A Semitic/Afrasian Gathering in Remembrance of Albert Ehrman,* ed. Y. Arbeitman, Current Issues in Linguistic Theory 58 (Amsterdam: John Benjamins, 1988).

43. S. Moscati, ed., *An Introduction to the Comparative Grammar of the Semitic Languages,* Porta Linguarum Orientalium (Wiesbaden: Otto Harrassowitz, 1964), 32; ibid. for Syriac; *cf.* Petráček (n.6), 31.

44. W. Lehn, "Emphasis in Cairo Arabic," *Language* 39 (1963): 29–39.

45. C. T. Hodge, "Indo-European Consonant Ablaut," *Diachronica* 2 (1986): 143–62.

46. C. T. Hodge, "Indo-European and Afroasiatic," in *Sprung from Some Common Source,* ed. S. M. Lamb and E. D. Mitchell (Stanford: Stanford University Press, 1991), 141–65.

2

Egypt and Nubia: Old, Middle, and New Kingdom Eras

FRANK J. YURCO

✳

E vidence about Egypto-Nubian relations has increased markedly in the last quarter century. Much of this originated in the accumulation of fresh evidence coming from archaeological excavation and research, but some represents reinterpretation of earlier data. Nubia, in particular, was impacted by the intense survey and archaeological salvage work that followed Egypt's decision to build the Aswan High Dam; the dam created large Lake Nasser, which flooded all of Lower Nubia, and even part of Upper Nubia. A world-wide effort was mounted to salvage the threatened temples, to excavate and survey undocumented areas, and to collect all inscribed materials, from the entire area to be flooded by the lake.[1] Much of this work was carried out between 1964 and 1975, but the publications have in some cases lagged behind, partly owing to the necessarily rushed schedule of the salvage work, but sometimes due to other factors.

The state of knowledge about Nubia was summarized masterfully by W. Y. Adams, in his *Nubia: Corridor to Africa*, 2d ed. (Princeton: Allen Lane, 1984). Since that great survey, fresh evidence has been found that has added to the overall state of knowledge. This chapter is an effort to summarize these recent findings, and to integrate them into the earlier body of data, and to discuss their impact on the understanding of Egypto-Nubian history.

This survey begins with the dramatic evidence found by the Oriental Institute of the University of Chicago at Qustul, near the southern limit

of Lower Nubia at Wady Halfa. (See fig. 2.1ab.) There the expedition led
by Keith Seele found a cemetery with large tombs of a scale comparable
with those of Abydos and Saqqara of the Archaic Period. Though badly
plundered, enough material remained to show that these were royal

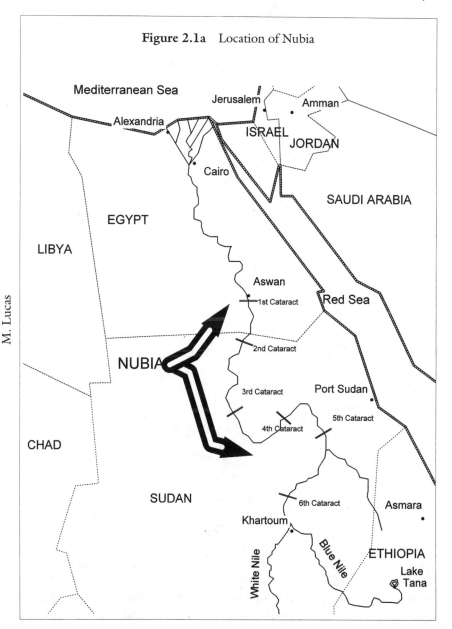

Figure 2.1a   Location of Nubia

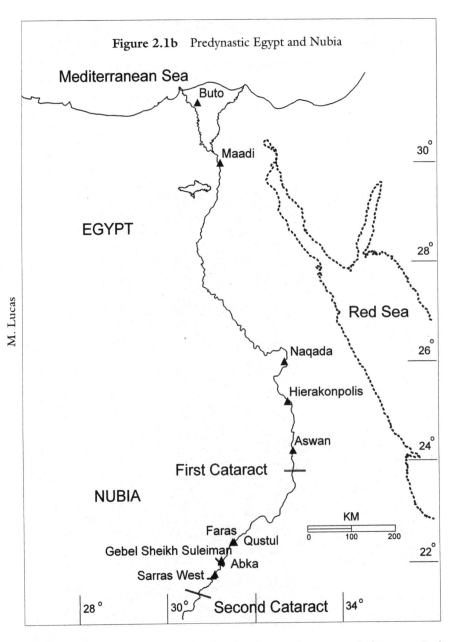

Figure 2.1b   Predynastic Egypt and Nubia

M. Lucas

tombs. After Seele's untimely death, the project passed first to Carl
DeVries, and finally to Bruce Williams who researched and interpreted the
materials, and made the electrifying discovery that the kings buried in the
Qustul cemetery were veritable proto-pharaohs, datable to Naqada IIIa,
ca. 3300 B.C.[2] The objects recovered included incised and decorated

incense burners, one of which depicted a water-borne victory procession of one of the Qustul proto-pharaohs. (See fig. 2.2ab.) That these kings were proto-pharaohs is beyond dispute, for the iconography carved on the incense burner was entirely pharaonic, and included the earliest known Egypto-Coptic hieroglyphs: depicting the king riding in a boat wearing the White Crown (of Upper Egypt), protected by a flying falcon (the god Horus) with the whole procession moving toward a building with a palace-facade type entry, the royal *serekh*.[3] The name *serekh*, an early type, is like the *serekhs* depicted on Naqada IIIa pottery from Egypt, all without a royal name. The Qustul documents helped elucidate other A-Group finds, such as the Sayala macehead and handle and sealings from Siali that provided more examples of the *serekh*. They also contained the name of the A-Group Nubian kingdom, *Ta-Seti*, "Land of the Bow," again in proto Egypto-Coptic hieroglyphs.[4] They clarified the date and significance of the Gebel Sheikh Suleiman rock inscription, that now can be assigned to

Figure 2.2a   Qustal incense burner from Tomb L-24, clay minerals, c. 3300 B.C. with scene of royal procession, A-Group Nubian. Courtesy of the Oriental Institute, University of Chicago.

Figure 2.2b   Drawing of Qustul incense burner. Note serekh shaped gateway, the king wearing the White Crown, a falcon overhead, and a falcon above the name *serekh*. Courtesy of the Oriental Institute, University of Chicago.

the *Ta-Seti* kingdom and no longer to the First Dynasty of Egypt.[5] Other seals from Nubia also were related to the Qustul material, specifically some from Faras and Sarras West, both with *serekhs*, or other parts of royal rituals that Williams and Logan have termed the Early Pharaonic Cycle.[6] The conclusion that may be drawn from this material is that the A-Group elite who developed into proto-pharaohs were culturally Naqadans, as all their monuments and artifacts are part of the emerging pharaonic tradition attested throughout the Naqada IIIa culture of Upper Egypt; they also may be the earliest ancestors of the kings who eventually unified Egypt, ca. 3100 B.C.[7]

This conclusion raises the question of the origin of the A-Group Nubians. The late prehistoric culture of Nubia was called A-Group because its archaeological remains represented a blend of Nubian and Egyptian traditions, sufficiently distinct from Upper Egyptian Naqadan culture to merit distinction. The most recent evidence suggests that A-Group origins are from Abkan and Khartoum Variant traditions of the Sudan.[8] Now the material found at Qustul and elsewhere, and discussed above, is distinctly Egypto-Coptic and pharaonic in style, and yet it comes from A-Group contexts. The likeliest explanation is that in Naqada II times, Naqadans may have spread south of the First Cataract and intermingled with the Nubian population already there to produce the A-Group Classic culture.[9] Thus, A-Group would reflect both an Egyptian and a Nubian heritage and traditions.

Adams disputed whether Qustul was a fully developed pharaonic kingdom, and doubted its Egyptian nature.[10] His objections to the methodology of the excavation were answered effectively by Williams;[11] his doubts about the Gebel Sheikh Suleiman monument were resolved by Murnane's full epigraphic analysis of the monument, now in the Khartoum Museum.[12] The questions regarding the findspot and material of the incense burner found in tomb L-24 have been addressed nor is that incense burner the sole example found at Qustul.[13] Objections to the early date for the Qustul cemetery and associated materials were found to be unwarranted or to be based upon older, outdated references.[14] The early dating of the Qustul royal iconography in the developing tradition of pharaonic iconography throughout Naqada IIIa-b periods has been demonstrated clearly.[15] Finally, Adams's objection, echoed by Kemp,[16] that Lower Nubia lacked an adequate population and a sufficient resource base to support the emergence of a royal dynasty was answered in part by Williams,[17] but further observations may be added. In the time-frame of A-Group culture, 3500–3100 B.C., the Neolithic Wet Phase had not yet deteriorated to its maximum state of aridity. Thus there would have been more desert game resources, and also a better environment for cattle and small domestic animal pastoralism. Some estimate of the importance of cattle, sheep, and goats, can be gauged from the testimony of Pharaoh Sneferu's raid in Nubia, ca. 2680 B.C., documented in the Royal Annals. Sneferu brought away 7,000 human captives, and 200,000 cattle and small animals, and this in an era when both Williams and Adams would postulate a sparse population in Lower Nubia,[18] prior to the emergence of C-Group peoples. Extrapolating from this data, it may be surmised that pastoralism was one important base of the Qustul A-Group kingdom's wealth. Another base would have been trade. The materials found in the Qustul tombs were very eclectic, with a strong percentage of Naqadan Egyptian and Sudanese, and even some Syro-Palestinian Levantine material.[19] Qustul, also like Maadi and Buto in the northern part of Egypt, specialized in trade between the Naqadans and the Sudanese cultures south of the Second Nile Cataract region.[20] Qustul, like Maadi and Buto, was situated at the interface of Naqadan and non-Egyptian cultures. Just as at Qustul, at Maadi materials excavated were very eclectic, including Naqadan, indigenous, and Syro-Palestinian materials.[21] Recent excavations and discoveries at Buto in the central Delta indicate that Maadi focused on the overland trade with southern Canaan, whilst Buto handled sea-borne trade with the Amuq region in Northern Syria.[22] Qustul, by analogy, controlled the southern trade routes between Naqadan and Sudanese cultures farther south. Maadi and Buto shared the northern trade, yet it has been suggested that both became prosperous communities that even achieved proto-kingdom status.[23] A-Group material has even been excavated from Delta sites,[24] underscoring the widespread nature of this early long-distance trade. Just as these northern Egyptian centers became wealthy and prosperous through foreign trade, Qustul similarly was located with respect to trade from the South, from the Sudanese cultures and Africa beyond. Trade, and especially long-distance trade, became an important factor in Naqada II–III Predynastic Egypt, as Nekhen (Hierakonpolis) and Nubt (Naqada) developed social stratification and the beginnings of an elite social class.[25] It was this elite class that fueled the demand for foreign luxury goods, and soon items such as lapis lazuli, cedar wood and cedar oils were imported from Syria-Palestine[26] and helped make such middleman places as Buto and Maadi prosperous. What was the southern trade passing through Qustul? One might suggest ivory and ebony wood, amethyst stone, animal skins, and even incense and myrrh, goods that in later historic times were products from the south, or from Punt, by Red Sea voyages. At this early state of history, seaborne voyages to Punt are not yet attested and such traffic might have come downstream along the Nile. Another resource base Qustul might have tapped was the mineral wealth of Nubia. Amethyst already is attested in these early cultures, found in royal and elite tombs, and the Nubian source is Wadi el-Hudy.[27] Gold is harder to assess. Severe plundering of the Qustul tombs means that little gold was found, and there is also little evidence, so far, of A-Group extraction of gold in Nubia. Furthermore, gold was what helped make both Nubt and Nekhen prosperous in Egypt.[28] The pottery found at Qustul indicates that foodstuffs also were imported by the A-Group peoples.[29] Accordingly, my conclusion is that the Qustul monarchy was able to develop from the prosperity derived from cattle and small animal pastoralism, from the control of trade between Naqadan Upper Egypt and the Sudanese and African cultures farther south, and from limited mineral extraction. Finally, I would agree with Williams, that the Qustul documentation, and its early dating, suggests strongly that the mainstream pharaonic tradition stemmed from Qustul,[30] although clearly the Classic A-Group tradition is jointly Nubian and Upper Egyptian Naqadan.[31] Thus, as suggested by Williams, Nubia played a significant role in the development of the pharaonic Egyptian tradition and it is also the earliest known source for the kingship that later evolved in Upper Nubia (Kush). However, recent excavations at Abydos have pushed back the history of this royal cemetary to well before First Dynasty times. The earliest royal tomb found there now dates to King Scorpion.[32]

Archaic and Old Kingdom Egypt and Nubia
(3100–2230 B.C.)

As posited by Hoffman, one of the goals of the pharaohs who unified Egypt was to bring under royal monopoly the rich foreign trade in luxury goods. Maadi was overrun,[33] and likewise Buto, as indicated by pharaoh Narmer's macehead.[34] Qustul's turn came under pharaoh Aha.[35] In contrast to recent research, which disputes the evidence of an ivory label of king Aha (indicating the smiting of *Ta-Seti*, as the Nubian A-Group kingdom was known),[36] Williams found a steep decline of A-Group prosperity corresponding with the advent of the First Dynasty in Egypt.[37] His idea that the label may be a double commemoration is probably the best resolution of this conflicting evidence. Thus, the First Dynasty marks a new stage in Egypto-Nubian relations. Nubia now is alienated from Egypt politically. There is a strong scholarly consensus that A-Group Nubia experienced a sharp decline in population and prosperity after Egypt's unification.[38] Among several causes suggested, Aha's raid would be one.[39] Continued environmental deterioration might be another; during the First Egyptian Dynasty, the volume of Nile floods diminished[40] and for Nubia this meant a substantial lowering of the flood-plain, and a loss of agricultural lands. Deterioration of the Neolithic Wet Phase also put pressure on pastoral activities. Egyptian monopolization of the foreign trade with the south would have been a crowning blow. All these factors would impact negatively on the two major bases of Qustul's prosperity that were discussed above.[41] The sum of these factors would be a significant blow to Lower Nubia, such as Hoffman saw.[42] Williams has seen in the altered burial customs, type of grave goods, and altered hair styles, the possibility that the surviving population was from a different tradition than the A-Group.[43] All of this made it easier for the consolidating kingdom of Egypt to engage in the exploitation of Nubia which a short time later they set out to do. A fragmentary victory stela of Pharaoh Khasekhemwy (end of the Second Dynasty) may indicate another military raid into Nubia.[44] About this time, or shortly later in the Third Dynasty, Buhen was founded as an Egyptian base in Nubia, possibly to exploit mineral deposits of copper or to serve as a trading station for commerce with Upper Nubia to the south.[45] The earliest level at Buhen was not heavily fortified. This might reflect a sparse and dispersed local population that has been postulated for Nubia in this period. By Pharaoh Sneferu's time (early Fourth Dynasty) the Egyptians evidently felt that another military raid was needed. As the Royal Annals record, 7,000 people and 200,000 cattle and small animals were taken and brought back to Egypt. Various explanations for this raid have been attempted. Adams saw in it a raid against a pastoral population.[46] Trigger, following a suggestion by Kemp, felt that it was directed against a population located south of Buhen in an Egyptian effort to secure trading routes south to the Dongola Reach.[47] However, judging by the episodic nature of these Nubian raids, it seems likeliest that they were intended to prevent a buildup of population and resources in Nubia that would interfere with Egypt's exploitation of Lower Nubia. After Sneferu's raid, the Buhen base was rebuilt, again only lightly fortified, and the exploitation of minerals resources was expanded, with the quarrying of diorite above Toshka started by Pharaoh Khufu.[48] Semiprecious gem stones were quarried from near Toshka as well, and this activity of the Old Kingdom continued into the reign of Djedkare-Isesi of the later Fifth Dynasty. Lack of any defensive arrangements around the quarries reflects the thoroughness of Sneferu's raid, and perhaps the generally sparse population of lower Nubia during this era.[49]

Summing up the activities of Dynasties I–V, it may be said that Egypt established a long-standing policy towards Nubia and its peoples. Nubia was visited episodically with military raids by the pharaohs. These upset any incipient political development or growth of population and prosperity. This made it easy for the Egyptians to begin the exploitation of the mineral riches of Nubia. Lastly, Egypt began to take manpower away from Nubia, commencing with Sneferu's raid. The deported Nubians, it has been suggested, or their descendants, appear as titled servants of Old Kingdom nobles in the Fifth Dynasty.[50] Other Nubians in Egypt may have descended from these captives. One, possibly, is the woman, with non-Egyptian, distinctly Kushite features, buried in Giza mastaba no. 4440, in the reign of Khufu, with her Egyptian husband and prince.[51] Another possibly is Ny-ankh-Pepy-the Black of Meir, whose painted statue, now in the Cairo Museum, depicts him as quite dark in skin color with wooly hair and elongated limbs.[52] Known as Governor of Meir, his nickname perhaps was given to him because he stood out among his lighter brown-skinned neighbors and subjects at Meir. That both these individuals held elevated status and moved in court circles indicates that Nubians were easily integrated into Egyptian society. It is possible though, that if these Nubians and Sneferu's captives represent a final relic of A-Group people, or people descended from A-Group, then they may have been related distantly to the Egyptians, particularly in light of Williams' analysis of A-Group Qustul as proto-pharaohs, who used pharaonic iconography and wrote in the earliest known forms of Egypto-Coptic hieroglyphs. Alternately, they might be "Egyptianized" Nubians, with the wife of the prince at Giza being perhaps the daughter of some Nubian potentate. Regardless of which view is accurate, these two individuals offer eloquent testimony that Nubian origin was no barrier to social advancement and high ranking status among the nobility and even the royalty of Old Kingdom Egypt.

The Sixth Dynasty marked a changed policy towards Nubia. Buhen, Toshka, and possibly other sites like Qubban, were abandoned by the Egyptians and the operation of trade and other relations with the Nubians fell now to the governors of Upper Egypt and the governors, or nomarchs, of Aswan. Evidence of these relations is found in several autobiographies, particularly Weni's and Harkhuf's.[53] Weni dealt with Nubians while serving as a general in campaigns against Asiatic Sand Dwellers. The army he commanded included Egyptians and Nubians from several districts of Nubia. These included Irtjet, Medja, Yam, Wawat, Kaau, and Tjemeh, the last usually considered southern Libyans.[54] All these foreign troops were under commanders who included bilingual Egyptians, titled *Imy-r ʿw*.[55] In light of Weni's army of Nubians and Egyptians, the translation of the term as "overseer of foreigners," makes good sense.[56] Clearly, since they dealt with foreigners, these officials also might have been bilingual interpreters, as suggested by Fischer.[57] All this data implies that the Nubians whom Weni dealt with spoke a different language from Egypto-Coptic, perhaps an early form of Nubian. This would mark the emergence of distinct Nubian languages at this early date.[58] The name Yam perhaps is also reflected in the Meroitic name Irm.[59] It has also been suggested that ancient Yam lay in the Kerma region,[60] as that toponym is related to Irm. Next, as governor of Upper Egypt, Weni states that he had the chiefs of Irtjet, Wawat, Yam, and Medja cut acacia timber for barges that Weni needed to transport granite blocks from Aswan to Saqqara, for use in Merenre's pyramid. The chiefs built seven boats, towboats and barges, using wood from Wawat. It is of considerable interest that Wawat at this time had adequate acacia timber for such a project, an indicator perhaps of resource survival from the Neolithic Wet Phase.

Although Wawat was later a name for the whole of Lower Nubia, at the time of the Sixth Dynasty it included only the region closest to Aswan. (See fig. 2.3.) In the middle of Lower Nubia lay Irtjet, and farther south, Satjet, near the second Nile Cataract.[61] It has been confirmed by recent excavations at Karma by Charles Bonnet's expedition that Yam lay farther south, in the Kerma basin. The Medja were the Eastern desert nomads, ancestors of today's Bedja. The Kaau Nubians are hardest to locate, but Trigger would locate them south of Satjet and north of Yam.[62] So, Weni's autobiography is a valuable geographical source that also demonstrates the use of Nubians as mercenaries in Egypt's armies. The Sixth Dynasty initiated this use of Nubians as mercenaries and certain Egyptian officials who left their titles and names on the rocks at Tomas probably came to recruit Nubians, as suggested by the title, "overseer of mercenaries/inter-

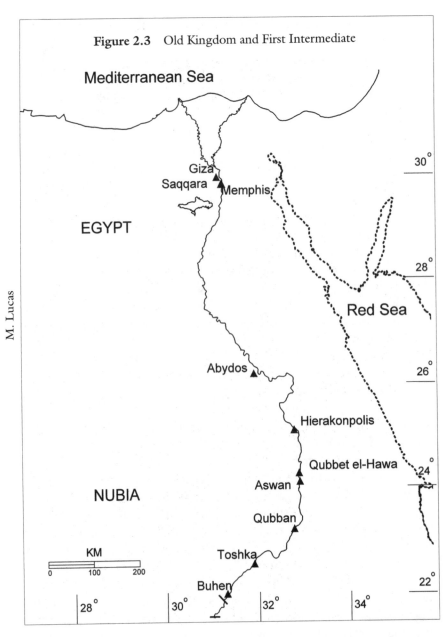

Figure 2.3   Old Kingdom and First Intermediate

preters."[63] (See fig. 2.4.) The next Egyptian involved with Nubia is Harkhuf, whose autobiography, carved on the outer walls of his tomb chapel at Qubbet el-Hawa, Aswan, includes a description of four trading voyages he made to Yam.[64] His titles indicate that he was not only governor of Upper Egypt, but also governor of the mountain lands belonging

Figure 2.4 Autobiography of Harkhuf at Qubbet el-Hawa, Aswan, Fourth Dynasty, sandstone. Courtesy of F. Yurco.

to the southern regions. He was also "overseer of mercenaries/inter-preters," as had been his father, Iri.[65] Harkhuf's career differs from Weni's in that he was concerned strictly with Nubian affairs. He probably is dat-able to a generation or so after Weni. Posted at Aswan, where his tomb still stands, Harkhuf's first voyage came under pharaoh Merenre, the last king Weni had served. It was made together with Iri, his father, who was on the eve of retirement.[66] The voyage took seven months and acquainted Harkhuf with the land of Yam. On his second voyage, Harkhuf, now alone, took the Elephantine Oasis desert road descending back to the Nile at Mekher and Terers, subdistricts of Irtjet. This voyage lasted eight months and Harkhuf returned via Satjet and Irtjet. On his third voyage, Harkhuf set out again on the Oasis Desert road, but from This, in Mid-dle Egypt. He found his trading partner, the chief of Yam, gone on a ven-ture to smite the Tjemeh-Libyans.[67] Harkhuf pursued the chief after send-ing notice of his actions to the pharaoh, and convinced the chief, probably with the proverbial veiled fist,[68] to desist from war and focus on trade with Harkhuf. On the return trip, Harkhuf descended into the river valley between Satjet and Irtjet, where he discovered Wawat, Irtjet, and Satjet confederated under one chief. This was ominous, but Harkhuf's Egypt-ian escort, and a second unit of Yamite recruits enroute to Egypt with him, convinced the federation's chief to receive Harkhuf with hospitality and send him back on to the desert track unharmed. This voyage indicates that besides trade, Harkhuf could make a show of force and collect intelligence data.[69] Did he take the desert route outbound because he had informa-tion about the Yamite chief's expedition, or on the return route take the river-route because of information about the coalescing of the confeder-ation? It almost seems so. During his fourth voyage Harkhuf acquired a pygmy in Yam,[70] said to be from the land of the Horizon Dwellers, one who could perform the "dances of the god." This supports the idea that in this context Egyptian *dng* means "pygmy." These sources indicate the episodic nature of the event, and the nature of the acquisition of these people. Why would Pepy II, or his mentors, trouble to write a very excited letter to Harkhuf about this *dng*, and recall an earlier episode when another *dng* from the land of Punt had been brought to Egypt in Djed-kare-Isesi's reign some one hundred years earlier if Harkhuf's *dng* and the earlier one were but dwarfs? Dwarfs were common in Old Kingdom Egypt (see fig. 2.5) judging by the regular representation of them in the mastabas of the nobles. So why would yet another dwarf, albeit from foreign regions, cause such excitement? Considering this and the southerly regions from which both *dngs* were brought, areas that would have access

Figure 2.5   Dwarfs at work as jewelers. From the tomb of Mereruka at Saqqara, Sixth Dynasty, limestone. Courtesy of F. Yurco.

to the tropical rainforest where pygmies live, it seems reasonable that in these two instances *dng* means "pygmy," regardless of how the term was used in other periods. The usage could be an extended one, inasmuch as pygmies have the same short stature as dwarfs.

Adams dismissed many Egyptian texts as hyperbolic and overly embellished, but he did acknowledge the value of the autobiographies.[71] Egyptologists also have debated their meanings. As Kadish noted,[72] there indeed are cases of boasting in these two autobiographies, but they result from the exceptional nature of the situations in which these two nobles found themselves. Weni's boasts stem from the fact that he was granted great responsibilities while holding relatively minor rank, and that the king placed great reliance upon him. To substantiate his boast, Weni gives much supporting detail from the operations he engaged in. Weni's positions would be a source of rightful pride in anyone's résumé. He served as judge, court supervisor for the king, army commander, governor of Upper Egypt and quarrying expedition leader. His skills included the ability to deal with people from varied backgrounds. Above all, he had a facility of movement among leaders and rulers that marked him as a man of trust who served three successive pharaohs. He deftly commanded a large, complex army, and exhibited a knack for military strategy, executing the first attested flanking maneuver known in history. He also knew how to deal and negotiate with Nubian chieftains and get them to acquire wood for him and build boats for his use. Again, as Kadish proposed, Harkhuf's autobiography is far less boastful when the verb *wb3*, "drill, open up" is given a more extended interpretation as "review, inspect, make the rounds" than its usage in Weni's and Harkhuf's autobiographies seems to require.[73] Harkhuf emerges as a deft and observant merchant and diplomat who moved easily and smoothly among Egyptian officialdom and the Nubian chieftains with whom he dealt, or whose territories he had to cross. The slight variations of his travel routes to and from Yam show that he was adjusting constantly to the shifting realities of Nubia's chiefdoms. Yet he also represented the Egyptian interest and pharaoh's authority in these foreign lands. On his third voyage, when he found the chief of Yam on the brink of war, he managed to persuade him to desist and return to trade. This achievement was a masterpiece of diplomacy, even when described with the inherent ambiguities of the verb *shtp*, "satisfy, pacify" as Kadish has analyzed.[74] Harkhuf also collected intelligence on developments among Nubia's local rulers, as when, on the third voyage, he discovered the confederacy of Wawat, Irtjet, and Satjet under a single chieftain. Such information was vital in keeping the trade routes to Yam open and Egyptian interests in Nubia safe. Indeed, the emergence of the confederacy in Lower Nubia in Harkhuf's time should give pause to those doubting the ability of the Qustul monarchy to emerge in Lower Nubia.[75] This is the same area that composed A-Group *Ta-Seti*, only now, in the Sixth Dynasty, Egypt was a far more potent state with the ability to meddle in the political affairs of Nubia than was Naqada III's Nekhen, *Ta-Seti's* northern neighbor in A-Group times. Yet neither this nor the less amenable climate and riverine regime during the Sixth Dynasty kept these C-Group chieftains from attempting a political confederation as populations grew and prospered.

Several other documents need to be considered to fully assess Egypt's relations with Nubia in this period, the late Old Kingdom. At Aswan, two royal inscriptions have been found that involve the Egyptian pharaoh with the Nubian chieftains. Both date to Merenre's reign, a pharaoh who both Weni and Harkhuf served. The first is dated year 5 and depicts pharaoh's appearance at Aswan, opposite El-Hessah Island.[76] The chiefs who presented themselves and did obeisance were from Medja, Irtjet, and Wawat. Another similar scene and inscription lacks a date, but it shows one of the Nubian chieftains standing before pharaoh, who again is described as

being present in person.[77] Thus, even in the Sixth Dynasty, if these
pharaohs did not raid Nubia militarily, they left little doubt about Egypt's
hegemony over at least Lower Nubia. It is noteworthy that Satjet and Yam
both are absent from the Merenre scenes and texts, and little wonder, for
they lay farther south where the power of pharaoh was a bit more distant.
In the light of this, Harkhuf's dealings with the chief of Yam emerge more
clearly. Yam was the remotest and most independent of these Nubian
chiefdoms, yet Harkhuf had the best and smoothest relations with its
chief. Indeed it was the Yamite recruits who accompanied Harkhuf back
on his third voyage that made the chief of the newly emergent confederacy in Lower Nubia more receptive to Harkuf and eager to hasten his party
along the way.[78] This underlines another of Harkhuf's responsibilities.
Like his father, Iri, and Weni's subcommanders, he was "overseer of for-
eigners/interpreters" and thus responsible for recruitment of Nubian
manpower. Harkhuf's autobiography also lists what was traded with Yam.
He mentions incense, ebony, ivory (elephant tusks), panther skins, throw-
ing sticks, and *hknw* oil.[79] This list largely parallels what was suggested
above as the trade obtained via Qustul in A-Group times, and now veri-
fied by artifacts and materials discovered in elite and royal tombs of
Naqada III and the First Dynasty.

Two other autobiographies from Aswan, much less well known, are
datable to the Sixth Dynasty, those of Pepy-nakht (also called Heka-ib)
and Sabni, son of Mekhu. Both date to Pepy II's reign, a very long one of
over ninety years. Pepy-nakht probably followed Harkhuf as "governor of
the foreign lands" and was likely posted to Aswan for the last part of his
career,[80] since his tomb is located there. His titles indicate that he had
served as scribe for the priestly phyles of the pyramid of Pepy II, as governor of the pyramid city of Pepy I and as chief of the priestly phyle for
the pyramid of Merenre. He had also been judge at Nekhen, and lord of
Nekheb. His role at Aswan included "overseer of foreigners who bring
products to his lord," and "he who sets the terror of Horus among the
countries," echoing Harkhuf's titles.[81] His name Pepy-nakht suggests that
he was born in the reign of Pepy I. All this indicates that after spending
his earlier career in Memphis and Nekhen-Nekheb, Pepy-nakht was
Harkhuf's successor to the Aswan governorship.[82]

The Nubian portion of his autobiography states that the pharaoh sent
Pepy-nakht with an army to hack up Wawat and Irtjet and that he slew many,
including children of the chiefs and commanders, and brought away others
as prisoners to Memphis.[83] On a second mission he pacified (*shtp*) Wawat
and Irtjet. As part of the mission he convinced two Nubian chieftains to

come to the Egyptian court.[84] His third mission was to the land of the Asiatics to retrieve the body of An-nakht, "overseer of foreigners/interpreters," who, with his troops, had been attacked and slain by Asiatics (Sand Dwellers) while engaged in building a ship for a voyage to Punt.[85] This engagement occurred somewhere in the Gulf of Suez area, where the Egyptians often launched their Punt expeditions.[86] It is tempting to see in Pepy-nakht's first two missions to Nubia, a response by Egypt to the emergence of "a veritable king of Lower Nubia" in the confederation of Wawat, Irtjet, and Satjet mentioned by Harkhuf. The Egyptians were not about to relinquish Lower Nubia and the trade to Yam to a resurgent middleman state in Lower Nubia. Just as in the case of Aha, Khasekhemwy, and Sneferu, Egypt once more exercised her hegemony over Lower Nubia with the unveiled fist. The second autobiography is not as well preserved. It is by Sabni, son of Mekhu.[87] Sabni's titles were "count" and "governor of the South," indicating that he held the same offices as Harkhuf and Pepy-nakht. He reports that he received news of the death of his father, Mekhu, from a ship's captain and "overseer of foreigners/interpreters." Sabni then loaded 100 donkeys with ointments, honey, clothing, oil, and other goods and set out with an escort of his troops. He notified the Elephantine garrison that he was enroute to recover the body of his father, Mekhu, from Wawat and Wetjetj, the latter possibly a subdistrict of Wawat. He then states that he "pacified" (*shtp*) these countries. Recovering his father's trade goods, he arranged his father's burial and sent a royal attendant with two of his own retainers to deliver the trade goods, consisting of elephant tusks, incense, hides, and clothing, to the court. This list agrees largely with that presented by Harkhuf. Mekhu's mummification was arranged, and authorization to bury him in his tomb north of Nekheb (El-Kab) was issued by pharaoh. Finally the king rewarded Sabni with land for his efforts and success in retrieving the trade goods. The disposition of the 100 donkey-loads of goods is recorded in a poorly conserved section of the text, and scholars have differed over its interpretion.[88] The quantity of goods is rather large and may have served several purposes. Perhaps part was a reward to those Nubians who had retrieved Mekhu's body and had safeguarded his trade goods, and part was ransom.[89] Yet that Sabni was able to recover his father's trade goods suggests that Mekhu was not murdered for plunder, but perhaps died accidentally while on the return journey from Yam. So *shtp* in this case would be closer to "reward" than to the threat of the veiled fist, as proposed by Kadish.[90] The damaged state of the text, however, makes any conclusion tentative.

In conclusion, the Old Kingdom Egyptians exercised hegemony over

Lower Nubia, by diplomacy whenever possible, but with force, episodically, whenever they felt their interests threatened or when the Nubians
showed too much independence. Merenre's texts at Aswan and Pepy-
nakht's hauling of two Nubian chieftains to court imply that the chiefs
owed some measure of fealty to the pharaoh. Such fealty could also
account for their ready cooperation with Weni when he needed to build
boats. Trade and the recruitment of Nubians as mercenaries also figured
into the relations. The level of recruitment was quite intense to judge by
the number of Nubians in Weni's army and the numerous references to
"overseers of foreigners/interpreters." Yam and Satjet retained greater
independence from Egypt. Neither were shown doing fealty before
Merenre, nor subjected to Pepy-nakht's smiting. Egypt's interest in Yam,
though, was keen for the recruitment of mercenaries, and also because
Yam was Egypt's southernmost trade partner and gave access to products
from farther south in Africa. The earlier Old Kingdom pharaohs who led
military raids also had interests in manpower, and likewise in the exploitation of minerals and stone. They also developed an alternate route by Red
Sea voyages to Punt for the incense trade. Finally, the Egyptians used
magic to deal with the Nubians. The earliest known execration texts were
written against Wawat, Irtjet, Satjet, Medja, and even Yam.[91] Egypt's relations with Nubia in the late Old Kingdom do not show any measure of
relaxation or of more egalitarian dealings with the emerging C-Group
chieftains.[92] It is more a change of style than substance.[93] If pharaoh was
now willing to appear at the border as Merenre did, he still demanded
obeisance, and leaving the enforcement of hegemony to the governor of
the South simply reflects the decentralized style of government of the later
Old Kingdom. Yet all the governors, whether Harkhuf, or Pepy-nakht, or
Mekhu and Sabni, acted at the behest of the pharaoh, reported to the royal
palace, and delivered the trade goods they had acquired and the mercenaries they had recruited to the royal residence.

The C-Group People of Nubia

Following the A-Group decline in the early First Dynasty, some surviving
population remained in Lower Nubia. Its traditions reflect both continuity from A-Group, and also distinctness. Many problematic, so called
B-Group, tombs might also fall into this period.[94] By the Fourth Dynasty,
following Sneferu's raid, even this sparse population is diminished, as
shown by the unfortified and minimally defended Buhen complex, the

Qubban and the Toshka quarries, and their river loading point. This suggests a very cowed population of Nubians, or a very sparse population that posed no threat to the Egyptians.

Earlier scholars were wont to see all sorts of foreign influence on the succeeding C-Group population which moved into Lower Nubia during the Fifth and Sixth Dynasties. There have even been claims of a Caucasoid element in the population.[95] Such claims have been invalidated by later researchers.[96] The A- and C-Horizon Nubians are now understood to be a very closely related and homogenous population with more continuities than differences in their cultural backgrounds. Naqadan and A-Group intermingling had made the A-Group somewhat distinct,[97] and related them to the Egyptians. The Egyptian First Dynasty unification, though, and the subsequent alienation of Nubia made the survivors of A-Group again distinct culturally.[98] Ethnically, however, even the Egyptian Naqadan-A-Group intermingling had no major impact on the population, for, as both Adams and Keita have observed, Naqadan Egyptian, A-Group and C-Group peoples were very similar and interrelated.[99] In the burial tradition there is striking similarity between A-Group and Naqadan Egypt. Intact A-Group burials, with superstructures preserved, were found at cemetery 268 at Tunqala West. They are circular tumuli, built of dry, undressed stone with rubble fill, and with an offering place of upright stone slabs at right angles to the tumulus, featuring offering jars and uninscribed grave stelae.[100] While no intact Egyptian Naqadan tomb superstructure has been found, it is notable that among the proposed reconstructions offered for the Abydos royal tombs of the Zero and First Dynasties, is a tumulus with a stone revetment, a niche, or offering place, and grave stelae, the latter actually found and documented for both the royal and the subsidiary tombs.[101] The circular tumulus and associated chapel recurs in C-Group burials,[102] and the circular tumulus in the Kerma culture burials.[103] The simplest model for C-Group origins, accordingly, is that they are closely related to A-Group and also to Kerma culture, but they represent a group that survived the A-Group by being outside the area of Egyptian military depredation. After Egypt had almost completely eliminated the A-Group and their survivors, the C-Group moved into Lower Nubia in late Fifth to early Sixth Dynasty.[104] Because the later Old Kingdom pharaohs were content with receiving the fealty of the chieftains, the C-Group survived. Thus the chieftains with whom Weni, Harkhuf, Pepy-nakht, and Mekhu and Sabni dealt were C-Group Nubians. As the Egyptian documents show, although the C-Group spoke a language not understood by the Egyptians they were speakers of an early form of Nubian.

First Intermediate Period and Middle Kingdom
(2230–1786 B.C.)

It has been observed by Adams that the periods of Lower Nubia's greatest prosperity were usually those of Egypt's greatest weakness.[105] The change in Egypt came dramatically with the collapse of the monarchy, precipitated by the overly long reign of Pepy II, who had probably experienced an extended period of senility.[106] His successors had ephemeral reigns attempting to regroup the Eighth Dynasty, but collapsing finally with the onset of the first severe Sahel drought as the Neolithic Wet Phase ended and the full desert regime started. This brought catastrophic low Nile floods with ensuing hardship, famine, and civil war.[107] When the Eighth Dynasty collapsed the provincial nobility gained considerable local power. The Ninth Dynasty, arising at Heracleopolis, tried to reformulate the kingship but its kings had to rule in the company of powerful provincial nomarchs, and their hold on southern Upper Egypt was tenuous at best, although the first Heracleopolitan kings won limited recognition.[108] Ankhtify, local nomarch of Hefat, near Gebelein, was nominally loyal to one of the Heracleopolitan kings named Neferkare, or Kaneferre. He restored a semblance of order to Nekhen and Nekhbet and the three southernmost nomes, but only with the force of arms; he also fought Denderah over the Theban nome.[109] All this activity required troops, and Nubians found a ready market for their martial skills, especially archery. Nomarchs in Upper Egypt, and those in Middle Egypt, loyal to the Heracleopolitans all used them, as evidence from Aswan, Assiut and Hermopolis shows.[110] Either Ankhtify, or the later independent Theban nomarchs settled a community of Nubians at Gebelein (see fig. 2.6), where they intermarried with local Egyptian women.[111] Ankhtify even supplied food to Wawat during a bout of famine, no doubt out of ties developed in recruiting Nubians.[112] Although the trade with Yam had ended with the collapse of the kingdom in Egypt, Lower Nubia's C-Group graves now exhibited great prosperity and a large percentage of Egyptian goods, reflecting wages for mercenary services remitted back home.[113] Nubians also moved into the Aswan region, forming a C-Group settlement at Kubaniyeh North.[114] Some time after Ankhtify's demise, around 2134 B.C.,[115] Thebes proclaimed kingship under a local nomarch named Intef, son of Montuhotep, and revolted from Heracleopolitan rule. This soon after led to intermittent civil war, and the Nubians found increased opportunity for employment. The boundary between Heracleopolis and Theban territory lay in the vicinity of This, just north of Abydos.[116]

Figure 2.6   Funerary stela of the Nubian mercenary, Nenu, with his Egyptian wife, Gebelelein. Eleventh Dynasty, sandstone. Purchased by A. M. Lithgoe. Courtesy of the Museum of Fine Arts, Boston.

Thebes now also consolidated its hold over Nubia. An Egyptian general from Gebelein in service to Thebes, named Djemi, claims on his autobiographical stela that he subjugated Wawat for his overlord; garbled names found in Lower Nubia, possibly of Theban nomarchs may be further evidence of this renewed dominion.[117] Pharaoh Montuhotep II reinvigorated the Theban drive to reunify Egypt, and by his 39th regnal year had defeated the Heracleopolitans, ca. 2020 B.C. Again, many Nubians served in his armies, and one, named Tjehemau, left inscriptions in Lower Nubia at Abisko, mentioning the capture of the entire land by his majesty, and another expedition against Djaty in Nubia.[118] The Abisko texts suggest that some of the Nubians returned home somewhat Egyptianized. Their author Tjehemau expresses a sort of jibing of the Theban soldiers, claiming that at Djaty, while the Thebans showed their backs to the enemy, he faced the enemy, insuring pharaoh's victory.[119] The same sort of good-natured ethnic jibing is attested in the stela of a soldier named Qedes, from Gebelein. He claims that he was swiftest in his town among both Egyptians and Nubians.[120] These texts offer rare glimpses into the minds and attitudes of the common soldiers, Egyptians and Nubians, who fought in the civil wars of the First Intermediate Period.

After unifying Egypt, Montuhotep II launched campaigns to reestablish Egypt's prestige and hegemony abroad. Fragmentary inscriptions refer to campaigns in Sinai, against the Libyans, and against Wawat. In Wawat he went beyond Old Kingdom rulers by annexing Wawat and receiving submission of chieftains from Wawat and the Medja Eastern Desert tribal peoples.[121] Tjehemau's inscriptions confirm independently the Nubian campaign against Djaty and another against *Bn*, identified by some as Buhen.[122] Montuhotep II's chancellor led several expeditions to Nubia, and in one text mentions ships assigned for Nubian service.[123] In Nubia, corresponding decline in the wealth of C-Group graves, especially in Egyptian goods, may reflect renewed Egyptian depredations.[124] Montuhotep II also had several high-ranking priestesses of Hathor, Kushites, to judge by their dark complexions, buried behind his funerary complex at Deir el-Bahri. (See fig. 2.7.). Although Trigger doubted serious Egyptian occupation of Nubia,[125] all the Eleventh Dynasty activity outlined above foreshadows more the policy of the Twelfth Dynasty than the Late Old Kingdom policy. Further, as always, trade and the recruitment of mercenaries figured in relations between Egypt and Nubia.

The founder of the Twefth Dynasty, Amenemhat I (1991–1961 B.C.),[126] according to the Prophecy of Neferti, was a son of a woman from Ta-Seti and a southern Upper Egyptian father.[127] Scholars have debated his ancestry, some seeing his mother as Nubian,[128] others consider her to be from the first Upper Egyptian nome where the population was intermingled with Nubians. Extant royal portrait heads depict Amenemhat I with strongly Nubian features,[129] and such features recur among his successors. (See fig. 2.8abc.)[130] Following Montuhotep II's policy, Amenemhat I resumed the outright conquest of Nubia. An inscription at Korosko, in Nubia, stating: "we came to overthrow Wawat," was dated year 29.[131] Senwosret I, (see fig. 2.9) his successor, extended this conquest. He erected mudbrick fortresses at Ikkur, Qubban, and Aniba, and refurbished and enlarged Buhen; (see fig. 2.10) other fortresses at Kor, Faras, Serra East and Mirgissa (Iken) (see fig. 2.11) were begun.[132] A stela, dated year 18 by general Montuhotep, found at Buhen, records a campaign and victory over Nubian lands, including Kush, Sai Island and Ashmeik.[133] The Nomarch, Ameni, of Beni Hasan was on this campaign according to his autobiography.[134] This also is the first known Egyptian reference to Kush, a land evidently south of the Third Nile Cataract in the

Figure 2.7   Kemsit, priestess of Hathor, and Pharaoh Montuhotep II's favorite. From her sarcophagus at Deir el-Bahri. Eleventh Dynasty, painted limestone. Courtesy of the British Museum.

vicinity of Kerma and Old Kingdom Yam.[135] It is the first solidly attested Egyptian thrust so far southward. For the Twefth Dynasty, Kush, the Nubian state of the Middle Kingdom era with its capital at Kerma, becomes a major focus for the Egyptians.[136] Senwosret I's aims in this thrust southward are discerned less easily. The nomarch at Beni Hasan, Ameni, states that the campaign was to advance the boundary southward.[137] An offering stone with Senwosret I's cartouche was found on Argo Island, south of Kerma,[138] yet, so portable an object is of unreliable value, especially since the later Kushites brought Egyptian objects of Middle Kingdom date back to Kerma as booty.[139] Other suggestions have

Figure 2.8a The head of King Amenemhat I. Twelth Dynasty, quartzite.
Courtesty of the Metropolitan Museum of Art, a gift of J. Pierpont Morgan,
1912 [12.183.6].

included the goal of gaining control of the southern trade routes, or simply the destabilization of Kush, so that Egypt's exploitation of Nubia
might be easier.[140] The forts may offer a clue to the problem. The southernmost fort built by Senwosret I probably was the lower fortress at Mirgissa, ancient Iken.[141] A smaller fort on Dabenarti Island, opposite Mirgissa, was evidently unfinished,[142] and may, with Mirgissa, have been
designed to form a frontier bastion such as the Semna group formed under
Senwosret III. Mirgissa lay at the southern head of the Kabuka Rapids of
the Second Nile Cataract and south of Buhen and Kor.[143] On the western
desert north of Mirgissa, remains of a mud-paved slipway were found with
traces of the dragging of keels and footprints. [144] (See fig. 2.12.) Thus

Figure fig 2.8b   The head of King Amenemhat I. From the Lisht Pyramid complex. Twelth Dynasty, limestone. Courtesy of the Metropolitan Museum of Art, Museum Excavations and Rogers Fund, 1908 [08.200.2].

access to Mirgissa was assured even at low water. An armory inside the fortress permitted the garrison to manufacture shields and weapons.[145] All this suggests a forward base that had secured access from the rear, and self-sufficiency in armaments. Thus it may be concluded that Senwosret I advanced the boundary to Mirgissa (Iken), a conclusion that Ameni's autobiography supports. The difficult Kabuka Rapids would have formed a barrier to any Kushite ships trying to advance northward beyond Mirgissa, especially at times of low water. Indeed, the enemy that this elaborate fortification system protected against was predominantly the state of Kush.[146] Yet Kush could also be a trading partner for the Egyptians, as

Figure 2.8c Sphinx with the head of Amenemhat III. Twelth Dynasty, Cairo
Museum, quartzite. Courtesy of F. Yurco.

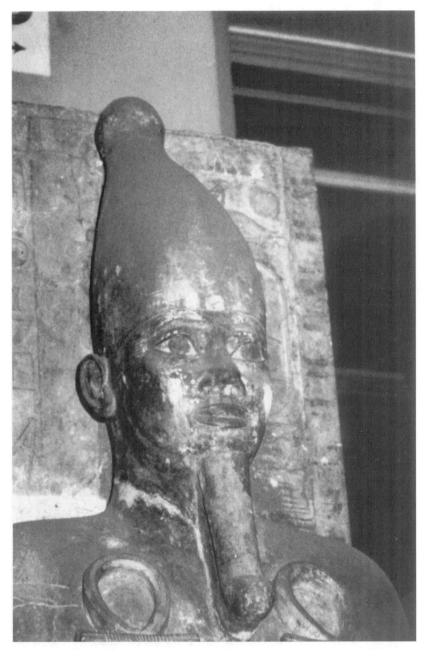

Figure 2.9   Senwosret I. Cairo Museum, limestone. Courtesy of F. Yurco.

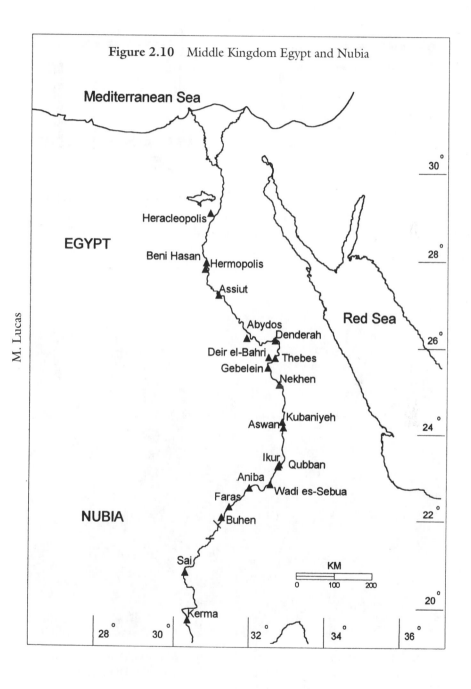

Figure 2.10 Middle Kingdom Egypt and Nubia

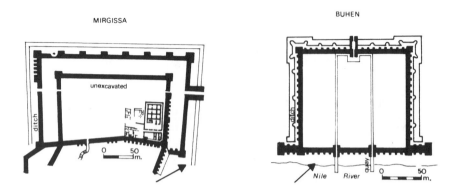

Figure 2.11   Plans of the fortresses at Buhen and Mirgissa in Nubia. Twelfth Dynasty, reign of Senwosret I (1961–28 B.C.). From B. Trigger, Nubia under the Pharaohs (London: Thames and Hudson Ltd., 1976). Courtesy of Thames and Hudson Ltd.

Figure 2.12   caption: Mud-brick paved slipway at Mirgissa, around the Batn el-Haggar region of the Second Cataract of the Nile. Twelfth Dynasty. Courtesy of Jean Vercoutter and Thames and Hudson, Ltd.

Senwosret III's reign would demonstrate. The fortresses also guarded Lower Nubia, now annexed firmly to Egypt. What the Egyptians found in Lower Nubia to protect so zealously were rich gold deposits. Ameni, the nomarch, had already gone on a second and third mission to fetch gold.[147] Gold mining in the Eastern desert of Nubia is attested widely,[148] and the east bank Qubban fortress at the mouth of the Wadi el-Allaqi, the gold-mining route, served specifically to control and collect the extracted gold.[149] Other minerals were also sought. Copper was mined and smelted at Abu Seyal; and Buhen and Qubban fortresses also handled copper working.[150] Amethyst, diorite, and perhaps carnelian were quarried.[151] Buhen had the strongest fortifications, special out-buildings, and the nearby settlement of Kor. It served as the headquarters for Egyptian administration in Nubia.[152] The whole of Nubia was under the jurisdiction of the nomarch of Aswan, entitled "overseer of all foreign lands."[153] Another special function of these early forts built by Senwosret I was the defense of the riverine traffic as illustrated by their disposition along the banks of the Lower Nubian Nile.[154] Other functions are suggested by a late Middle Kingdom papyrus that names the fortresses.[155] Among those north of the Second Nile Cataract most have local geographic names, but one, Serra East, was called "repelling the Medjau," and so was probably used to check the movements of these eastern desert tribesmen.[156] This fort was built also with a sheltered basin that enabled ships on the river to dock within the safety of its walls.[157]

The C-Group population that lived in Lower Nubia was largely unaffected by the Egyptian military presence. Their villages and tombs continued to be built along traditional Nubian lines.[158] Some were employed by the Egyptians to wash gold ore, and a cattle tax was likely assessed.[159] Trigger doubts the importance of the cattle tax, but hides may have been used to manufacture shields as was done at Mirgissa,[160] and the meat could have fed the fortress garrisons. The Egyptian garrisons are estimated at 300 men plus dependents per fortress.[161] The garrisons initially were Egyptian, but eventually Nubians also seem to have been recruited to man them.[162] There were some cattle reared in the fortresses and some residents had small garden plots, suggesting that dairy, meat, and vegetable supplies were produced locally, but grain probably was shipped upriver from Egypt.[163] That the local C-Group population continued to live around the fortresses supports the idea of a mild Egyptian regime. Few objects of Egyptian origin, besides beads, were found in C-Group graves of this period.[164] The Nubian C-Group society remained relatively egalitarian, but a policy to segregate them from the Kushites seems to have been followed.[165] Nevertheless, the

Egyptian surveillance and control of the Medja tribesmen probably gave the C-Group a measure of security and the number of C-Group settlements seems to have increased.[166] Still, while the local C-Group enjoyed relative autonomy under the Egyptians, the mining of minerals and the exploitation of trade with the Kushites were pharaoh's monopoly.

The reigns of pharaohs Amenemhat II and Senwosret II passed uneventfully in Nubia, but Senwosret III (1878–1843 B.C.) (see fig. 2.13) undertook a major expansion and restructuring of Egypt's Nubian realm. In a series of military campaigns he extended the Egyptian frontier to Semna at the southern end of the Second Nile Cataract, marking it as his border in year 8. That same year this pharaoh had the Aswan cataract cleared to aid passage of Egypt's riverine fleet.[167] Additional campaigns were launched against Kush in years 10,[168] 12, 16, and 19. To back up his claims, Senwosret III built six strategic fortresses, (see fig. 2.14) irregu-

Figure 2.13 Sphinx with the head of King Senwosret III. Twelth Dynasty, Gneiss. Courtesy of the Metropolitan Museum of Art, gift of Edward S. Harkness, 1916–17 [17.9.2].

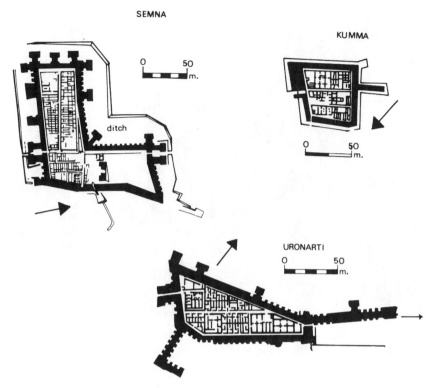

Figure 2.14 Plans of the fortresses at Semna, Kumma, and Uronarti in Nubia. Reign of Senwosret I (1961–28 b.c.). Twelfth Dynasty. From B. Trigger, *Nubia under the Pharaohs* (London: Thames and Hudson Ltd., 1976). Courtesy of Thames and Hudson Ltd.

larly shaped to take full advantage of topography on the islands and rocky eminences of the Second Cataract. Three fortresses were built at Semna South, Semna North, and Kumma to confront Kush where the cataract narrowed to a constricted passage.[169] Uronarti (see fig. 2.15), Shalfak, and Askut were built on islands or rocky eminences within sight and signaling distance of the Semna group, and also within range of Mirgissa to the North.[170] Mirgissa was enlarged with an upper fortress, while the lower area was developed into a trade market named Iken.[171] Atop rocks around Buhen and Kor, signal stations were situated that could communicate with Mirgissa.[172] Finally, year 8 and 16 inscriptions of Senwosret III make clear the main function of the border and forts: "Southern boundary made in year 8 . . . to prevent any Nubian (Kushite) from passing it, downstream or overland, or by boat, also any herds of Nubians (Kushites), apart from

Figure 2.15   Mud-brick fortress at Uronarti, Nubia. Reign of Senwosret III, Twelfth Dynasty. Courtesy of the Museum of Fine Arts, Boston.

any Nubian (Kushite) who shall come to trade in Iken, or an envoy."[173] This makes clear that a major function of the forts at Semna was to regulate Kushite trade, channeling it into pharaoh's entrepot, Iken (Mirgissa). Clearly the forts were to keep out all other Kushites, save envoys, from Egyptian-held territory. For that purpose they had the most sophisticated defenses, fortifications, and a protected access to water supply.[174] (See fig. 2.16.). Again, Senwosret III's year 16 inscription states: "as for any son of mine who shall maintain this boundary which my majesty has made, he is my son and was born to me . . . but he who shall destroy it and fail to fight for it, he is not my son and was not born to me." [175] (See fig. 2.17.) Clearly Senwosret III had extended the border once again to Heh, the area of Semna. The forts also served to track the movements of Kushites and Medja peoples[176] and to signal intelligence back to Buhen. Nile inundation levels inscribed on the Semna Cataract rocks (see fig. 2.18) suggest that signaling could have been used also to communicate advance word to Egypt about inundation heights. In the late Twelfth Dynasty and early Thirteenth Dynasty these were significantly above standard heights for this period.[177] Finally, Semna offered a more forward base in a superbly

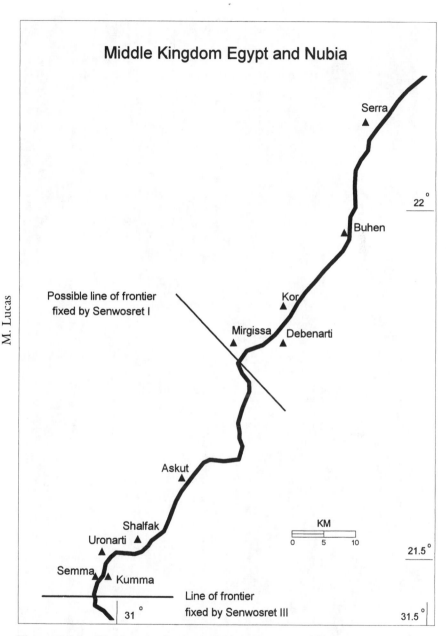

Figure 2.16 The frontier fortresses of Senwosret I and Senwosret III near the 2nd Cataract in Nubia, facing the state of Kush.

Figure 2.17   Stela of Year 16 of Senwosret III from Nubia. Courtesy of Ägyptisches Museum, Berlin.

Figure 2.18 Rock inscription recording the Nile's inundation heights. Semna, 2nd Cataract area. Late Middle Kingdom. Courtesy of the Museum of Fine Arts, Boston.

defensive area that provided forward defense for the trading complex at Iken (Mirgissa), and could also serve as a springboard for operations against Kush. Additionally, gold deposits were situated along the Nile banks between Buhen and Kerma, and indeed, a Twelfth Dynasty gold mine has been located at Saras.[178] Gold weighing scales and weights were found in Semna and Uronarti fortresses.[179]

In summarizing Thirteenth Dynasty activity in Nubia, Adams characterized the massive Egyptian fortresses as an example of material hypertrophy, which is typical of Egyptian civilization, and as glorified customs posts.[180] Yet, in view of the discussion above noting the multiple functions described for these forts, and in view of the strength of the Kushite state they faced, the forts not only made good sense, but were a brilliant example of military architecture and adaptation to a peculiar and difficult, but strategic, terrain. Events in the Thirteenth and Seventeenth Dynasties would make Senwosret III a prophet in his view of Kush as a formidable foe. Again, as in the Old Kingdom, magical execration texts and ceremonies were composed to counteract the enemies of pharaoh, and Kush stood preeminent among them.[181] Little wonder, then, that Senwosret III was made into a god of Nubia in the New Kingdom period.[182]

Second Intermediate Period and The Kushite State (ca. 1786–1570 B.C.)

The reigns of Amenemhat III, Amenemhat IV, Queen Sobek-noferu and the early Thirteenth Dynasty kings are marked by a succession of extraordinarily high Nile floods, which damaged some of the forts and other Egyptian installations in Nubia.[183] As suggested above, recording of these floods at Semna may have been meant to relay early advance notice to Egypt about exceptionally high floods; it is noteworthy that no evidence suggests that Egypt suffered from these.[184] Damage in Nubia included the burial of Semna South fort's glacis under a layer of silt.[185] Debenarti's foundations experienced water erosion; the lower town at Mirgissa suffered extensive flooding, up to six meters above earlier Middle Kingdom levels; Serra East's riverine harbor silted up and footings around the earlier Twelfth Dynasty Lower Nubian forts required stone protective coverings.[186]

The Thirteenth Dynasty in Egypt represented a new, bizarre form of government with, for the most part, ephemeral kings and powerful viziers forming their own dynasty.[187] Nonetheless, for some three-fourths of a century, strong central government prevailed until a rival Asiatic Fourteenth Dynasty split off in the Delta around 1700 B.C.[188] The frontier in Nubia at Semna continued to be held and the Nubian fortresses were adequately garrisoned, at least until the reigns of Khasekhemre-Neferhotep and his brother, Khaneferre-Sobekhotep, ca. 1740–20 B.C. A statue of the latter king found on Argo Island was likely transported there from one of the forts by the Kushites as booty.[189] There probably was even an Egyptian campaign to Sai Island, south of Semna, in the later Thirteenth Dynasty.[190] Dispatches from Semna attest to continued tracking of the Medja people.[191] At Uronarti fort some 4,500 mud seals with impressions from scarabs and stamp seals, including one of the Hyksos king Ma'at-ib-re, have been found.[192] All of this suggests continued Egyptian occupation of the forts to the very eve of the Hyksos invasion of Egypt.

In the meantime the Kushite state of Kerma also grew in power.[193] The history of Kush has been elucidated only since the 1920s and the work of the archaeological surveys and the Reisner expedition to Kerma. Recent excavations on Sai Island, site of a major Kushite-Kerma cemetery, have allowed the development of a general chronology of the Kerma culture.

Early Kerma is now equated roughly with Nubian A-Horizon, Middle Kerma to Nubian early C-Group, Classic and Late Kerma to later Nubian C-Group (Second Intermediate Period to the Eighteenth Dynasty).[194] The Kushites who encountered Senwosret I and III then would represent Kerma Middle to Late-Middle Kerma culture. The excavations at Kerma have demonstrated that this was the Kushite king's capital. A well fortified town with a defensive ditch and stone and mud-brick walls,[195] it included a large mud-brick structure termed the "Western Deffufa." This structure served several varied purposes over its history, the last being a stronghold or castle. The cellars yielded seal impressions from pots, baskets, and packages with the names of several Hyksos rulers, including Jakob-her, Sheshi, Ma'at-ib-re and a queen Ineni all in Hyksos-style design.[196] Some of the seals came from Nubian pottery containers, but others are clearly imports from Hyksos-occupied Egypt.[197] Buildings around the Deffufa probably mark industrial areas where a lot of Egyptian-style glazed material was produced (see figs. 2.19 and 2.20), including beads and ornaments. Many have assumed that the strong Egyptian influence is evidence of Egyptian artisans and even officials working for the Kushite monarch.[198] It is the Kerma royal burials that really demonstrate the power and status of the Kushite kings. They were buried in large, circular tumuli, with a central burial chamber for the ruler, and a corridor in which, at the time of the burial, up to several hundred sacrificed men and women courtiers and retainers, and rams were disposed.[199] (See fig. 2.21ab.) The grave goods were extraordinarily rich, as befits a king. The king was buried on a bed (in one example, of glazed quartz), with sacrificed women dressed in leather and cloth adorned with mica ornaments, jewelry, and crowns of silver or gold. They were surrounded by a plundered, eclectic collection of Egyptian Middle Kingdom statuary or artifacts, and heavy gold-plated furniture.[200] At least two of the tumuli had funerary temples attached, built of mud-brick (see fig. 2.22), with Egyptian-style faience inlay,[201] and even a granite door-lintel with the winged sun-disk carved on it (though this might have been plundered from a Middle Kingdom Egyptian site). The inner walls of the temples had painted scenes, including animals and, significantly, fleets of sailing ships. Thus, Kush, like Egypt, was a riverine power with great military strength in its riverine fleets. Finally, the widespread distribution of Kerma-type pottery shards, from the Butana Steppe[202] to the Gash River delta (see fig. 2.23) near the Ethiopian border,[203] suggests a widespread, powerful state with access to the rich gold mines of Upper Nubia.[204] This assessment of the Kushite state confirms the value of Senwosret III's powerful fortifications,

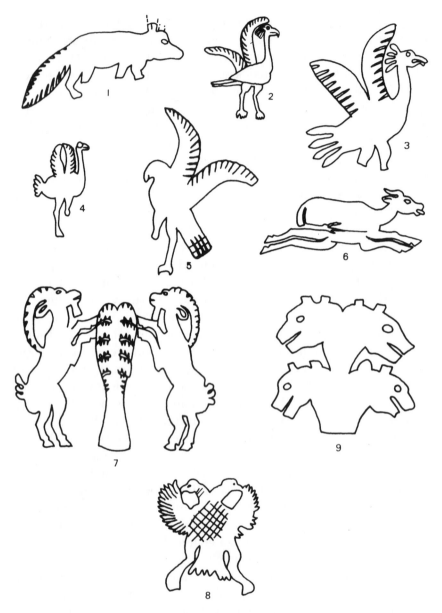

Figure 2.19   Ivory and mica furniture and clothing inlays and appliqués. Kerma-Kushite c. 1650 b.c. From B. Trigger, *Nubia under the Pharaohs* (London: Thames and Hudson Ltd., 1976). Courtesy of Thames and Hudson Ltd.

Figure 2.20   Bed with ivory inlays from a royal Kerma-Kushite burial. c. 1650
B.C. Courtesy of the Museum of Fine Arts, Boston.

confronting the Kushite state, but it also supports the evidence, continuing to accumulate, that Kush was a great trading partner too; and the evidence that Kush was also a riverine power depending on strong riverine
fleets helps explain the overwhelmingly riverine nature of the Egyptian
fortresses and pharaoh's tight control of the Kushite trade.

   The collapse of the Egyptian administration in Nubia corresponds
roughly to the collapse of the Thirteenth Dynasty before the Hyksos, ca.
1665 B.C., when the Hyksos ruler, Salatis (or Sharek), seized *It-Tawy*, the
Egyptian capital, and set up the Fifteenth Dynasty.[205] This was a traumatic
event for the Egyptians, forcing the survivors to retreat to Upper Egypt.
It has been suggested that Egyptian garrisons of the forts in Nubia were
withdrawn to help cope with the Hyksos onslaught.[206] Other views hold
that some Egyptians in Nubia were stranded by the Thirteenth Dynasty's
collapse and others fled to Nubia to escape the Hyksos.[207] The abandonment of the fortresses poses even larger questions. Arkell proposed that
resentful C-Group peoples burned them.[208] Yet the generally good treatment of the C-Group by the Twelfth Dynasty, and the numbers of Egyptians remaining behind in Nubia, makes this unlikely. Emery thought that
the Kushites had attacked and burned the forts.[209] Others doubt this and
propose withdrawing Egyptians as those who fired the forts.[210] One or
more of these ideas may have validity. There also is evidence indicating the

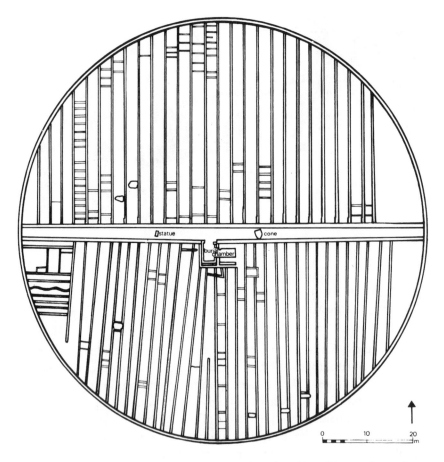

Figure 2.21a   Tumulus K III, royal tomb of Kushite king, Kerma. Second Intermediate Period. From B. Trigger, *Nubia under the Pharaohs* (London: Thames and Hudson Ltd., 1976). Courtesy of Thames and Hudson Ltd.

Kushites as the ones who burned the forts during a raid. Among the royal Kerma tumuli, Tumulus K-III contained diverse Middle Kingdom goods, ranging from statues of a nomarch of Assiut and his wife, a jar-lid bearing Amenemhat III's name, an ivory wand, and scarabs of Thirteenth Dynasty date. Such an eclectic collection has suggested that these items were collected by the Kushites during a raid into Egypt,[211] or perhaps were goods traded to the Kushites by the Hyksos.[212] There is other evidence that indicates a Kushite raid into Egypt. Kerma-style burials have been found at Mirgissa, dated 1650–1580 B.C.,[213] at Saras East, Shalfak, and at Abu Sir Rock;[214] also near Qubban, Ikur and Buhen forts, in Nubian C-Group

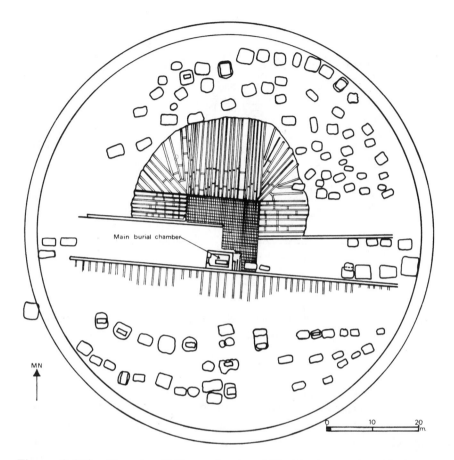

Figure 2.21b Tumulus K X, another royal Kushite Kerma burial. Second Intermediate Period. From B. Trigger, *Nubia under the Pharaohs* (London: Thames and Hudson Ltd., 1976). Courtesy of Thames and Hudson Ltd.

cemeteries, and within Egypt proper, as far north as Abydos.[215] Such graves are not so numerous as to denote an occupation of any length, especially those north of Aswan in Egypt, but they may mark a temporary Kushite penetration into Egypt. Such a raid might be envisioned just after the Hyksos onslaught that toppled the Thirteenth Dynasty. Kushite graves in Lower Nubia are more numerous; Trigger postulates that they represent traders, and that the Kushite monarch struck up alliances with the C-Group chieftains and some surviving Egyptians.[216] Adams thought that the burials represented Kushite garrisons posted in the forts.[217] Indeed, in the Seventeenth Dynasty, Kamose and his courtiers admitted that the

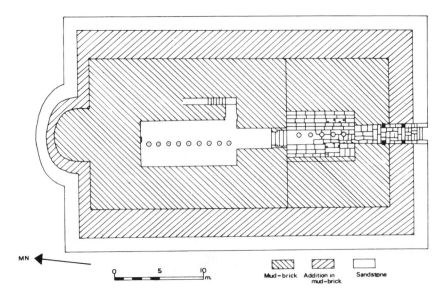

MN

Mud–brick   Addition in   Sandstone
            mud–brick

Figure 2.22   Plan of a royal funerary chapel, Kerma. From B. Trigger, *Nubia under the Pharaohs* (London: Thames and Hudson Ltd., 1976). Courtesy of Thames and Hudson Ltd.

Kushite monarch ruled south of Aswan.[218] Moreover, some surviving Egyptian officials were loyal to the King of Kush,[219] confirming Kamose's admission. Also suggesting more than just trade is the arrangement of some C-Group house clusters into defensive perimeters, complete with guard-houses and archers' loopholes in the perimeter walls, as at Wadi es-Sebua[220] (see fig. 2.24). Another fortified village at Amada with C-Group clustered dwellings dates to the Late Middle Kingdom period[221] as does another fortified site at Karanog.[222] Trigger viewed these as chieftains' abodes,[223] but the Wadi es-Sebua camp especially appears more like a for-tified village. The only power capable at this time of offensive action against the Nubians was the Kushite state. The evidence of C-Group graves is ambiguous. Kerma and Medja influences appear[224] (see fig. 2.25), yet in the grave goods, Egyptian, not Kushite, materials predomi-nate.[225] Trigger suggested that C-Group Nubians collected tolls from trade between Egyptians and Kushites, but after the forts collapsed, along with their Egyptian administration, the Kushite trade with Egypt ceased and the Kushites began to trade and maintain diplomatic contacts directly with the Hyksos.[226] It is more likely that the Egyptian goods that appear among the C-Group came from surviving resident Egyptians who now willingly cooperated with their C-Group Nubian neighbors.[227] The grow-

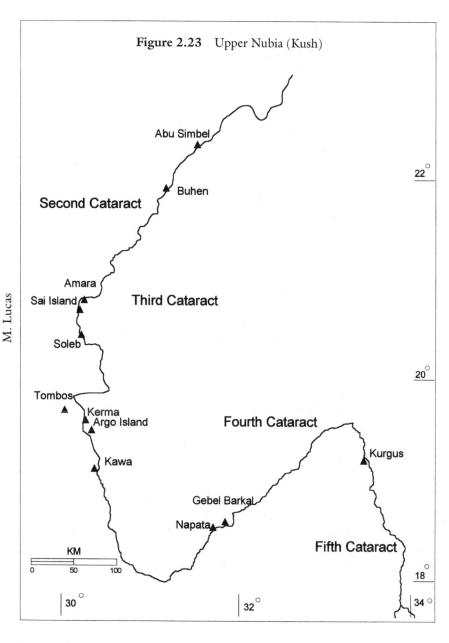

Figure 2.23 Upper Nubia (Kush)

ing trend among C-Group Nubians to copy Egyptian style of architecture might also indicate Egyptian-C-Group interaction, and indeed, the fact that C-Group Nubians did not adopt more Kerma-Kushite customs, such as sacrifice burials, has been ascribed to possible Egyptian influence.[228]

The sum of this often conflicting evidence seems to be that Lower

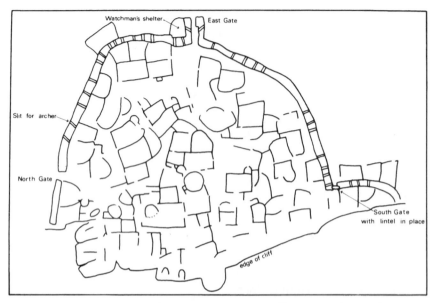

Figure 2.24   Plan of a fortified Nubian C-Group village at Wady es-Sebua. Late Second Intermediate Period. From B. Trigger, *Nubia under the Pharaohs* (London: Thames and Hudson Ltd., 1976). Courtesy of Thames and Hudson Ltd.

Nubia was subject to the Kushite monarch,[229] and that some resident Egyptians became his loyal subjects, or mercenaries. Other Egyptians, though, cooperated with the indigenous C-Group population, cut off as they were from Egypt. Long, tolerant associations between the C-Group and Egyptians perhaps helped such bonds. Kushite trade shifted away from the impoverished Upper Egyptian vassals to the Hyksos, as seals found at Kerma denote. However, Kushite trade did not shift to the C-Group Nubians of Lower Egypt. The likeliest scenario is that surviving Egyptians, who did not support the Kushites, and the C-Group Nubians supported each other. The resident Kushites and those Egyptians who were loyal to them were overlords and troops, probably not traders.

The New Kingdom Period (ca. 1570–1080 B.C.)

The Hyksos Period was the low point of ancient Egyptian pharaonic history.[230] The Thirteenth Dynasty ended ingloriously in exile in Upper Egypt. The Hyksos set up their capital at Avaris and ruled directly in the Delta and the Memphis-Fayum area through vassals of their own, or by

Figure 2.25 Nubian C-Group pottery and artifacts. Late Second Intermediate Period. From B. Trigger, *Nubia under the Pharaohs* (London: Thames and Hudson Ltd., 1976). Courtesy of Thames and Hudson Ltd.

cooperative Egyptians in Middle Egypt. They allowed the indigenous princes at Thebes a tenuous existence as vassals in southern Upper Egypt. The presence of the names of Hyksos kings on blocks from a temple at Gebelein, south of Thebes, suits this view.[231] Further evidence includes Hyksos dedications of a sistrum from Denderah and an adze for Sobek, lord of Sumenu, south of Thebes.[232] These are religious dedications by the Hyksos kings, normally a prerogative of pharaoh. Likewise, the Rhind Mathematical Papyrus is dated year 33 of the Hyksos king, Aa-weserre Apepy, and is said to be from Thebes.[233] Only a few functions remained to the indigenous Egyptian rulers. Transfer of the governorship of El-Kab was executed under the Seventeenth Dynasty king Sewadjenre-

Nebiryaw;[234] and a later king, Nubkheperre Intef, ordered the expulsion of a priest guilty of sacrilege from the temple of Min at Coptos.[235] This suggests a limited autonomy, yet the real situation can be grasped by noting the Hyksos sector of control and the Kushite king's domain and their respective capitals, Avaris[236] and Kerma. Both, now excavated, show large, prosperous cities and richly appointed royal graves. These contrast with provincial Seventeenth Dynasty Thebes and the meager burials of the Theban rulers.[237] It remains unclear why the Hyksos did not finish off the Thebans. They certainly took over the royal monopoly of trade with Kush, as demonstrated by the seals with Hyksos royal names recovered from Kerma. Moreover the Hyksos and Kushite monarchs maintained diplomatic contact, as Kamose's second stela revealed. Perhaps the Hyksos felt that Thebes would wither on the vine, shorn of foreign trade, limited to but a part of Egypt, with a powerful Kushite state in diplomatic alliance with the Hyksos at the Egyptians' rear. The Hyksos surmise about the Thirteenth Dynasty was accurate. It sputtered to a close and was replaced by the Seventeenth Dynasty.[238] That dynasty also limped along for part of the 108-year Hyksos tenure until a new branch of the family, started by Queen Teti-sheri and King Senakhtenre Ta'a I, emerged, ca. 1600 B.C.[239] Their son, King Seqenenre Ta'a II, evidently launched the struggle to liberate Egypt from the Hyksos who may have been weakened by the effects of the eruption of Santorini Volcano in the Aegean, 1628 B.C.[240] He died in battle and his battered mummy displays head wounds caused by a distinctive Hyksos-type axe.[241] A Ninteenth Dynasty popular story, "Seqenenre and the Hyksos ruler Apepy," [242] poses the scene as a challenge by the Hyksos king to Seqenenre, setting one's wit against the other's. The story may have religious overtones, but it retains the notion that Seqenenre was a vassal of the Hyksos ruler and could be called upon to do the Hyksos king's bidding. Afterwards, Ahhotep, Seqenenre's widow, kept the resistance alive. Kamose, son, or perhaps brother, of Seqenenre,[243] next took up the struggle. Fragments of one stela, and a complete second stela (see pl. 31), recounting his exploits are still extant. In the first he puzzles over the Theban situation: "Give me to understand what this strength of mine is for. A king is in Avaris, another is in Kush, and so, I sit alongside an Asiatic and a Nubian. Each one has his slice of this Egypt, dividing up the land with me."[244] In stating that the Kushite king holds part of this Egypt, Kamose lays claim to part of Nubia.[245] Kamose's courtiers reply: "It is Asiatic territory as far as Cusae, . . . Elephantine is strong," thus admitting that indeed Nubia was under Kushite control.[246] The second stela opens with an attack on Nefrusy, a Middle Egyptian town governed by an Egyptian-Hyksos ally. After its capture the town was turned into ruins, so bitter was the hatred of Kamose for the turncoat ruler. Kamose proceeded next to raid the environs of Avaris, but he cautiously protected his flanks. He sent a force to seize Bahria Oasis, while he remained at Sako, south of Heracleopolis. The wisdom of this move was soon evident, for Kamose's forces captured a Hyksos envoy carrying a letter to Kush via the Oasis Road. Kamose quoted the intercepted letter: "Do you see what Egypt has done to me? The king of the place, Kamose, is attacking me on my ground. . . . He chooses to plague these two lands, mine and yours. He has ravaged them."[247] Then the Hyksos king invited the Kushite monarch to strike Kamose in the rear: "Come, journey downstream! Fear not! He is here with me, and there is no one who will stand up against you in that part of Egypt. Behold, I will allow him no road until you have arrived. Then we shall divide up the towns of that part of Egypt, and Khenetkhenefer (a name for Nubia) shall thrive in joy."[248] This letter demonstrates clearly the Hyksos-Kushite alliance. The letter also quotes the Hyksos king: "Why have you arisen as ruler without letting me know?"[249] Kamose had chosen his moment for attack carefully; a newly crowned, inexperienced king in Kush had provided an opportunity for a pre-emptive strike against Nubia, up to Buhen. Kamose appointed the earliest known Viceroy of Kush at this point.[250] The stela of Emhab also declares that the king reached Miu.[251] At least one scholar has suggested, based on this reference to Miu, that Kamose raided deep into Upper Nubia, perhaps to catch the Kushites in the rear.[252] Others believe that an advance so far south is speculative.[253] Kamose also solidified his position by recruiting Medja Nubians, this is specifically mentioned in his first Stela.[254] Notably, in this era, a foreign type of grave, the Pan grave, appears in Upper Egypt, co-terminous with territory held by the Thebans. The Pan graves are dissimilar from C-Group, Kushite and other known types, and probably are Medja graves.[255] Unplundered Pan graves often include Egyptian-style axes and daggers, gold and jewelry.[256] If Kamose had established good relations with the Medja, his raid deep into Upper Nubia might be envisioned going through their territory, and surprising the Kushites by an attack on their eastern flank. It has been suggested that some prominent New Kingdom families were of Medja ancestry, for instance the mayors of El-Kab.[257] Some scholars have even seen Nubian ancestry in the royal family of Seqenenre Ta'a II, especially based upon his mummy,[258] although as noted above, the southern Upper Egyptians were similar genetically to the Nubians, and there had also been substantial settlement of Nubians in southern Upper Egypt in the First Intermediate Period.

For Kush, the capture of the Hyksos king's letter meant a disaster. It drove home to the Egyptians the real menace that Kush presented at their rear, especially in alliance with the Hyksos. Between Kamose and Ahmose, the pharaohs, determined on the destruction of both enemies. The Egyptian thrust into Nubia and their alliance with the Medja threw Kush off balance. Discovery of the Hyksos' use of the Oasis Road to communicate with Kush and the Egyptian seizure of the oases broke that line of contact. The ease of the Egyptian penetration into Lower Nubia may suggest that surviving Egyptians and C-Group Nubians cast their lot with the Egyptians, although relatively light Kushite garrisons may have been a factor too.[259] Pan graves in Nubia indicate that Medja troops were among the new occupation forces that the Egyptians posted in the forts, once they were refurbished.[260] Certain Medja may even have served as local governors.[261] Kamose perhaps died prematurely, and Ahmose, ca. 1570–1548 B.C., his brother, or possibly son,[262] came to the throne as a minor.[263] Reaching maturity, he launched his campaigns against the Hyksos around years 10–11, taking Avaris about years 12–13, and then besieging Sharuhen, in southern Palestine, for three years.[264] Next he attacked Kush in year 22, winning a victory there, and quelling two rebellions in Lower Nubia.[265] Amenhotep I (1548–1524 B.C.) mounted a stronger attack against Kush (see fig. 2.26). A statement of the soldier Ahmose, son of Abana: "Then I conveyed King Djeserkare, the justified, when he sailed south to enlarge the borders of Egypt,"[266] shows without ambiguity that Kush was under attack. Pharaoh slew a Kushite commander and brought back prisoners and cattle. While Kush proper was not destroyed, the forts of Buhen, Uronarti, and Semna were refurbished.[267] In year 2 of Thutmose I (1524–1518 B.C.) the real onslaught against Kush occurred. The Kushite king was slain, his dependents carried off and pharaoh returned to Thebes with the Nubian king's body head downward on the prow of the royal flagship.[268] Thutmose I pushed on past the Fourth Nile Cataract, leaving his boundary text on a rock at Kurgus.[269] Some believe that Thutmose I pillaged and burned the Western Deffufa at Kerma.[270] He set up fortresses at Tombos and began to exploit gold deposits in the area.[271] Military garrisons were posted throughout Upper Nubia at key locations, and the Kushite realm was divided into five parts to dissuade rebellion.[272] No sooner was Thutmose I dead than a surviving chieftain of the Kushite kingdom, and two of his sons who had escaped Thutmose I, rebelled and tried to attack the Egyptian fortresses. Thutmose II (1518–1504 B.C.), the successor pharaoh, promptly led a new attack against the Kushite rebels; only one of the chieftain's sons survived, and he was brought cap-

Figure 2.26 Pharaoh Amenhotep I (1551–25 B.C.) alabaster from a relief in a chapel in the Karnak Temple, at Luxor. Courtesy of F. Yurco.

tive to Egypt.[273] After Thutmose II died, his minor son, Thutmose III (1504–1450 B.C.), succeeded, with Hatshepsut, Thutmose II's widow and his aunt, as regent. Before long, Hatshepsut (see fig. 2.27) elevated herself as pharaoh with young Thutmose III as coregent.[274] If the Nubians and others thought the female pharaoh unwarlike, they were in for a shock. Besides outfitting her well-known Punt expedition, she led three campaigns deep into Upper Nubia, securing direct Egyptian rule of the Abri-Dongola stretch of the Nile.[275] This broke the back of Kushite resistance, and future campaigns were sparse and episodic.[276] Thutmose III in his sole rule led seventeen campaigns into Syria-Palestine, but only one real campaign to Kush, in year 50, and that was more a tour of inspection.[277] (See fig. 2.28.) In his typically methodical fashion the old pharaoh charged the fishermen of Elephantine with the task of annually clearing out the canal through the Aswan Cataract,[278] a task previously performed when a campaign sailed south to Nubia. (See fig. 2.29.).

Thutmose I and II had already begun to build fortified towns in Nubia. Hatshepsut and Thutmose III expanded this construction to Upper Nubia (see fig. 2.30), founding Napata at Gebel Barkal (see fig. 2.31) in the Abri-Dongola area.[279] Sai Island had a fortress founded by Ahmose;[280] Amara may be a later Eighteenth Dynasty foundation[281] along with Soleb, Sesebi, and Kawa.[282] Sai, Amara, and Sesebi were initially walled towns, but later large temples began to be built in Amenhotep III's and later reigns, and only *temenos* walls are attested.[283] As noted by Adams, this shift from fortresses to walled towns, and eventually unwalled settlements with temples, denotes the pacification and gradual Egyptianization of Nubia.[284] By Thutmose III's era, Nubia was divided into two regions; Wawat (see fig. 2.32), extending up to the Second Nile Cataract; and Kush, extending from the southern end of the Second Cataract to the limits of Egyptian rule.[285] Nubia's government under the Viceroy of Kush included a deputy for Wawat, headquartered with the Viceroy at Aniba, and a deputy for Kush at Amara.[286] Local government was provided by mayors, equivalent in title to Egypt's mayors. Nubia had its own military forces, known as the Battalion of Kush, under the Viceroy, and there were also chief treasurers, overseers of cattle, overseers of granaries, and chief priests of the gods; in short, a complete administration based on that of Egypt.[287] Children of Nubian chiefs were sent to Egypt's royal court to be educated.[288] The policy of the New Kingdom pharaohs involved the destruction of the state of Kush and the exploitation of the rich gold deposits of Upper Nubia. The annals of Thutmose III make clear just how valuable the gold mining was.[289] Later military campaigns were aimed at keeping the gold mining areas safe from nomadic tribes under Thutmose

Figure 2.27 Queen Hatshepsut (1501–1480 B.C.). Limestone statue from Deir el-Bahri temple. Courtesy of The Metropolitan Museum of Art, Rogers Fund and Edward S. Harkness Gift, 1929 [29.3.2].

Figure 2.28 Thutmose III (1504–1450 B.C.), Luxor Museum, greywacke. Courtesy of F. Yurco.

Figure 2.29   Aswan Cataract from Sehel Island. Courtesy of F. Yurco.

IV and Amenhotep III.[290] Other campaigns were aimed at Irem and the southernmost reaches of the Egyptian empire and resulted in large numbers of captives.[291] Smaller numbers of slaves were mentioned in the annals of Thutmose III, but the greatest numbers came from military campaigns. These were transported to Egypt and were assigned to work on temple estates, royal estates, and to serve in the army. In the subsequent Ramesside period, slaves were also employed in building projects; the Wadi es-Sebua temple was built by Tjemeh-Libyan captives collected by the viceroy in a raid.[292] It also has been stated that slaves worked in the gold mines and quarries.[293] Legal texts specify that certain serious criminals be sent to the gold mines of Kush as punishment;[294] foreign rebels especially might end up there. Direct pharaonic control of Nubia assured the flow of other desired commodities, such as ebony wood, ivory, ostrich feathers, leopard and panther skins, oils, and gum resins, other minerals, and a variety of live African animals.[295]

Among the thorniest questions is what happened to the Nubians, especially the C-Group in Wawat (Lower Nubia), during the New Kingdom. It has been proposed that the Egyptians did not respect Nubian culture, religion, or customs, and expressed their attitude in literary barbs.[296] Royal inscriptions exhibit such phrases as "wretched Kush," or "vile

M. Lucas

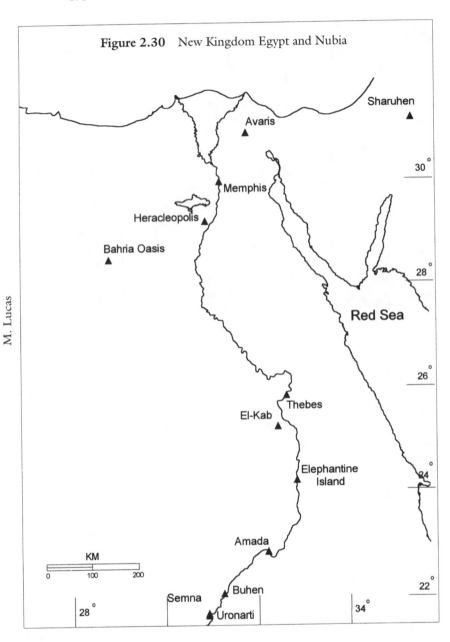

Figure 2.30 New Kingdom Egypt and Nubia

Kush," they scorned their Syro-Palestinian foes in similar terms.[297] While some Nubians were depicted "scantily clad,"[298] others are depicted in Egyptian dress or in their indigenous dress.[299] Again, as with depictions of Syro-Palestinians and Libyans, foreigners often are shown in indigenous dress.[300] In scenes depicting military victories, scorn is heaped upon the

Figure 2.31   Gebel Barkal, the "Holy Mountain" of Amun, for Kushites and Egyptians. Site of Napata. Courtesy of Museuum of Fine Arts, Boston.

foes (see fig. 2.33) by the victorious Egyptians.[301] But when, as in the tomb of Huy, Tutankhamun's Viceroy of Kush, foreigners are depicted on diplomatic or peaceful missions, they are depicted with dignity.[302] (See fig. 2.34.) Indeed, if, by Egyptian standards, status is reflected in burials, the ultimate honor and status was achieved by a Nubian named Maherpra, who was buried in the Valley of the Kings during the Eighteenth Dynasty.[303] The Nubians had their own, distinct dances, which were recognized and appreciated by the cosmopolitan New Kingdom Egyptians. Private tomb scenes of parties and temple and royal festivals, such as the Sed, or Opet at Thebes, feature Nubian dancers.[304] (See fig. 2.35.). So too, Asiatic and Libyan musicians and dancers were appreciated.[305] Egyptians were great practitioners of dance and even the pharaohs performed dances before the gods.[306]

In government the situation was more complex. Lower Nubia had been considered as Egyptian territory since Middle Kingdom times. Earlier it had been close to Egypt in A-Group times. In Upper Nubia, Kush had presented a great menace to Egypt during the Second Intermediate Period, and the early Eighteenth Dynasty pharaohs decided to dismantle it. Thutmose I subdivided Kush into five parts and tried ruling through

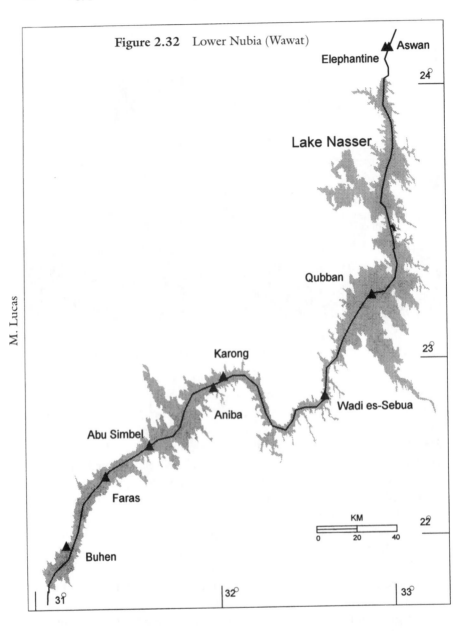

Figure 2.32   Lower Nubia (Wawat)

M. Lucas

indigenous chieftains or their sons. Some children of chiefs were shipped back to Egypt to be raised in the royal nursery and Egyptianized, a process also tried on Syro-Palestinian chieftains' sons.[307] The Kushite royalty proved very rebellious, as demonstrated by Thutmose I's, Thutmose II's and Hatshepsut's campaigns. Other Nubian chieftains in Lower Nubia

Figure 2.33   Nubian-Kushite prisoners from the Memphite tomb of Horemheb. Eighteenth Dynasty, reign of Tutankhamu (1334–25 B.C.), limestone relief. Courtesy of the Museo Civico Archeologico, Bologna.

were Egyptianized to some degree and ruled as part of the Egyptian administration.[308]

Among the deities worshipped in Nubia, Dedun, from remote antiquity, had Nubian associations, as did Anukis and Satis.[309] Senwosret III was made the patron deity of Nubia in the New Kingdom era because of his extensive activities there.[310] The distinctive Horus cults of Lower Nubia, at Qubban, Miam and Buhen may be distant echoes of Horus of *Ta-Seti,* seen on the A-Group pharaonic monuments. Other deities, such as Re-Horakhty, Ptah and Amun, were promoted in the Ramesside period as universal transcendent deities.[311] Akhenaton (1350–1334 B.C.) had also proclaimed such universality for Aton, and he built a shrine for this deity at Sesebi.[312] (See fig. 2.36.) In a great hymn to the Aton, Nubians, Egyptians and Syrians were declared as equals, all creatures of Aton, made with diverse skin colors and speech to distinguish them.[313] At Gebel Barkal, near Napata, the Egyptians recognized a Kushite ram deity, known since Kerma times, as their own deity Amun of Karnak. As a result, temples to Amun were started by both Hatshepsut and Thutmose III. As Trigger

Figure 2.34   Nubian and Kushite nobility in dignified procession with tribute for Egypt. Tomb of the Viceroy of Kush, Huy. Reign of Tutankhamun (1334–25 B.C.), painted plaster. Copyist: Charles K. Wilkinson. Courtesy of the Metropolitan Museum of Art [30.4.21].

notes, the worship of the living pharaoh was promoted by Amenhotep III and Ramesses II, both in Nubia, and in Egypt.[314] When temples were built in Nubia, as in Egypt, they were given land grants, staff, and peasants to cultivate the lands, including land in Nubia.[315] It has been suggested that many Nubians were assigned to such temple estates,[316] which may account for the local population's diminution.

Yet, C-Group and even Kerma-Kushite burial traditions continued in Nubia through the end of the Eighteenth Dynasty.[317] Egyptian-style houses containing C-Group pottery may reflect the Egyptianization

Figure 2.35   Nubian dancers from the Feast of Opet relief, Karnak Temple. Reign of Hatshepsut (1504–1482 B.C.). Courtesy of the Oriental Institute.

Figure 2.36   Akhenaton. Cairo Museum, sandstone. Courtesy of F. Yurco.

process. Egyptian-style graves in Nubia, containing weapons and jew-elry,[318] may be the tombs of Nubians serving in Egyptian armies and retiring back home after service. In Papyrus Anastasi I, of Ramesside date, the scribe Hori jibes at his colleague's military incompetence. For instance, in one division-sized unit, 5,000 soldiers, 880, or 18 percent of the division, were Nubians.[319] With four divisions standard in Ramesside armies, that works out to 3,500 Nubians in the Egyptian army, on average. In addition, the Viceroy of Kush had his own army, the Battalion of Kush, almost certainly recruited heavily from Nubia.[320] So common were Nubians in New Kingdom Egypt that Panehsy, "The Kushite," became a common man's name. A vizier, a viceroy, and a Hebrew in *Exodus* were so named.[321] The term Medja became the New Kingdom word for "police" because the Medja-Nubian desert people were regularly used in the military and police services. Members of the military and police were government employees and received pay and retirement bonuses. The soldiers might also receive battlefield awards for bravery.[322] Some of these veterans settled in Egypt, but others may have returned home to Nubia to settle, and they may be reflected in the wealthier, Egyptianized, graves. In the tomb of Huy, Tutankhamun's Viceroy of Kush, there is a scene of the grand procession of the Nubian tribute, already cited.[323] The procession shows a variety of Nubian and Kushite peoples, all distinctive as Nubians by complexion, features, and accoutrements, but otherwise dressed in Egyptian linen and finery. This documents some level of Egyptianization of Nubians, at least on the upper social levels. Other evidence indicates continuities from C-Group cemeteries to New Kingdom era Egyptianized cemeteries.[324] Still, the overall number of graves in Lower Nubia decreases from the early Eighteenth Dynasty to the Nineteenth Dynasty, and drops off most severely in the Twentieth Dynasty.[325] It has been suggested that there was an increased placement of Nubians on temple estates as *fellahin*.[326] There is also some evidence of Egyptians settling in Nubia, particularly from graves with totally Egyptian grave goods; some of these may reflect Egyptian personnel assigned to the administration and the temples and their estates.[327] Anthropological analysis of the human remains supports the idea of a mixed Egypto-Nubian population in Lower Nubia.[328] In the Nineteenth Dynasty, Ramesses II (1279–1212 B.C.) in his 44th year ordered a raid among the Tjemeh-Libyans to secure labor needed to build Wadi es-Sebua temple (see fig. 2.37) in Nubia.[329] This might suggest a lack of available population locally to draft for the project. Still, in Merenptah's 4th regnal year, ca 1208 B.C., the Nubians managed to raise a revolt that pharaoh suppressed brutally.[330]

Figure 2.37   Wadi es-Sebua temple, Nubia. Reign of Ramesses II, year 44, 1235 B.C. Courtesy of F. Yurco.

It is possible that environmental problems are partly to blame for the drop of population in Nubia in the late Ramesside period. The Twentieth Dynasty (1181–1070 B.C.) may have experienced lower Nile floods because of a drop in rainfall over the Blue Nile catchment area.[331] At Amara West, the Ramesside temple and town suffered considerably from wind-blown sand and erosion.[332] In Egypt itself, a rise in grain prices begins late in the reign of Ramesses III, and peaks in the middle of the Twentieth Dynasty before declining under Ramesses XI, again possibly reflecting poorer Nile inundations.[333] Lower Nubia had a more marginal environment throughout ancient history, so that problems in the Nilotic river regime would be amplified there. Even at the best of times, Egyptian military garrisons had to be supplied with grain shipped to Nubia from Egypt.[334] Nonetheless, Trigger has shown that some land remained cultivable in Lower Nubia during Dynasties XIX–XX, since land donations to temples are attested at Aniba, Faras, and Abu Simbel.[335] Also, some officials' tombs and monuments are dated to the Twentieth Dynasty.[336] Thus, some of the Nubian population may have remained in the vicinity of the larger settlements and temple estates. Stronger Nubian and Kushite traditions survived, most likely in Upper Nubia.[337]

The final act in Egypto-Nubian relations in the New Kingdom period came late in the Twentieth Dynasty, ca. 1090–1070 B.C. At this time the Viceroy of Kush had the most powerful army in southern Egypt and Nubia. The pharaoh was resident in distant Tanis. Libyans had established themselves in Middle Egypt and also in part of the Delta.[338] The mid Twentieth-Dynasty inflation in grain prices had caused hardship, and people in Thebes had increasingly resorted to tomb robbing. A corrupt administration turned a blind eye. During the Twentieth Dynasty, the High Priests of Amun had come to hold most of the administrative power in Upper Egypt, but they lacked military forces.[339] Early in the reign of Ramesses XI, a rebellion in Thebes ousted the High Priest of Amun, Amunhotep, and pharaoh called upon the Viceroy of Kush and his army to restore him.[340] The Viceroy, Panehsy, did this with his mostly Kushite army, and he forcibly crushed the Theban revolt and other rebellions farther north in Egypt.[341] At Thebes he even stormed the Medinet Habu temple (See pl. 46) where the rebels had taken up positions.[342] After seven or more years of Panehsy and his Kushite army's rule, Ramesses XI inexplicably reversed his decision and ordered the Viceroy of Kush to leave Thebes. A new commander, Herihor, appeared now in the Theban region, claiming the titles of vizier and High Priest of Amun, in addition to his military titles.[343] Ostensibly supporting pharaoh, he declared war on Panehsy in Nubia, but the viceroy had withdrawn his army successfully from Thebes and now successfully defended Nubia against Herihor and later his son, Payankh.[344] Although Herihor and his heirs claimed the title Viceroy of Kush, it was a hollow claim. Panehsy survived in Nubia, and was buried in his tomb at his capital, Aniba.[345] Once again, Egypt and Nubia parted ways. There is slim evidence that a regime, possibly started by Panehsy, survived in Nubia after the Twentieth Dynasty's demise. Some reliefs that look strikingly Ramesside might belong to this immediately post-Ramesside period.[346] (See fig. 2.38ab.) Perhaps it was these survivors who helped preserve Egyptian influence and religion at Gebel Barkal and Napata, which eventually had a deep impact on local Kushite chieftains ancestral to the later Napatan Dynasty.

Notes

1. See, for instance, Torgny Säve-Söderberg, *Temples and Tombs of Ancient Nubia* (Paris: UNESCO, 1987).
2. Bruce B. Williams, "The Lost Pharaohs of Nubia," *Archaeology* 33, no. 5

Figure 2.38a Blocks with a scene and inscription of King Men-Ma'at-Re, setep-en-Amun, from the Gebel Barkal Temple of Amun. Post-Ramesside, sandstone. Now in the Khartoum Museum. Courtesy of the Museum of Fine Arts, Boston.

Figure 2.38b   Blocks with a scene and inscription of King Men-Ma'at-Re, setep-en-Amun, from the Gebel Barkal Temple of Amun. Post-Ramesside, sandstone. Now in the Khartoum Museum. Courtesy of the Museum of Fine Arts, Boston.

(1980): 12–21. See also the final publication, Bruce B. Williams, *Excavations between Abu Simbel and the Sudan Frontier, Part 1: The Group Royal Cemetery at Qustul: Cemetery L*, Oriental Institute Nubian Expedition, vol. 3 (Chicago: Oriental Institute, 1986), hereafter OINE 3.

3. Williams, "The Lost Pharaohs of Nubia," 12–21, esp. figures on 16–17; Williams, OINE 3, 138–45, plate 34.

4. Williams, "The Lost Pharaohs of Nubia," 15; Williams, OINE 3, 177–79.

5. Williams, OINE 3, 179; for a full epigraphic study see William Murnane, "The Gebel Sheikh Suleiman Monument: Epigraphic Remarks," appendix C in Bruce Williams and Thomas J. Logan, "The Metropolitan Museum of Art Knife Handle and Aspects of Pharaonic Imagery Before Narmer," *JNES* 46 (1987): 282–84, and 263–64.

6. Williams and Logan, "Metropolitan Museum of Art Knife Handle," 256–59.

7. Ibid., 245–82; Williams, OINE 3, 163–82, esp. 177.

8. Fekri A. Hassan, "Chronology of the Khartoum 'Mesolithic' and 'Neolithic' and Related Sites in the Sudan: Statistical Analysis and Comparisons with Egypt," *African Archaeological Review* 4 (1986): 96; Bruce Williams, "Neolithic, A-Group, and Post-A-Group Remains from Cemeteries W, V, S, Q, T, and a Cave East of Cemetery K," *Excavations Between Abu Simbel and the Sudan Frontier,* Parts 2, 3, and 4, Oriental Institute Nubian Expedition, vol. 4 (Chicago: Oriental Institute, 1989), 135–36, hereafter OINE 4; Williams, OINE 3, 12–13.

9. Suggested by Williams, OINE 4, 135; a variant version of the idea proposed by William Y. Adams, "A Re-appraisal of Nubian Culture History," *Orientalia* n.s. 39, no. 2 (1970): 269–277, esp. 272.

10. William Y. Adams, "Doubts about the 'Lost Pharaohs,'" *JNES* 44 (1985): 185–192.

11. Bruce B. Williams, "Forbears of Menes in Nubia: Myth or Reality?" *JNES* 46 (1987): 15–26.

12. Murnane, "The Gebel Sheikh Suleiman Monument," 282–84.

13. Williams, "Forbears of Menes," 20–23; further, Williams and Logan, "Metropolitan Museum of Art Knife Handle," 252–53, 257; and final report on Qustul, Williams, OINE 3, 138–47, plates 33–34.

14. Williams, "Forbears of Menes," 16–20.

15. Williams, OINE 3, 172–79; Williams and Logan, "Metropolitan Museum of Art Knife Handle," 245–82.

16. Adams, "Doubts about the 'Lost Pharaohs,'" 191–92; Barry J. Kemp. *Ancient Egypt: Anatomy of a Civilization* (London: Routledge, Kegan-Paul, 1989), 52, 52n. 49, calling Williams's interpretation "an overstated case for its importance."

17. Williams, "Forbears of Menes," 24–25.

18. James Henry Breasted, *Ancient Records of Egypt,* vol. 1 (Chicago: University of Chicago, 1906), 65–66, 146 (hereafter *ARE* 1); Williams, OINE 4, 127, 136, 136n. 14; William Y. Adams, *Nubia: Corridor to Africa* (Princeton: Princeton University Press, 1977, 1984), 134–35; Bruce Trigger, *Nubia under the Pharaohs* (London: Thames and Hudson, 1976), 44–47.

19. Williams, "Lost Pharaohs," 14–15. Note that the Egyptian material was Naqada IIIab, mainly, see Williams, OINE 3, 108–37.

20. Trade already postulated as a factor by H. A. Nordström, *Neolithic and A-Group Sites,* Scandinavian Joint Expedition to Sudanese Nubia, vol. 3 (Stockholm: Scandinavian University, 1972), 31–32.

21. See for example, Michael Hoffman, *Egypt Before the Pharaohs,* 2d. ed. (Austin: University of Texas, 1991), 200–14. Timothy P. Harrison, "Economics with an Entrepreneurial Spirit: Early Bronze Age Trade with Late Pre-dynastic Egypt," *Biblical Archaeologist* 56, no. 2 (June 1993): 81–93.

22. Thomas Von der Way, "Investigations Concerning the Early Periods in the Northern Delta of Egypt," in *Archaeology of the Nile Delta: Priorities and Problems*, ed. E. C. M. van den Brink (Amsterdam: Netherlands Foundation for Archaeological Research in Egypt, 1988), 245–49. P. R. S. Moorey,"From Gulf to Delta in the Fourth Millennium B.C.," *Eretz Israel* 21 (1990): 62–69. Donald B. Redford, *Egypt, Canaan, and Israel in Ancient Times* (Princeton: Princeton University Press, 1992), 17–24, fig. 1.

23. Kemp, *Ancient Egypt: Anatomy of a Civilization*, 31–32; also Williams, OINE 3, 172–73 (citing Buto and Sais as possible proto-kingdoms).

24. See n. 22 above. Another Delta site was the find site of two examples of A-Group pottery in Naqada IIIa-b context, see Karla Kroeper, "The Excavations of the Munich East-Delta Expeditions in Minshat in Abu Omar," in *Archaeology of the Nile Delta: Priorities and Problems*, 15, 27 figs. 113–14.

25. For instance, Hoffman, *Egypt Before the Pharaohs*, 201, 338–39.

26. Ibid. For lapis lazuli in predynastic Egypt see W. M. F. Petrie, *Prehistoric Egypt and Corpus of Prehistoric Pottery and Palettes*, BSAE, vol. 31 (London: British School of Archaeology in Egypt, 1920), 44; also Kathryn Bard, "A Quantitative Analysis of the Pre-dynastic burials in Armant Cemetery 1400–1500," *JEA* 74 (1988): 45, 47.

27. See A-Group jewelry, Williams, "Lost Pharaohs," 19, plate; the probable source would be Wady el-Hudy amethyst quarries, see Ahmad Fakhry, *The Inscriptions of the Amethyst Quarries at Wadi el-Hudi* (Cairo: Government Press, 1952); for use of amethyst in predynastic times see Petrie, *Prehistoric Egypt*, 44.

28. Bruce G. Trigger, et al., *Ancient Egypt: A Social History* (Cambridge: Cambridge University Press, 1983), 39.

29. Ibid., 42–43; also Bruce G. Trigger, *History and Settlement of Lower Nubia* (New Haven: Yale University Press, 1965), 68–73.

30. Williams, OINE 3, 177; idem, "Forbears of Menes," 15–26.

31. Ibid.; Williams and Logan, "Metropolitan Museum of Art Knife Handle," 245–82.

32. Vijay Joshi, "Clay Tablets May Show Earliest Known Writing," *Chicago Sun Times*, 16 December 1998, 37 World.

33. Hoffman, *Egypt Before the Pharaohs*, 213–14; see also William K. Simpson, *Hekanefer and the Dynastic Material from Toshka and Arminna* (New Haven, Yale University Press, 1963), 48–49.

34. For instance, Nicholas Millett, "The Narmer Macehead and Related Objects," *JARCE* 27 (1990): 53–59. Frank J. Yurco, "Narmer: First King of Upper and Lower Egypt, A Reconsideration of his Palette and Macehead," *JSSEA* 25, no. 5 (1999): 85–95.

35. Walter B. Emery, *Archaic Egypt* (Harmondsworth: Penguin, 1961), 50–51, 51 fig. 11; also Trigger, *Nubia Under the Pharaohs*, 40–41, 40 fig. 8; and Williams, OINE 3, 183; Williams, OINE 4, 136; and Williams and Logan, "Metropolitan Museum of Art Knife Handle," 271.

36. Thomas Logan, "The Origins of the *Imy-wt* Fetish," *JARCE* 27 (1990): 61–69.

37. Williams, OINE 4, 127–28, 136.

38. See notes 34 and 36 above; also Trigger, *Nubia Under the Pharaohs*, 44–46; Adams, *Nubia: Corridor to Africa*, 136–37; although Adams posits that the decline came after the First Dynasty, but see Williams, "Forbears of Menes," 16–20; and Williams, OINE 4, 183.

39. See notes 34 and 38, above.

40. Barbara Bell, "The Oldest Records of the Nile Floods," *Geographical Journal* 136 (1970): 569–73; Trigger, *Nubia Under the Pharaohs*, 44–45.

41. Williams, OINE 4, 126–27.

42. Hoffman, *Egypt Before the Pharaohs*, 248.

43. Williams, OINE 4, 126–27.

44. Torgny Säve-Söderbergh, *Ägypten und Nubien* (Lund: Haken Ohlssons Boktryckeri, 1941), 7; Trigger, *Nubia Under the Pharaohs*, 46.

45. Trigger, *Nubia Under the Pharaohs*, 46, 46n. 17.

46. Adams, *Nubia: Corridor to Africa*, 139, 174, also partly to collect slaves.

47. Trigger, *Nubia Under the Pharaohs*, 47, 47n. 21.

48. Reginald Engelbach, "The Quarries of the Western Nubian Desert and the Ancient Road to Toshka," *ASAE* 38 (1938): 369–90.

49. Trigger, *Nubia Under the Pharaohs*, 48 and plate 9; Adams, *Nubia: Corridor to Africa*, 170–74. Buhen was a center for copper smelting.

50. Trigger, *Nubia Under the Pharaohs*, 47.

51. For her reserve head, see William Stevenson Smith, *Ancient Egypt as Represented in the Museum of Fine Arts, Boston*, 6th ed. (Boston: Museum of Fine Arts, 1960), 35 fig. 11.

52. See, for instance Jean-Pierre Corteggiani, *The Egypt of the Pharaohs at the Cairo Museum*, trans. Anthony Roberts (London: Scala Publications, 1987), 60, 60n. 27. The elongated torso and limbs that Corteggiani found bizarre might reflect an elongated physique such as found among some Nilotic pastoral peoples, or perhaps Egyptian provincial style.

53. See, for example, Miriam Lichtheim, *Ancient Egyptian Literature*, vol. 1 (Berkeley, Los Angeles, Calif.: University of California, 1973), 18–27, hereafter *AEL* 1.

54. Trigger, *Nubia Under the Pharaohs*, 54.

55. Scholars have debated the meaning of this title, rendered as "caravan leader," Raymond O. Faulkner, *A Concise Dictionary of Middle Egyptian* (Oxford: Oxford University Press, 1962), 39; "overseer of dragomans," Alan H. Gardiner, *Egypt of the Pharaohs* (Oxford: Oxford University Press, 1961), 96–99; "overseer of foreigners, or mercenaries," Hans Goedicke, "The Title *imy-r ꜥw* in the Old Kingdom," *JEA* 46 (1960): 60–64; and idem, "An Additional Note on 'ꜣ 'foreigner,'" *JEA* 52 (1966): 172–74; and "chief of interpreters," Henry G. Fischer, *Inscriptions from the Coptite Nome, Dynasties VI–XI*, Analecta Orientalia 40

(Rome: Pontifical, Biblical Institute, 1964), 29; and Lanny Bell, "Once more the '*w* 'interpreters' or 'foreigners,'" *Newsletter of the ARCE* 87 (1973): 33. Two Egyptian graffiti at Tomas call the officials "overseer of the army of Satjet" indicating further the use of Nubian mercenary troops, see Trigger, et al., *Ancient Egypt: A Social History,* 126.

56. Goedicke, "The Title *imy-r ʿw* in the Old Kingdom," 62; idem, "An additional note on *3* 'foreigner,'" 173; and Bell, "Once More the '*w* 'interpreters' or 'foreigners',", 33; supported also by Gerald E. Kadish, "Old Kingdom Egyptian Activity in Nubia: Some Re-considerations," *JEA* 52 (1966): 23–33.

57. Fischer, *Inscriptions from the Coptite Nome,* 29.

58. K. H. Priese, "Articula," *Études et Travaux* 7 (1973): 159–62; supported by Trigger, *Nubia Under the Pharaohs,* 57.

59. K. H. Priese, "*rm* and *3m,* das Land Irame: Ein Beitrag zur Topographie des Sudan in Altertum," *Altorientalische Forschungen* 1 (1974): 7–41; again supported by Trigger, *Nubia Under the Pharaohs,* 57; but see also David O'Connor, "The Location of Irem," *JEA* 78 (1987): 99–136 who disputes this identification; idem, "Egypt, 1552–664 B.C.," in *The Cambridge History of Africa,* vol. 1, ed. J. Desmond Clark (Cambridge: Cambridge University Press, 1962), 902–905, and 925–40.

60. Priese, "*rm* und *3m,* das Land Irame," 7–41; Elmar Edel, *Inschriften des alten Reiches V. Die Reiseberichte des Hrw-hwjf* (Herchuf), in *Ägyptologische Studien,* ed. Otto Firchow (Berlin: 1955), 51–75, esp. 62–68; idem, "Inschriften des alten Reiches XI. Nachtrage zu den Reiseberichten des Hrw hwjf," *ZÄS* 85 (1960): 18–23; idem, "Die Ländername Unternubiens und die Ausbreitung der C-Gruppe nach den Reiseberichten des Hrw-hwjf," *Orientalia* n.s. 36 (1967): 153–58; followed by Trigger, *Nubia Under the Pharaohs,* 54; and Trigger, et al., *Ancient Egypt: A Social History,* 129. Similar locations are advocated by Dean Dixon, "The Land of Yam," *JEA* 44 (1958): 40–55; but others have advocated a western desert or oasis locale, for instance, Jean Yoyotte, "Pour une localisation du Pays de Iam," *BIFAO* 52 (1953): 173–78 (favoring Dunkul Oasis), and Hans Goedicke, "Harkhuf's Travels," *JNES* 40 (1981): 1–20. David O'Connor, "The Locations of Yam and Kush and Their Historical Implications," *JARCE* 23 (1987): 27–50, figs. 2, 3, proposes for Yam a far more southerly locale in the Butana-Shendi area of the Upper Nile. He proposes also that Wawat comprised all of Lower Nubia, already in the Old Kingdom, and that Irtjet and Satjet lay in the Sai Island-Kerma region. This requires rejecting all Old Kingdom and Middle Kingdom rock inscriptions from Lower Nubia as having any geographical value. The utter lack of Old Kingdom inscriptions or other evidence from the Butana-Shendi area, or anywhere south of the Second Nile Cataract region renders his thesis highly speculative. For this paper, I will continue using Edel's location for Yam.

61. This geographic sequence is indicated by Harkhuf's autobiography; see Lichtheim, *AEL* 1, 18–27; also Edel, "Die Ländername Unternubiens und die

Ausbreitung der C-Gruppe nach Reiseberichten des Hrw hwjf," 133–58; also note 60, above.

62. Trigger, *Nubia Under the Pharaohs,* 54.

63. Ibid., citing Goedicke, and following Kadish and Bell's interpretation, see note 56 above.

64. Lichtheim, *AEL* 1, 23–27.

65. Kadish, "Old Kingdom Egyptian Activity in Nubia," 23–24; Iri was one of three officials who left their names on the rocks at Tomas.

66. Ibid., 24–25.

67. Ibid., 29; they lived west of the Nubian Nile, perhaps in the oases.

68. Ibid., 32–33.

69. Basically following Kadish's reasoning; see also Trigger, *Nubia Under the Pharaohs,* 59, for another view of this incident.

70. So, Faulkner, *Concise Dictionary of Middle Egyptian,* 314, s.v. *dng;* Lichtheim, *AEL 1,* 26–27, and 48 (citing Pyramid Texts Utterance 517); Gardiner, *Egypt of the Pharaohs,* 58–59, n. 1; also Kadish, "Old Kingdom Egyptian Activity in Nubia," 26; disputed by Kent Weeks, "Art, Word, and the Egyptian World View," in *Egyptology and the Social Sciences* (Cairo: American University Press, 1979), 72–73, 72–73nn. 65–68, 80, who would see *dng* as a dwarf used for ceremonial performances, followed by Trigger, *Nubia Under the Pharaohs,* 56–57.

71. Adams, *Nubia: Corridor to Africa,* 140, 144.

72. Kadish, "Old Kingdom Egyptian Activity in Nubia," 27–28.

73. Ibid., 26–30.

74. Ibid., 28–32.

75. Trigger, et al., *Ancient Egypt: A Social History,* 126, suggest this C-Group confederacy's chief as a "veritable king of Lower Nubia."

76. Breasted, *ARE* 1, 145–46, 316–17.

77. Ibid, 146, sec. 318. Breasted suggested, n. 1, that the 'm' of M[edja] was visible, and part of the verb "praise." This text is located opposite Philae Island, on the East Bank road.

78. Kadish, "Old Kingdom Egyptian Activity in Nubia," 32–33.

79. Lichtheim, *AEL 1,* 26.

80. Like Weni, perhaps his civil career preceded his post as governor of Aswan.

81. Breasted, *ARE 1,* 162; compare with Lichtheim, *AEL 1,* 25; see Kadish, "Old Kingdom Egyptian Activity in Nubia," 31, 31n. 6, mentioning a suggestion by John A. Wilson, that Pepynakht had copied Harkhuf's title.

82. Harkhuf having started service under Pharaoh Merenre, with his fourth voyage coming under Pepy II, year 2, see Lichtheim, *AEL 1,* 25–27.

83. Breasted, *ARE 1,* 163, sec. 358.

84. Ibid., 163, sec. 359; Säve-Söderbergh, *Ägypten und Nubien,* 29.

85. Breasted, *ARE 1,* 163, sec. 360; Säve-Söderbergh, *Ägypten und Nubien,* 29.

86. Trigger, *Nubia Under the Pharaohs,* 59; Säve-Söderbergh, *Ägypten und Nubien,* 29; and Kadish, "Old Kingdom Egyptian Activity in Nubia," 31, all reflected Pepy-nakht's campaigns. Adams, *Nubia: Corridor to Africa,* overlooked them.

87. Breasted, *ARE 1,* 164–69; Trigger, *Nubia Under the Pharaohs,* 59.

88. Trigger, *Nubia Under the Pharaohs,* 59; Säve-Söderbergh, *Ägypten und Nubien,* 19–21, 29, saw it as a case of tongo payment for safe passage to the local chiefs, but Kadish, "Old Kingdom Egyptian Activity in Nubia," 31n. 9, 32n. 7, doubts the idea of tongo payment.

89. Trigger, *Nubia Under the Pharaohs,* 59, allows for both possibilities.

90. Kadish, "Old Kingdom Egyptian Activity in Nubia," 32.

91. A. M. Abu Bakr and J. Osing, "Achtungstexte aus dem Alten Reich," *MDAIK* 29 (1973): 97–133; idem, "Achtungstexte aus dem Alten Reich," *MDAIK* 32 (1976): 133–85. Georges Posener, "À la recherche de nouveaux textes d'evoûtement," in *Proceedings of the Vth World Congress of Jewish Studies* (Jerusalem: World Union of Jewish Studies, 1971), 144–49.

92. As claimed by Adams, *Nubia: Corridor to Africa,* 174–75; also Edel, *Inschriften den Alten Reich V,* 53–54; Dixon, "The Land of Yam," 40–55; Gardiner, *Egypt of the Pharaohs,* 100, 100n. 1; and even Säve-Söderbergh, *Ägypten und Nubien,* 20–21.

93. Kadish, "Old Kingdom Egyptian Activity in Nubia," 29–33, and recognized also by Trigger, *Nubia Under the Pharaohs,* 59–60; and Jean Leclant, "Egypt in Nubia during the Old, Middle, and New Kingdoms," in *Africa in Antiquity,* vol. 1, ed. S. Hochfield and E. Riefstahl (Brooklyn, N.Y.: The Brooklyn Museum, 1978), 63.

94. Williams, OINE 4, 127; Manfred Bietak, "The C-Group and the Pan Grave Culture in Nubia," in *Nubian Culture Past and Present,* ed. T. Hagg (Stockholm: Almqvist and Wiksell, 1987), 113–17.

95. For instance, A. J. Arkell, *A History of the Sudan to 1821,* 2d ed. (London: Athlone Press, 1961), 46.

96. Adams, *Nubia: Corridor to Africa,* 91–95; Ahmed Batrawi, "The Racial History of Egypt and Nubia," *Journal of the Royal Anthropological Institute of Great Britain and Ireland* 76 (1946): 131–56; Trigger, *Nubia Under the Pharaohs,* 52–54; Bietak, "C-Group and the Pan Grave Culture in Nubia," 113–17.

97. Williams, OINE 4, 135–36.

98. Ibid., 126–27.

99. Adams, *Nubia: Corridor to Africa,* 94, 94fig. 12; Shomarka O. Y. Keita, "Studies of Crania from Northern Africa," *American Journal of Physical Anthropology* 83 (1990): 35–48.

100. Adams, *Nubia: Corridor to Africa,* 128–29; H. S. Smith, "The Nubian B-Group," *Kush* 14 (1966): 69–124, esp. 124.

101. Barry J. Kemp, "Abydos and the Royal Tombs of the First Dynasty," *JEA* 52 (1966): 13; the Egyptian tumuli, though, were rectangular.

102. Adams, *Nubia: Corridor to Africa,* 128, 128fig. 15; Trigger, *Nubia Under the Pharaohs,* 49–50, 49 fig. 12; Bietak, "C-Group and Pan Grave Cultures in Nubia," 119.

103. For example, David O'Connor, "Ancient Egypt and Black Africa-Early Contacts," *Expedition* 14, no. 1 (fall 1971): 6–7, 6–7figs. 2, 3; Trigger, *Nubia Under the Pharaohs,* 88–93, 91–92 figs. 28, 29.

104. Bietak, "C-Group and Pan Grave Culture in Nubia," 115–16.

105. Adams, *Nubia: Corridor to Africa,* 141.

106. Trigger, et al., *Ancient Egypt: A Social History,* 112; Georges Posener, "Le conte de Néferkarè et du Géneral Siséné," *Revue d'Égyptologie* 11 (1957): 119–37.

107. Barbara Bell, "The Dark Ages in Ancient History, I: The First Dark Age in Egypt," *AJA* 75 (1971): 1–26. Autobiographies of the period mention low Niles, famine, and relief efforts; see Lichtheim, *AEL 1,* 83–90 for examples.

108. Willam C. Hayes, "The Middle Kingdom in Egypt, Internal History from the Rise of the Heracleopolitans to the Death of Ammenemes III," in *Cambridge Ancient History,* vol. 1, 3d ed., pt. 2 (Cambridge: Cambridge University Press, 1971), 464.

109. Ibid., 465, 474; and Lichtheim, *AEL 1,* 85–86; J. Vandier, *Mo'alla: La tombe d'Ankhtifi et la tombe de Sebekhotep* (Bibliothèque d'Étude, 18; Cairo: Institut Français d'Archéologie Orientale, 1950), 163–66 (inscription 2), 185–206 (inscriptions 5–7), and 263 (inscription 16).

110. Trigger, *Nubia Under the Pharaohs,* 61, and plate 13.

111. H. G. Fischer, "The Nubian Mercenaries of Gebelein during The First Intermediate Period," *Kush* 9 (1961): 44–80, and plate x; Lechtheim, *AEL 1,* 90.

112. Jean Vercoutter, "Upper Egyptian Settlers in Middle Kingdom Nubia," *Kush* 5 (1957): 61–69, esp. 69.

113. Trigger, *Nubia Under the Pharaohs,* 60, and Adams, *Nubia: Corridor to Africa,* 169, see these as trade goods of the Dynasties VI–XI, but as noted by David O'Connor, "Political Systems and Archaeological Data in Egypt: 2600–1780 B.C.," *World Archaeology* 6 (1974): 29–30, most Egyptian goods in early C-Group graves date precisely to the First Intermediate Period: Sixth Dynasty trade mainly was with Yam, not with Lower Nubia.

114. Hermann Junker, *Bericht über die Grabungen von El-Kubaniyah-Nord,* Akademie der Wissenschaften in Wien, Philosophisch-historische Klasse Denkschriften 64, no. 3 (Vienna: A. Holder, 1920); Trigger, *Nubia Under the Pharaohs,* 61.

115. Following the traditional chronology. Herbert E. Winlock, *Rise and Fall of the Middle Kingdom in Thebes* (New York: Macmillan, 1947), 2; also, Richard A. Parker, "The Sothic Dating of the Twelfth and Eighteenth Dynasties," in *Studies in Honor of George R. Hughes,* ed. E. F. Wente and J. Johnson, S.A.O.C. 39 (Chicago: University of Chicago Press, 1976), 177–89.

116. Lichtheim, *AEL 1,* 102–3 (Teaching for Merykare); 105, 90–93.

117. Säve-Söderbergh, *Ägypten und Nubien,* 45, 46–50; Trigger, *Nubia*

Under the Pharaohs, 62; O'Connor, "Political Systems and Archaeological Data," 30.

118. Edward Brovarski and William J. Murnane, "Inscriptions from the Time of Nebhepetre Mentuhotep II at Abisko," *Serapis* 1, no. 1 (1969): 11–33; Hayes, "The Middle Kingdom in Egypt," 470–71; and Leclant, "Egypt in Nubia during the Old, Middle, and New Kingdoms," 63.

119. Brovarski and Murnane, "Inscriptions from the Time of Nebhepetre," 11.

120. Lichtheim, *AEL 1,* 90.

121. Hayes, "The Middle Kingdom in Egypt," 480.

122. Brovarski and Murnane, "Inscriptions from the Time of Nebhepetre," 11; Säve-Söderberg, *Ägypten und Nubien,* 58–60; Leclant, "Egypt in Nubia during the Old, Middle, and New Kingdoms," 63; but see Trigger, *Nubia Under the Pharaohs,* who doubts that Bn is Buhen.

123. Säve-Söderbergh, *Ägypten und Nubien,* 57.

124. O'Connor, "Political Systems and Archaeological Data," 30; Trigger, *Nubia Under the Pharaohs,* 62–63.

125. Trigger, *Nubia Under the Pharaohs,* 63.

126. Following the traditional chronology, Dynasties XI–XII, see note 115 above.

127. Lichtheim, *AEL I,* 143.

128. For instance, Walter B. Emery, *Lost Land Emerging* (New York: Scribner's, 1967), 189; William C. Hayes, *The Scepter of Egypt* (New York: Metropolitan Museum of Art, 1953), I, 171, 176; but doubted by Georges Posener, *Littérature et politique dans l'Égypte de la XIIe Dynastie* (Paris: H. Champion, 1956), 47–48; and Trigger, Kemp, O'Connor, and Lloyd, *Ancient Egypt: A Social History,* 79; and Trigger, *Nubia Under the Pharaohs,* 64. Even if the lady was not from Nubia, the population around Aswan has always been strongly intermixed with Nubians, and never more than in early Dynasty XII, after numerous Nubians settled in Upper Egypt; see Fischer, note 111 above.

129. Cyril Aldred, *Middle Kingdom Art in Egypt* (London: Alec Tiranti, 1969), 38, 38n. 19, and plate 19. Also, Cyril Aldred "Some Royal Portraits of the Middle Kingdom in Ancient Egypt," *Metropolitan Museum of Art Journal* 3 (1970): 27–50, esp. 35 fig. 13.

130. For instance, Senwosret I, see Frank J. Yurco, "Were the Ancient Egyptians Black or White?" *Biblical Archaeology Review* 15, 5 (Sept.–Oct., 1989), 15, and plate at bottom; Senwosret III and Amenemhat III, Aldred, "Some Royal Portraits of the Middle Kingdom in Ancient Egypt," 41–42, 41 fig. 21, 42 fig. 22, 48–49, 48–49 fig. 34–36; also Aldred, *Middle Kingdom Art in Egypt,* 54–55, plates 77–78.

131. Breasted, *ARE I,* 223, sec. 473.

132. Trigger, et al., *Ancient Egypt: A Social History,* 130–31; Trigger, *Nubia Under the Pharaohs,* 64–65.

133. Breasted, *ARE I,* 248–49, sec. 512; the inscription records burning of tents and hurling of grain into the Nile. Note, however, that this campaign was

against Kush, and not the C-Group Nubians; contra Adams, *Nubia: Corridor to Africa*, 176, who equates these XIIth Dynasty operations to IInd–IVth Dynasty raids that took many captives from Lower Nubia, eventually depopulating the region.

134. Breasted, *ARE I*, 251, sec. 519; Säve-Söderbergh, *Ägypten und Nubien*, 70–71; Gardiner, *Egypt of the Pharaohs*, 134.

135. Georges Posener, "Pour une localisation du pays Koush au Moyen Empire," *Kush* 6 (1958): 39–68; see also footnote 60 above.

136. Trigger, *Nubia Under the Pharaohs*, 65. Leclant, "Egypt in Nubia during the Old, Middle, and New Kingdoms," 64–66; Barry J. Kemp, "Old Kingdom, Middle Kingdom and Second Intermediate Period in Egypt," in J. Desmond Clark, ed. *The Cambridge History of Africa*, (Cambridge: Cambridge University, 1982), 1:715–17.

137. Breasted, *ARE*, vol. I, 251, sec. 519, also see note 134 above.

138. Säve-Söderbergh, *Ägypten und Nubien*, 72; Trigger, *Nubia Under the Pharaohs*, 65.

139. Trigger, *Nubia Under the Pharaohs*, 91–92; O'Connor, "Political Systems and Archaeological Data," 31–32.

140. Trigger, *Nubia Under the Pharaohs*, 65–66.

141. Jean Vercoutter, ed., *Mirgissa*, Mission archéologique française au Soudan, (Paris: P. Geuthner 1970), 1:170; suggested already by Säve-Söderbergh, *Ägypten und Nubien*, 76; see too Jean Vercoutter, "La stèle de Mirgissa IM. 209 et la localisation d'Iken (Kor ou Mirgissa?)," *Revue d'Égyptologie* 16 (1964): 179–91; idem, *Mirgissa*, 1:187.

142. J. W. Ruby, "Preliminary Report of the University of California Expedition to Dabenarti, 1963," *Kush* 12 (1964): 54–56.

143. Trigger, *Nubia Under the Pharaohs*, 69, 69fig. 18, and 72–73, 73 fig. 20.

144. A. Vila, "Les vestiges de la plaine," in Vercoutter, ed., *Mirgissa*, 1:204–14; Trigger, *Nubia Under the Pharaohs*, 71, 76 fig. 21, and pl. 20. The date of the slipway is uncertain; it may have already been operational under Senwosret I.

145. A. Vila, "L'armement de la fortresse de Mirgissa-Iken," *Revue d'Égyptologie* 22 (1970), 171–99; Trigger, *Nubia Under the Pharaohs*, 71.

146. Trigger, *Nubia Under the Pharaohs*, 75; idem, "The Reasons for the Construction of the Second Cataract Forts," *JSSEA* 12.1 (1982): 1–6, advocates trade and defense.

147. Breasted, *ARE I*, 251–52, sec. 520–21; Gardiner, *Egypt of the Pharaohs*, 134.

148. Säve-Söderbergh, *Ägypten und Nubien*, 73; Jean Vercoutter, "The Gold of Kush," *Kush* (1959): 120–53; Trigger, et al., *Ancient Egypt: A Social History*, 122–23.

149. Vercoutter, "The Gold of Kush," 133–35; Trigger, *Nubia Under the Pharaohs*, 66–67, and map, 66 fig. 17.

150. A. Lucas and J.R. Harris, *Ancient Egyptian Materials and Industries,* 4th ed. (London: Edward Allen, 1962), 207–9.

151. Trigger, et al., *Ancient Egypt: A Social History,* 123.

152. Ibid., 131; Walter B. Emery, *Lost Land Emerging* (New York: Scribner's, 1967), 197–99. Implied also by the presence there of General Montuhotep's stela of year 18 Senwosret I.

153. Säve-Söderbergh, *Ägypten und Nubien,* 67–69; Trigger, *Nubia Under the Pharaohs,* 65.

154. Trigger, *Nubia Under the Pharaohs,* 71, 74, and map, 69 fig. 18, .

155. Alan H. Gardiner, "An Ancient List of Fortresses of Nubia," *JEA* 3 (1916): 184–92.

156. Trigger, *Nubia Under the Pharaohs,* 71, 74, and map, 69 fig. 18, .

157. Emphasizing the riverine nature of the defense, see James Knudstad, "Serra East and Dorginarti," *Kush* 14 (1966): 165–86; Trigger, *Nubia Under the Pharaohs,* 75, and pl. 28.

158. Adams, *Nubia: Corridor to Africa,* 147–52, 148–51figs. 18–20, also 160; Trigger, *Nubia Under the Pharaohs,* 77–81; Manfred Bietak, *Studien zur Chronologie der Nubischen C-Gruppe,* Österreichische Akademie der Wissenschaften, Philosophisch-historische Klasse Denkschrift 97 (Vienna: Bohlau in Komission, 1968), 98–105; Leclant, "Egypt in Nubia during the Old, Middle, and New Kingdoms," 66, proposed passive resistance among the C-Group Nubians, but their non-adoption of Egyptian goods may simply indicate that the C-Group were not much involved with trade or interaction with the Egyptians of Dynasty XII, see David O'Connor, "Nubia before the New Kingdom," in *Africa in Antiquity,* S. Hochfield and E. Riefstahl, eds. (Brooklyn: Brooklyn Museum, 1978), 1:56.

159. H. Å. Nordström, "Excavations and Survey in Faras, Argin, and Gezira Dabrosa," *Kush* 10 (1962): 34–61, esp 40–41; Trigger, *Nubia Under the Pharaohs,* 79; Adams, *Nubia: Corridor to Africa,* 161–62; and Säve-Söderbergh, *Ägypten und Nubien,* 74.

160. Trigger, *Nubia Under the Pharaohs,* 79; Nordström, "Excavations and Survey in Faras, Argin, and Gezira Dabrosa," 40–41. Also note 145 above.

161. Vila, "L'armement de la fortresse de Mirgissa-Iken," 198–99; Adams, *Nubia: Corridor to Africa,* 182, 182nn. 60–62.

162. Jean Vercoutter, "Upper Egyptian Settlers in Middle Kingdom Nubia," *Kush* 5 (1957): 61–69; Adams, *Nubia: Corridor to Africa,* 182, 182n. 59.

163. Trigger, *Nubia Under the Pharaohs,* 71.

164. Ibid., 77–79; O'Connor, "Political Systems and Archaeological Data," 30.

165. Trigger, *Nubia Under the Pharaohs,* 80–81.

166. Ibid., 80: also Trigger, *History and Settlement in Lower Nubia,* 159–61.

167. Gardiner, *Egypt of the Pharaohs,* 135; Säve-Söderbergh, *Ägypten und Nubien,* 76.

168. Jean Vercoutter, "Nile Levels at Kumma," *Kush* 14 (1966): 164; for the other campaigns, see Trigger, *Nubia Under the Pharaohs*, 68.

169. Trigger, *Nubia Under the Pharaohs*, 72–73, and fig. 20; Trigger, et al., *Ancient Egypt: A Social History*, 131–32, 133 fig. 2.3; for full reports see: G. Reisner, D. Dunham, and J.M.A. Janssen, *Semna, Kumma. Second Cataract Forts*, vol. 1 (Boston: Museum of Fine Arts, 1960); G. Reisner, N. F. Wheeler, and D. Dunham, *Uronarti, Shalfak, Mirgissa. Second Cataract Forts*, vol. 2 (Boston: Museum of Fine Arts, 1967); Jean Vercoutter, "Semna South Fort and the Records of Nile Levels at Kumma," *Kush* 14 (1966): 125–64; Louis Žabkar, "The Egyptian Name of the Fortress of Semna South," *JEA* 58 (1972): 83–90.

170. Trigger, *Nubia Under the Pharaohs*, 74; Alexander Badawy, "Preliminary Report on the Excavations by the University of California at Askut," *Kush* 12 (1964): 47–53.

171. Vercoutter, ed., *Mirgissa*, 1:70, 187; Trigger, *Nubia Under the Pharaohs*, 72–73, 73 fig. 20d, plates 25–26.

172. Harry S. Smith, "The Rock Inscriptions of Buhen," *JEA* 58 (1972): 43–61, esp. 55–57.

173. Gardiner, *Egypt of the Pharaohs*, 135; Vercoutter, ed., *Mirgissa*, 1:187; Trigger, et al., *Ancient Egypt: A Social History*, 132. Adams, *Nubia: Corridor to Africa*, 185, citing Walter B. Emery, *Egypt in Nubia* (London: 1965), 129, translates *nhsy* as "Negro," an imprecise, outmoded, racial usage. "Nubian," or "Kushite" more precisely, would be the correct translation of the term, considering the purpose of the Semna fortresses, and who they were meant to regulate.

174. Trigger, *Nubia Under the Pharaohs*, 68–77, with figs. 19, 20, 21, and 23.

175. Gardiner, *Egypt of the Pharaohs*, 135.

176. See Smither, "The Semnah Dispatches," 3–10.

177. Barbara Bell, "Climate and History of Egypt: The Middle Kingdom," 223–69; Trigger, *Nubia Under the Pharaohs*, 82–83, 83 fig. 23.

178. Trigger, et al., *Ancient Egypt: A Social History*, 123.

179. Vercoutter, "The Gold of Kush," 132–35.

180. Adams, *Nubia: Corridor to Africa*, 185, 187; see Trigger, *Nubia Under the Pharaohs*, 74–75.

181. Trigger, et al., *Ancient Egypt: A Social History*, 132–36; A. Vila, "Un rituel d'evoûtement au Moyen Empire égyptien," in *L'Homme, hier et aujourd'hui, Recueil d'études en hommage à Andre Leroi-Gourhan, avant-propos de Marc Sauter* (Paris: Éditions Cujas, 1973), 625–39; idem, "Un dépôt de textes d'evoûtement au Moyen Empire," *Journal des Savants* 3 (1963): 135–60; Reisner, Wheeler, and Dunham, *Uronarti, Shalfak, Mirgissa*, pls. 31–32; see also, Georges Posener, *Princes et Pays d'Asie et de Nubie* (Brussels: Fondation Égyptologique Reine Elisabeth 1940), 48–54.

182. Gardiner, *Egypt of the Pharaohs*, 136.

183. Bell, "Climate and History of Egypt: The Middle Kingdom," 223–69;

Badawy, "Preliminary Report on the Excavations by the University of California at Askut," 52. For a possibly related high inundation, see John Baines, "The Inundation Stela of Sebekhotpe VIII," *Acta Orientalia* 36 (1974): 39–54; idem, "The Sebekhotpe VIII Inundation Stela: An Additional Fragment," *Acta Orientalia* 37 (1976): 11–20; Labib Habachi, "A High Inundation in the Temple of Amenre at Karnak in the Thirteenth Dynasty," *Studien zur altägyptischen Kultur* 1 (1974): 207–14.

184. Trigger, et al., *Ancient Egypt: A Social History*, 181–82, propose that the high floods led to the decline of Middle Kingdom culture, yet the fact is, the XIIIth Dynasty represents only a change in government structure with no immediate decline in Egypt's prestige or influence. The decline came suddenly, with the Hyksos inruption after 1710 B.C., see 149–52.

185. Vercoutter, "Semna South Fort and the Records of Nile Levels at Kumma," 125–64; Trigger, *Nubia Under the Pharaohs*, 82–83, 83 fig. 23.

186. See A. Hesse, "Introduction géophysique et notes techniques," in *Mirgissa*, J. Vercoutter, ed., 1:51–67; Bell, "Climate and History of Egypt: The Middle Kingdom," 232–35. The idea that a barrage was built at Semna, causing these high floods, (Jean Vercoutter, "Égyptologie et Climatologie. Les crues du Nil à Semneh," *Cahiers de Recherches de l'Institut de papyrologie et d'Égyptologie de Lille* 4 [1976]: 139–72) is nullified by the attestation of high floods and siltation farther north throughout Lower Nubia and Egypt.

187. Trigger, et al., *Ancient Egypt: A Social History*, 154; Jurgen von Beckerath, "Notes on the Viziers 'Ankhu and Iymeru in the Thirteenth Egyptian Dynasty," *JNES* 17 (1958): 20–28; and William C. Hayes, "Notes on the Government of Egypt in the Late Middle Kingdom," *JNES* 12 (1953): 31–39, esp. 38–39.

188. Regarding Dynasty XIV, see Donald B. Redford, "The Hyksos Invasion in History and Tradition," *Orientalia* n.s. 39 (1970): 21; idem, *Pharaonic Kinglists, Daybooks, Annals, and Kinglists* (Mississauga, Ont: Benben, 1986), 239–40.

189. Säve-Söderbergh, *Ägypten und Nubien*, 119–20; Trigger, et al., *Ancient Egypt: A Social History*, 160; Trigger, *Nubia Under the Pharaohs*, 84.

190. Säve-Söderbergh, *Ägypten und Nubien*, 119–20; also Jean Leclant, "Fouilles et Travaux en Égypte et au Soudan, 1971–72," *Orientalia* n.s. 42 (1973): 429.

191. Smither, "The Semnah Dispatches," 3–10.

192. A. W. Lawrence, "Ancient Egyptian Fortifications," *JEA* 51 (1965): 69–94, esp. 86n. 1; Olga Tufnell, "Seal Impressions from Kahun Town and Uronarti Fort," *JEA* 61 (1975): 67–101.

193. Trigger, *Nubia Under the Pharaohs*, 85; Trigger, Kemp, O'Connor, and Lloyd, *Ancient Egypt: A Social History*, 162.

194. Brigitte Gratien, *Les Cultures Kerma: Essai de classification* (Lille: Université de Lille, 1978); Adams, *Nubia: Corridor to Africa*, 2nd ed., xxiii. Now

generally confirmed by excavations at Kerma, see Charles Bonnet, "Fouilles archéologiques de Kerma (Soudan)," *Genava* n.s. 28 (1980): 31–72, esp. 50–58.

195. Bonnet, "Fouilles archéologiques à Kerma (Soudan); rapport préliminaire de la campagne 1977–1978," 107–27; idem, "Remarques sur la ville de Kerma," in *Hommage à la Mémoire de Serge Sauneron, 1927–1976*, (Cairo: Institut Français d'Archéologie Orientale, 1979), 1:3–10.

196. George A. Reisner, *Excavations at Kerma, Parts I–III, IV–V* (Cambridge: Harvard University, 1923), I–III:38–39, and IV–V:81.

197. Trigger, et al., *Ancient Egypt: A Social History*, 163, inexplicably claim that these seals originated in Kerma! Yet on 162, Uronarti seals from a similar context are stated correctly to come from packages delivered to the fort from outside. The normal procedure was to apply seals to guarantee the contents and identify the sender. Assuredly, the same explanation should apply to the Hyksos seals at Kerma. Indeed, page 95 of Trigger, *Nubia Under the Pharaohs*, notes: "The sealings bearing the names of Hyksos rulers that were found in the rooms around the base of the Western Deffufa indicate that early in the Fifteenth Dynasty extensive trade went on between Kush and Lower Egypt."

198. Trigger, et al., *Ancient Egypt: A Social History*, 167.

199. See O'Connor, "Ancient Egypt and Black Africa-Early Contacts," 6–8, 7 fig. 3, for a depiction of a Kushite royal burial.

200. Trigger, et al., *Ancient Egypt: A Social History*, 164–65, 165 fig. 2.13.

201. William Stevenson Smith, *Interconnections in the Ancient Near East: The Arts of Egypt, the Aegean, and Western Asia* (New Haven, London: Yale University, 1965), 39–40, fig. 60.

202. Anthony Marks, A. Mohammed-Ali, T.R. Hays, and Y.M. Elamin, "Butana Archaeological Project: 1981 Fieldwork," *Nyame Akuma* 21 (1982): 39–40.

203. Rodolfo Fattovich and Marcello Piperno, "Survey of the Gash Delta: November, 1980," *Nyame Akuma* 19 (1981): 29–30.

204. For example, besides the gold in the Kerma tumuli, an Egyptian mercenary serving the Kushite king for six years returned to Edfu with sufficient gold to buy land; see Trigger, et al., *Ancient Egypt: A Social History*, 162 and 167.

205. Ibid., 158, and note 1, but following the higher chronology of the New Kingdom, in *Studies in Honor of George R. Hughes*, E.F. Wente and J. Johnson eds., S.A.O.C. 39 (Chicago: Oriental Institute, 1977), 216–17, esp. 225 and table 1, 218 (Ahmose I, 1570–46 B.C.), expulsion of the Hyksos about year 12–13, 1558–57 B.C.

206. Trigger, *Nubia Under the Pharaohs*, 85.

207. George A. Reisner, *The Archaeological Survey of Nubia for 1907–1908*, 2 vols. (Cairo: National Printing Dept., 1910), 2:346.

208. Arkell, *A History of the Sudan to 1821*, 54.

209. Emery, *Egypt in Nubia*, 102, 167; see also Harry S. Smith, *The Fortress of Buhen; the Inscriptions*, Egypt Exploration Society Memoir 48 (London: EES, 1976), 80–82.

210. Adams, *Nubia: Corridor to Africa*, 190.

211. Säve-Söderbergh, *Ägypten und Nubien*, 110–14; Trigger, *Nubia Under the Pharaohs*, 91; O'Connor, "Political Systems and Archaeological Data," 31–32.

212. O'Connor, "Political Systems and Archaeological Data," 31–32.

213. Vercoutter, *Mirgissa*, 1:183–84.

214. A. J. Mills and H. Å. Nordström, "The Archaeological Survey on the West Bank of the Nile: Third Season, 1961–1962," *Kush* 11 (1963): 19–21.

215. Bietak, *Studien zur Chronologie der Nubischen C-Gruppe*, 123, 154.

216. Trigger, *Nubia Under the Pharaohs*, 97–98.

217. Adams, *Nubia: Corridor to Africa*, 214.

218. Säve Söderbergh, *Ägypten und Nubien*, 141; Gardiner, *Egypt of the Pharaohs*, 166.

219. Torgny Säve-Söderbergh, "A Buhen Stela from the Second Intermediate Period," *JEA* 35 (1949): 50–58; J. W. Barns, "Four Khartoum Stelae," *Kush* 2 (1954): 19–25; see now Smith, *The Fortress of Buhen; the Inscriptions*, 72–76, and 80–85.

220. Serge Sauneron, "Une village fortifié sur rive orientale de Quadi es-Sebou," *BIFAO* 63 (1965): 161–67; Trigger, *Nubia Under the Pharaohs*, 101–2, 100fig. 33.

221. Trigger, et al., *Ancient Egypt: A Social History*, 159.

222. Georg Steindorff, *Aniba* (Gluckstadt: J.J. Augustin, 1937), 2:35.

223. Trigger, *Nubia Under the Pharaohs*, 102.

224. Bietak, *Studien zur Chronologie des Nubischen C-Gruppe*, 149–53; Trigger, *Nubia Under the Pharaohs*, 98–100. Also Labib Habachi, *The Second Stela of Kamose and the Struggle Against the Hyksos Ruler and his Capital* (Glüchstadt: J. J. Augustin, 1972) and Harry A. and S. Smith, "A Reconsideration of the Kamose Texts," *ZÄS* 103 (1976): 48–76.

225. Trigger, *History and Settlement in Lower Nubia*, 165.

226. Torgny Säve Söderbergh, "The Nubian Kingdom of the Second Intermediate Period," *Kush* 4 (1956): 54–61, esp. 59.

227. Trigger, *Nubia Under the Pharaohs*, 98.

228. Ibid., 102.

229. Adams, Nubia: *Corridor to Africa*, 214–15.

230. Redford, "The Hyksos Invasion in History and Tradition," *Orientalia* N.S. 39 (1970): 1–51.

231. Trigger, et al., *Ancient Egypt: A Social History*, 159.

232. Ibid.

233. Ibid.

234. Ibid., 160; see Pierre Lacau, *Une Stèle juridique de Karnak* (Cairo: Organisation Égyptienne Générale du Livre 1949); also, A. Théodoridès, "Mise en ordre chronologique des éléments de la stèle juridique de Karnak, avec ses influences sur la procédure," *Revue Internationale des Droits d'Antiquité* 21 (1974): 31–74.

235. Trigger, et al., *Ancient Egypt: A Social History*, 160.

236. Manfred Bietak, "Vorlaüfiger Bericht über die erste und zweite Kampagne der österreichischen Ausgrabungen auf Tell ed-Dab'a im Ostdelta Ägyptens (1966–1967)," *MDAIK* 23 (1968): 79–114; idem, "Vorlaüfiger Bericht über die Dritte Kampagne der österreichischen ausgrabungen auf Tell ed-Dab'a im Ostdelta Ägyptens (1968)," *MDAIK* 26 (1970): 15–42; idem, *Tell el Daba,* vol. 2 (Vienna: Österreichische Äkademie der Wisessenschaft 1975); idem, "Die Haupstadt der Hyksos und die Ramesesstadt," *Antike Welt* 6 (1975): 28–43; idem, *Avaris and Piramesse: Archaeological Exploration in the Eastern Nile Delta* (Mortimer Wheeler Archaeological Lecture, 1979); *Proceedings of the British Academy* 65 (1979): 225–90.

237. Herbert E. Winlock, *The Rise and Fall of the Middle Kingdom in Thebes* (New York: Macmillan, 1947), 93–103, 105–49, and pls. 14–20.

238. Ibid.

239. James E. Harris and Edward F. Wente, eds., *An X-Ray Atlas of the Royal Mummies* (Chicago and London: University of Chicago, 1980), 122–23.

240. See Yurco, "Black Athena: An Egyptological Review," M. Lefkowitz and G. MacLean Rogers, eds., *Black Athena Revisted* (Chapel Hill: University of North Carolina, 1996), 62–100.

241. Manfred Bietak, "Die Totumstände des Pharaos Seqenenre (17e Dynastie)," *Annuaire naturhistorisches Museens Vienna* 78 (1974): 29–52.

242. See William Kelly Simpson, ed., *The Literature of Ancient Egypt* (New Haven: Yale University, 1973), 77–80.

243. Harris and Wente, *X-Ray Atlas of the Royal Mummies,* 122–27.

244. Trigger, et al., *Ancient Egypt: A Social History,* 162.

245. Claude Vandersleyen, *Les Guerres d'Amosis, fondateur de la XVIIIe Dynastie,* Monographies Reine Elisabeth 1 (Brussels: Fondation Égyptologique Reine Elisabeth, 1971), 53–56; J. Vercoutter, ed., *Mirgissa,* 1:184–86.

246. Trigger, et al., *Ancient Egypt: A Social History,* 162.

247. Independent documentation of a raid on Avaris and Nubia by Kamose comes from the stela of Emhab, a soldier of Kamose. See Jaroslav Černy, "Stela of Emhab from Tell Edfu," MDAIK 24 (1969): 87–92; John Baines, "The Stela of Emhab: Innovation, Tradition, Hierarchy," *JEA* 72 (1986): 41–53.

248. Habachi, *The Second Stela of Kamose,* 39; Säve Söderbergh, "The Nubian Kingdom of the Second Intermediate Period," 54–61; Smith and Smith, "A Reconsideration of the Kamose Texts," 48–76; Trigger,et al., *Ancient Egypt: A Social History,* 162 and 173–74.

249. Habachi, *The Second Stela of Kamose,* 39.

250. Year 3 building inscription at Buhen, H. S. Smith, *The Fortress of Buhen;* the Inscriptions, 8, plate II.1, plate LVIII.1, no. 488; Viceroy's graffito at Arminna, Simpson, *Heka-Nefer,* 34; Trigger, *Nubia Under the Pharaohs,* 104–5, fig. 35.

251. Near Aniba? So, Vandersleyen, *Les guerres d'Amosis,* 161–63, and n. 247 above.

252. L. Störk, *Die Nashörner* (Hamburg: Borg, 1977), 101, 241–85 locates Miu between the fourth and fifth Nile Cataracts, K. Zibelius. *Africanische Orts*

and Völkernamen in Hieroglyphischen und Hieratischen Texten (Wiesbaden: O. Harrassowitz, 1972), 120, preferred a more northerly locale for Miu, but Barry J. Kemp, "Imperialism and Empire in New Kingdom Egypt (ca. 1575–1087 B.C.)," in P.D.A. Garnsey and C. R. Whittaker, eds., *Imperialism in the Ancient World* (Cambridge: Cambridge University, 1978), 290, n. 68, would locate Miu in the Berber-Shendi area of the Upper Nile.

253. David O'Connor, "The Location of Irem," *JEA* 73 (1987): 122–24.

254. Habachi, *The Second Stela of Kamose*, 48; Alan H. Gardiner, "The Defeat of the Hyksos by Kamose: The Carnarvon Tablet, no. 1," *JEA* 3 (1916): 105–6, 108.

255. Torgny Säve Söderbergh, "The Hyksos Rule in Egypt," *JEA* 37 (1951): 70, and 69 fig. 4; Trigger, *Nubia Under the Pharaohs*, 104–5; Trigger, et al., *Ancient Egypt: A Social History*, 170–71.

256. Trigger, *Nubia Under the Pharaohs*, 105.

257. Based upon the linguistic elements in their names. Vandersleyen, *Les guerres d'Amosis*, 24–25; Wolfgang Helck, *Die Beziehungen Ägyptens zu Vorderasiens im 3. und 2. Jahrtausend vor Chr*, 2nd ed.(Wiesbaden: O. Harrassowitz, 1971), 101, thought of the family as of Asiatic ancestry, but one member actually was named *Md3y-s*, "Medja-man," so J. J. Tylor and F. Ll. Griffith, *The Tomb of Paheri at El-Kab*, Egypt Exploration Fund, Memoir no. 11 (London: Egypt Exploration Fund, 1894), pl. VII; Trigger, *Ancient Egypt: A Social History*, 171, 171n. 2, demonstrating their Medja relationship.

258. James E. Harris, and Kent R. Weeks. *X-Raying the Pharaohs* (New York: Scribner's, 1973), 123, 123n. 1.

259. Trigger, *Nubia Under the Pharaohs*, 104; Adams, *Nubia: Corridor to Africa*, 217 (although he fails to note Kamose's Nubian campaign, see note 248 above).

260. Trigger, *Nubia Under the Pharaohs*, 107, and 117; also, Simpson, *Heka Nefer*, 36–43, and pl. XXII.

261. Trigger, *Nubia Under the Pharaohs*, 117.

262. Claude Vandersleyen, "Une Stèla de l'an 18 d'Amosis à Hanovre," *Chronique d'Égypte* 52 (1977): 223–44, esp. 237–38, considers Kamose a younger brother of Seqenenre Ta'a II. See Harris and Wente, *X-Ray Atlas of the Royal Mummies*, 124–27 for other views.

263. Harris and Wente, *X-Ray Atlas of the Royal Mummies*, 243–44.

264. Biography of Ahmose, son of Abana: Lichtheim, *AEL*, 2:12–13; Vandersleyen, *Les guerres d'Amosis*, 64–80.

265. Lichtheim, *AEL*, 2:12–13; Vandersleyen, *Les guerres d'Amosis*, 64–80; Adams, *Nubia: Corridor to Africa*, 217.

266. Lichtheim, *AEL*, 2:13–14.

267. Trigger, *Nubia Under the Pharaohs*, 107–8; Säve Söderbergh, *Ägypten und Nubien*, 146.

268. Lichtheim, *AEL*, 2:14; Trigger, *Nubia Under the Pharaohs*, 108–9.

269. Säve Söderbergh, *Ägypten und Nubien*, 145–46; A. J. Arkell, "Varia

Sudanica," *JEA* 36 (1950): 36–39; Trigger, *Nubia Under the Pharaohs,* 108, fig. 38.

270. Fritz Hintze, "Das Kerma-Problem," *ZÄS* 91 (1964): 79–86, esp. 85; Trigger, *Nubia Under the Pharaohs,* 108.

271. Vercoutter, "The Gold of Kush," 135.

272. Retrospectively, from the stela of Thutmose II. See Gardiner, *Egypt of the Pharaohs,* 180; see also, O'Connor, "The Location of Irem," 115, 115n. 74, 125; Säve Söderbergh, *Ägypten und Nubien,* 150–52.

273. Gardiner, *Egypt of the Pharaohs,* 180.

274. Ibid., 181, quoting Ineni; also Trigger, et al., *Ancient Egypt: A Social History,* 218–19.

275. Donald B. Redford, *History and Chronology of the Eighteenth Dynasty: Seven Studies* (Toronto: University of Toronto, 1967), 58–62, Thutmose III leading one campaign, during which a rhinoceros was bagged; also W. F. Reineke, "Ein Nubienfeldzug unter Königen Hatschepsut," in *Ägypten und Kush,* E. Endesfelder, et al., eds. (Berlin: Akademie Verlag, 1977), 369–76; and O'Connor, "The Location of Irem," 99–136, esp. 114, 114n. 73, 126–27.

276. Redford, *History and Chronology of the Eighteenth Dynasty,* 57–59, and 61; Trigger, *Nubia Under the Pharaohs,* 109; O'Connor, "The Location of Irem," 125.

277. Breasted, *ARE,* 2:259–60, 649–50, but see note 275 above for another campaign to Nubia he partook in under Hatshepsut.

278. Ibid.

279. Trigger, *Nubia Under the Pharaohs,* 129; Dows Dunham, *The Barkal Temples* (Boston: MFA, 1970); Adams, *Nubia: Corridor to Africa,* 228. Certainly established by Amenhotep II's reign, see Gardiner, *Egypt of the Pharaohs,* 199–200.

280. Jean Vercoutter, "Excavations at Saï, 1955–57 *Kush* 6 (1958): 155: Vercoutter, et al., "La XVIIIe Dynastie à Saï en Haut Nubie," *Études sur L'Égypte et le Soudan anciens, CRIPEL* 1 (1973): 7–38; and Michel Azim, "Quatre campagnes de fouilles sur la fortresse," *Études sur L'Égypte et le Soudan anciens, CRIPEL* 3 (1975): 91–125.

281. H. W. Fairman, "Preliminary Report on the Excavations at 'Amarah West, Anglo-Egyptian Sudan, 1938–9," *JEA* 25 (1939): 143.

282. Adams, *Nubia: Corridor to Africa,* 227–28; M. Schiff Giorgini, *Soleb I* (Florence: Sanconi, 1965); M. Schiff Giorgini, *Soleb II,* Les Necroples (Florence: Sanconi, 1971); Trigger, *Nubia Under the Pharaohs,* 126–27, 127 fig. 47.

283. Adams, *Nubia: Corridor to Africa,* 221 fig. 34, 227.

284. Ibid., 218–29, 231–32.

285. Ibid., 229–32; exemplified by the deliveries of annual tribute imposts from Nubia in Thutmose III's annals, see Breasted, *ARE,* 2:201–17, 475–539.

286. Arkell, *A History of the Sudan to 1821,* 98–100; George A. Reisner, "The Viceroys of Ethiopia," *JEA* 6 (1920): 28–55, and 73–78; Säve Söderbergh, *Ägypten und Nubien,* 177–84; Trigger, *Nubia Under the Pharaohs,* 111.

287. Säve Söderbergh, *Ägypten und Nubien,* 175–84; Trigger, *Nubia Under the Pharaohs,* 111.

288. Arkell, *A History of the Sudan to 1821*, 98–100; the policy was initiated by Thutmose II or III, see note 273 above.

289. Vercoutter, "The Gold of Kush," 120–53; Breasted, *ARE II*, 201–17, sec. 475–539; Adams, *Nubia: Corridor to Africa*, 231–35.

290. Säve Söderbergh, *Ägypten und Nubien*, 156–59, and 228.

291. Trigger, *Nubia Under the Pharaohs*, 112–13, but see now, O'Connor, "The Location of Irem," 99–136 for the extreme southern locations of Irem and Miu.

292. Emery, *Egypt in Nubia*, 200–2; Säve Söderbergh, *Ägypten und Nubien*, 196–97; Gardiner, *Egypt of the Pharaohs*, 270; and Trigger, *Nubia Under the Pharaohs*, 125.

293. For example, Adams, *Nubia: Corridor to Africa*, 233; Vercoutter, "The Gold of Kush," 135n. 55, 140.

294. David Lorton, "The Treatment of Criminals in Ancient Egypt," *JESHO* 20, part 1 (1974): 32–36, 38.

295. Trigger, *Nubia Under the Pharaohs*, 111.

296. Ibid., 109–10, citing a pun, that in Kush monkeys dance, and the king dances, cited from Henri Wild, "Une danse nubienne d'époque pharaonique," *Kush* 7 (1959): 86–87.

297. See for example, Gardiner, *Egypt of the Pharaohs*, 180, "vile Kush;" 167, "base Asiatic;" 190, "vile enemy of Kadesh;" 199, for Amenhotep II's letter to his viceroy, scorning Asiatics and Nubians equally; and 254, "vile enemy who was in the town of Hamath."

298. Trigger, *Nubia Under the Pharaohs*, 110, and pls. 45–56.

299. Ibid, pl. 47, and pl. 53.

300. For instance, Frank J. Yurco, "3,200 year Old Pictures of Israelites Found in Egypt," *Biblical Archaeology Review* 16, 5 (Sept.-Oct., 1990), 29–35 (Canaanites, Israelites, and Shashu).

301. Geoffrey Martin, *The Hidden Tombs of Memphis* (London: Thames and Hudson, 1991), 67–72, pls. 35, 40–41, and 42.

302. Trigger, *Nubia Under the Pharaohs*, pl. 47 and pl. 53; and idem, "Nubian, Negro, Black, Nilotic?" in *Africa in Antiquity*, vol. 1, S. Hochfield and E. Riefstahl, eds. (Brooklyn: The Brooklyn Museum, 1978), 32 fig. 12 (caption on p. 34, fig. 14 is in error).

303. Corteggiani, *The Egypt of the Pharaohs at the Cairo Museum*, 93–95, no. 53, plates on 93–94. Titled "fan bearer and child of the nursery," he was probably one of the sons of Kushite chieftains brought to Egypt for education at the court. He never left Egypt, but becoming a close companion of one of the XVIIIth Dynasty pharaohs, he was granted the highest possible status burial that a non-royal person might expect in ancient Egypt. Another sign of equality in Egypt is the vizier's remark in a XXth Dynasty marriage case: "Said the vizier: even if it had not been his wife, but a Syrian or Nubian whom he loved and to whom he gave

property of his, who should make void of what he did?" Jaroslav Černy and T. Eric Peet, "A Marriage Settlement of the Twentieth Dynasty," *JEA* 13 (1927): 32.

304. Wild, "une danse nubienne d'époche pharaonique," 76–90; also *Lexikon der Ägyptologie,* W. Helck and E. Otto, eds. (Wiesbaden: O. Harrassowitz, 1985), vol. 6, *s.v.* "tanz," 223 and n. 88, hereafter LdÄ; Donald B. Redford, *Akhenaten: The Heretic King* (Princeton: Princeton University, 1984), 53 fig. 3.5, 118 fig. 7.11, 128–29.

305. LdÄ, 222–23, *s.v.* "tanz."

306. Ibid., 222–24.

307. Trigger, *Nubia Under the Pharaohs,* 114–15.

308. Ibid., 116–17.

309. Manfred Lurker, *The Gods and Symbols of Ancient Egypt,* trans. by Barbara Cummings (London: Thames and Hudson, 1980), 28, 104; Trigger, *Nubia Under the Pharaohs,* 118.

310. Trigger, *Nubia Under the Pharaohs,* 118, and pl. 56.

311. Exemplified best in the Report of Wenamun, see William Kelly Simpson, *The Literature of Ancient Egypt,* 142–55.

312. Trigger, *Nubia Under the Pharaohs,* 127; H. W. Fairman, "Preliminary Report on the Excavations at Sesebi (Sudla) and 'Amārah West, Anglo-Egyptian Sudan, 1937–8," *JEA* 24 (1938): 151–56.

313. Lichtheim, *AEL,* 2:98.

314. Trigger, *Nubia Under the Pharaohs,* 118–19; Säve Söderbergh, *Ägypten und Nubien,* 200–5.

315. For instance, Sety I's Abydos temple, see F. Ll. Griffith, "The Abydos Decree of Seti I at Nauri," *JEA* 13 (1927): 193–208; W. F. Edgerton, "The Nauri Decree of Seti I. A Translation and Analysis of the Legal Portion," *JNES* 6 (1947): 219–30; Alan H. Gardiner, "Some Reflections on the Nauri Decree," *JEA* 38 (1952): 24–33; also Trigger, *Nubia Under the Pharaohs,* 125.

316. Adams, *Nubia: Corridor to Africa,* 237.

317. William Y. Adams, "Post-Pharaonic Nubia in the Light of Archaeology," *JEA* 50 (1964): 102–220, esp. 105.

318. Adams, *Nubia: Corridor to Africa,* 237–38, 238 fig. 36.

319. Edward F. Wente, *Letters from Ancient Egypt,* ed. Edmund Meltzer (Atlanta: Scholar's Press, 1990), 98–131, esp. 106.

320. See Bell, "Once More the *w* 'interpreters' or 'foreigners,'" 33; also Trigger, *Nubia Under the Pharaohs,* 111; and Trigger, et al., *Ancient Egypt: A Social History,* 231.

321. *Exodus* 6:25 (Phineas). Moses too had a Kushite wife (*Numbers* 12:1); Panehsy, the vizier, served under Merenptah, and Panehsy the viceroy under Ramesses XI.

322. See, for example, Ahmose, son of Abana, Lichtheim, *AEL;* 2:12–14.

323. See note 302 above, and fig. 40.

324. Adams, *Nubia: Corridor to Africa*, 237.

325. Ibid., 236; Trigger, *Nubia Under the Pharaohs*, 133, 135; Adams, "Post-Pharaonic Nubia in the Light of Archaeology," 106, and 106n. 1.

326. Adams, *Nubia: Corridor to Africa*, 237.

327. Ibid., 239.

328. O. Vagn-Nielsen, *Human Remains,* Scandinavian Joint Expedition to Sudanese Nubia Publications 9 (Copenhagen: Murksgaard, 1970), 86–87.

329. See 30, and note 292 above.

330. Kenneth A. Kitchen, *Pharaoh Triumphant: Life and Times of Ramesses II* (Mississauga: Benben, 1982), 215.

331. Karl Butzer, *Environment and Archaeology*, 2nd ed. (Chicago: University of Chicago, 1971), 338–39.

332. H. W. Fairman, "Preliminary Report on the Excavations at 'Amarah West, 1938–9," *JEA* 25 (1939): 139–44; idem, "Preliminary Report on the Excavations at Amarah West, Anglo-Egyptian Sudan, 1947–8," *JEA* 34 (1948): 3–11.

333. Trigger, et al., *Ancient Egypt: A Social History*, 228–29. Another volcanic eruption, Hekla III in Iceland, 1159 B.C., also may be implicated, see Yurco, "Black Athena: An Egyptological Review," 83–86.

334. Trigger, *Nubia Under the Pharaohs*, 130.

335. Ibid.; also Säve Söderbergh, *Ägypten und Nubien*, 149; and C.M. Firth, *Archaeological Survey of Nubia, Report for 1910–1911* (Cairo: National Printing Department, 1927), 28.

336. Trigger, *Nubia Under the Pharaohs*, 136.

337. Adams, *Nubia: Corridor to Africa*, 240.

338. Trigger, et al., *Ancient Egypt: A Social History*, 231.

339. Ibid., 229–30.

340. Edward F. Wente, "On the Suppression of the High-Priest Amenhotep," *JNES* 25 (1966): 73–87.

341. Ibid.; also Bell, "Once More the *w* 'interpreters' or 'foreigners,'" 33.

342. Wente, "On the Suppression of the High-Priest Amenhotep," 73; Trigger, et al., *Ancient Egypt: A Social History*, 231–32.

343. Wente, "On the Suppression of the High-Priest Amenhotep," 86–87.

344. Trigger, et al., *Ancient Egypt: A Social History*, 231–32.

345. Steindorff, *Aniba*, 2:241; Trigger, *Nubia Under the Pharaohs*, 136–37.

346. For the reliefs, see Peter James, et al., *Centuries of Darkness*, forward by Colin Renfrew (London: Jonathan Cape, 1991), 216–18, 218 fig. 9.5. The royalty includes a king Men-ma'at-re, setep-en-Amun, and a queen Karimala. This king's name is also strongly reminiscent of Ramesses XI's prenomen, Men-ma'at-re, setep-en-Ptah. Considering Herihor's and Smendes' seizure of power in Egypt and ignoring of Ramesses XI, Panehsy perhaps felt justified in declaring himself the sole surviving legitimate heir to the Ramesside kings. The epithet setep-en-Amun could well refer to Amun of Napata.

3

Egypt and the Kushites: Dynasty XXV

EDNA R. RUSSMANN

❋

Kushites

"The Kingdom of Kush furnishes a classic example of a successor state: a barbarian people assuming the mantle and the burdens of empire from the hands of their former overlords."[1] The Twenty-fifth Dynasty, the period of Kushite rule in Egypt (ca. 716-656 B.C.), is one of the earliest and most interesting post-colonial episodes. It is the first to be fairly well documented. In addition to contemporary texts, both Egyptian and Kushite, important archaeological evidence has been found (some of which is yet to be fully explored). Some further information is provided by contemporary Assyrian documents, by a few passages in the Bible, and by several classical authors who, although they wrote several centuries later, seem to have had access to continuous oral traditions and to written records. There is, finally, the fact that we know a great deal (though not, of course, as much as we would wish) about ancient Egyptian culture, religion, social organization, etc. Kushite studies by Egyptologists have been criticized, sometimes with justice, as Egyptocentric. Much, however, has been learned about the Kushites by analyzing unorthodoxies in their version of Egyptian culture. Better, more sophisticated techniques for comparing the two societies could yield further information.

Kush is a toponym of indigenous origin, applied by Egyptians of the Middle Kingdom to a part of the Nile Valley well south of their border at

Aswan. This territory included the key sites of Kerma and Gebel Barkal. Their importance may explain the expansion of the term Kush, in the New Kingdom, to designate the southern regions generally.[2] The rulers of the independent kingdom that subsequently arose in this area called themselves Kushites. Kashta, the name of the first to claim sovereignty over Egypt, means "The Kushite."[3]

Classical writers called the Kushites and their Meroitic descendants Ethiopians. This term continues to be applied to the Kushites by some modern scholars, especially those writing in French. However, since Ethiopia has been adopted as the name of a modern state that has no connection to Kush or the upper Nile valley, continued use of this name for the ancient culture or its homeland is unnecessarily confusing. A better modern designation for the region is Nubia, from the Nubian languages now or formerly spoken by many of the region's current inhabitants.[4] Although anachronistic in terms of ancient history, the name Nubia does relate to native peoples. It has the further advantage of expressing the geographical and cultural continuum of a stretch of the Nile Valley now politically divided between Egypt and the Sudan. (See fig. 3.1.).

The Kingdoms of the Kushites

Virtually nothing is known of the Kushite state until the early eighth century B.C., at which time it controlled the Nile Valley from at least as far north as Gebel Barkal to Meroe in the south. Its king was selected from among the eligible men of the ruling family. The process of selection may have been influenced or even controlled by a powerful priesthood, but a normal sequence of succession appears to have proceeded from elder to younger brother, and thence to the elder brother's sons.[5] This pattern of inheritance, like other aspects of Kushite culture, such as bed burial under a tumulus, is clearly non-Egyptian. Scholars are now virtually unanimous in recognizing the Kushite state as an indigenous development,[6] possibly descended from the great Kerma culture of the eighteenth to mid-sixteenth centuries B.C.[7]

The kingdoms of Kerma and Kush are separated, however, by a long interval of Egyptian occupation of much of Nubia, during the New Kingdom. In taking over the region, Egypt's main interests were to secure its southern frontier and to monopolize the rich trade, pre-eminently in local gold, but also including exotic products from farther south. The techniques developed for controlling Kush were efficient and in some respects

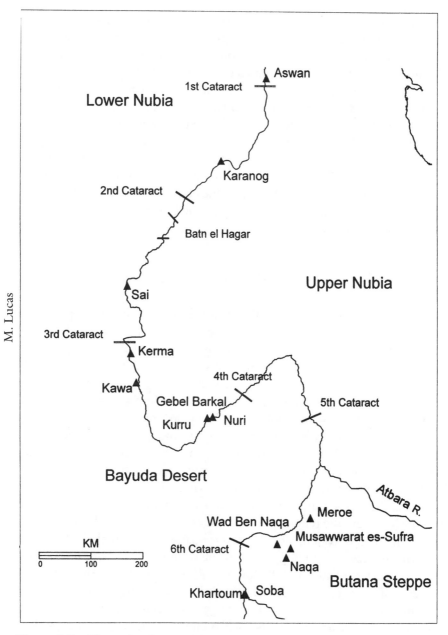

Figure 3.1 The region between the First and Sixth Cataracts.

prophetic of modern colonial practices. An Egyptian bureaucracy, headed by the King's Son of Kush,[8] operated out of Egyptian administrative towns, supported by resident garrisons at fortified strategic points. The loyalty of local rulers was encouraged, not just with the material benefits of imported Egyptian goods,[9] but by involving some of them in local administration and by sending their offspring to the Egyptian court.[10] The Egyptians also built temples and established priesthoods at a number of sites. In these New Kingdom Nubian temples, the cult of pharaoh as a god was far more prominent than in Egypt proper. The propagandistic qualities so evident at Abu Simbel suggest that such emphases were calculated, at least in part, to impress and overawe the natives. For later Kushites, they will have provided the most concrete and vivid evidence of the kings whose succession they claimed by divine right.[11]

The Egyptianization of the Kushites

A considerable degree of Egyptianization is attested in northern Nubia from the Eighteenth Dynasty, in the careers and the Egyptian-style tombs and other monuments of local chieftains.[12] The process of Egyptianization in the more remote heartland of Kush is still largely undocumented, but it persisted long after Egypt's withdrawal from Nubia at the end of the New Kingdom. In the eighth century B.C., Kushite kings appear to have spoken the Egyptian language. They worshipped the Egyptian pantheon, with a special and fervent devotion to the god Amun, whose cult, established at Gebel Barkal since the Eighteenth Dynasty, had become intertwined and even identified with their own dynastic destiny. Egypt's political weakness and infighting may have made that country ripe for a takeover, but the southern incursion seems to have been prompted at least as much by genuine religious conviction as by calculated self-interest.

Nonetheless, to judge from the very sparse documentation, the earliest Kushite claims to the Egyptian throne seem rather equivocal. The first recorded ruler, Alara (ca. 780–760 B.C.),[13] is known only from the monuments of later generations. His name is written in a royal cartouche, but it is preceded by partial (or pseudo-) Egyptian royal titles, which raise the suspicion that Alara did not himself pretend to be king of Egypt. His brother and successor, Kashta (ca. 760–747 B.C.), certainly did.[14] A few of Kashta's monuments have been found in Egypt; they show a pharaonic titulary, including the explicit title "King of Upper and Lower Egypt." His only important attestation, however, is the fragment of a stela dedicated in the temple of Khnum at Aswan,[15] on the southern border of Egypt, a location that suggests Kashta controlled all of Nubia up to the frontier, but may not have penetrated Egypt proper.[16]

Piankhy's Conquest of Egypt

Kashta's son and successor, Piankhy (ca. 747–716 B.C.),[17] reiterated his father's claims, but for almost two decades he remained in Kush without attempting to enforce them. Only when Tefnakht, the ruler of Sais in the Delta, began an aggressive expansion southward did Piankhy move into Egypt, about 730 B.C. His campaign is vigorously described in a long inscription on a stela found at Gebel Barkal and now in Cairo.[18] Full of religious and cultural nuances and unmistakably propagandistic in tone, the text nonetheless provides a circumstantial and apparently accurate account of his conquest of Egypt. Whatever the dynasty's prior relations with Egypt, it is clear that, by the time he moved against Tefnakht and his allies, Piankhy was able to rely on the loyalty of southern Egypt and specifically of Thebes. He does not seem to have been eager to leave home, and initially just sent his army north against the enemies he is careful to characterize as rebels. Unsatisfied with the progress of his troops, he eventually came to lead them in person, timing his trip to permit a stopover in Thebes for the Opet festival of Amun. A formidable warrior and—to read between the lines—a canny manipulator of weak and potentially treacherous petty rulers, Piankhy proceeded systematically northward. His campaign was climaxed by the bold, well-orchestrated capture of the seemingly impregnable Memphis. With Memphis taken, the Delta began inevitably to fall before him, until Tefnakht himself capitulated. A vignette at the top of Piankhy's stela shows the reigning kinglets of the north bowing to the ground before their overlord.[19] Then, for reasons that remain unexplained, the Kushite conqueror packed up and went back home to Kush. There is no evidence to suggest that he made even token provision for deputies or surrogates to function in his stead. Left in place and in possession, the petty princes of the north were quite predictably prompt to restore the *status quo ante*.

The XXVth Dynasty

Piankhy's successor, his brother Shabako (ca. 716–702 B.C.),[20] almost at once found it necessary to travel to Egypt to re-establish Kushite control, in about 715 B.C. The inscription on a scarab preserves his claim to have defeated rebels in Upper and Lower Egypt,[21] but no documentation comparable to the Piankhy stela has survived to provide details of his reconquest. There seems little doubt that, like his predecessor, Shabako was able to depend on Thebes. As before, the source of rebellion was the Libyan dynasty at Sais, under Tefnakht's successor, Bocchoris (Bakenrenef).[22] Manetho says that Shabako sealed his victory over this ringleader by burning him alive. The historical accuracy of this much-discussed passage is not confirmed by other evidence, and some scholars dismiss it altogether. However, even if Manetho's story is rejected as fact, it may well preserve the memory, among the Delta princes, of a bitter, and perhaps brutal, defeat.[23]

Shabako remained in Egypt and may thus be considered the true founder of the Twenty-fifth Dynasty.[24] Although the significance of his reign has been overshadowed by the better-documented career of his nephew Taharqa, it is clear that almost all the distinctive characteristics of Kushite rule in Egypt, in administrative control, royal regalia, iconography, and artistic style, were formulated under Shabako. The determination to establish his dynasty firmly throughout Egypt is attested by traces of his temple building or donations in the Delta (Bubastis, Athribis), at Memphis, Dendera, Thebes (Karnak, Luxor, Medinet Habu), and farther south (Esna, possibly Edfu).[25]

Shabako was succeeded by Shebitku (c. 702–690 B.C.), who was probably his nephew.[26] Shebitku resided at Memphis; this site and Thebes provide almost all of the sparse evidence of his reign. One can surmise that he carried on Shabako's domestic policies with reasonable success, but with less interest in temple construction and similar high-profile activities. His energy may, however, have been redirected abroad: Shebitku initiated an active policy of foreign intervention against Assyria in Syro-Palestine. Given the obvious threat of this aggressively expanding power, such a policy may have seemed—and perhaps even been—unavoidable; but it was to set the stage for the dynasty's ultimate expulsion from Egypt. It was as his field commander that Shebitku brought from Kush the young Taharqa, Piankhy's son, thus choosing (or acknowledging) him as the heir apparent.

Taharqa

Taharqa (690–664 B.C.)[27] was crowned in Memphis, and resided there. (See fig. 3.2.). He has left a record of his coronation, an event for which his mother traveled all the way from Kush.[28] Taharqa was by far the most

Figure 3.2 Sphinx with the head of Taharqa from Temple T at Kawa. Courtesy of the British Museum.

ambitious builder of his dynasty. As with his predecessors, his generosity within Egypt was most lavishly extended to Memphis and Thebes. The best-known of his constructions, the column of Taharqa in the first court at Karnak, is the remnant of a monumental gateway, one of four that he built at the temple's cardinal points. Some of his structures completed or replaced the work of his predecessors: the "Lake Edifice of Taharqa" incorporated blocks from an earlier structure of Shabako beside Karnak's Sacred Lake.[29] Other traces of Taharqa's activities have been found from the Delta to Philae on the southern border.

At the same time, Taharqa was the first Kushite ruler of Egypt to turn such attentions also to his homeland.[30] At Gebel Barkal, Sanam, Kawa, and a number of other sites, he built temples and enlarged others on a scale unprecedented since the New Kingdom. Part of this work was carried out by craftsmen sent from Memphis.

Even so brief a survey of Taharqa's monuments gives the strong impression of an unusually vigorous, able, and well-organized regime. Ironically, however, Taharqa is best known to history through his opposition to the Assyrians, which is mentioned in the Bible.[31] His actions brought the Assyrians into Egypt, and precipitated the dynasty's fall. Esarhaddon invaded as far south as Memphis in 671 B.C. and celebrated his triumph with the erection of a victory stela at Sinjirli, representing the conquered Taharqa or (more likely) his captured son.[32] Taharqa recovered from this onslaught, but a second invasion, under Ashurbanipal, drove him south, presumably all the way back home, for his successor, Tanwetamani, was crowned in Napata.

The Assyrian Attacks

Tanwetamani (664–656 B.C.)[33] may have been a son of Shebitku. In the so-called Dream Stela of his first regnal year,[34] he recorded his god-given mission to win back Egypt and set off at once to do so. His trip north, with pauses for ritual sacrifices at Elephantine and Thebes, then on to Memphis, is reminiscent of Piankhy's incursion. Like his great forebear, Tanwetamani penetrated the Delta, defeated an archfoe—the Assyrian protégé Necho I of Sais—and received the submission of other princes. But Ashurbanipal attacked at once, conquering Memphis and pushing on to Thebes, which was sacked in 663 B.C. Tanwetamani fled back to Kush. There he continued to rule for an undetermined length of time, maintaining his claim to the throne of pharaoh, but never returning to Egypt.

Before withdrawing from Egypt, Ashurbanipal installed (or reinstated) Delta kinglets as his vassals, including Necho's son, Psamtik I of Sais. Thebes, however, remained loyal to Tanwetamani until 656 B.C., when Psamtik I, long free of the Assyrians and fully in control of the north, negotiated a peaceful reunification. The Twenty-sixth, or Saite, Dynasty was to rule Egypt until the Persian conquest in 525 B.C. For many generations the dynasty of Kush maintained its claim to Egypt, each successive ruler adopting pharaonic titles and regalia. However, there was never again any chance of reconquest. The dynasty was reduced to its ancestral holdings, centered around Gebel Barkal in the district of Napata.

This post-Egyptian phase of the Kushite kingdom is conventionally called Napatan. It cannot have presented any real threat to Egypt and it is therefore unclear what prompted Psamtik II to send an army against Kush in 593 B.C.[35] He followed his victory with a program of usurping or destroying the Kushite monuments in Egypt, which had been respected by his predecessors.[36] Psamtik's troops may have penetrated as far south as Gebel Barkal; they undoubtedly accelerated a natural shift of Napatan culture toward the south. Meroe became the effective capital, although royal burials continued in the ancient cemeteries near Gebel Barkal until the fourth century B.C. Then even this tradition ended; physically isolated from an Egypt which itself looked increasingly to the north, the Meroitic civilization became progressively more self-contained and less Egyptianized.

Gebel Barkal

Three places had peculiar significance for the Kushite dynasty, and each of these places exerted strong and perceptible influences. A consideration of each of these sites may offer the best approach to understanding the unique Kushite amalgam of indigenous and Egyptian elements.

Rising in dramatic isolation from the desert plain, Gebel Barkal[37] is a high, rounded plateau with a partially separated spire on the western face. Investigating persistent claims of earlier visitors that the spire was the eroded remnant of a colossal statue, Timothy Kendall has recently succeeded in reading an inscription carved just below its tip. Made by Taharqa and restored by the Napatan king Nastasen, this rectangular patch of hieroglyphs once glittered under gold foil, held in place by bronze nails hammered into the rock face; a ledge below it may have held a statue of the king.[38] Kendall found no evidence that the main body of the spire had been sculpturally worked. But he argues very convincingly that the ancient Egyptians, from at least the New Kingdom, saw in its slender, irregularly vertical form the semblance of a rearing cobra—an uraeus at the "forehead" of the hill, emblematic of the special holiness of this place at the edge of Egypt's southernmost expansion.[39] The Egyptians made Gebel Barkal a major cult center of their state god Amun, thus creating the basis for the fervent Amun worship of the Kushites. The unique royal regalia of the later dynasty reflected the peculiarities of this local cult; thanks to Kendall's discoveries, we can now begin to see how closely these were tied to the physical properties of Gebel Barkal itself.

Instead of the single uraeus cobra worn at the brow of Egyptian kings since the Old Kingdom, Kushite kings are represented with a pair of snakes.[40] The double uraeus is unique to kings of this dynasty,[41] and has often been presumed to allude to their rule over both Egypt and Kush. The Kushite uraei often wear the crowns of Upper and Lower Egypt, however, and I have argued that they can refer only to the traditional union of the "Two Lands" of Egypt.[42] The reason for the doubling is undoubtedly to be found in the monumental "uraeus" at Gebel Barkal, which was sometimes represented with the crown of Upper Egypt. Egyptians of the New Kingdom considered it to mark the southernmost limit of Upper Egypt, and the inheritance of this long-outmoded imperial doctrine by the Kushites goes far to explain their belief in their legitimacy within Egypt.[43] Gebel Barkal, whence they derived their status and their power, was still Egypt to them, possibly in a religious or even mystical sense. The double uraeus reinforced the orthodox Egyptian symbolism, at the same time alluding to their own sacred place of origin, and thus to their divine legitimacy.

Kendall makes a strong case for the ancient perception of Gebel Barkal as the top of a uraeus-bearing head. If this hypothesis proves correct, the image may clarify the nature of the so-called Kushite cap. Although they were represented wearing most of the traditional Egyptian crowns, the headdress most characteristic of Kushite kings, one with particularly close associations to the double uraeus,[44] is an un-Egyptian-looking, head-hugging form usually assumed to be a skullcap.[45] However, closer examination strongly suggests that it was, in fact, a bare head with close-cropped hair.[46] A skullcapped mountain presents, of course, a fairly ludicrous vision. More significantly, a punning reference to Gebel Barkal seems to describe it as a bare, uncapped head, like that of the king.

The god Amun was normally represented in human form, but he could be manifested in a ram. For reasons that we do not understand, the aspect of Amun as a ram was heavily emphasized in his cult at Gebel Barkal.[47] This local variation in religious imagery is probably a visible sign of otherwise unknown variations in cult practices, and perhaps even beliefs, at Gebel Barkal, differences which may have evolved or accelerated during its relative isolation from Egypt through much of the Third Intermediate Period. Kushite devotion to the ram of Amun is very noticeable. Statues representing a Twenty-fifth Dynasty king before the protecting figure of a ram have been found not only in Kush,[48] but also at Karnak itself.[49] In addition, they were frequently represented wearing a ram's head as an amulet on a cord. Like the double uraeus, this kind of necklace, with one or three ram's head amulets, is unique to the Kushite kings.[50]

The mystique of Gebel Barkal helps to explain why the Kushite rulers of Egypt never felt any need to present themselves as ethnic Egyptians. As in their regalia, so also in the faces of their statues and reliefs, they exhibit the idealized but unmistakable features of non-Egyptians from the south.[51]

Kurru

In death, the Kushite kings were sent home for burial in the ancestral cemetery at Kurru, some ten miles down the Nile from Gebel Barkal.[52] Of the Kushite rulers of Egypt, only Taharqa is buried elsewhere; his tomb at Nuri, about six miles upstream from Gebel Barkal, inaugurated a second royal cemetery, which remained in use until the fourth century B.C.[53]

Following very ancient Nubian tradition,[54] the earliest burials at Kurru were marked by large tumuli.[55] From at least the time of Piankhy, however, both kings and queens appear to have been buried under pyramids.[56] Since funerary practices are notoriously conservative, this change in superstructure was significant, and must be related to the dynasty's claim to Egyptian kingship and its awareness that pyramids were the tombs of pharaohs in the distant and venerated past. The pyramid tomb was used for royal burials until the end of the Meroitic kingdom, making it among the longest-lived of the borrowings from Egypt. However, although this inspiration was undoubtedly royal, the form of Kushite and Meroitic pyramids with their small size, steeply sloped sides, and offering chapel attached to the eastern face, closely resembles the small pyramids erected over New Kingdom private tombs at Thebes, and also in Nubia.[57]

The burials themselves were Egyptian in many respects. The bodies had been mummified and laid in anthropoid wooden coffins; canopic jars were provided for the separately preserved internal organs, and *shawabtis*—surrogate figures of the deceased—were present in large quantities. There were, however, strikingly non-Egyptian features, most especially the elaborate horse burials, in pits carefully dug to support the animals in a standing position.[58]

Thebes

There can be no doubt of Thebes' genuine loyalty to the Kushite cause, nor that it was based on a common devotion to Amun as the state god. The roots of rapprochement between Thebes and Kush must lie in the Third Intermediate Period, during which southern Egypt was not just independent, but increasingly dissociated from the north. There is no evidence, however, to show how or when relations were actually established. Since Thebes controlled all of southern Egypt, Kashta's royal titles on his stela at Aswan suggest that he already had Theban support.

The one formal act of Kushite kingship recorded at Thebes is

Piankhy's provision that his sister be adopted as successor to the reigning high priestess known as the Divine Consort of Amun.[59] The adoption followed due legal precedents, and it apparently took place well before Piankhy's invasion of Egypt.[60] Symbolically, the significance of the Divine Consort was very potent, not only because she was in some sense Amun's earthly wife, but also because, by tradition established in the Third Intermediate Period, the office was held by princesses of the official royal lineage.[61] A succession of Kushite Divine Consorts spans the Twenty-fifth Dynasty; they are the only Kushite royal women represented at Thebes.[62] Their adoptions must have been interpreted as some form of naturalization, for these women, unlike their royal fathers and brothers, were buried at Thebes.[63] The estate of the Divine Consorts was administered by Great Stewards whose extravagant tombs testify vividly to the power and wealth under their control.[64] It is interesting, therefore, that the two known Great Stewards of the Kushite Period were native Thebans.[65]

Direct control may have been exercised at Karnak by the two Kushite High Priests of Amun, Shabako's son Horemakhet and the latter's son Horkhebi.[66] It should be noted, however, that the appointment of royal sons to this top priestly office was another precedent set by Third Intermediate Period kings.[67] More unusual, and more significant in political terms, was the appointment, early in the dynasty, of the Kushite Kelbasken as Mayor of Thebes.[68] This office, the hereditary possession of one of the great Theban families, had evolved during the late Third Intermediate Period to become the virtual rulership of southern Egypt. As interesting as Kelbasken's insertion into this lineage, however, is the fact that after him it reverted to the Theban line, to culminate, at the end of the Kushite Period, in the redoubtable and highly autonomous Mentuemhat.[69] If the Kelbasken interlude was a Kushite experiment with direct rule at Thebes, it was soon rejected in favor of non-interference.

Nonetheless, there was a noticeable Kushite presence in southern Egypt during the Twenty-fifth Dynasty. Besides Kelbasken, other Kushites made prominent careers at Thebes.[70] And, in what has very much the look of a diplomatic union, Mentuemhat took a Kushite woman as his third wife.[71] Apart from inscriptions giving the filiation of Divine Consorts, Kushite kings were not named, either in the tombs or on the statues of their Theban subjects, at all as frequently as were the succeeding kings of the Twenty-sixth Dynasty. This difference must be meaningful, but has yet to be analyzed: it might simply reflect a rather casual acceptance of the Kushites, but it might equally signal a circumspect disaffection.

Memphis

The choice of Memphis as residence by Shabako, Shebitku, and Taharqa, might have been dictated by strategic considerations alone. The city's founding in the First Dynasty and its almost uninterrupted history as Egypt's governmental capital were a result of its pivotal location just above the intersection of the Nile Valley with the Delta. For the Kushite kings, needing always to keep an eye on turbulent Delta politics, there could be no better vantage point. However, there is abundant evidence to show that this traditional capital of Egypt, home of the great pyramid-building kings of remote antiquity, had a far greater significance for them than mere utility. As the ancestral seat of the legitimacy they claimed so insistently, Memphis was in a real sense more important than Thebes, and they went to great lengths to associate themselves with the city and its past.[72]

The virtual obliteration of Late Period religious structures at Memphis has helped to obscure the extent of Kushite activity, although future excavations may well provide more information. Recent work at the site of the so-called Apis House in the southeastern corner of the Ptah temple compound, has yielded evidence to suggest that an early version of this important structure—perhaps, indeed, the first—dates to the Twenty-fifth Dynasty.[73] The majority of known Kushite remains from Memphis, however, are statues and isolated inscriptions without context. Shabako, Shebitku, and Taharqa are all represented.

The central importance of Memphis to the Kushite Dynasty, and some of the meaning it had for them, are given concrete expression on the so-called Shabako Stone found at Memphis and now in the British Museum.[74] This worn and fragmentary inscription, bearing the name of Shabako, purports to reproduce an ancient text on papyrus, wormhole lacunae and all. It contains an exaltation of Memphis, and of its god Ptah as the great creator god.

The Kushite kings set themselves, not just to seek out, but also to resurrect and emulate royal monuments from the Pyramid Age of the Old Kingdom. A tendency toward archaizing imitation of early monuments was already present in northern Egypt during the Third Intermediate Period; under the Kushite kings, this became a full-fledged movement with an emphasis on Memphite/Old Kingdom characteristics. The pyramids of Kush, with their provincial-looking, steep-sided forms, are among the least sophisticated examples of Kushite archaizing. The relief decoration in Taharqa's temples at Gebel Barkal and Kawa, however, includes detailed copies of scenes from Old Kingdom pyramid temples near Memphis,[75] done in a creditable imitation of Old Kingdom style; to achieve this, the king had skilled craftsmen sent all the way from Memphis.[76]

The proportions, anatomical details, costume, and poses of Kushite royal statues simulate Old Kingdom royal work with great success.[77] This strong Old Kingdom quality, combined with ethnic references and indigenous regalia, such as the double uraeus, all seamlessly blended in work of very high quality, make the statues of the Twenty-fifth Dynasty kings unique among Egyptian sculpture.

Bibliography

The Brooklyn Museum. *Africa in Antiquity: The Arts of Ancient Nubia and the Sudan.* 2 vols. Brooklyn, The Brooklyn Museum, 1978.

Helck, Wolfgang, et al., eds. *Lexikon der Ägyptologie.* 6 vols. Wiesbaden: Otto Harrassowitz, 1972–1986. Individual entries as cited in endnotes, especially those by Jean Leclant; these constitute the most complete compendium available of historical and archaeological data on the Kushite Period.

Kendall, Timothy. "Kingdom of Kush." *National Geographic* 178, no.5 (1990): 96–125.

Kitchen, Kenneth A. *The Third Intermediate Period in Egypt (1100–650 B.C.).* 2nd ed. Warminster: Aris and Phillips, 1986.

Leclant, Jean. "Kushites and Meroïtes: Iconography of the African Rulers in the Upper Nile Valley." In *The Image of the Black in Western Art I From the Pharaohs to the Fall of the Roman Empire,* edited by J. Vercoutter, et al., 89–132. New York: William Morrow and Co., 1976.

Russmann, Edna R. *The Representation of the King in the XXVth Dynasty.* Brussels: Fondation Égyptologique Reine Élisabeth; Brooklyn: The Brooklyn Museum, 1974.

Notes

1. W. Y. Adams, *Nubia: Corridor to Africa* (London: A. Lane, 1977), 293.

2. T. Säve-Söderbergh, "Kusch," in *Lexikon der Ägyptologie* [hereafter *LA*], 6 vols., ed. W. Helck, et al. (Wiesbaden: Otto Harrassowitz, 1972–86), 3:888–93.

3. J. Leclant, "Kuschitenherrschaft," *LA,* 3:893.

4. Adams, *Nubia: Corridor to Africa,* 45.

5. Leclant, "Kuschitenherrschaft," 893. *cf* Adams *Nubia,* 259–60.

6. For the earlier, discredited theory that it was founded by foreigners, see the remarks of Stanley M. Burstein in this symposium: "The Kingdom of Meroe." *Cf.* Adams, *Nubia,* 257.

7. Leclant, "Kuschitenherrschaft," 893.

8. This was an appointive office equivalent to viceroy, and did not imply actual royal filiation; see L. Habachi, "Königssohn von Kusch," *LA,* 3:630.

9. An interesting example is the New Kingdom faience bowl found in one of the Kurru tumuli; see note 55 below.

10. O'Connor, "New Kingdom and Third Intermediate Period, 1552–664 B.C.," in *Ancient Egypt: A Social History,* ed. B. G. Trigger (Cambridge: Cambridge University Press, 1983), 263. Young Nubian hostage/courtiers are shown in the tomb of Tutankhamun's viceroy of Kush, Huy (Theban tomb 40): ibid., 264, fig. 3.21/2.

11. It is probably significant that the Kushite kings are sometimes shown wearing a ram's horn, an Egyptian emblem of divine royalty represented much more frequently in New Kingdom Nubian temples than in Egypt proper; E. R. Russmann, *The Representation of the King in the XXVth Dynasty* (Brussels: Fondation Égyptologique Reine Élisabeth; Brooklyn:The Brooklyn Museum, 1974), 27.

12. O'Connor, *Ancient Egypt,* 266–67.

13. R. Drenkhahn, "Alul," *LA,* 1:169.

14. St. Wenig, "Kaschta," *LA,* 1:353–54.

15. J. Leclant, "Kushites and Meroïtes: Iconography of the African Rulers in the Upper Nile Valley," in *The Image of the Black in Western Art I: From the Pharaohs to the Fall of the Roman Empire,* ed. by J. Vercoutter, et al. (New York: William Morrow and Co., 1976), 91 fig. 67.

16. The occurrences of his name at Thebes, as father of the Divine Consort Amenirdas I, mean nothing in this regard, since she was almost certainly installed in office by her brother, Piankhy.

17. J. Leclant, "Peye," *LA,* 4:1045–52. K. H. Priese has convincingly demonstrated that native speakers of this Kushite name did not vocalize the ankh sign with which it is written. On these grounds, the name is better transcribed as Piye; this form has become almost standard in the subsequent literature. However, inasmuch as this account deals primarily with Egyptian history and monuments, I prefer to retain an Egyptian transliteration of the name in the belief that Piankhy (demonstrably a canny propagandist) would have recognized and, if possible, exploited the symbolic importance and the numerous Egyptian royal precedents of the ankh sign in his name; *cf.* G. Vittmann, "Zur Lesung des Königsnamen . . . ," *Orientalia* 43 (1974): 12–16.

18. Cairo Museum JE 48862: N. C. Grimal, *La stèle triomphale de Pi('ankh)y au Musée du Caire,* MIFAO 105 (Cairo: Institut Français d'Archéologie Orientale, 1981); for an English translation, see M. Lichtheim, *Ancient Egyptian Literature III: The Late Period* (Berkeley, Los Angeles, London: University of California Press, 1980), 66–84.

19. This detail is well illustrated in W. S. Smith, *The Art and Architecture of Ancient Egypt* (Baltimore: Penguin Books, 1958), pl. 174B, and (much less satisfactorily) in the revised edition with additions by William Kelly Simpson (New Haven, London: Yale University Press, 1998), 233 fig. 389.

20. J. Leclant, "Schabaka," *LA*, 5:499–513.

21. The authenticity of this scarab was long doubted, but has been convincingly defended: ibid., 503.

22. H. De Meulenaere, "Bokchoris," *LA*, 1:846. Tefnakht and Bocchoris are conventionally designated the Twenty-fourth Egyptian Dynasty.

23. The legend is not, therefore, necessarily incompatible with a tradition that remembered Shabako more benignly, as a lawgiver: Leclant, "Kuschitenherrschaft," 897.

24. Of the Kushite rulers, Manetho recognized only Shabako, Shebitku, and Taharqa: ibid., 898 n. 12.

25. Kushite reliefs from a ceremonial gateway, found reused under the court of Edfu temple in 1984, apparently do not preserve any royal names. Their provincial-looking style suggests a date as early as Shabako, but this cannot be confirmed without further study. The most complete preliminary publication is J. Leclant, "Fouilles et travaux en Égypte et au Soudan, 1985–1986," *Orientalia* 56 (1987): 349, pls. 43–45, figs. 56–59.

26. It is probable, but not certain, that he was Piankhy's son; J. Leclant, "Schabaka," 514–20.

27. J. Leclant, "Taharqa," *LA*, 4:156–84. Note that these and later regnal dates are certain.

28. Leclant, "Kuschitenherrschaft," 895.

29. R. A. Parker, J. Leclant, J. C. Goyon, *The Edifice of Taharqa by the Sacred Lake of Karnak* (Providence: Brown University Press; London: Lund Humphries, 1979).

30. Piankhy had done substantial building at Gebel Barkal; Smith, *The Art and Architecture of Ancient Egypt* (1958), 238–39, pls. 173A-B, 174A.

31. 2 Kings 19:9; Isaiah 37:9. For the chronological problem of these references in connection with the campaign of Sennacherib see Leclant, "Taharqa," *LA*, 6:183 n. 242.

32. Russmann, *Representation*, 22.

33. J. Leclant, "Tanutamun," *LA*, 6:211–15.

34. Cairo, JE 48863; N. C. Grimal, *Quatre stèles napatéennes au Musée du Caire*, MIFAO 106 (Cairo: Institut Français d'Archéologie Orientale, 1981), 3–20.

35. *Cf.* Burstein's essay; for the text of the Shellal victory stela erected after this campaign, see Lichtheim, *Ancient Egyptian Literature III*, 84–86. Greek graffiti on the leg of one of the colossal seated figures of Ramesses II at Abu Simbel were carved by Greek mercenaries in Psamtik II's army: S. Sauneron and J. Yoyotte, "La campagne nubienne de Psammétique," *BIFAO* 50 (1952): 187–88.

36. J. Yoyotte, "Le martelage des noms royaux éthiopiens par Psammétique II," *RdE* 8 (1951): 215–39.

37. I am deeply indebted to Dr. Timothy Kendall for his generosity in sharing with me conclusions, still only partially published, drawn from his recent discoveries at the site of Gebel Barkal. Dr. Kendall's interpretation of the evidence is

compelling in its main arguments, and in many of its details. Such important and even revolutionary findings will require much further investigation to fully elucidate their meaning and significance, but they already represent a major contribution to our understanding of the Kushite dynasty; they have substantially influenced my remarks in this section. For a preliminary publication of this work, see T. Kendall, "Kingdom of Kush," *National Geographic* 178.5 (November, 1990): 96–125.

38. Kendall, "Kingdom of Kush," 110.

39. Ibid., 111, 122.

40. Russmann, *Representation*, 35 ff.

41. It should not be equated with the queen's double uraeus, worn from the Eighteenth Dynasty through the Ptolemaic Period: ibid., 39.

42. E. R. Russmann, "Some Reflections on the Regalia of the Kushite kings of Egypt," *Africa in Antiquity: The Arts of Ancient Nubia and the Sudan*, Meroitica 5 (Berlin: Akademie-Verlag, 1979), 51–52; cf. L. Török, *The Royal Crowns of Kush* Cambridge Monographs in African Archaeology 18 (Oxford: BAR, 1987), 6–7.

43. It may also help to explain the notable infrequency with which they refer to themselves as King of Kush.

44. Russmann, *Representation*, 35.

45. So described in ibid., 28 ff.

46. Russmann, "Regalia," 49–51. This suggestion has been rejected without discussion by Leclant and others: for example, Leclant, "Kushites and Meroïtes," 96. Such adamant resistance to the possibility of kings (Egyptian or Kushite) going bareheaded reflects most curiously on our own cultural preconceptions. Only Török, *Royal Crowns*, 4–6, has essayed a systematic defense of the Kushite skullcap, but his graphic examples are erroneous and his inscriptional evidence ambiguous. In the meantime, excavations at Abusir have uncovered Fifth Dynasty royal statues whose incontrovertibly bare heads demonstrate that this form of headdress was acceptable for Egyptian kings during the Old Kingdom. See M. Saleh and H. Sourouzian, *Official Catalogue: the Egyptian Museum Cairo* (Munich: Prestel-Verlag; Mainz: von Zabern, 1987), no. 38.

47. For the rarity of ram imagery of Amun in Egypt, as compared with Kush, see R. A. Fazzini, *Egypt: Dynasty XXII–XXV*, Iconography of Religions XVI, fasc. 10 (Leiden: E. J. Brill, 1988), 17.

48. Russmann, *Representation*, 49–51 nn. 15, 17, 19, 20.

49. R. A. Fazzini, "A Sculpture of King Taharqa (?) in the Precinct of the Goddess Mut at South Karnak," *Mélanges Gamal Eddin Mokhtar*, Bibliothèque d'Études 97.1; (Cairo: IFAO, 1985), 293–306.

50. Russmann, *Representation*, 25–26.

51. The evidence of ethnicity has been remarked by many commentators, but it is not always very easy to analyze. An initial attempt to describe the complex interplay of elements in the incorporation by Egyptian artists of Kushite ethnic features into an Egyptian royal context, may be found in E. R. Russmann,

Egyptian Sculpture: Cairo and Luxor (Austin: University of Texas Press, 1989), 166–68; see also Russmann, *Representation,* 24.

52. Dows Dunham, *El Kurru,* The Royal Cemeteries of Kush I (Cambridge: Harvard University Press, 1950), 5, 6 Map 1. For this cemetery, see also the excellent summary by Timothy Kendall, *Kush: Lost Kingdom of the Nile,* Exhibition catalogue (Brockton, Mass: Brockton Art Museum/Fuller Memorial, 1982), 21.

53. Dows Dunham, *Nuri,* The Royal Cemeteries of Kush II (Boston: Museum of Fine Arts, 1955), 2–3.

54. Dunham, *El Kurru,* 121–22.

55. Estimated to cover five consecutive generations, designated A through E; summarized ibid., 2–3. However, Kendall, pointing out that an imported Egyptian object from the earliest of the tumuli is of late New Kingdom manufacture has suggested that these first burials should probably be placed considerably more than five generations earlier: Kendall, *Kush,* 22 no. 1.

56. The tomb of Kashta, probably Ku. 8, may have had the transitional (?) form of a mastaba (Dunham, *El Kurru,* 46). Most tomb superstructures in this cemetery had been virtually obliterated (ibid., 12), but their traces seem to be early versions of the standard Kushite pyramid, ibid., 121 ff. The tombs of Piankhy and later kings were identifiable through associated finds.

57. For private pyramid tombs in Nubia, see Leclant, "Kuschitenherrschaft," 896. Pyramids continued to be associated with private tombs at Thebes after the Kushite Dynasty: D. Eigner, *Die monumentalen Grabbauten der Spätzeit in der thebanischen Nekropole,* text vol. and boxed plates (Vienna: Verlag der Österreichischen Akademie der Wissenschaften, 1984), 102 ff.

58. Dunham, *El Kurru,* 110 ff.

59. M. Gitton and J. Leclant, "Gottesgemahlin," *LA,* 2:792–812, especially 797–801.

60. Fazzini, *Egypt,* 4.

61. Gitton and Leclant, "Gottesgemahlin," 797.

62. For their representations in poses and roles previously reserved to kings, see Fazzini, *Egypt,* 20.

63. Their mortuary chapels are at Medinet Habu: B. Porter and R. L. B. Moss, *Topographical Bibliography of Ancient Egyptian Hieroglyphic Texts, Reliefs, and Paintings II, Theban Temples,* 2nd ed. (Oxford: Clarendon Press, 1972), 476 ff.

64. Eigner, *Die monumentalen Grabbauten der Spätzeit in der thebanischen Nekropole,* passim.

65. They were: (1) Harwa, owner of Theban tomb 37: E. R. Russmann, "Harwa as Precursor of Mentuemhat," *Artibus Aegypti. Studia in Honorem Bernardi V. Bothmer,* H. De Meulenaere and L. Limme, eds. (Brussels: Musées Royaux d'Art et d'Histoire, 1983), 137–46; G. Vittmann, *Priester und Beamte im Theben der Spätzeit,* Beiträge zur Ägyptologie 1 (Vienna: Veröffentlichungen der Institut für Afrikanistik und Ägyptologie der Universität Wien, 1978), 101–2; (2) Akhamenru, owner of Theban tomb 404: B. V. Bothmer, comp., *Egyptian*

Sculpture of the Late Period (700 B.C. to A.D. 100) (Brooklyn: The Brooklyn Museum, 1960), 6–7 n. 6, pl. 6; Vittmann, *Priester,* 102–3. For Divine Consorts and their officials, also see E. Graefe, *Untersuchungen zur Verwaltung und Geschichte der Institution der Gottesgemahlin des Amun vom Beginn des Neuen Reiches bis zur Spätzeit,* 2 vols. Ägyptische Abhandlungen 37 (Wiesbaden: Otto Harrassowitz, 1981).

66. Leclant, "Kuschitenherrschaft," *LA,* 3:894.

67. Fazzini, *Egypt,* 3.

68. Kelbasken is the owner of Theban tomb 391; for his date, see M. L. Bierbrier, review of *Priester und Beamte im Theben der Spätzeit,* by G. Vittmann, *Bibliotheca Orientalis* 36 (1979): 307.

69. M. L. Bierbrier, "Montemhet," *LA,* 4:204; the definitive work on his career and monuments remains: J. Leclant, *Montouemhat, Quatrième Prophète d'Amon* (Cairo: IFAO, 1961).

70. Most of the foreigners are identified by their Kushite names; they include Iriketakana, represented in a statue, Cairo Museum JE 38018: E. R. Russmann, *Egyptian Sculpture,* no. 81, pp. 175, 178; Leclant, "Kushites and Meroïtes," 117 fig. 115, ; and Karakhamun, owner of Theban tomb 223: B. Porter and R. L. B. Moss, "Private Tombs," in "The Theban Necropolis Part 1," in *Topographical Bibliography of Ancient Egyptian Hieroglyphic Texts, Reliefs, and Paintings I* (Oxford: Griffith Institute, 1960), 324.

71. For this wife, see now E. R. Russmann, "Mentuemhat's Kushite Wife (Further Remarks on the Decoration of the Tomb of Mentuemhat, 2)," *JARCE* 34 (1997): 21–39.

72. The role of Memphis in the Twenty-fifth Dynasty is seldom sufficiently appreciated; see, however, Leclant, "Kuschitenherrschaft," *LA,* 3:894 with n. 25.

73. This conclusion is based partly on blocks with Kushite inscriptions (usurped in the following dynasty), reused in a later stage of the structure (M. Jones and A. M. Jones, "Apis Expedition at Mit Rahinah: Preliminary Report of the Fourth Season, 1984," *JARCE* 22 [1985]: 23–28), and partly on my own unpublished examination of the earliest of the "lion beds" at the site. Further work at this site should be given a high priority.

74. British Museum EA 498: H. Altenmüller, "Denkmal memphitischer Theologie," *LA,* 1:1065–69; illustrated in Fazzini, *Egypt,* pl. 34. Scholars do not agree about the date of the original document copied onto the stone: some think it was late Old Kingdom, but others would place it as late as the Ramesside Period (Ibid. 7). There is little reason to doubt that the Kushites themselves thought they were preserving a text of the highest antiquity.

75. Ibid., 6–7, pl. 2.

76. Russmann, *Representation,* 22 n. 6.

77. Ibid., 22–23.

4

The Kingdom of Meroe

STANLEY M. BURSTEIN

❀

Located roughly six hundred miles south of the first cataract of the Nile at Aswan, just below the junction of the Nile and Atbara rivers, Meroe was well known in the first millennium B.C.E. and the early first millennium C.E. as an important center of civilization. (See fig. 4.1.). Hellenistic Greek writers made it the capital of a vast legendary empire ruled by Cepheus, the father of Andromeda, that extended from the Sudan to Syria[1] and claimed that it had been visited by the philosopher Democritus, who translated into Greek Meroitic books written in Egyptian hieroglyphs.[2] They also told stories of a romance between Alexander the Great and a queen of Meroe.[3] Some late Jewish writers claimed that Moses' Cushite wife was a member of the Meroitic royal family[4] as was also the Queen of Sheba.[5] More prosaically, Meroe was the southernmost of the seven cities whose latitudes were used by classical geographers to define the limits of the *oikumene,* the civilized world known to the Greeks.[6]

Despite its fame in antiquity, the kingdom of Meroe occupies little space in modern histories of the ancient world for understandable reasons. Of the once extensive ancient written evidence in a variety of languages including Greek, Latin, Egyptian, and Meroitic, little remains. For example, Pliny the Elder mentions six men who visited Meroe, most probably in the third century B.C.E., including a certain Dalion who lived in the city for six years and published accounts of their experiences. Only meager fragments of their works survive, however, in the form of quotations and summaries in the works of later writers such as the first century B.C.E. universal historian Diodorus, the first and second centuries C.E. geographers

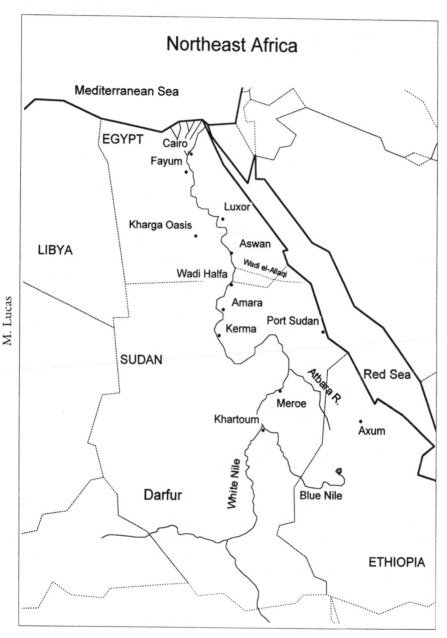

Figure 4.1 Northeast Africa

Strabo and Ptolemy, and the Latin encyclopedist Pliny the Elder.[7] Scattered references by a wide range of classical authors from Herodotus in fifth century B.C.E. to Procopius in the sixth century C.E. contribute further information.

Sources of Meroe

But even had the full *corpus* of ancient writing on Meroe survived, the situation for the modern historian would still have been unsatisfactory. Meroe's geographical position on the extreme southern periphery of the ancient civilized world, separated from Egypt by the harsh and forbidding terrain of lower Nubia,[8] ensured that the history of contact between it and its northern neighbor would be episodic in character. This history was marked by long periods of relative peace broken by occasional military intervention into one another's territory whenever the opportunity of gaining some advantage seemed to beckon. It is not surprising in this situation that Greek and Roman interest in Meroe was more ethnographic than historical, concerned more with describing the culturally "other" than recording the history of the kingdom of Meroe. Equally unsurprising is the fact that allusions to historical events are few and imprecise as is illustrated by the fact that the names of only two of the long line of Meroitic kings are mentioned in classical sources, Aktisanes[9] and Ergamenes, and the former is misdated by over a millennium! Nor can we place in the balance native written sources. Meroitic historical inscriptions written in Egyptian end in the late fourth or early third century B.C.E. The last religious inscriptions in Egyptian are less than a century later in date. Worst of all, although the Meroitic script was deciphered by F. Ll. Griffith early in the twentieth century C.E.,[10] little progress has been made in understanding the Meroitic language itself or identifying its linguistic affinities. Even the seemingly most solid analyses of Meroitic texts remain tentative and open to question.[11] That it has nevertheless been possible to reconstruct the main outlines of the history of the kingdom of Meroe is one of the triumphs of modern archaeology.

The Archaeology of Meroe

The history of Meroitic archaeology has been a checkered one ever since the rediscovery of the site of Meroe, unknown to western geography since the end of antiquity, by the explorer James Bruce in 1772.[12] Bruce noted the great extent of the ruins and the finding of numerous fragments of statues and other antiquities by the local Arabs.[13] But the unsettled political conditions of the 19th century Sudan made it difficult for scholars to take advantage of his identification of the site of Meroe. Still, a thin stream of travelers including F. Calliaud, Linant de Belfonds, G. A. Hoskins, and, above all, the great German Egyptologist Karl Richard Lepsius, visited Meroe and other Meroitic sites, sometimes at the risk of their lives, and left descriptions and drawings of what they saw that remain of fundamental importance both as a record of the condition of the ruins of the major centers of Meroitic civilization at the time of their discovery, and sometimes as the sole surviving evidence of monuments now destroyed.[14] Less praiseworthy was the work of the first archaeologists to work at the major sites of the central Sudan. The excavation of the Italian doctor, Joseph Ferlini, at Meroe in 1834 was little more than a treasure hunting expedition and resulted in serious damage to the site including the destruction of several pyramids.[15] Excavations by "professional" archaeologists, such as those of E. A. W. Budge in the pyramid fields of Meroe[16] and that of Sir John Garstang[17] in the royal city of Meroe in the late nineteenth and early twentieth centuries c.e., were hardly less destructive, being marred by the use of masses of inadequately trained and supervised diggers and poor record keeping.

George Reisner

Only with the pathbreaking excavations at Napata and Meroe, carried out between 1916 and 1925 under the sponsorship of the Museum of Fine Arts in Boston and Harvard University by the great American Egyptologist George Reisner,[18] was a sound foundation laid for the further progress of Meroitic studies. His findings were made available to scholars by his assistant, Dows Dunham, three decades later in the five magisterial volumes of *The Royal Cemeteries of Kush*.[19]

As Flinders Petrie had done before him in Egypt, Reisner introduced modern archaeological standards and methods to the Sudan in his excavations of the royal pyramids at Napata and Meroe and their associated noble cemeteries.[20] (See fig. 4.2.). The sites were conceived of and excavated as a whole, each tomb was methodically dug and planned, its principal architectural features drawn and analyzed, and its contents carefully recorded. By applying the same principles of stylistic evolution that Petrie had used to bring order to the archaeological history of predynastic Egypt, Reisner similarly organized the history of Meroe, first, by reconstructing

Figure 4.2   Pyramids at Meroe. Photograph by S. Sidebotham.

the developmental history of Cushite funerary architecture and then by using the resulting architectural history of the Meroitic royal pyramids as the key to the restoration of the list of the kings of Meroe. (See fig. 4.3.). As a result, it became possible for the first time since antiquity to reconstruct the outlines of the history of the kingdom of Meroe. Inevitably, the passage of time has modified the details of Reisner's scheme. His kinglist has had to be adjusted to accommodate additional kings as excavations at sites such as Kawa, Mussawerat es-Sufra, and even Philae have produced new royal names. Reconsideration of the chronological position of particular tombs by later scholars including F. Hintze,[21] S. Wenig,[22] and especially I. Hofmann[23] has led to further revision of Reisner's architecturally based kinglist. The core of his work, however, remains intact and still provides the indispensable framework for all reconstructions of Meroitic history.

In the reconstructions of Reisner and his followers, the history of Meroe took the form of the story of a millennium long cultural decline interrupted by brief renaissances. In Reisner's formulation, "the civilization was Egyptian, not native, and the subsequent history is one of loss, not of gain—of the gradual fading of the tradition of the arts and crafts and of the knowledge of the Egyptian language and the sacred texts."[24] Central to Reisner's vision was the idea that Napata, and later Meroe, were

Figure 4.3   Statue of King Aspelta from the Gebel Barkal temple, sixth century
B.C.E., black granite. Courtesy of The Museum of Fine Arts, Boston.

not independent cultural centers but outposts of Egyptian civilization planted in a hostile inner African environment so that their isolation from their Egyptian roots resulted in the using up of Meroe's "cultural capital" and, hence, in the inevitable decline and disintegration of Meroitic civilization.

Reisner divided the history of Meroitic civilization into four main phases.[25] The first, or Napatan period, began with the expulsion of the last Cushite ruler of Egypt, Tanwetamani, by Psamtik I, the founder of the Twenty-sixth dynasty, in 654 B.C.E., and lasted until the early third century B.C.E. The period was marked by an increasingly unsuccessful struggle to maintain the Egyptian character of Napatan culture that had been reinvigorated by Egyptian artists and craftsmen imported by the kings of the Twenty-fifth dynasty and was sustained, during the next three centuries, by the Egyptian priests who staffed the old Eighteenth dynasty temples of Amon and the other Egyptian gods that clustered around the base of the sacred mountain of Gebel Barkal.

The second phase, which marked the beginning of Meroitic history proper, opened with the transfer of the spiritual as well as the political capital of the kingdom to Meroe, by the Hellenized king Ergamenes, following a violent conflict with the priests of Amon of Napata. Politically, the period was characterized by rivalry between opposing factions of the royal lineage and the repeated division of the realm into two rival kingdoms, one based at Napata and one at Meroe, first in the late third century B.C.E. and again in the first century B.C.E. Culturally, the central feature of the period was the growing prominence of local, specifically Meroitic, cultural phenomena, such as the replacement of Egyptian with Meroitic as the language of government and religion, the substitution of bed burial for Egyptian style mummification, and the revival of the practice of retainer sacrifice. This occurred despite the renewed infusion of Egyptian influence during the third century following the establishment of close ties with Ptolemaic Egypt by Ergamenes and his successors. This phase of Meroitic history ended with the decisive reunification of the kingdom following the Roman sack of Napata in 24 B.C.E.

The subsequent signing of the treaty of Samos between Meroe and the Roman emperor Augustus in 20 B.C.E. heralded the beginning of a period of prosperity for Meroe that was based on the kingdom's control of the lucrative caravan trade between sub-Saharan Africa and Roman Egypt. (See fig. 4.4ab.). This brief "Indian summer" of Meroitic civilization saw significant building activity at Napata, Meroe and other Meroitic

Figure 4.4a Bronze head of Agustus found at Meroe. London 1911 (9.1.1).
Courtesy of The British Museum.

Figure 4.4b   Amon Temple at Naga. Photograph by S. Sidebotham.

sites and a final reinvigoration of the Egyptian aspects of Meroitic culture caused once again by the importation of Egyptian artisans by the rulers of Meroe.

A gradual decline, however, set in after the early first century C.E., which accelerated dramatically in the fourth and final period of Meroitic history with the collapse in the third century C.E. of the critical luxury trade with Roman Egypt, and the consequent impoverishment of Meroitic society and culture as evidenced by the tiny size and meager contents of the last Meroitic royal pyramids. Meroitic history itself finally ended in the mid-fourth century C.E. with the destruction of the now enfeebled kingdom through a combination of invasions by the barbarian Noba peoples and attacks by the kingdom of Axum in modern Ethiopia which had replaced Meroe as Rome's principal trading partner in northeast Africa.

The Reconstruction of Meroitic History

"All history is contemporary history" and "every generation must write its own history." So hold familiar clichés. The chronological foundation Reisner laid for the reconstruction of Meroitic history still remains largely intact. Not so his interpretation of that history which inevitably reflected the historical and anthropological models and views of his time. History was conceived as a political chronicle based on written sources. Accordingly, his reconstruction, and those of scholars writing in the tradition of scholarship established by him, tended to emphasize the political development of the Meroitic state. Because of the priority assigned to literary sources in this model, topics were selected for analysis not necessarily because of their intrinsic historical significance but because of the chance survival of written evidence so that, for example, more attention was given to occasional military conflicts such as that with Rome in the 20s B.C.E. and the Axumite invasion in the mid-fourth century C.E., than to the analysis of the character and evolution of Meroitic civilization. Equally important, political interpretations of archaeological phenomena, such as the alternation of royal burial sites between Napata and Meroe, were privileged over other possible explanations. In addition, cultural development was interpreted in essentially political terms with causal priority being given to the role of external forces, especially invasions. Thus, the foundation of the Napatan and, hence, the Meroitic state was explained as the result of the migration into Nubia of an Egyptianized Libyan family from which the kings of Napata and Meroe were descended.[26]

Similarly, the artistic revivals of the third century B.C.E. and first century C.E. resulted from the importation of a few Egyptian craftsmen whose presence could be deduced from the sudden improvement of the quality of art objects produced in those periods. Still more unfortunate was the fact that Reisner, writing in the heyday of European imperial expansion in Africa and the "racial science" of Douglas Derry and Grafton Elliot Smith,[27] could not avoid framing his analyses of Meroitic history in terms of the racial interpretations so fashionable at that time. So, faced with the portrayal of Taharqa with clearly negroid features on the victory stela of Esarhaddon, Reisner dismissed it as an "oriental boast" because "Tirharqa was not a negro, for the statues of both himself and his descendants show features which might be Egyptian or Libyan but certainly not negro."[28] The evidence of Meroitic creativity suggested by the creation of the Meroitic alphabet was accounted for with the observation that "it was the use of writing which marked the difference between the negroes . . . and the Ethiopians and Abyssinians" who were, as today, "dark colored races in which brown prevails . . . but not . . . African negroes." At the same time its significance was discounted by placing it in the general context of declining Meroitic understanding of Egyptian.[29] The influence of the native population was admitted only when required to account for the appearance of negative aspects in Meroitic culture such as the revival in the Hellenistic and Roman periods of retainer sacrifice or "sati-burial" in Reisner's terminology which he pointed out was a custom "still practiced by certain African tribes."[30] So much for the past; what about the present state of Meroitic historiography?

Recent Nubian Archaeology

At first glance, much remains familiar. Reisner's seriation of the royal pyramids still provides the chronological underpinning of all accounts of Meroitic history. Archaeology has not aided the Meroitic historian in recent years to the same extent that it has scholars of other periods of Nubian history, and for good reason. Nubian archaeology has been dominated by the need to record archaeological sites threatened with destruction by the successive increases in height and capacity of the Aswan dams. Beginning in 1907, each raising of the dams has been accompanied by a parallel campaign of salvage archaeology that reached a climax with the unparalleled international effort organized by UNESCO in the 1960s to survey and/or excavate all major and minor archaeological sites in lower

Nubia before they were drowned by the rising waters of Lake Nasser.[31] Consequently, lower Nubia has become archaeologically the most thoroughly explored region of Africa and has produced numerous historically important discoveries such as that of possible A Group royal tombs at Qustul, the seemingly unlimited treasures of Qasr Ibrim, the spectacular X-Group royal tombs at Ballaña and Qustul, and the remarkable Christian frescoes and inscriptions of the cathedral of Faras.

No similar sense of urgency has fueled archaeology in the central and southern Sudan. As a result, except for the exploration of the residential areas of Meroe by the University of Calgary and the work of the East Germans at Musawwerat es-Sufra, archaeological exploration of the Meroitic heartland has been limited. (See figs. 4.5 and 4.6.). Indeed, some of the most profitable "excavation" work in recent years has been in the storerooms of museums where material discovered early in this century is being rediscovered and finally made available to scholars.[32] That the potential for significant discoveries remains great, however, is illustrated by finds such as that of a first-century C.E. royal palace at Wad ben Naqa,[33] a series of four processional shrines at Meroe,[34] and the identification of remains of the sculptural program of the temple of Amon at Napata and the true character of the pinnacle of Gebel Barkal.[35] (See figs. 4.7 and 4.8.). Until that potential is realized, and the current unsettled political situation in the Sudan unfortunately makes that unlikely any time soon, the historian of the kingdom of Meroe will continue to face the unfortunate fact that the material and, to some extent, intellectual culture of the northern periphery of the Meroitic empire are far better known than that of the heartland of the kingdom itself. Nevertheless, there have been significant and positive changes in the state of Meroitic studies since the publication of *Africa in Classical Antiquity,* most of which have flowed from the fact that Meroitic studies has emerged as a distinct and recognized field of scholarship.

Meroitic Studies

The emergence of a separate field of Meroitic studies was an unanticipated bonus from the international effort to save the antiquities of lower Nubia. In addition to the United Arab Republic and the Republic of the Sudan, twenty-five countries mounted archaeological expeditions to the Sudan. For over a decade Nubian archaeology enjoyed unprecedented notoriety, being kept in the public eye by hundreds of books and articles and a major traveling exhibit of Meroitic art.[36] Numerous scholars, drawn from disciplines

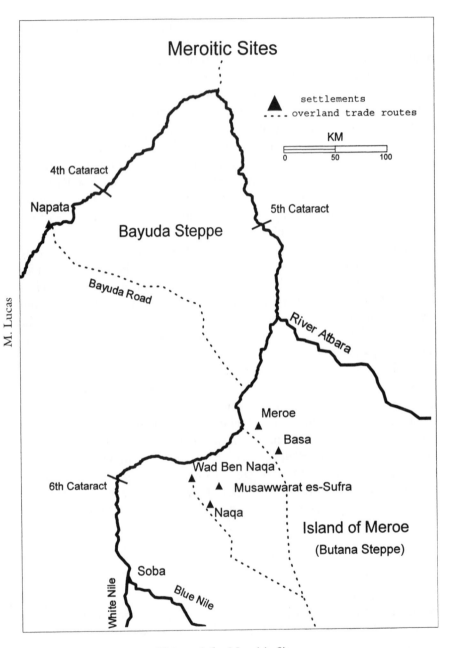

Figure 4.5 Meroitic Sites

Figure 4.6   Lion Temple at Musawerat es-Sufra. Photograph by S. Sidebotham.

as disparate as classics and cultural and physical anthropology, became active participants in a field that hitherto had been the private preserve of a handful of Egyptologists. More important, these scholars continued actively researching Meroitic topics after the completion of the UNESCO campaign, attending international meetings of specialists in the field, publishing papers in new journals devoted to Nubian studies, and assuring the future survival of the field by encouraging graduate students to do Ph.D. dissertations on Meroitic subjects. Perhaps the best testimony to the magnitude of the changes that have overtaken Meroitic studies is the fact that, while the notes to L. H. Thompson's article in *Africa in Classical Antiquity* cite only twenty-eight scholarly works, most of which were written in English, dealing with Meroitic themes,[37] the similar survey of Meroitic history published in 1987 by L. Török in *Nubian Culture: Past and Present,* the proceedings of the Sixth International Conference for Nubian Studies,[38] is accompanied by a nine-page bibliography of works in most of the scholarly languages of the modern world. As important as the growth in the number of scholars actively involved in Meroitic studies has been the transformation of the perspective from which the history of Meroe has been studied, caused by the increasingly interdisciplinary character of the field. Particularly important has been the contribution of

Figure 4.7   Gebel Barkal. Photograph by S. Sidebotham.

scholars trained in the fields of art history and cultural anthropology, who have taught a scholarly world, made receptive by the post-World War II decolonization of Africa and the emergence of an independent Republic of the Sudan, to treat Meroitic civilization as an analytically separate and coherent cultural entity with its own distinctive style whose primary creators were the Meroites themselves.[39]

Every aspect of Meroitic studies has been affected by these developments. The most dramatic change has been the disappearance or marginalization of topics that had been previously prominent in Meroitic scholarship. Examples are the once common discussions of invading people as responsible for each new phase of ancient Nubian history[40] and the racial identity of the populations of the kingdom of Meroe. Both were victims of the recognition that Meroitic civilization was largely the creation of the indigenous Nubian population, a population that, racially, was essentially the same as the modern non-Arab people of the Sudan.[41] Also largely gone are the various grandiose theories that, with little evidence, made Meroe the center from which such central features of African civilization as iron working and sacral kingship diffused to the furthest corners of the African continent. Freed of the incubus of what Bruce Trigger called in a fundamental study of Meroitic iron working the "pseudo-history" of Meroe,[42] a version of Meroitic history has begun to emerge in the last several

Figure 4.8 Kiosk at Naqa. Photograph by S. Sidebotham.

decades that differs markedly from the grim history of almost continuous decline temporarily interrupted by brief renaissances inspired by contact with Egyptian culture that was propounded by Reisner in the early twentieth century and was still apparent in the treatment of Meroitic history offered in *Africa in Classical Antiquity* in 1969.[43]

New Interpretations

No period of Meroitic history has been left untouched by these changes. Thus, the discovery of evidence pointing to extensive building at Meroe as early as the eighth century B.C.E. has confirmed the theory that the city was an important royal center already, under the Twenty-fifth dynasty.[44] In addition, study of the Aswan stela together with evidence for extensive destruction at Napata during the reign of Aspelta makes it likely that the transfer of the capital from Napata to Meroe is best explained as a defensive response to hostilities between Nubia and Twenty-sixth dynasty Egypt that began with the raid of Psamtik II in 593 B.C.E.[45] The hostilities continued intermittently until the fall of the dynasty and the recognition by Meroe of the suzerainty of the new Persian rulers of Egypt in the late 520s B.C.E.[46] Most dramatically affected, however, have been Reisner's second and third phases of Meroitic history, that is, the period from approximately the mid-third century B.C.E. to the early third century C.E.

The distinguished Hungarian Meroiticist, L. Török, has recently characterized the third century B.C.E. as the period of the "early Meroitic miracle"[47] and with reason. Much that would typify Meroitic culture for the rest of antiquity emerged during this period including the final eclipse of Napata by Meroe as the spiritual center of the realm, the building of the first "lion temples," the rise to prominence in the pantheon of specifically Meroitic gods, such as Apedemak, Arensnuphis and Sebiumeker, and the development of the Meroitic alphabet. Moreover, a passage of the first-century B.C.E. Greek historian Diodorus[48] seems to suggest that fundamental changes also occurred in the political structure of the Meroitic state at this time:

> Of all their customs the most astonishing is that which obtains in connection with death of their kings. For the priests at Meroe who spend their time in the worship of the gods and the rites which do them honor, being the greatest and most powerful order, whenever the idea comes to them, dispatch a messenger to the king with orders that he die. For the gods, they add, have revealed this to them, and it must be that the command of the immortals should in no wise be disregarded by one of mortal frame. And this order they accompany with other arguments, such as are accepted by a simple minded nature, which has been bred in a custom that is both ancient and difficult to eradicate and which knows no argument that can be set in opposition to commands enforced by no compulsion. Now in former times the kings would obey the priests, having been overcome, not by arms nor by force, but because their reasoning powers had been put under a constraint by their very superstition; but during the reign of the second Ptolemy the king of the Ethiopians, Ergamenes, who had had a Greek education and had studied philosophy, was the first to have the courage to disdain the command. For assuming a spirit which became the position of a king he entered with his soldiers into the unapproachable place where stood, as it turned out, the golden shrine of the Ethiopians, put the priests to the sword, and after abolishing this custom thereafter ordered affairs after his own will (Loeb translation by C.H. Oldfather).

Much remains uncertain about the events described in this passage, including the reality of the reported custom of royal suicide and the identity of the king called Ergamenes (most scholars identify him with a king named Arakakamani, the first Meroitic ruler known to have been buried at Meroe). The central fact, however, seems clear, namely, that a Meroitic king with close ties to the Ptolemaic government of Egypt reacted violently to a challenge from the priesthood of Amon, the guardians of Meroe's Egyptian traditions. He then reorganized the Meroitic state so as to strengthen the position of the king, as is revealed by the increase in royal patronage of deities closely connected with the office of the king who lack identifiable Egyptian backgrounds, such as Apedemak and Arensnuphis.

But was there also a connection between the cultural and political developments of the period? Reisner believed there was and argued that Ergamenes and his successors followed a policy characterized by the maintenance of close relations with Ptolemaic Egypt and a deliberate strengthening of Egyptian influence in Meroe that accounted for the cultural revival of the period.

Other scholars, such as L. Thompson, who claimed that Meroe was transformed into "an approximation of a Hellenistic kingdom,"[49] agreed as to the basic thrust of Meroitic policy, but identified the primary cultural influence as Greek and with some reason. Greek luxury goods, including metal vessels and wine amphorae, appear in Hellenistic Meroitic royal and noble burials. Masons' marks and the use of the Greek systems of measurements indicate that the Meroitic kings employed Greek artisans and architects on some of the most important building projects of the period, including a number of royal pyramids, much of the great enclosure at Musawwerat es-Sufra, and the nearby temple of Apedemak.[50] Contemporary Meroitic scholarship paints a more complex picture, one that emphasizes the independent and creative character of the Meroitic response to contact with Ptolemaic Egypt in both the political and cultural spheres.[51]

Politically, evidence from Philae and lower Nubia indicates that, in fact, the kings of Meroe tried to pursue an independent policy toward Ptolemaic Egypt, even exploiting the outbreak of civil war between the Ptolemies and their Egyptian subjects in the last decade of the third century B.C.E. to expand Meroitic influence in the area immediately south of Aswan.[52] Likewise, except for the amphorae and related vessels such as wine strainers, the bulk of the Greek imports found in Meroitic tombs belong to categories of objects that are attested as well established components of pre-hellenistic Meroitic burials. Similarly, the buildings built by Greek artisans and architects in Meroitic service were not typical Hellenistic edifices but buildings such as the so-called lion temples that were superficially Egyptianizing in their general decor but had no exact Egyptian prototypes and served as shrines to local deities, particularly, the royal war god Apedemak. Moreover, studies by L. Žabkar on the cult of Apedemak[53] and J. Yellin on the role of

Anubis in Meroitic funerary cult[54] have revealed similar Meroitic adaptions of Egyptian texts and iconography made available by contact with Ptolemaic Egypt to express specifically Meroitic religious ideas.

Even the invention of the Meroitic alphabetic script, surely the most remarkable cultural achievement of Hellenistic Meroe, is most likely the result of a similar use of Meroe's Egyptian heritage to meet a specific local need, namely, the desire of the Hellenistic kings of Meroe to free themselves of dependence on the Egyptian educated priesthood of Amon for literate officials. It was not, as has usually been suggested, an attempt to compensate for declining Meroitic understanding of Egyptian as evidenced by the supposedly "barbaric" character of Late Napatan hieroglyphic texts. The reasons for this conclusion are twofold. First, claims of the "corruption" of late Napatan Egyptian texts have been shown to be greatly exaggerated.[55] Second, inscriptions in Meroitic hieroglyphs first appear in the early second century B.C.E. at a time when Meroitic knowledge of Egyptian and access to sources of Egyptian texts and persons capable of composing them were both high.[56] Clearly, Hellenistic Meroe did not experience a simple revival of its Egyptian heritage made possible by contact with Ptolemaic Egypt as suggested by Reisner, but instead it took advantage of the opportunities afforded by that contact to select and adapt elements of that heritage to create its own distinctive voice and style.

Equally far reaching has been the revision of the history of Meroe during the early centuries C.E. Reisner described the period as a brief renaissance followed by a long decline. Recent scholars view it in more positive terms, noting evidence of prosperity and cultural innovation and expansion of Meroitic influence into both lower Nubia and the southern Sudan. Indeed, one scholar, Fritz Hintze, has even described it as a "golden age."[57] The reasons for this remarkable *volte face* in scholarly opinion are complex. One key consideration, however, is chronology. The archaeological record is clear that during the joint reign of king Natakamani and queen Amanitare, a remarkably ambitious construction program took place that included most of the known examples of the so-called lion temples, the Amon temple at Naga and the palace at Wad ben Naqa together with extensive repair work on the Amon temple at Meroe. Reisner's dating of their reign to the late first century B.C.E. was crucial to his interpretation so that redating it to the second half of the first century C.E., as most current scholars do,[58] made his thesis of a "brief renaissance followed by a long decline" untenable. At the same time evidence of Meroitic initiative throughout the kingdom's territory has been steadily accumulating. Clearest is the situation in Lower Nubia, which had been largely depopulated for much of the first millennium B.C.E. During this period, however, resettlement of the area, aided by peace with Meroe's northern neighbor, Roman Egypt, and, as Adams has repeatedly pointed out,[59] probably also by the introduction of improved agricultural technology in the form of the *saqia,* accelerated dramatically. Likewise, the numerous *hafirs,* circular stone structures intended to store water in the Butana, the steppe region south of Meroe, suggests similarly deliberate efforts by the Meroitic government to improve agriculture in the Meroitic heartland. Nor was innovation limited to the political and economic spheres. In his monumental study of Nubian pottery, *Ceramic Industries of Medieval Nubia,*[60] Adams demonstrated that the remarkable Meroitic tradition of fine painted pottery began during these same centuries, while the recovery of Meroitic texts at Qasr Ibrim on a variety of materials including papyrus, ostraca, and wood points to growing literacy among, at least, the official class.[61] Add the prosperity resulting from trade with Roman Egypt implied by the numerous imported luxury goods found in Meroitic graves throughout the Sudan, goods, given the looted character of virtually all Meroitic cemeteries, that surely represent a tiny remnant of what once existed,[62] and the description of the period as the "golden age" of Meroitic civilization clearly has considerable justification.

By contrast, the final century or so of Meroitic history has, for understandable reasons, attracted comparatively little scholarly interest during the past two decades. Little new archaeological evidence datable to this period has been discovered that would call into question the picture of growing poverty, isolation, and political weakness created by the tiny brick pyramids of the late third and fourth centuries C.E.

If the general picture of this period has not changed, it has been significantly nuanced in two ways. First, reconsideration of the evidence of the two long known Axumite inscriptions concerning Meroe in the light of newly discovered texts has made it clear that the destruction of the organized Meroitic state by Ezana sometime shortly after 350 C.E. was the final act in an extended period of growing Axumite power over Meroe. That period had been marked by at least two earlier military interventions, and not the sudden and unprecedented act of foreign aggression that scholars had traditionally assumed it to have been.[63] Second, it has become increasingly clear that the Meroitic settlements in Lower Nubia, whose history and governmental and social structure have been masterfully analyzed by N. Millet[64] and L. Török,[65] did not experience the same extreme impoverishment and political debilitation as the capital. In fact, Meroitic authority in its northern province may even have continued after the fall of Meroe itself for an indeterminable period of time. That would account for the clear evidence of the survival of Meroitic political and religious ideas that is apparent in the tombs of the rulers of the first post-Meroitic successor states at Ballana and Qustul,[66] but that speculation takes me beyond the limits set for this paper.

Interdisciplinary fields such as Meroitic studies are not without their tensions. Representatives of the various concerned disciplines understandably differ over the relative evidential value to be assigned to different categories of sources and the most appropriate interpretative models to be used by scholars. Philologists, art historians, and archaeologists argue whether priority should be assigned to textual or material evidence.[67] Anthropologists and historians seek to reconcile synchronic and diachronic approaches to the same material.[68] More important than such disputes, which are inevitable in a field in which scholars working within different disciplinary paradigms study the same subject, is the principal achievement of the past two decades of scholarship. The agreement of scholars of all backgrounds that the history of Meroe is the history of an independent civilization with its own specific cultural style and not the story of the preordained millennium long decline of a forlorn outpost of Egyptian civilization that had been assumed by Reisner and those who followed in his footsteps. Filling in the details of that history in all its variety is the task for the future.

Bibliography

Adams, William Y. *Nubia: Corridor to Africa*. Princeton: Princeton University Press, 1977.

Africa in Antiquity: The Arts of Ancient Nubia and the Sudan. 2 vols. Brooklyn: Brooklyn Museum, 1978.

Agatharchides of Cnidus. *On the Erythraean Sea*. Edited and translated by Stanley M. Burstein. London: Hakluyt Society, 1989.

Burstein, Stanley, ed. *Ancient African Civilizations: Kush and Axum*. Princeton: Markus Wiener Publishers, 1998.

Dunham, Dows. *The Royal Cemeteries of Kush*. 5 vols. Boston: Museum of Fine Arts, 1950–1963.

Shinnie, P. L. *Meroe: A Civilization of the Sudan*. London: Thames and Hudson, 1967.

———. "The Culture of Meroe and its Influence in the Central Sudan," *Sahara:* 2 (1989): 21–30.

Török, László. *Der meroitische Staat 1*. Meroitica 9. Berlin: Akademie Verlag, 1986.

———. "Kush and the External World," Meroitica 10. Berlin: Akademie-Verlag, 1989; 49–216.

———. *The Kingdom of Kush: Handbook of the Napatan-Meroitic Civilization.* Leiden: Brill, 1997.

Welsby, Derek A. *The Kingdom of Kush: The Napatan and Meroitic Empires.* London: British Museum Press, 1996.

Žabkar, L. V. *Apedemak: Lion God of Meroe.* Warminster: Aris and Phillips, 1975.

Notes

1. Pliny the Elder *Natural History* 6.182.

2. Diogenes Laertius *Lives of the Philosophers* 9.49.

3. Ps. Callisthenes *Alexander Romance* 3.18–24.

4. Josephus *Jewish Antiquities* 2.252–253.

5. Josephus *Jewish Antiquities* 8.165, 175.

6. O. A. W. Dilke, *Greek and Roman Maps* (London: Thames and Hudson, 1985), 64, 177–78.

7. Pliny *Natural History* 6.183. The surviving fragments of the classical writers on Nubia are collected in Felix Jacoby, *Die Fragmente der Griechischen Historiker,* Vol. 3C1 (Leiden: Brill, 1958), 666–73. The textual sources for Meroitic institutions have been collected in László Török, *Der meroitische Staat 1,* Meroitica 9 (Berlin: Akademie Verlag, 1986); and Tormod Eide et al., *Fontes Historiae Nubiorum: Textual Sources for the History of the Middle Nile Region between the Eighth Century* B.C. *and the Sixth Century* A.D., 3 vols. (Bergen: University of Bergen, 1994–98). For a full critical evaluation of the evidence for Meroitic history see László Török, "Geschichte Meroes. Ein Beitrag uber die Quellanlage und den Forschungstand," *Aufstieg und Niedergang der römischen Welt,* 2.10.1 (Berlin: W. de Gruyter, 1988), 106–341.

8. *Cf.* Claude Vandersleyen, "Des obstacles que constituent les cataractes du Nil," *BIFAO* 69 (1969): 253–66.

9. Diodorus 1.60.2. The context suggests a date in the second quarter of the second millennium B.C.E.

10. *Cf.* P. L. Shinnie, *Meroe: A Civilization of the Sudan* (London: Thames and Hudson, 1967), 132–40 for a brief account. The most comprehensive recent account of the Meroitic language is Fritz Hintze, *Beiträge zur meroitischen Grammatik,* Meroitica 3 (Berlin: Akademie Verlag), 1979.

11. So the interpretation of the so-called "Great Stela of Akinidad" as containing the Meroitic account of the war with Rome in the 20s B.C.E. generally accepted since the masterful analysis of this important text by F. Ll. Griffith in "Meroitic Studies IV," *JEA* 4 (1917): 159–73, has been called into question by Karl Heinz-Priese, "'rm und '3m, das land Irame. Ein Beitrag zur Topographie des Sudan im Altertum," *Altorientalische Forschungen,* Schriften zur Geschichte und Kultur des alten Orients 1 (1974), 10–12.

12. Although a comprehensive overview of the history of Nubian archaeology is lacking, there are useful brief surveys in William Y. Adams, *Nubia: Corridor*

to Africa (Princeton, N.J.: Princeton University Press, 1977), 65–90, and "Paradigms in Sudan Archaeology," *Africa Today* 28 (1981): 15–24; P. L. Shinnie, "Changing Attitudes toward the Past," *Africa Today* 28 (1981): 25–33; and Bruce G. Trigger, "Reisner to Adams: Paradigms of Nubian Cultural History," in *Nubian Studies: Proceedings of the Symposium for Nubian Studies Cambridge 1978,* J. M. Plumley, ed. (Warminster: Aris and Phillips, 1982), 223–26.

13. Quoted from Basil Davidson, *The African Past* (London: Longmans, 1964), 258–59.

14. *Cf.* E. A. Wallis Budge, *The Egyptian Sudan: Its History and Monuments* (London: Kegan, Paul, Trench, Trübner, 1907) 1:1–63; and Shinnie, *Meroe,* 24–27, for accounts of the early travelers in the Sudan.

15. *Cf.* Budge, 1:285–320.

16. Budge, 1:321–56.

17. Only the first volume of the final report was ever published, John Garstang, *Meroe, The City of the Ethiopians* (Oxford: Clarendon Press, 1911) together with five preliminary reports in the *Liverpool Annals of Archaeology and Anthropology* between 1911 and 1916. The evidence for Garstang's excavations has been collected and analyzed in László Török, *Meroe City: An Ancient African Capital, John Garstang's Excavations in the Sudan,* 2 vols. (London: Egypt Exploration Society, 1997).

18. For an entertaining autobiographical account of Reisner's excavations see Dows Dunham, *Recollections of an Egyptologist* (Boston: Museum of Fine Arts 1972), 16–28.

19. Dows Dunham, *The Royal Cemeteries of Kush,* 5 vols. (Cambridge, Mass.: Harvard University Press, 1950–63).

20. There is a good brief account of Reisner's excavation methods in Neil Asher Silberman, *Digging for God and Country: Exploration, Archaeology, and the Secret Struggle for the Holy Land, 1799–1917* (New York: Knopf, 1982), 172–78.

21. Fritz Hintze, "Meroitic Chronology: Problems and Prospects," *Meroitica* 1 (1973), 127–44.

22. S. Wenig, "Bemerkungen zur Chronologie des Reiches von Meroe," *Mitteilungen des Instituts für Orientforschung* 13 (1967): 1–44.

23. Inge Hofmann, *Beiträge zur meroitischen Chronologie,* Studia Instituti Anthropos, vol. 31 (Bonn: Anthropus-Inst., 1978).

24. G. A. Reisner, "The Pyramids of Meroe and Candaces of Ethiopia," *Sudan Notes and Records* 5 (1922): 178.

25. For Reisner's reconstruction of the history of Meroe see in particular "The Pyramids of Meroe and the Candaces of Ethiopia," 173–94; and the identically titled article in the *Museum of Fine Arts Bulletin,* 21, 124 (April 1923), 12–27. For a somewhat different interpretation of Reisner's scheme see Dows Dunham, "Notes on the History of Kush: 850 B.C.–A.D. 350," *AJA* 50 (1946): 378–88; and "Outline of the Ancient History of the Sudan," *Sudan Notes and Records* 28 (1947): 1–10.

26. G. A. Reisner, "Outline of the Ancient History of the Sudan: Part IV: The First Kingdom of Ethiopia," *Sudan Notes and Records* 2 (1919): 41–43.

27. *Cf.* Adams, *Nubia*, 91–95, for the "racial question" in Nubian Studies.

28. G. A. Reisner, "Outline of the Ancient History of the Sudan: Part IV," 50. The claim recurs in A. J. Arkell, *A History of the Sudan to 1821,* 2nd edition (London: Athlone Press 1961), 128, although Arkell concedes that he "may have had some negroid blood in his veins."

29. Reisner, "Candaces (*M.F.A.B.*)," 24–25.

30. Ibid., 21.

31. The fullest account of the UNESCO salvage campaign and its results is Torgny Säve-Söderbergh, ed.,*Temples and Tombs of Ancient Nubia* (New York: Thames and Hudson 1987).

32. Good examples are the publication of a Meroitic copy of a Ptolemaic astronomical text discovered by Reisner by Janice W. Yellin, *An Astronomical Text from Beg. South 503,* Meroitica 7 (1984), 577–82; and of a column drum with a Greek inscription found by Garstang in the Royal City at Meroe by A. R. Millard, "BGD . . . Magical Spell or Education Exercise?" *Eretz Israel* 18 (1985): 39*–42*.

33. Jean Vercouter, "Un palais des 'Candaces', contemporain d'Auguste (Fouilles à Wad-ban-Naga 1958–60)," *Syria* 39 (1962): 263–99.

34. No details have yet been published concerning these structures; *cf.* Rebecca Bradley, "Meroitic Chronology," *Meroitische Forschungen 1980,* Meroitica 7 (Berlin: Akademie-Verlag, 1984), 209.

35. Only a popular account of these finds has so far appeared in Timothy Kendall, "Kingdom of Kush," *National Geographic* 178, no. 5 (November 1990): 125.

36. The catalogue of this exhibit together with a volume of valuable essays was published under the title *Africa in Antiquity: The Arts of Ancient Nubia and the Sudan,* 2 vols. (Brooklyn: Brooklyn Museum, 1978). The proceedings of a symposium held in connection with this exhibit were published under the same title as Meroitica 5. Also valuable is the catalogue of a small exhibition of Cushite art held at the Brockton Art Museum between 1981 and 1984 by Timothy Kendall, *Kush: Lost Kingdom of the Nile* (Brockton, Mass.: Brockton Art Museum 1982).

37. L. A. Thompson, "Eastern Africa and the Graeco-Roman World (to A.D. 641)," *Africa in Classical Antiquity,* edited by L. Thompson and J. Ferguson (Ibadan: Ibadan University Press 1969), 26–61. A fuller version of the section of this article dealing with Kush was published under the title "The Kingdom of Kush and the Classical World," *Nigeria and the Classics* 11 (1969), 26–53.

38. László Török, "The Historical Background: Meroe, North and South," *Nubian Culture Past and Present: Main Papers Presented at the Sixth International Conference for Nubian Studies in Uppsala,* 11–16 August 1986, edited by Thomas Hägg (Stockholm: Almquist and Wiksell 1987), 208–16.

39. Good statements of this new perspective are W. Y. Adams, "Continuity

and Change in Nubian Cultural History," *Sudan Notes and Records* 48 (1967): 1–32; and B. G. Haycock. "The Place of the Napatan-Meroitic Culture in the History of the Sudan and Africa," *Sudan in Africa,* edited by Yusuf Fadl Hasan (Khartoum: Khartoum University Press 1971), 26–41.

40. For a good account of the decline of "invasionism" in archaeological explanation in general and Nubian studies in particular see William Y. Adams, "Invasion, Diffusion, Evolution?," *Antiquity* 42 (1968): 194–215.

41. *Cf.* Dennis P. Van Gerven, David S. Carlson, and George J. Armelagos, "Racial History and Bio-Cultural Adaptation of Nubian Archaeological Populations," *JAH* 14 (1973): 555–64; and David S. Carlson and Dennis P. Van Gerven, "Diffusion, Biological Determinism, and Biocultural Adaptation in the Nubian Corridor," *American Anthropologist* 81 (1979): 561–80.

42. Bruce Trigger, "The Myth of Meroe and the African Iron Age," *AHS* 2, no. 1 (1969): 23–50.

43. *Cf.* Thompson, "Eastern Africa," 45.

44. Rebecca J. Bradley, "Meroitic Chronology," Meroitica 7 (1984), 197–203, 207–8.

45. Serge Sauneron and Jean Yoyotte, "La campagne de Psammétique II et sa signification historique," *BIFAO* 50 (1952): 157–207.

46. For relations between Meroe and Persia see Stanley M. Burstein, "Herodotus and the Emergence of Meroe," *JSSEA* 11 (1981): 1–5.

47. Török, "Meroe, North and South," 154.

48. Diodorus 3.5. Diodorus' source is the lost *On Affairs in Asia* of the second century B.C.E. Greek historian Agatharchides of Cnidus; *cf.* Agatharchides of Cnidus, *On the Erythraean Sea,* edited and translated by Stanley M. Burstein (London: Hakluyt society 1989), 19–21.

49. Thompson, "Eastern Africa," 36; "Kush," 32.

50. Friedrich W. Hinkel, "Ägyptische Elle oder griechischer Modul?: Metrologische Studien an historischen Bauwerken im mittlern Niltal," *Das Altertum* 33 (1987): 150–62; and "Saule und Interkolumnium in der meroitischen Architektur; Metrologische Vorstudien zu einer Klassifikation der Bauwerke," *Meroitica* 10 (1989), 231–67.

51. I have discussed these matters more fully in a paper entitled "The Hellenistic Fringe: The Case of Meroe" which is my contribution to the volume *Hellenistic History and Culture,* edited by Peter Green (Berkeley: University of California Press, 1993), 38–54.

52. Erich Winter, "Ergamenes II., seine Datierung und seine Bautätigkeit in Nubien," *MDAIK* 37 (1981): 509–13; *cf.* Stanley M. Burstein, "The Ethiopian War of Ptolemy V: An Historical Myth?" *Beiträge zur Sudanforschung* 1 (1986): 17–18.

53. L. V. Žabkar, *Apedemak: Lion God of Meroe* (Warminster: Aris and Phillips 1975).

54. J. Yellin, "The Role of Anubis in Meroitic Religion," *Symposium for Nubian Studies* (Warminster: Aris and Phillips, 1982), 227–34.

55. *Cf.* the observation by F. Hintze in *Meroitica* 1, 171, that the peculiarities of these inscriptions can be explained as the result of translating texts written in Demotic into Hieroglyphs.

56. The inscriptions of the late third century B.C.E. Lion Temple at Musawwerat es-Sufra are in good Ptolemaic hieroglyphs (*cf.* Török, "Geschichte Meroes," 144). Evidence for Meroitic contact with Upper Egyptian priests is provided by Papyrus Berlin P. 15527, a papyrus from Elephantine dated to the year 187 B.C.E. which refers to a priest taking refuge in Nubia to escape reprisals following the reestablishment of Ptolemaic power in southern Egypt after two decades of native Egyptian rule (Karl-Theodor Zauzich, ed., *Papyri von der Insel Elephantine* [Berlin: Akademie Verlag 1978], 1:1–3).

57. Fritz Hintze, "The Meroitic Period," *Africa in Antiquity*, 1:98.

58. *Cf.* Hofmann, *Chronologie*, 115–34.

59. His views are most readily accessible in Adams, *Nubia*, 345–56.

60. William Y. Adams, *Ceramic Industries of Medieval Nubia*, Memoirs of the UNESCO Archaeological Survey of Sudanese Nubia (Lexington: University Press of Kentucky, 1986), 1:50.

61. William Y. Adams, "The 'Library' of Qasr Ibrim," *The Kentucky Review* 1 (1979): 16–17.

62. The fullest list of imported goods found in the Sudan is provided by László Török, "Kush and the External World," *Meroitica* 10 (1989), 117–50.

63. *Cf.* Tomas Hägg, "A New Axumite Inscription in Greek from Meroe. A Preliminary Report," *Meroitica* 7 (1984), 436–41; Stanley M. Burstein, "Axum and the Fall of Meroe," *JARCE* 18 (1981): 47–50; "The Axumite Inscription from Meroe and Late Meroitic Chronology," *Meroitica* 7 (1984): 220–21.

64. Nicholas B. Millet, "Social and Political Organisation in Meroe," *ZÄS* 108 (1981): 124–41. Unfortunately, Dr. Millet's important thesis "Meroitic Nubia" (Yale Dissertation, 1969) remains unpublished, but may be obtained through University Microfilms International (Ann Arbor, 1983).

65. L. Török, *Economic Offices and Officials in Meroitica Nubia (A Study in Territorial Administration of the Late Meroitic Kingdom)*, Studia Aegyptiaca 5 (Budapest: Archaeological Institute of the Hungarian Academy of Sciences, 1979); *Late Antique Nubia*, Antaeus 16 (Budapest, 1988).

66. The last Meroitic royal inscription, the inscription of King Kharamadoye from Kalabscha in lower Nubia, is now generally agreed to postdate the fall of Meroe (*cf.* Török, *Geschichte Meroes*," 288–89 for the most recent discussion of this text). The recent excavations of what appears to be a post-Meroitic royal tomb at El Hobagi near Khartoum suggests that the end of a unified Nubian state ruled from Meroe was followed by the emergence of similar local successor states in the southern portion of the former Meroitic kingdom, albeit ones lacking the sort of

extensive contacts with late Roman Egypt that are attested at Ballana and Qustul. *Cf.* Patrice Lenoble and Nigm ed Din Mohammed Sharif, "Barbarians at the Gates?: the royal mounds of El Hobagi and the end of Meroe, *Antiquity* 66 (1992): 626–35.

67. *Cf.*, for example, Török, "Kush and the External World," 86–92; and my commentary in Stanley M. Burstein, "Kush and the External World: A Comment," *Meroitica* 10 (1989), 225–30.

68. These issues are clearly stated and discussed in William Y. Adams, "Three Perspectives on the Past: The Historian, the Art Historian, and the Prehistorian: Comments on Session II," *Nubian Culture Past and Present,* 285–91.

5

The Ballaña Kingdom and Culture: Twilight of Classical Nubia

WILLIAM Y. ADAMS

❋

The collapse of Kushite imperial power, sometime in the fourth century A.D., ushered in what is often regarded as a dark age in Nubian and Sudanese history. So far as the central Sudan is concerned, this perception appears to be justified. The old Kushite heartland areas of Napata and Meroe were overrun by invading tribesmen who left no literary record of themselves, and apparently rather little in the way of an archaeological record that can be securely identified. Nor can we glean much useful information from Classical writers, who seem to have lost all interest in the remote lands of inner Africa once the city and the civilization of Meroe had fallen.

The same cannot be said of the most northerly portion of Kush, on the immediate frontiers of Egypt. Here, in the region between the First and Third Nile Cataracts,[1] vestiges of Kushite civilization lived on, blending with influences from Byzantine Egypt to form a distinctive local civilization which represents the twilight of the Classical era in the northern region of Nubia. Today we call this the Ballaña culture, and the people the Ballaña people,[2] though earlier authors had other names for them. The Ballaña people, unlike their Kushite predecessors, had no indigenous written language, and their only written testimony consists of a handful of inscriptions in a kind of pidgin Greek. But, unlike the peoples of more southerly territories, they did not escape the notice of foreign chroniclers. There are about two dozen currently known Classical texts which refer in one way or another to events and conditions in post-Kushite Nubia;[3] until about 100 years ago they provided our only knowledge of this somewhat enigmatic chapter in history.

The Textual Record

In the volume *Africa in Classical Antiquity,* Professor L. A. Thompson did a superb job of summarizing what was, and still is, known about post-Kushite Nubia on the basis of Classical texts.[4] Very little can be added to what he wrote more than 30 years ago, and I will therefore give only a brief synopsis of his account here.

Classical authors speak of two peoples in northern Nubia in the immediate post-Kushite period: the Blemmye and the Nobatae or Nobadae. At least by implication, both are identified as invaders into the former territories of Kush, respectively from east and west of the Nile Valley. The Blemmye were nomadic tribesmen from the Red Sea Hills—kinsmen to the modern-day Beja tribes of the same area, while the Nobadae were said to come from oases in the Western Desert. Both peoples quite obviously settled as peasant farmers in the Nile Valley, adopting many of the lifeways of their Kushite predecessors. Both were warlike, and their incursion was in fact the reason for Diocletian's decision to abandon the Roman outposts in Lower Nubia and to withdraw the imperial frontier to Aswan.[5] Occasionally the two peoples made common cause in attacking the Roman settlements in southern Egypt, but most of the time they seem to have been at war with each other for the control of Nubia itself. Eventually the Nobadae were triumphant; their King Silko claimed to have driven the Blemmye out of Nubia altogether. This accomplishment is recorded in a very ungrammatical Greek inscription on the walls of the old Roman Temple of Kalabsha.[6]

Despite the mutual hostility of Blemmye and Nobadae, the texts do not hint at much cultural difference between the two immigrant peoples. Apparently neither group had been peasant farmers prior to their entry into the Nile Valley. After the immemorial fashion of settled nomads, they simply adopted the existing lifeways of the peasant population among whom they settled, which means that both groups became, in a sense, both "Kushized" and "Byzantinized."

One cultural feature that was evidently common to Blemmye and Nobadae was the worship of the ancient Egyptian goddess Isis, who clearly was their most important deity. Both peoples regularly made pilgrimages to the Temple of Isis at Philae, just within the Roman frontier, and when the Roman governor attempted to close the temple as part of a general suppression of pagan worship, they mounted a joint attack against the garrison at Aswan. The attack was defeated, but the governor relented to the extent of keeping the temple open for the benefit of the Nubian votaries of Isis.[7]

From the Classical texts, a good deal has been inferred about the nature and structure of the Blemmyan "state." In the words of Thompson, "their state was organized as a confederation of tribes, each with its own chief or king bearing the Greek title *basiliskos,* and with a supreme king entitled *basileus.* Blemmye inscriptions in Greek, found at their capital Kalabsha and at Gebelein, give the names and titles of several chiefs and officials of the Blemmye state: among them 'Charachen, *basiliskos* of the Blemmyes,' and 'Pachytimme, most illustrious *basiliskos.*' The state officials bear Byzantine titles, such as *domesticus, protector, curator, comes,* and *grammateus.* These and other titles indicate a state-organization copied from Byzantium, and an economic organization based on the use of Byzantine coinage."[8]

The extent of Byzantinization in the Blemmyan state must nevertheless be regarded as problematical, based as it is on the evidence of non-Blemmyan, Graeco-Egyptian scribes. The propensity of Greek observers to see everything in the world through Greek eyes, and to translate foreign titles and foreign practices into their nearest Greek equivalents, is well illustrated in the case of Herodotus, and the same may well have been true of the scribes in Byzantine Egypt. Monneret de Villard has also warned that the mere borrowing of Greek titles should not be taken as evidence that the individuals who bore them had functions equivalent to those of similarly titled officials in the Byzantine state.[9]

One Greek historian, a certain Olympiodorus, actually claimed to have visited the Blemmyan kingdom at the invitation of their "pagarchs and prophets," and to have traveled as far south as Qasr Ibrim.[10] However, Olympiodorus was not highly regarded as an authority in his own time.[11]

Despite their enigmatic nature, a picture clearly emerges from the Classical texts of a rather complex political system combining Byzantine and indigenous traditions. What is conspicuously lacking, however, is any suggestion of a survival of Kushite imperial traditions. What we seem to perceive is a pseudo-Byzantine frontier state, not a Kushite successor-state.

The Archaeological Record

While Thompson's survey of historical sources was so complete that very little can be added to it now, the same is not true in regard to archaeological information. It is primarily from this source that we have been able to enlarge significantly our knowledge of post-Kushite Nubia. Some of the archaeological information was already available in Thompson's time, but much has come to light from excavations and surveys in the last three decades. Because it makes a kind of interesting archaeological detective story, I propose in the next few pages to review chronologically the development of our knowledge of post-Kushite culture as it has come to light through archaeology.[12]

Early in the twentieth century, the Government of Egypt began construction of what today we call the Aswan Low Dam, a few miles upstream from the city of Aswan. The structure, when completed, was to create a lake about 90 miles long, inundating a considerable part of the historic land of Lower Nubia. In advance of the rising waters, the Egyptian Survey Department launched a major program of archaeological survey and salvage—the first such project undertaken anywhere in the world. The Archaeological Survey of Nubia was originally organized and directed by the distinguished Egyptologist George A. Reisner.[13]

Reisner began the survey in the expectation that in Nubia he would encounter remains not very much different from those that had long been familiar to archaeologists in Egypt. While the Nubians were acknowledged to be a people different from the Egyptians, with a language and a history of their own, it was also conventional wisdom among Egyptologists that Nubian culture at all times in history was hardly more than a provincial imitation of the Egyptian.[14]

That expectation proved wrong almost at once. Within weeks of beginning the survey, Reisner undertook the excavation of an enormous cemetery at Shellal, just upstream from the damsite. Here he encountered no fewer than four different kinds of graves, each containing distinctive pottery types and other funerary equipment, which had never previously been found in Egypt. Reisner concluded, correctly, that these were interments of indigenous Nubian populations, following distinctive Nubian cultural traditions, and belonging to different periods in prehistory and history. Three of the grave types could be dated by their contents to a very high antiquity, coeval with the earliest pharaonic dynasties, and these were named by Reisner the A, B, and C Groups. The fourth group of graves, however, while non-Egyptian in type, contained objects of Roman and even Byzantine manufacture, and obviously dated from a much later era. Yet they could not be identified with any specific population group known to history, and so Reisner designated both the graves and their occupants as the "X-Group."[15]

For better or worse the name took root, and it continues to appear in archaeological and historical literature down to the present day.[16] Yet it is certainly no longer justified to speak of the "Mysterious X-Group,"[17] merely on the basis of archaeological remains that did not fit into a convenient and familiar historical niche. Excavations in the last quarter-century have filled in a great many gaps in our knowledge, and allow us to reconstruct with some confidence the lifeways of these last Nubians of the Classical era. We now know that they were successors, both politically and culturally, to the great Empire of Kush, and were also the immediate predecessors and ancestors of the Christian Nubians of the Middle Ages. Their culture thus forms a connecting link—indeed almost the only connecting link—between the two greatest civilizations of Nubia, the Kushite and the Medieval.

We know too that these "X-Group" people, or at least many of them, were subjects of a powerful kingdom whose rulers may have resided at the fortress-city of Qasr Ibrim, though they were buried some distance further to the south, in the great royal cemeteries of Ballaña and Qustul. Because so much archaeological knowledge of the people and their culture came, initially, from those tombs, it has become common to speak of the Ballaña people and culture, replacing the increasingly inappropriate "X-Group" designation of Reisner. (See fig. 5.1.). In this paper "X-Group" will continue to be used as a typological designation for certain kinds of graves, pottery, and houses, while "Ballaña" will be used as the designation for the people and their culture.[18] (See fig. 5.2.)

The First Archaeological Survey

In the years between 1907 and 1911, the first Archaeological Survey of Nubia encountered and excavated a total of 28 cemeteries and 418 individual graves that were assigned to Reisner's "X-Group" people and culture.[19] The graves were mostly rather modest, containing an abundance of locally made redware pottery that was clearly inspired by late Roman traditions, but there was little in the way of items of wealth such as furniture or ornate jewelry. Weaponry in the form of bows, arrows, and quivers was, however, rather prominent in the graves, in comparison to those of the immediately preceding Meroitic period. The graves were mostly located in cemeteries that had already been used by earlier Nubian populations, but the grave types themselves were distinct both in their contents and in the fact that the interments were usually contracted rather than extended, as had been the Nubian practice for many centuries previously.[20]

The First Archaeological Survey did not investigate any townsites,

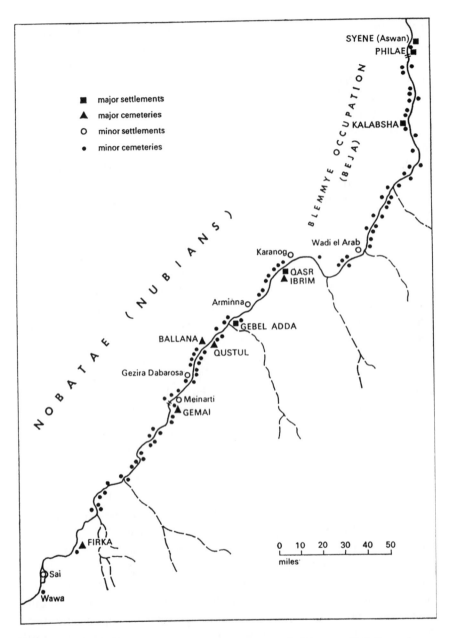

Figure 5.1   Northern Nubia, showing locations of all known Ballaña archaeological sites. From W. Adams, *Nubia: Corridor to Africa* (Princeton, N.J.: Princeton University Press, 1977). Courtesy of Princeton University Press.

Figure 5.2   Typical "X-Group" pottery vessels. Courtesy of W. Adams.

fortifications, or temples that could be assigned to the "X-Group." Thus, after four years of excavation, the newly discovered culture was really known only as a mortuary complex. Since Classical authors had made reference both to Blemmye and to Nobadae in post-Kushite Nubia, it seemed clear enough that the "X-Group" graves should be identified with one or the other of those peoples. Debate however arose as to which one,[21] and to some extent it has persisted right to the present day.

Karanòg

Concurrently with the First Archaeological Survey of Nubia, an expedition from the University of Pennsylvania Museum was at work in a number of sites farther upriver in Nubia. These included a very large and rich cemetery and also a townsite at the Nubian village of Karanòg, not far from Aneiba. The townsite, which we now know to have been partly of Ballaña date, included a number of substantially built mud brick houses, in many cases surrounded by much flimsier constructions, and also an extraordinary three-story brick castle.[22] Unfortunately the value of this excavation as a source of information about the "mysterious X-Group people" was largely overlooked, because the excavators believed the houses and castle to be coeval with the nearby Meroitic cemetery.[23] They gave the rather odd designation "Romano-Nubian" to both sites. It was only a reexamination of the pottery at a much later time which disclosed that the cemetery of Karanòg is Meroitic in date, while the townsite at least in considerable part is post-Meroitic.[24]

The Second Archaeological Survey

The original Aswan Dam was heightened in the early 1930s, extending the impounded Nile reservoir another 90 miles upriver, to the borders of the Sudan. Consequently, a second archaeological survey was launched, and was in the field from 1929 to 1934. Twenty more "X-Group" cemeteries, containing 178 individual graves, were investigated.[25] The graves found during the initial seasons were little different from those excavated in the First Archaeological Survey. In 1931, however, the archaeologists began work in a series of very large earthen mounds at the Nubian villages of Ballaña and Qustul, close to the Sudanese border. A number of previous observers had considered these to be natural formations,[26] but excavation soon proved that they were enormous earthen tumuli covering very elaborate and rich burials, obviously of nobles or rulers. (See fig. 5.3.). Beneath the tumuli were brick-lined chambers containing an extraordinary wealth of gold and silver jewelry, furniture, objects of everyday use, and pottery vessels which had contained foodstuffs, oils, honey, and wine. Additionally, the royal dead were accompanied by numbers of sacrificed animals, including horses decked out with fancy bridle trappings, and many sacrificed human retainers. Eight of the burials were accompanied by jeweled silver crowns whose general style was Byzantine, but which also exhibited elements of Kushite royal iconography including the sacred *uraeus* cobra.[27] (See fig. 5.4.).

The Second Archaeological Survey also investigated a single village site attributable to the Ballaña people, as we may now call them. The houses, usually comprising three or four rooms, were of mud brick, and were virtually the same as those found in townsites of the preceding, Meroitic period.[28] Yet the Ballaña graves were different in a number of respects from Meroitic graves, and the Ballaña people did not continue use of the Meroitic system of writing. Indeed, it was thought at the time that they had abandoned the use of writing altogether.

In the political sphere, then, the picture that emerged from the Sec-

Figure 5.3   One of the larger Ballaña royal tumuli, before excavation.
Courtesy of W. Adams.

ond Archaeological Survey was not of a pseudo-Byzantine bureaucratic
state but of a highly centralized barbarian chiefdom, which owed much
more to the older imperial traditions of Kush than it did to Byzantium.
Still, very little was known about most details of everyday life, about relations with Egypt, or about religion. In addition, the debate over ethnic
identity remained unresolved. Because Ballaña and Qustul lie well to the
south of the Blemmyan territory as described by Classical authors, most
scholars concluded that the Ballaña rulers were Nobadae. Nevertheless
W. B. Emery, the principal excavator of the royal tombs, always insisted
on a Blemmyan identity, arguing that the features of "X-Group" culture
that had been established archaeologically were in accord with Classical
descriptions of the Blemmye.[29]

Excavations in the Sudan

Although prior to 1960 there was no systematic archaeological survey
south of the Aswan reservoir, archaeologists were at work in various parts
of the northern Sudan in the early twentieth century, and here too they
noted the presence of "X-Group" or Ballaña cemeteries. Eventually it was
determined that the culture, and perhaps the Ballaña Kingdom, had
extended as far south as the island of Sai, between the Second and Third
Cataracts of the Nile. The full territorial extent of the culture, from Aswan

Figure 5.4　One of the Ballaña royal crowns, showing Kushite iconography. Courtesy of W. Adams.

in the north to Sai Island in the south, was therefore just over 300 miles. On the other hand, no remains even remotely resembling those of the Ballaña have ever been found outside the Nile Valley.

Most of the Ballaña graves found in the Sudan, like most of those in Egyptian Nubia, seemed quite clearly to be the interments of workaday peasants, possessed of few luxury goods. However, at Gemai[30] and at Firka[31] there were clusters of conspicuously larger and richer tombs, though none in any way approached the opulence of the Ballaña and Qustul interments. Whether Gemai and Firka represent the seats of *basiliskoi,* or of rulers wholly independent of Ballaña, has not been determined.

The High Dam Survey

In 1959 construction began on the Aswan High Dam, which pushed the impounded waters of the Nile back 110 miles into the Republic of the Sudan. Again a massive archaeological salvage program was launched, this time extending over a period of more than a decade and involving the work of more than 50 separate archaeological missions.[32] While much additional salvage work was required in Egyptian Nubia, the most important new discoveries were naturally made in the Sudan, where there had been no previous archaeological survey. Altogether, more than 100 new Ballaña sites were discovered and excavated, and for the first time these included a substantial number of settlements.[33] In particular, the survey expedition mounted by the Sudan Government Antiquities Service made a conscious effort to find and excavate Ballaña settlements, for it was one of the aims of this expedition to fill in gaps in the existing archaeological picture rather than to replicate what was already known.[34]

Prominent among the townsites excavated by the Sudan Government team was the stratified mound of Meinarti, which had been occupied continuously from Meroitic times to the end of the Middle Ages. Here the Ballaña phase was represented by three occupation levels, underlain by a Meroitic level and overlain by a succession of Christian Nubian levels.[35] It was evident however that there had been no abrupt changes in the town's development, such as might have signaled the coming of a new population. On the contrary, the finds at Meinarti and at several other habitation sites pointed strongly to a continuity of population and to gradual rather than revolutionary changes in the northern Nubian culture from Meroitic to Ballaña to Christian times. Whoever the Ballaña folk were, ethnically speaking, it began to seem evident that they were direct descendants of the folk who had been in northern Nubia in the last centuries of Kushite rule.[36] The idea of the "X-Group" as a new and mysterious people was thus pretty much put to rest. Everyday peasant life, it seemed, had carried on in northern Nubia after the fall of the Kushite Empire, but some of the more elaborate features of Kushite civilization, and especially the state religion, were abandoned. However, many questions about the Ballaña culture still remained unanswered, and the problem of ethnic identity was not wholly resolved.

Wadi Qitna and Kalabsha

As a contribution to the High Dam salvage campaign, a Czechoslovak expedition in 1964 and 1965 excavated two enormous cemeteries in the vicinity of Kalabsha, the place identified in a number of texts as the Blemmyan capital. Altogether more than 2000 graves were excavated.[37] The graves belonged clearly to the post-Kushite period, and exhibited many of the features, including familiar pottery types, found in other "X-Group" graves throughout Nubia. At the same time there were certain previously unfamiliar features, including some quite distinctive pottery types that had not been found elsewhere. This led Eugen Strouhal, one of the excavators, to suggest that the Wadi Qitna and Kalabsha graves should be attributed specifically to the Blemmye, in contrast to more typical "X-Group" graves which should be attributed to the Nobadae.[38] Strouhal went on to suggest that a careful re-examination of other, previously excavated cemeteries in the most northerly part of Nubia would show that they too were more nearly similar to the Kalabsha cemeteries than to the so-called "Classic X-Group" type. This is, thus far, the only indication of an *archaeologically* visible distinction between Blemmye and Nobadae.

Qasr Ibrim

Qasr Ibrim is a fortified citadel, about five acres in extent, situated high on a bluff overlooking the Nile, in the southern part of Egyptian Nubia. It is mentioned several times in Classical texts[39] in connection with both the Blemmye and the Nobadae, as well as with their Kushite predecessors, and was clearly one of the most important strongpoints in Lower Nubia. Although the site lies within the region inundated in the 1930s, its elevated situation precluded any danger of destruction at that time. Consequently, no excavation was undertaken on the citadel prior to the time of the High Dam campaign. Excavations were begun by the Egypt Exploration Society in 1963, and have continued intermittently down to the present time.[40]

The excavations have disclosed that Qasr Ibrim was occupied, perhaps continuously, from at least the Egyptian New Kingdom until the beginning of the nineteenth century A.D. Surprisingly, the Ballaña occupation levels are some of the richest and best-preserved on the site, yielding a wealth of material goods including bronze and pottery vessels, basketry and wooden objects, and a wide variety of textiles both locally made and imported. The site furnishes a picture of daily life vastly different from that at the previously excavated villages of Karanòg, Wadi el-Arab, and Meinarti, for Qasr Ibrim was obviously a market town rather than a peasant village. Stoutly built, mostly two-story houses of stone were ranged along narrow, but regular and straight, streets. Most of the structures seem to have had store rooms and perhaps business rooms on the lower floor, with living quarters on the floor above. One building, which stood at the intersection of two main streets, was quite clearly identifiable as a tavern.[41] (See fig. 5.5.).

Qasr Ibrim has provided at least one clue to the apparent prosperity of northern Nubia in the otherwise chaotic post-Kushite era. On the site there was a flourishing weaving industry in cotton, attested by the finding of innumerable weaving instruments such as spindles, shuttles and loom weights, as well as by actual hanks of raw cotton. Cotton cultivation had come to the upper Nile Valley from Ethiopia several centuries previously, but in Ptolemaic and Roman times the crop had not yet been introduced in Egypt. While proper Egyptians always insisted on the wearing of linen, this was evidently not true of the Greek and Roman immigrants in the country, and the provision of cotton garments for them evidently provided economic opportunity for the Nubians.

Figure 5.5   View over excavated Ballaña houses at Qasr Ibrim. Courtesy of W. Adams.

The Qasr Ibrim excavations have very substantially enlarged our understanding of the religious life of post-Kushite times. There had been on the site a fairly large Meroitic stone temple, built perhaps in the second century A.D., and it was the practice of worshippers to place small offerings of Roman coins on the stone-flagged floor and to pour a libation of oil over them. More than 150 of these coins were recovered in the course of excavations, and a study of their dates shows that the practice of making monetary offerings continued at least into the early fifth century A.D.[42] Kushite religious practices, and presumably a Kushite priesthood, therefore persisted at least into the early part of the Ballaña period. Unfortunately nothing can be said about the dedication of the temple, for it was almost completely razed to provide stone for the Qasr Ibrim Cathedral in the seventh century. Only the original floor and a few foundation blocks were left *in situ*.

(Parenthetically, it may be noted that the coins found in the Qasr Ibrim temple furnish the only confirmation, so far, for the assertion by Classical authors that Byzantine coinage circulated in Nubia.[43] No coins have yet been found in any other archaeological context, nor, significantly, were they among the riches found in the Ballaña tombs. Indeed, most evidence tends to suggest that the economy of the Ballaña period was not monetized.)

An even more interesting find, dating from later in the Ballaña period, was a relatively modest mud brick temple that had rather obviously been dedicated to the worship of Isis.[44] The cult that was observed here, however, was not the traditional Egyptian funerary cult of Isis, but the Graeco-Roman Isis cult with its accretion of Near Eastern elements, made familiar to us through the writings of Lucius Apuleius and other Classical authors.[45] Among the many extraordinary finds in the temple were two horned altars of Near Eastern type, statues and statuettes of Osiris, Isis, and Horus, a large number of faience votive plaques, twenty-four wooden plaques bearing painted depictions of various birds, animals, and snakes accompanied by texts *in the Meroitic language,* and many kinds of textiles. Among the latter were a number of small tied-up bundles that had evidently been soaked in milk.[46]

Although both the earlier and the later levels at Qasr Ibrim have been rich in textual finds,[47] the same has not been true of the Ballaña levels. They have yielded a small number of fragmentary Meroitic inscriptions on papyrus and wood; unfortunately these, like other Meroitic inscriptions, cannot be deciphered. The number of Greek inscriptions is smaller still. One of them, however, is of outstanding political significance, for it is a letter from a certain Blemmyan King Phonen to a certain Nobadian King Abourni.[48] The latter was evidently a successor to the Nobadian Silko whose victory inscription at Kalabsha has long been known.[49] In the document found at Qasr Ibrim, the Blemmyan king seems to be responding to an offer of peace by Abourni; he states his willingness to negotiate, providing the Nobadians will return the Blemmyan lands taken by Silko in his previous campaigns. The text, although written this time by, or rather for, a Blemmye, is in the same kind of barbarized or pidginized Greek as is Silko's inscription.

The letter of Phonen is important for confirming the historicity of Silko's campaigns and victories. At the same time it shows that he was premature in claiming to have driven the Blemmye out of the Nile Valley altogether. Finally it shows that there was a connection between the Nobadian rulers and Qasr Ibrim, dispelling any suggestion that Ibrim (at least at this time) was a Blemmyan settlement, as reported by Olympiodorus.[50]

It must be acknowledged however that nothing identifiable as a palace has yet come to light at Qasr Ibrim, although excavation of the Ballaña stratigraphic levels is not yet complete. The houses, though stoutly built and imposing in comparison with those in other Ballaña communities, are certainly not of the magnitude or grandeur that one would expect of the rulers buried with such ostentation at Ballaña and Qustul. Indeed, it is doubtful if any one house at Qasr Ibrim could have held all of the treasure found in the grandest of the Ballaña tombs. The letter of King Phonen was in fact found on the floor of a quite ordinary house, different in no important respect from others along the same street.[51]

But where, if not at Qasr Ibrim, could the Nobadian capital have been? Certainly not at any of the small village sites uncovered during the High Dam surveys. The surveys were, moreover, so intensive that it is unthinkable that any really important townsite went undiscovered. But there were two other major towns in Lower Nubia that apparently included significant Ballaña remains: Gebel Adda, a few miles to the south of Qasr Ibrim, and Faras, close the present Egyptian-Sudanese border. Both places are somewhat nearer to the Ballaña and Qustul burial grounds than is Qasr Ibrim, and from that perspective are perhaps slightly more logical possibilities for the Ballaña royal residence. Unhappily, both Faras and Gebel Adda were allowed to go under water with their Ballaña stratigraphic levels largely uninvestigated.

The Current Picture and Its Problems

The excavations at Qasr Ibrim have brought us to our current state of knowledge regarding the Ballaña kingdom and people. Happily they are not necessarily the last word, for there are still substantial unexcavated deposits at Ibrim, and the possibility still exists of finding additional temples, important texts, and just possibly the Ballaña royal residence. In addition there are many unexcavated cemeteries, and probably also village sites, in Sudanese Nubia, upstream from the head of the Aswan reservoir.

The current state or knowledge presents us with a curious paradox, or in fact a set of paradoxes. For the Blemmye we seem to have a fairly rich textual record, which was already well known and was very effectively surveyed by Thompson over 20 years ago. The record offers us a picture of a strongly Byzantinized, bureaucratic polity, with very little surviving Kushite influence, except perhaps in the continuing worship of Isis. Yet we still have very few archaeological remains that can be specifically identified with these people as distinguished from their Nobadian neighbors. For the Nobadians we have a rich archaeological record, but little in the way of supporting texts. From the archaeological remains we derive a picture of a highly centralized chiefdom retaining many of the traditions of imperial Kush, without much evidence of Byzantine influence except in certain kinds of material goods.

If we turn our attention from the royal remains to the common folk, another paradox confronts us. All of the Classical texts indicate, or at least imply, that both Blemmye and Nobadae were newcomers to the Nile Valley, who presumably displaced or absorbed their Meroitic predecessors. Yet the immigrants continued to occupy the villages and even the houses of the Meroites, made pottery and other goods clearly akin to those of late Meroitic times, and even buried their dead in the Meroitic cemeteries. In most cemeteries, the Ballaña graves simply begin where the Meroitic graves leave off. On the basis strictly of archaeological evidence, we would surely have concluded long ago that the Nubian people of post-Kushite times were simply the Kushites at a later stage of cultural development.

But at this point language confronts us with another paradox. The Nobadians certainly spoke a language akin to and ancestral to modern Nubian,[52] which belongs to the Eastern Sudanic group of African languages.[53] Of equal certainty the Beja spoke a "Cushitic" language,[54] related to the Beja, Oromo, and Somali languages of the East African highlands and coast.[55] But the fairly numerous Meroitic inscriptions, both from northern Nubia and from the Kushite heartland, are in a language that shows no clear affinities with either Eastern Sudanic or Cushitic. Linguistic evidence therefore seems to support the idea of the Ballaña peoples as invading newcomers, ethnically distinct from their Kushite predecessors.

The problem is one of seeming linguistic (and therefore ethnic) discontinuity contrasting with obvious social and cultural continuity. The solution which I proposed some years ago was to suggest that the Nobadae were already present and were the principal residents in Lower Nubia during late Kushite times, having migrated eastward to the Nile from the Kordofan region in the late centuries B.C. or the first century A.D.[56] They used Meroitic as their written language because it was the language of the empire to which they were subject, but it was not their spoken language. (In just the same way they later used Greek as a written language, though this also was clearly not spoken.) When the Empire of Kush broke up, the Nobadians found themselves politically independent, and they established in northern Nubia a successor-kingdom based largely on Kushite precedents. Their geographic situation on the frontier of Byzantine Egypt allowed them to continue the prosperous trade with the northern country which had developed in late Meroitic times, and it was this same relationship which induced them, as a matter of convenience, to use Greek in their few written texts.

While the foregoing hypothesis takes care of the Meroitic versus Nobadae problem, it still leaves the Blemmye unaccounted for. Strouhal's interpretation of the Wadi Qitna and Kalabsha graves may hold a part of the answer,[57] and seems to confirm a previously common notion that the Blemmye were installed only in the far north of Lower Nubia, immediately beyond the Roman and Byzantine frontier, while the Nobadae held the country from about Wadi Sebua southward. It must be noted however that the Wadi Qitna and Kalabsha graves have been dated largely or entirely from the third to fifth centuries A.D.,[58] which is to say from the earlier part of the Ballaña period. From the later part of the period it seems impossible to make any distinction of grave types or of populations based on archaeological evidence. It would appear, therefore, that over time the two warring peoples became assimilated to a common culture and lifestyle.

My own hunch is that the number of ethnic Blemmye was never very large. Following the withdrawal of the Roman frontier to Aswan in A.D. 297, one or more Blemmye chieftains and some of their cohorts moved into the newly relinquished valley territory, where they established hegemony over an already settled, presumably Nobadian, population. The rulers retained their separate ethnic identity, and possibly also their Cushitic language, but over time their Blemmyan subjects merged and intermarried with their Nobadian subjects, and the cultural distinction between the two peoples disappeared. Thus, the warring kingdoms of Phonen and Abourni can be likened to the warring Greek city-states, involving conflict between politically distinct but culturally identical peoples.

Postlude: The Christianization of Nobadia

The Christianization of Nubia in the sixth century has been described by four medieval chroniclers.[59] Their accounts are not in total agreement, but points of difference need not concern us here. What they do agree on is that there was only a single polity, Nobadia, in northern Nubia at the time of conversion, between 540 and 580 A.D. Mention is made of Blemmyes (who were also evangelized) in the Red Sea Hills, but not anywhere in the Nile Valley. We have to conclude, therefore, that sometime during or after the reign of Abourni the Blemmyan rulers were finally dislodged, and their subjects fully absorbed into the Nobadian population.

Another point of consensus is that the evangelization of the Nobadians proceeded very rapidly, and was complete well before the end of the sixth century. This might be dismissed as the biased perception of ecclesiastical historians, but it finds extraordinary confirmation in the Nubian cemeteries. There is no transition from pagan to Christian burial ritual, nor can we find zones where pagan and Christian graves are intermixed. On the contrary the use of funerary offerings, of contracted burial, and of above-ground tumuli seem to have disappeared as if overnight.[60] We can also identify a fairly substantial number of churches that seem to have been built at least in the sixth century.[61]

Less than a century after the Christianization of Nubia came the Arab conquest of Egypt, followed almost immediately by two separate invasions whose aim was to add Nubia to the Islamic dominions. Both were successfully resisted, and in the process the warlike prowess of the Nubians won the admiration of the invaders, who previously had defeated the imperial armies of Persia and of Byzantium.[62] A treaty was negotiated which allowed the Nubians to retain both their political independence and their Christian faith, free from Islamic incursion, for the next 600 years, although it was at the cost of paying an annual tribute to Egypt.[63] The warlike Ballaña period gave way to one of the most peaceful eras in Nubian history. And early in that period the once truculent kingdom of Nobadia allowed itself to be absorbed, apparently without a struggle, by the more southerly Nubian Kingdom of Makouria, about which we have no knowledge in pre-Christian times.[64]

Although there was no change in the Nubian population, the cultural transformation from Ballaña to Christian times was one of the most profound and dramatic in the long history of Nubia and the Sudan. The Ballaña period is symbolized for us by the barbarously opulent royal tombs at Ballaña, and by the truculent victory proclamation of Silko: "for those who strive with me, I do not permit them to sit in their own country unless they esteem me and do homage to me. For in the Lower Country I am a lion and in the Upper Country a bear."[65] The Christian period is symbolized by the longest peace in Nubian history, and by countless representations of a heavenly king, but no single monument nor tomb of any earthly king. There should be evidence here, if any were needed, that national character is the product of history and not of heredity.

Notes

1. This region comprises what today we call Lower Nubia and the most northerly portion of Upper Nubia; it also lies today partly in Egypt and partly in the Republic of Sudan. To avoid cumbersome terminology, I shall hereafter refer to the region under discussion as northern Nubia.

2. For discussion of the nomenclature problem see William Y. Adams, *Nubia, Corridor to Africa* (London: A. Lane 1977), 390–92.

3. For a conspectus of these see C. L. Woolley and D. Randall-MacIver, *Karanòg, the Romano-Nubian Cemetery,* University of Pennsylvania Museum, Eckley B. Coxe Junior Expedition to Nubia, vol. 3 (Philadelphia: University Museum, 1910), 99–105; See also Ugo Monneret de Villard, *Storia della Nubia Cristiana.* Orientalia Christiana Analecta 118; (Rome: Pontificium Institutum Orientalium Studiorum, 1938), 24–60.

4. L. A. Thompson and J. Ferguson, eds., *Africa in Classical Antiquity* (Ibadan, Nigeria: Ibadan University Press, 1969), 45–52. Thompson's account is based in large part on the previous scholarship of Ugo Monneret de Villard.

5. See W. B. Emery, *Egypt in Nubia* (London: Hutchinson, 1965), 234–35.

6. For the original text see Woolley and Randall-MacIver, 104–5. For a translation see Adams, *Nubia,* 422–23.

7. See L. P. Kirwan in *University of Liverpool Annals of Archaeology and Anthropology* 24 (1937): 82–83.

8. Thompson, 50.

9. Monneret de Villard, 189–91.

10. His account survives only in a fragmentary paraphrase by Photius. For the surviving text see Woolley and Randall-MacIver, 103. For a partial translation see Emery, 236.

11. See Kirwan, 77.

12. For a fuller review see Adams, *Nubia,* 390–419.

13. For details see ibid., 71–74.

14. *Cf.* George A. Reisner, *Archaeological Survey of Nubia, Report for 1907–1908* (Cairo: National Print. Dept., 1910), I, 348.

15. See George A. Reisner in *Archaeological Survey of Nubia, Bulletin* no. 5 (Cairo: National Print. Dept., 1909), 3–6.

16. *Cf.* Adams, *Nubia,* 390–92.

17. *Cf.* L. P. Kirwan in Edward Bacon, ed., *Vanished Civilizations* (London: Thames and Hudson, 1963), 55–78.

18. For discussion of the nomenclature see Adams, *Nubia*, 390–92.

19. See ibid., 72.

20. For more detailed discussion of "X-Group" grave types see Emery, 241–44, and Adams, *Nubia*, 393–97.

21. See Adams, *Nubia*, 419–24.

22. C. L. Woolley, *Karanòg, the Town*, University of Pennsylvania Museum, Eckley B. Coxe Junior Expedition to Nubia, vol. 5 (Philadelphia: University Museum 1911).

23. Ibid., 3.

24. See Adams, *Nubia*, 352.

25. See ibid., 76.

26. See W. B. Emery, *The Royal Tombs of Ballana and Qustul* (Cairo: Government Press 1938), 3–4.

27. For the complete excavation report see ibid.

28. See W. B. Emery and L. P. Kirwan, *The Excavations and Survey between Wadi es-Sebua and Adindan* (Cairo: Government Press, 1935), 108–22.

29. W. B. Emery, *The Royal Tombs*, 18–24; Emery, *Egypt in Nubia;* 244–45.

30. Oric Bates and Dows Dunham in *Harvard African Studies* 8 (1927), 19–121.

31. L. P. Kirwan, *The Oxford University Excavations at Firka* (London: Oxford University Press, 1939).

32. See Adams, *Nubia*, 78–88; Torgny Säve-Söderbergh, *Temples and Tombs of Ancient Nubia* (London: Thames and Hudson, 1987).

33. See Adams, *Nubia*, 397–401; Bruce G. Trigger, *History and Settlement in Lower Nubia*, Yale University Publications in Anthropology 69 (New Haven: Yale University Press, 1965), 116.

34. See especially William Y. Adams in W. C. Ackerman, G. F. White and E. B. Worthington, eds., *Man-Made Lakes: Their Problems and Environmental Effects*, Geophysical Monograph Series 17 (Washington: American Geophysical Union, 1973), 826–35.

35. See William Y. Adams in *Kush* 12 (1964): 222–41; *Kush* 13 (1965): 148–76; and in K. C. Chang, ed., *Settlement Archaeology* (Palo Alto: National Press Books, 1968), 174–207.

36. See especially Adams, *Nubia*, 420–22.

37. See Eugen Strouhal, *Wadi Qitna and Kalabsha South*, vol. 1 (Prague: Charles University, 1984).

38. Ibid., 268–70.

39. Usually under the name Primis; occasionally as Prima or Premnis. It also appears in Meroitic texts as Pedeme.

40. The situation of Qasr Ibrim is so elevated that most parts of the site have been spared from destruction even by the High Dam waters (Lake Nasser). For a conspectus of what has been learned from the Qasr Ibrim excavations see William

Y. Adams in J. Martin Plumley, ed., *Nubian Studies* (Warminster: Aris and Phillips, 1982), 25–34.

41. See J. Martin Plumley and William Y. Adams in *JEA* 60 (1974): 217–19.

42. See J. Martin Plumley in *JEA* 61 (1975): 16.

43. *Cf.* Thompson, 50.

44. Boyce N. Driskell, Nettie K. Adams and Peter French in *Archéologie du Nil Moyen* 3 (1989): 11–54.

45. See especially R. E. Witt, *Isis in the Graeco-Roman World* (Ithaca: Cornell University Press, 1971).

46. Driskell, Adams and French, 27–28.

47. See, e.g., J. Martin Plumley in Kazimierz Michalowski, ed., *Nubia, récentes recherches* (Warsaw: Musée National, 1975), 101–7.

48. For the text and commentary see John Rea in *ZPE* 34 (1979): 147–62.

49. See n. 6.

50. See n. 10.

51. For the report of the original find see J. Martin Plumley, William Y. Adams and Elisabeth Crowfoot in *JEA* 63 (1977): 44–45.

52. More specifically to the Mahas-Fadija dialect of Nubian; see William Y. Adams in Christopher Ehret and Merrick Posnansky, eds., *The Archaeological and Linguistic Reconstruction of African History* (Berkeley: University of California Press, 1982), 11–38.

53. According to the linguistic classification of Joseph Greenberg; see *The Languages of Africa* (Bloomington: Indiana University Press, 1966), 85.

54. The unfortunate choice of the name "Cushitic" by modern linguistic scholars obscures the fact that the Beja, Galla, and Somali for the most part were not subjects of the Empire of Kush, and were certainly not its rulers.

55. Greenberg, 48–49.

56. See William Y. Adams, *Meroitic North and South*, Meroitica 2 (Berlin: Akademie Verlag 1976), 21–25. See also Adams, op. cit. (n. 52).

57. See n. 38.

58. Ibid., 265.

59. See Adams, *Nubia*, 69, 440–44.

60. Ibid., 444.

61. *Cf.* William Y. Adams in *JARCE* 4 (1965): 101–6.

62. See Adams, *Nubia*, 450–51.

63. Ibid., 451–53.

64. See ibid., 462–63; also William Y. Adams in W. Vivian Davies, ed., *Egypt and Africa; Nubia from Prehistory to Islam* (London: British Museums, 1991), 257–63.

65. Adams, *Nubia*, 422–23.

6

The Berbers of the Maghreb
and Ancient Carthage

REUBEN G. BULLARD

❂

North Africa has been the stage of interaction between an "indigenous" people and colonizers/invaders from the East and North for nearly three millennia. An amazingly resilient character, however, has been exhibited by the Berber people, who came to the Maghreb before the better known colonizers appeared. The natural stage upon which the superimposition of a number of cultures occurred has a remarkable physical history.

The Natural Setting of Western North Africa

The geographic area is mainly that of Morocco, Algeria, Tunisia and Libya and possesses a geologic setting which has molded its settlement patterns and the occupational traits of all its human history.

Thick Mesozoic and Cenozoic sedimentary strata representing Jurassic, Cretaceous and Tertiary Rock Systems lie largely undeformed on the crustal basement of the African continental interior south of the Maghreb.

In the Maghreb (western North Africa), on the other hand, these same rock systems composed of both terrestrial and marine deposits, were caught up in Alpine (Late Tertiary–or geologically relatively recent) orogenic tectonics, forming the chains of the folded Atlas Mountains and intermontane basins. These sedimentary strata (limestones, sandstones and shales) were folded, faulted and overthrust in a number of diastrophisms (crustal deformations). (See fig. 6.1.)

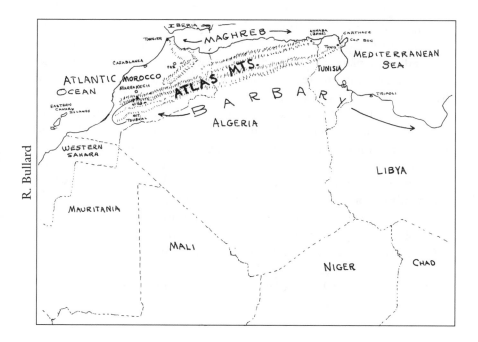

Figure 6.1 The Maghreb (western North Africa).

Along the southern Atlas Mountain flank, the folding is less complex and these ranges are spaced with broad intermontane tablelands. Tunisia, Algeria, and Morocco are punctuated with limestone mountains, some of which are incipiently marmorized, and inter-mountane down folded/faulted synclinal/basinal depressions.

Some of these depressional troughs were connected to the sea. In time, these depo-centers were cut off by coastal shore-zone processes and were no longer open to the sea, forming sebkhets, where saline percolation and evaporation have been filling/drying them up to the present time.

Quaternary (Pleistocene and Holocene Stages) sedimentation in these basinal areas, along the Libyan littoral and southward has consisted of marine, lacustrine, alluvial and aeolian derived material.

The coastal areas of the Maghreb, both Atlantic and Mediterranean shore-zones, show such geomorphic features as embayed beach coasts, straight beaches with spits, and embayed headland areas, often with localized beaches and linear cliffs. Some coasts are highly depositional (the western coast of the bay of Carthage, south of the Medjerda River delta) with sandy beach plains and baymouth bars isolating the depressions described above.[1, 2]

Climatological considerations of the Maghreb, drawn from the observations recorded in this century show an annual rainfall of 20 to 40 inches up to 50 miles inland in Tunisia and Algeria. The same level of precipitation is measured in an area of higher elevations south and southwest of the horn of Morocco to a distance of nearly 300 miles (that area known as the Rif, and the Middle and High Atlas Mountains). A zone of 10 to 20 inches of rainfall (semi-arid conditions) covers up to 125 miles from the coast inland to Tunisia and elsewhere, the zone continues west-south-west to a distance of 250 miles due south of the coast of Casablanca and Morocco. Some snow fall does occur on the High Atlas of Morocco which has an altitude of up to 4165 meters at Jebel Toubkal.[3]

The native vegetation of the Maghreb consists of a narrow band of steppe grasslands along the interface of the southern slopes of the Atlas and the northern edge of the Sahara. Nearer the coast in the north, *maquis,* a dense Mediterranean-type shrub community exists on the lower Atlas levels while the High Atlas Mountains abound in a forest-cover of pine, cedar or oak.[4]

Introduction to the Modern Research of the Carthage Area

There is no area of study of Mediterranean cultures that is significantly richer in material remains than the area we know as ancient Carthage and the region controlled by her.

> [Unlike Egypt,] ancient Tunisia was deeply marked by the superimposing of several civilizations: Berber, Punic, Hellenistic, Roman, Vandal (Gothic), Byzantine, Arab, Spanish, Turkish and French. It was a great crossroad of civilization. The country's geographical position makes it, in fact, a place of passage between Africa and Europe and a privileged link between the east and the west. Tunisia's population has been constantly renewed in a continuing mixing common to all residents of the Mediterranean area. Favorable topography has always facilitated cultural exchange, which has continually enriched and not destroyed the country. Conquerors attempting to dominate have had to renounce imposing their values. The natives accepted from foreign civilizations only traits that have become universal or those that could be assimilated into their own traditions. Ancient Tunisia's unity remained deep despite the apparent diversities.[5]

Tensions associated with modern salvage archaeological operations arose in the Carthage area of Tunisia because of ever expanding urbanization in the second half of the twentieth century. Building projects undertaken by Tunisians, especially by citizens from the city of Tunis who had prospered or by wealthy non-Tunisians who sought the lovely lands of the Carthage tombolo,[6] have destroyed or concealed ancient structures. Parts of attractive architecture, including mosaic and *opus sectile* floors and even cemeteries, have been discovered and reburied under cement foundations and basements for villas. Prompt action by those authorities sensitive to these losses resulted in an effort to save the antiquities of Carthage. The Tunisian Institute of Art and Archaeology appealed to UNESCO in 1972 for international assistance. Various nations manifested an interest in the preservation of these archaeological treasures. Countries sending in teams of specialists were Britain, Bulgaria, Canada (an English team and a French team), Denmark, France, Italy, Poland, Germany and the United States. These expeditions joined an already vigorous research effort by the Tunisian Institute and specifically by Dr. Abdelmajid Ennabli, Curator of the Site of Carthage, who was the coordinator of all these international operations. Some of the expeditions had research facilities which concentrated on the flood of information and materials coming forth from the field work, for example, the German School in Rome, whose expeditions director was Dr. Rekov. This writer is especially grateful to Dr. Ennabli for his generous permission and help to pursue scientific investigations and field work as they related to his historical/archaeological/geological and environmental studies.

Modern research in the history of Carthage and the Maghreb relies not only on historical writings as sources, but also draws heavily from the evidence generated by archaeological and scientific research. Because of such investigations, we may read of the defensive walls of Punic Carthage in the ancient literature, but realize now that such construction material was not available to the Punic inhabitants of the Carthage tombolo. They had to obtain the stone for defensive wall stone from a vast quarry near the northeastern tip of the Cap Bon Peninsula. We may therefore more fully appreciate the stone that was used, its source, the enormous effort to extract, ship and shape it, its petrographic and structural properties and, importantly, why it was used.[7]

Berber Beginnings and Culture

The culture of the earliest people of Western North Africa is Berber (from Greek *barbaros,* "foreign," "strange") also termed Libyan in Tunisia and the broader Maghreb [Libya, Tunisia, Algeria and Morocco]. The

Berbers, considered indigenous by some scholars, became well established by the mid-second millennium before the Common Era.[8] Various theories exist in the historical writings of the past 100 years concerning the origin of the Berber people.

Moreover, analysis of their physical character shows that, where mixing has been minimal, anthropologically, they are not a dark-skinned people, but have affinity with western Asiatic stock. Some early views, however, have been put forth proposing that Berbers were part of a Mediterranean racial group that included Celtic-Iberians and Semitic peoples (*e.g.*, Phoenicians from the Levant); others have viewed the Berbers as Aryans or as a Caucasian stock which had mingled with "indigenous Libyans."[9] Another view of this 100-year old source held that there was a "close relation" of the Berbers with the ancient Egyptians, and considered them as forming together the "White African race."[10]

> By 8000 B.C. the ethnic and linguistic maps of the continent as we know it began to take shape. Berbers occupied North Africa and the Sahara . . . each had its individual cultural traditions and developed those skills and patterns of social and economic behavior that were dictated by the record of the past and the exigencies of the surroundings . . . these new civilizations and cultures were also influenced by external factors, but they were nonetheless essentially African, with their roots buried deep in the land of Africa.[11]

Thus, there appears to be no evidence that the Berbers were not the earliest settled human inhabitants of the Maghreb.[12] S. Schaar points out in support of Ghaki cited above, that ancient inscriptions "seem to have been written by the ancestors of the modern Berbers [which have been discovered in the Sinai Peninsula and in the Nile Delta.]" He notes that some researchers believe that this ethnic group moved into Africa from western Asia. Modern analysis of African languages gives some support to this position. Joseph Greenburg has clustered the many Berber dialects, individually variable throughout the Maghreb and Sahara, with the larger Afro-Asiatic language family including Egyptian, Somali, Galla, Hebrew and Arabic.[13]

The ancient Berber language with its alphabet of 23 consonants is no longer remembered. A powerful modern tribe, the Tuareg Berbers, have partially drawn their own oral and written language traits from ancient sources. The Tuaregs, who use this alphabet cannot interpret the many Berber inscriptions written during the Roman dominance of their territories.[14]

Historical and Ethno-archaeological Characteristics
of the Berbers

Indigenous ethnic/physical characteristics in Berber peoples have been affected by environmental changes. The increasingly arid conditions prevailing in the Sahara, from about 5,500–3,000 B.C. initiated a Negroid people's migration northward, verging on the surviving oases.

> These tribes presumably later intermarried with the ancestors of the Berbers and the Egyptians of North Africa. . . . Such migrations and communications across once-navigable rivers, probably aided in the diffusion in surrounding areas of social and cultural institutions.[15]

That the Berber culture is one of great antiquity is demonstrated by the writings of the Roman author Sallust, who records ancient Numidian and Mauretanian names, which find meaning in certain Berber expressions contemporary with him. These words seem to have Semitic affinities.

Berber consists of the language spoken by these peoples in Mauretania, Morocco, Algeria, Mali, Nigeria and in small pockets across northern Africa, *e.g.*, Tamasheq and Zenati. [16]

Geographic areas occupied by the Berbers, especially the Mediterranean coastal region, were historically given the name Barbary (alternatively the area known by the Greek name "Libya" after the capital called Lebu Berbers), mentioned above, by the Arabs. They did (or do) not call themselves Berbers, but rather *Imazighen*, which denotes "free men."[17]

Before the European conquest, the Canary Islands were inhabited by a people known as the Guanches, whose culture, Murray says, was related to that of North African Berbers.[18]

An anthropology of the Berbers would include their physical characteristics and their social traits. Various Berber tribal groups differ in their characteristics, "but they are all fine men, tall, straight and handsome."[19]

Except in areas where intermarriage with dark-skinned people from the south occurred, the Berbers kept a light-skinned ethnic make-up. They are described as a highly "energetic and vigorous people . . . [and one considered by certain modern ethnologists to be] . . . a race which has many resemblances to the ancient Etruscans. They are quite like the pictures also of some of the ancient Egyptian dynasties."[20]

By contrast, Schaar writes that numerous ancient authors scorned the Berber peoples as "uncivilized, violent, impassionate people who lacked subtlety . . . and showed sensuality, apparent cruelty, turbulence, laziness, love of raiding and pillaging, and [having] double standards of truth." But other Greek and Roman writers sometimes described them as being courageous, sober and persevering.[21]

When the Phoenicians made the first contacts as traders with the Berbers along the North African coast during the twelfth century B.C., they found them as nomadic shepherds and cattle herders.[22]

Beyond question the Berbers have always been the "true overlords" of the mountain regions of the Maghreb, their "homeland," and of numerous oases of the Sahara, where their lifestyles embraced that arid environment. Wherever they settled, a fierce love of independent self, community freedom and liberty were exhibited. No later invader/colonizer of North Africa was able to subjugate them entirely over a long period of time.[23]

The more fertile areas of the Maghreb hosted the sedentary Berber farmers, while along the Sahel (*Sahil*, Arabic, meaning coast) that is the "shore-zone" of the desert, intermittent occupation by "transhumant" pastoralist and Saharan salt traders prevailed. Here such tribal traits as "elaborate caste like forms of social stratification" were carried out.[24] Modern ethno-archaeological studies indicate that the more familiar Berber groups include *Kabili, Kabyle, Shluh* and *Tuareg* had a total 1981 population of ten million.[25]

Arrival of the Phoenicians
and the Beginning of Carthage

A legend cited by Strabo[26] is that Queen Dido or Elissa of Tyre along with a company of Phoenician colonists came in the ninth century B.C. to North Africa where she was claimed as the wife of the Berber king Maxitani. A famous story has her settling on land granted by the king which was to become Carthage. His assignment of land was as much as that which could be covered by the hide of an ox. She cleverly cut the hide into thin strips which when strung out would circumscribe an area sufficient to serve as a fortified acropolis, the Byrsa. But then desiring no part of the king she cast herself on a funeral pyre.[27]

Within 100 years of its founding, Carthage was paying an annual tribute to nearby Berber leaders as a form of rent for the land it occupied. This continued off and on until the agreement was revoked in 450 B.C.[28]

The colonization of the Maghreb by the Phoenicians was driven by the prospects of acquiring deposits of copper, tin, silver, and lead ores in

Iberia (Spain). Thriving from this resource exploitation, *Kart Hadasht* = Carthage, or the "new city" grew from a small settlement and became independent from Phoenicia and its other colonies. Carthage eventually grew into a mighty challenger of Rome.[29]

The ensuing growth of trade between a nascent Carthage and the Berber societies was based upon the exchange of agricultural products, which in turn stimulated demand for Mediterranean goods.[30] Moreover, the population of North Africa was sufficient to provide "a cheap, local supply of farm labor." In this interaction between these two societies, the Berbers, who were unable to afford slaves, accomplished their own labor needs by means of their "women [who] did most of the hard labor amongst [them] . . ."[31]

Both Punic and Roman civilizations reached the Berbers by means of the activity of their own kings. These dynasties molded the foreign, social and religious traits to their own cultural interests.

The Phoenician cities, especially Tyre and Sidon, received goods funneled shoreward from the eastern inland and desert routes through the mountains of Lebanon to these ports. The goods of Syria, Mesopotamia, and Arabia became the resources of trade to be trans-shipped to the western colony ports. Of these, Carthage came to be the most important and powerful.

> However, it is clear that the great majority of Phoenician settlements in the West were not founded with a view to the exploitation of a fertile hinterland. Their classic situation was an off-shore island or a peninsula with landing places on either side suitable for use in almost all winds. In other words, the colonists looked to the sea rather than the land.[32]

Punic occupation spread throughout Tunisia as Carthage and other cities grew in prosperity and size. Carthage was able to stop Greek advances in the western Mediterranean in the sixth century and along North Africa beyond Cyrene. The Carthaginian empire covered nearly all of modern Tunisia, and also Tipasa and Hippo in Algeria. Beyond Africa, her empire dominated a portion of western Sicily, Sardinia, the Balearics, Malta, and the southern regions of Spain.[33] Two judges (called suffets) were elected yearly to deal with the administrative and political affairs of Carthage. The Senate was convened by them. They directed the debates taking place over proposals and carried out the decisions of the Assembly of the People. Moreover, they also held important judicial functions. There is little question as to the amount of power these individuals wielded over their society.

Carthaginian men of wealth controlled the political life, but their money contrasted with the city-state's difficulties in finance and public support for some of the military causes to which they seemed to be committed.[34]

The lower classes of Carthage were composed of farm workers, sailors and dock workers, and craftsmen. Slaves were present as field hands and domestics, who had the right to worship their gods at all times. By the 400's B.C., Carthage obtained major city-state status as the "foremost maritime commercial power" in the west. Carthage also controlled Greek colonial expansion there by its systematic use of marine power. The source of its influence upon North Africa, and even Spain, lay in its bases on Sicily from which attacks were launched against its enemies.[35]

The position of the city-state of Carthage was typical of Phoenician colony placements. Situated on a tombolo, a former island later connected to the mainland on the west, the city was established on the southwestern part of the semiprotected waters of the Gulf of Carthage.[36] The Punic (Latin for Phoenician) community had two headlands or sea cliffs facing east and northeast (Cap Carthage—with the modern village of Sidi bou Said and Cap Gammart). Besides these promontories, there was the acropolis or citadel of the Byrsa overlooking the harbor areas. This peninsula was formed geologically by the union of an island with the mainland and featured an isthmus, not more than three miles wide where it was most narrow. This was the work of the Medjerda River and its sediments which were carried southward from the delta system cusp by shore currents to form the Carthage tombolo, with its land-bridge to that former island mass.

Founded at the time of colonization on the open gulf waters to the north and south of the sediment bridge, the site was exposed to shallow waters. In what is presently the Lake of Tunis (El-Bahira) and also what is now the Sebkhet (a dry or near-dry evaporate basin cut off from the sea), Er-Riana, early Carthage, could beach her ships on the island which was linked to the mainland during these Punic and later Roman times by the main isthmus. Later, these portions of the waters of the Gulf of North Carthage were captured and contained by the sand bars of marine shore zone processes. Here the sandy beaches, both northwest and southwest of the Carthage headland were "harbor centers" of trade activity. From the sea, the southern portion of the upland of the former island rose gently to an elevation of about 200 feet on the Byrsa hill.[37] (See fig. 6.2.)

Since these ancient beaches were exposed to northerly and easterly winds, the Bay of Le Kram to the south took on some importance. In Punic times this bay was protected by an offshore bar and spit extending south from the Carthage headland. "It can hardly be doubted that it was at this sheltered spot that the Phoenician traders first anchored and the

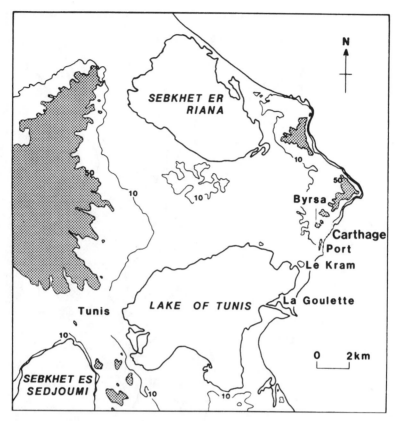

Figure 6.2 Location of the ancient city of Carthage. From G. Rapp and J. Gifford, eds., *Archaeological Geology* (New Haven, Conn.: Yale University Press, 1985). Courtesy Yale University Press.

earliest colony disembarked."[38] What was first a back-bar lagoon later received sediments, both storm-washed and wind-blown from the beaches to the east. It was in this setting that the earliest artificial harbors of Carthage were dug and walled.[39]

The southern or "rectangular" harbor was the anchorage of merchant men, while a connecting channel to the north provided access to the cothon or circular harbor where men-of-war were dry-docked. These facilities were investigated by American (see below) and British teams. The harbors were entered from the bay on the south side of the tombolo through a linking channel.[40] These harbors afforded both naval vessels and trade ships protection, giving Carthage a distinct advantage in the maintenance and utilization of her fleet in all seasons. (See fig. 6.3.)

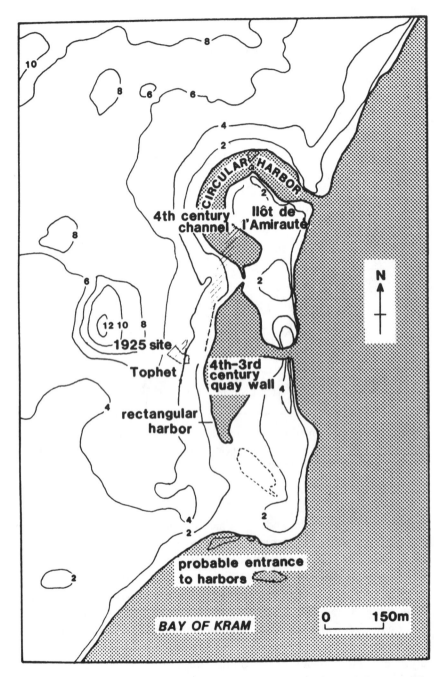

Figure 6.3 Topography of the harbor area of Carthage. From G. Rapp and J. Gifford, eds., *Archaeological Geology* (New Haven, Conn.: Yale University Press, 1985). Courtesy Yale University Press.

A valuable historical witness to these facilities was recorded by Appian of Alexandria who depended on Polybius:

> The harbors had communication with each other, and the common entrance from the sea was 70 feet wide, which could be closed with iron chains. The first port was for merchant vessels, and here were collected all kinds of ship's tackle. Within the second port was an island and great quays were set at intervals around both the harbor and the island. These embankments were full of shipyards which had the capacity for 220 vessels. In addition to them were magazines for their tackle and furniture. Two Ionic columns stood in front of each dock, giving the appearance of a continuous portico to both the harbor and the island. On the island was built the admiral's house from which the trumpeter gave signals, the herald delivered orders, and the admiral himself overlooked everything. The island lay near the entrance to the harbor and rose to a considerable height so that the admiral could observe what was going on at sea, while those who were approaching by water could not get any clear view of what took place within. Not even incoming merchants could see the docks at once, for a double wall enclosed them, and there were gates by which merchant ships could pass from the first port to the city without traversing the dockyards. Such was the appearance of Carthage at that time.[41]

The construction of the Punic quay walls was a work of considerable enterprise. A stone of excellent working properties, isotropic in cutting characteristics—nearly without bedding planes or joint partings—was discovered about 70 km up the eastern coast of the Bay of Carthage near the northern tip of the Cap Bon Peninsula, practically at the water's edge. This stone is composed of course-sand to granule-size bioclastic (shell fragments) and quartz grains bonded with calcite cement. The porous rock was cut and shaped by hammer and chisel with ease.

The Punic quarrying activity is amazing to behold: vertical shafts cut down through a one-to-two meter weathered zone and another three-to-four meters into the massive uniformly textured rock below. In modern collapse and exposure examples, these vertical tunnels show lateral cutting and chamber enlargements in the rock extraction process and the cut-stone blocks were hoisted up through them. The shafts show a "belling-outward and downward" excavation activity with parallel and sub-parallel chisel marks raking out most of the remaining quarry chamber facades. The product of these quarries is frequently termed El-Haouria stone in contemporary references. I prefer to call it Ghar el-Khebir sandstone (it is locally conglomeratic) for the actual place name given to the Punic quarry cavities by Arabic speaking inhabitants. Many of these were later cut into laterally by Roman stepledge quarrying techniques. Some of the Punic chambers have collapsed.[42] This stone was utilized in building construction in the harbor area.[43]

French excavation exposures of Punic buildings on the Byrsa and German excavations near the present shoreline south of the Carthage museum reveal appreciable utilizations of the Ghar el-Khebir stone in wall construction, especially that of Opus Africanum architectural design. This structural form may have been employed to dampen seismic shock. Both horizontal and vertical ashlars were employed. However, this lithic was never observed in any usage as a wear/abrasion surface (e.g., a threshold).

Another major use of the Ghar el-Khebir stone was for funerary stelae in the Tophet area close to the merchant harbor. Here these burial markers were never put in place with plain surfaces on all sides. They show architectural moldings and often depict a view through portals into a shrine probably of Baal Hammon [a pillar] or of Tanit [a female figure]. Signs of the sun and moon are also nearly always present. There is evidence that some of them were covered with plaster painted to accent the sculptured surface. The Ghar el-Khebir stelae were much more massive in size than the funerary markers used in later Punic history.

A biomicritic[44] [foraminiferal packstone] limestone, having a fine-grain texture, was employed by the Punic Carthaginians to mark urn burials. This was quarried from the foothills of Djebel bou Kornine in a southeastern spur called Djebel Jemaa. Here strata of both green and maroon limestone occur. These were intentionally quarried for use at Carthage and elsewhere. Although weathered and groundwater-leached, some of the stelae from the Carthage tophet still show this colored internal fabric when freshly broken or chipped (accidentally). No significance of this color variation is known.[45] Both strata sets were extensively quarried and there is a massive waste pile from initial shaping on the mountain side below the outcrop. Significantly, the bedding plane thickness for the strata most exploited is about the thickness of the individual stelae or cippus. The worked faces were always parallel to the bedding planes of the rock layers in the mountain.

The Djebel Jemaa colored lithic material shows excellent textural receptivity for relief sculpturing, both in paleo-Phoenician script and later symbol/totem rendering. The Roman funerary stelae continued the earlier burial traditions, but, of course, without infant sacrifices!

Leaving the geology of the stelae, the objects of their commemoration are an important consideration. Sacrifices were found buried in urns, the morphology of which varies through time. The evidence of fire is clearly and universally present among the charred bones. Both children and animals were present, attesting to the fact that this was no ordinary children's cemetery (a very rare thing anyway in the ancient world). No adult bone, unburned or burned has been found in this precinct. Our excavations unearthed about 200 of these interments. Many others were excavated by the French and the University of Michigan expeditions earlier this century.[46]

Larry Stager, Project Director, holds that the burned animals were intended as substitute sacrifices for children. In the lowest (earliest—seventh century B.C.) burials, the ratio between children and animals was three to one, but in the middle levels (fourth century B.C.) interments showed an increased ratio of ten children to one animal.[47]

The whole story of Punic art and architecture has yet to be told in a synoptic master work, into which her material science is carefully integrated. For all North African cultures, the mosaic of historical, cultural interrelationships and the intrinsic dependence upon the environmental geology also await full and careful analytic exposition.

Berber Kings and Kingdoms

Carthage, which was a Phoenician/Punic city, was surrounded by Berber kingdoms, particularly of Numidia to the west and south. The city's history involved not only its historic conflicts with the Romans for mastery of the Mediterranean Sea, but also its relationships with various Berber kings.

The early history of Berber leadership portrays the selection of chieftains upon the occasion of hostilities or for the duration of a single year. As loyal followers were drawn to him and as he gathered allies he was regarded as a prince. After demonstrating valor in battle and achieving victory over enemies he could assume power over others and make his territory and his family the care of a nascent state.[48] As a result, such a chief could become a king, with the potential of setting up a dynastic rule.

Much of this came about during the first millennium B.C. as iron was made available and the horse was introduced into North Africa, two innovations that enhanced the military and technological strength of those who possessed power. For example, beginning at this time, kingship was inherited by the Lebu, a Berber people in North Africa to the west of Egypt in the modern state of Libya, where diverse lineages were unified under a single authority.[49]

Once established, the Berber monarchy emerged historically as follows. The Berbers who dwelt in the mountains were environmentally protected from the raids of nomads (frequently *other* Berber tribes) who pillaged from time to time those kingdoms occupying the plains. But to check rebellion and potential treason, Berber kings took as hostages, members of powerful families in their realms. Wives were taken from among the daughters of tribal chieftains. In addition, the sons of important royal families were frequently retained as bodyguards to the kings.[50] The death of the ruler of a Berber kingdom constituted a major crisis. Outcries for revenge and civil wars occasionally broke forth. Thus beset from many sides, the kings sought to hold on to their authority over their subjects. Attempts to legitimize their sovereignty even included celebration of the "divinity" of preceding rulers.[51]

By the third century B.C., that region of the Maghreb included in Morocco, Algeria, and Tunisia was under the rule of three large Berber kingdoms. These were, from west to east, 1) the Moors (Latin Mauri) who made up the kingdom of Mauritania (Morocco), 2) the Massaesylins in the region east of the Moulouga River to Numidia (which included the territory of Oran), and 3) The Massylins, Numidia proper, a smaller realm, which extended to the borders of Carthage.[52]

The Massaesylian King Spax (d. 201 B.C.) was the first Berber monarch about whom any reliable historical data is preserved. The Roman historian, Titus Livy calls him "The wealthiest of the African princes." Before King Sphax was defeated by the Romans in 203 B.C., he controlled all of the desert regions of what is now the modern state of Algeria. The two centers of his kingdom were Siga in the westernmost part of the province of Oran, and Cirta (modern Constantine) in the east. Although both Rome and Carthage sought to make Sphax their ally, the king tried to play one state against the other, by acting as an arbiter. Livy records that Sphax even tried to imitate hellenistic monarchs by wearing a crown and having coins minted with his image. Such was the level of his importance that one of the most influential Carthaginian families gave a daughter for him to marry.[53]

King Massinissa is called one of the "greatest Berber personalities in history." During his rule, he extended his control over the lands of King Sphax to the west of his Massylin kingdom and became an ally of Rome. He is worthy of the characterization which Schaar gives of him:

> This intelligent, fearless and subtle man is shown on contemporary coins
> as a man in his forty or fifties with sharp features, wide eyes, thick eye-

brows and long hair and a pointed beard. He led an extraordinary vigorous life, at 80 he could still jump on his horse without aid and ride bareback. At the age of 86 one of his wives bore him a son, bringing the total of his male progeny to 44. Several of them survived him when he died at the age of 90.[54]

Massinissa's dynasty ruled Numidia for 100 years after which its control was extended over Mauretania for another 60 years. Having observed the Roman legions in Spain, he had foreseen that they would come and rule over all the Maghreb. He judiciously became an ally to Rome, a move which made him an enemy of King Sphax and Carthage, who were allies at the time.[55] It was the expansion of his territorial control that ultimately gave Rome a pretext to wipe Punic Carthage off the face of the earth in 146 B.C.[56]

There is good evidence that Berber kings lived in the opulent luxury of their day:

> Massinissa possessed a palace at Cirta, where in the manner of Carthaginians he gave lavish banquets complete with silver dishes, gold baskets, and Greek musicians to entertain his guests. Although he was raised in the tradition of the Berbers—indeed his mother had become a popular Berber prophetess—he knew the refined culture of Carthage, where he perhaps spent some of his early years.[57]

Massinissa took for a wife the daughter of a leading Carthaginian family, and schooled his sons in Greek education. Apparently the Carthaginians of high rank held in considerable regard and respect such Berber kings as Spax and Massinissa. They did not believe that they were lowering their social status by giving their children in marriage to the Berber princes.[58]

The principal source of wealth for the Berber kings was the agricultural products generated by their sedentary subjects living on the North African plains. Thus, farming was favored because it created greater taxes for them than other revenue sources. As a result, as often as possible, they coerced nomadic Berbers to settle and become growers of crops instead of wandering about seeking water and foraging for their flocks and herds. In fact, Schaar affirms that "a primary function of the [Berber] king was to protect farmers against nomadic (often other Berber) raids (pillages) and town-dwellers against foreign invasions.[59]

These monarchs were continually challenged in antiquity. While the Berber tribes, who occupied mountainous terrain, were themselves protected against attack upon their villages by their inaccessibility, these mountain warriors on the other hand, did not hesitate to raid those Berber (and other) cities on the plains which had no such natural defenses.[60] Armies of the king kept watch over nomadic movements and aided in the collection of taxes on their migrating herds. When unable to exercise authority over turbulent areas, the princes imposed control upon rebellious Berbers by threatening to cut off market access. The Berber kings sought to create commercial trade and assure the circulation of goods and products in their realms. Their royal treasuries were enlarged by revenue taken from marketing. Customs duty was added to these resources also. These kings became among the greatest merchants in their realms. They sold a full range of commodities such as wheat, wool, leathers, livestock and horses, wild animals, ivory, woods, building stone, and slaves to other states such as Carthage and, especially later, to Rome.[61]

One Berber king stands out above them all: Jugurtha. He was a grandson of King Massinissa and, in contra-distinction to the politics of his predecessors, he won against Rome (during the Jugurthine War, 111–105 B.C.). He set out to take all of Numidia from Rome, using bribery of Roman senators. After the plot was discovered, he accepted a summons to Rome, and is quoted as saying, "Rome is a city for sale and doomed to perish if it can find a purchaser."[62]

The Roman historian and politician, Sallust, provides some clues concerning Jugurtha's charisma. He writes:

> As soon as Jugurtha grew up, endowed as he was with great strength and handsome looks, but above all with a powerful intellect, he did not let himself be spoiled by luxury or idleness, but took part in the national pursuits of writing and javelin-throwing and competed with other young men in running; and though he outshown them all he was universally beloved. He also devoted much time to hunting; and was always to the fore at the killing of lions and other wild beasts. His energy was equalled by his modesty: he never boasted of his exploits . . . [later when fighting in Spain] by dint of hard work and careful attention to duty, by unquestioning obedience and the readiness with which he exposed himself to risk, he won such renown as to become the idol of the Roman soldiers and the terror of the enemy. He was in fact both a tough fighter and a wise counsellor . . . qualities extremely hard to combine.[63]

Jugurtha was eventually defeated by Marius and Sulla. After the kingdom of Jugurtha was divided in 105 B.C., descendants of Masinissa, who were loyal to Rome, were rewarded with Numidian territories. They became client states of the Romans, who themselves colonized the lands of Carthage which were then made the Province of Africa.

In the Roman revolution, the Berber kingdoms of Numidia became caught supporting Pompey and fell victim to annexation by Julius Caesar and his supporters in 46-40 B.C. During A.D. 40, the last king of Mauretania was assassinated by the Emperor Caligula.[64]

Roman Africa

Roman Africa, essentially the former territory dominated by Carthage, became a senatorial province, covering a region of about five thousand square miles. Meager concern was shown by the senators and settlement was minimal. Bordering areas controlled by Berbers were spared from the burden of Roman taxation and essentially enjoyed autonomy. These "indigenous" people were given considerable freedom because of their utility to Rome's wishes politically and militarily. Latin penetration into her north African frontier was facilitated by the princes of these Berber people who opened up trade and commerce in servicing Roman merchants by selling them grain. But the Berber rulers could never be regarded as easily dominated vassals, rather, their status as allies was carefully guarded with favorable treatment.[65]

Juba II, a Berber king, whose death occurred in A.D. 23, took as his wife Cleopatra Selene, the offspring of Anthony and Cleopatra. Juba, a Berber from Algerian territory, was educated in Greek studies at Rome and learned appreciation for art. Although he produced some fifty writings, none are extant. Pliny the Elder described Juba's forty-eight year reign over Mauretania as showing "glory as a scholar [which] was greater than his reputation as a sovereign."[66] His reign was filled with revolts by the Berbers and was only sustained through the help of Rome. He even sought to "establish himself as a living god" which, however, did not prevent rebellions.[67]

Cleopatra Selene seems to have brought the Egyptian cult of Serapis and Isis, mother goddess of fertility, to Mauretania. This cult spread to Tripolitania where, through the influence of Roman soldiers it was brought into the Berber Pantheon. The Berbers tied Serapis with Baal Hammon or Saturn, and Isis with the Punic goddess Tanit. Later in the context of Christianity "statues of Isis would readily become identified with the Virgin Mary and of Isiac rituals [which found] . . . their correlation in Christian practice."[68]

By the end of the reign of the Emperor Caligula, Roman mastery of Numidia and Mauretania had eliminated the Berber ruling families. In the meantime, the senatorial aristocracy, through money and political intrigue, took over the holdings of former Berber royal estates.[69]

Early in the empire, Egypt and the Maghreb supplied two-thirds of the grain requirements of Rome. Later, when other sources declined, the surpluses of Barbary produced enough wheat to feed the whole city of Rome, thus assuring the total absorption of North African produce as "the grainery of Rome."[70]

Roman successes in achieving the inclusion of Berber people into the urban provincial culture were limited in spite of some intermarriages and even an example of a well known Berber countryman such as Septimius Severus of Leptis Magha (A.D. 193–211) becoming emperor.[71] Later in the 300s A.D., about 7,500 Numidan and 15,000 Mauretanian Berber auxiliaries were pressed into service by Rome to maintain order in those territories.[72]

Persistent Berber attempts for self-rule and even "revenge against the rich masters" occurred during the fourth century A.D. Rome had to bring in European forces to put down an insurrection which had its beginnings with unrestricted nomads and mountaineers. Raids descended into the lowland agricultural areas from the mid-third century to about A.D. 370 when the mountaineer chieftain, Firmus from Kabylia, initiated a devastating revolt throughout Numidia. Such uprisings were approved by the growing heretical Christian communions, e.g. the Donatists who themselves attacked Christian settlements from their Numidian strongholds.[73]

Christian Berbers

From Berber foundations, "the two great sects of the early church of the fourth and fifth centuries, known as Donatists and the Circumcellions, are descended."[74] Considered by the historian Schaar as a type of Christian nihilism, they later became a force which overwhelmed senatorial towns and villages, and ultimately sapped the vitality which yielded to a later invasion of the sword and of a variant belief.[75]

Berber farm workers and city people of lower social levels became a nascent Barbary Christianity. From this beginning the Faith had expanded throughout many towns of the Maghreb by the fourth century with the establishment of some six hundred bishops ("more than Gaul and Egypt combined"). Out of this great Christian community, famous Berber church fathers arose: Tertullian, Cyprian and Augustine. Contemporary missionary activity even sought converts amongst the Jews in North African settlements, whose ancestors had fled the destruction of Jerusalem and its temple in A.D. 70.[76]

Orthodox Christians were terrorized by the Circumcellion and Donatists countrymen, and these sectarians even sought persecution as a form of martyrdom.[77] Thus Donatism, beginning "as a simple heresy within a puritanical tradition, . . . emphasized martyrdom, unremitting faith, morality and poverty," was supported by many Berbers who had been strongly influenced by it.[78] Suicide came to be regarded as a legitimate expression of martyrdom. The historical consequence was a large schism in the growing church resulting in a branch loyal to Rome and a "puritanical African branch supported by many Berbers." The Donatists' activity was later rendered illegal in Barbary in A.D. 412.

During his episcopate, St. Augustine, (born in A.D. 354) became bishop of Hippo [Annaba, formerly known as Bone in Algeria], "one of the foremost theologians of all time."[79] Augustine enlisted the support of Rome for an assault upon the Donatists, which ultimately annihilated the sect.[80] Augustine held his hierarchical office at Hippo until his death, in August, A.D. 430 when the Vandals were besieging the city.[81]

Mosaics and Ceramics

I want to link this famous Christian churchman with my Carthage/Tunisian research by setting down Augustine's words on the material culture of his time.

> [In some rich dwellings] . . . how many gold and silver vases there are! Finally what delight the house gives, with its paintings, its marble, its paneled ceilings, its pillars, its courts and chambers.[82]

There is a delightful array of Roman/Byzantine art and architectural material made available to us through archaeological research. It exists both in excavated sites (some of which are nearly ghost towns) and in museums especially the Bardo in Tunis.

I want to give honorable mention to authorities in Tunisian mosaic research which lie within the bounds of the author's acquaintance. They are Margaret Alexander, Katherine Dunbabin and Aicha Ben Abed Ben Khader, who wrote the following:

> Tunisia has the world's richest collection of mosaics. Thousands of mosaic pavements and cut marble floors have been unearthed in the last century, and the search for new examples continues. It is a rare excavation that does not result in the discovery of one or more mosaic pavements having

simple, geometric, floral, figural, monochrome, bichrome, or poly-
chrome design. The discoveries have greatly aided archaeologists and historians to gain knowledge of Roman civilization—especially its provincial aspects.[83]

UNESCO sponsored research at Carthage has prompted reconsideration that normal mosaic flooring construction known as *Opus Tessalla-
tum* originated at Morgantina, Sicily in the mid-third century B.C. Indeed,
fifth-century mosaics have recently been found at Carthage and *Opus
Figlinum* (square ceramic pieces laid flat) with fourth-century Attic pottery beneath.[84]

Especially significant is the beginning of the *Opus Signinum* or *Pavi-
menta Punica* in which bits of crushed ceramic or tile were laid in a mortar (lime and sand). Characteristically, these included inlays of 2 × 5 or 6
cm. pieces of limestone, marble, and sometimes glass. Patterned inlays of
white stone were fashioned as a geometric design using plants, the symbol of Tanit and the crescent on a staff.[85]

A strong influence from Rome appears in the second half of the second century A.D. in which simple monochrome or bichrome (black and
white) tesserae are featured, e.g. such as was prevalent at Ostia in Italy.
During the second half of the second century, African innovations began
with a gradual introduction of multiple colors and the integration of plant
and geometric designs.

> An excellent summary of this development is seen, at Thuburbo Maius,
> some 60 kilometers from Carthage, recent excavations have shown that
> new quarters (in the east and west areas of the city) constructed in the
> Fourth Century were devoted to houses that were the equal of the most
> beautiful in Charthage. The same was true at Bulla Regia and Douga.
> The African bourgeoisie had undisputed taste for grandeur and beauty,
> and commissions encouraged mosaicists to express their creativity; this
> resulted in great masterpieces at Carthage, Sidi Ghrib, Nabeul, Kelibia,
> Thuburbo Maius, Bulla Regia, Douga and elsewhere.[86]

Ceramic production matched the growing agricultural output for
containers in which to ship the oil, wine and grain. Many household items
were also made of ceramic/terra cotta composition. The manufacture of
lamps at Carthage has received considerable attention, both on account
of its design and art work.[87]

Certain areas are rich in ceramic clays. The author found a high quality clay deposit northwest of Gammert (on the Carthage headlands).

Other notable finds with their production centers are Kairouan, Hejep-Al, Aioun, El-Aouja and El-Jem. While these localities did not have fertile fields, ineffective crop growth was economically compensated in the pottery production from the clay deposits nearby.[88]

Masses of terra cotta statues were used in burial rites and terra cotta tiles featuring sculptured reliefs on them appeared on the walls and ceilings of fifth and sixth-century Christian basilicas. Equally important was the North African red slip ware in the form of plates, bowls, and saucers. Often, stamped decorations enhanced this ware which sometimes showed the potter's attempt to imitate silver examples.[89]

Founded at the interface between land and sea, Carthage emerged from the interplay of earth materials and forces. Indeed, there is no other site in the Mediterranean that offers a greater challenge for a full range of environmental studies than ancient Carthage.

Roman Exploitation of Lithic Resources

A study of Roman accomplishments in Carthage and Tunisia would never be complete without notice of the architectural acquisitions of materials. The headlands of the Carthage tombolo offer really very little quality construction materials, all of which were certainly discovered and utilized by the Punic occupants. (See figure 6.4.)

There are no quality architectural building stones in the tombolo hills and certainly not along the beaches either. Friable, sandstone and hard quartz pebble conglomerates outcrop on the Cap Carthage headland and near the Hamilcar Hotel. But this stone has only been found in Punic slurry mortar and rock fill walls of cisterns (which were usually plastered).[90]

In the Roman Province of Africa, most of the lithic material exposed on the surface of mountains, hills, headlands, plains and valleys ranges from resistant, locally slightly marmarized, Jurassic limestones and dolomites through resistant Cretaceous sandstones, softer limestones and lower Paleocene limestones to Miocene sands and sandstones and Pliocene clays and mudstones. Almost without exception, the topographic highs are resistant limestones, incipiently marmorized limetones and sandstones, for example, Jebel Ressas, Jebel Bou Kornine, Jebel Oust, Jebel Zaghouan, Jebel Aziz, Jebel Ben Kleb, and Jebel Rouas. These are known to have been of special significance to Roman architects and builders.[91]

Because there was almost no suitable building stone sources on the Carthage tombolo, the Romans opened quarry sites in the mountains

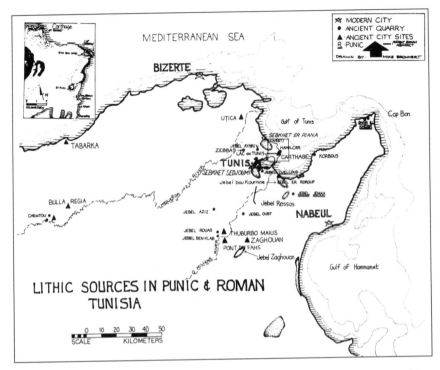

Figure 6.4   Lithic sources in Punic and Roman Tunisia. From G. Rapp and J. Gifford, eds., *Archaeological Geology* (New Haven, Conn.: Yale University Press, 1985). Courtesy Yale University Press.

which ringed Carthage on the west (Jebel Ayari), on the south (Jebel Djelloud), and southeast (the foothill spur of Jebel bou Kornine, Jebel er-Rorouf, on the coast in Hammanlif). The Romans also utilized the former Punic quarry site, Ghar el-Khebir, where a quarrying technique different from that of the Punic method was employed, the step-ledge extraction method. These stones constituted a basic commodity which the Romans used in walls, pavements and thresholds.

More distant resources were called upon especially to meet those architectural and artistic designs requiring aesthetically pleasing color or geometric effects. This building stone was brought from the uplifted, slightly recrystalized, mountain masses, the (Jurassic) rock lying to the west, north and northeast of Thuburbo Maius. Here these beautiful crypto-crystalline sub-marbles are gray with lensate streaks of pink and of white calcite. Other variations include banded travertines of diverse warm hues. The significance of these sources is seen the architectural utilization at Thurburbo Maius, Utica, Bulla Regia, and Carthage as well as elsewhere.[92]

Ultimately, the Roman builders and their architects were not satisfied by the spectrum of colored lithics available in Tunisia. They went to the Apennine Mountains of Italy for finely crystalline luminescent white Carrara marble, and to the Greek islands for Naxian, Parian, and Euboean varieties. Their quest also brought them to the western littoral of Asia Minor where exciting marble breccias and exotically variable color expressions were found.

Three decorative stone sources are especially worthy of note: 1) Chemtou marble—(exhibiting golden yellows and salmon-colored pinks) a sizeable portion of a mountain has been quarried away more than 100 kilometers west of Carthage, up the Medjerda River Valley. 2) Taygetus Mountains, 20 kilometers southwest of Sparta in the Peloponnesus offer a spectacular dark and light green bichrome crystalline Andesite porphyry with large greenish-white feldspar crystals (or Phenocrysts). This stone is used to accentuate *Opus Sectile* flooring geometric pattern. The lithic is known architecturally as Antika Verde. 3) A royal purple trachytic porphyry was extracted from a volcanic site known as Djebel Dokhtan, 50 kilometers north of Thebes in the eastern desert of Egypt. This stone was in great demand as demonstrated by the frequency of its occurrence in Roman sites. I have seen it in sculptures at Carthage and at Caesarea Maritima, in flooring at Tell er-Ras at Shechem and at Carthage, and in numerous Italian *Opus Sectile* church floors. The purple color is accentuated by small pink feldspar phenocrysts giving statues carved from this material a royal elegance.[93]

The wealth and ability of Romans to seek, quarry and cut these lithic construction materials is a manifestation of the success of their quest for architectural stones which not only provided strength but also beauty to their buildings. In a sense, I suppose, this is a measure of the mastery and domination of the larger world by Rome.

Research in connection with environmental studies at Carthage has not only been conducted from a geological framework, anthropological reconnaissance has also been explored. Joseph A. Greene, of the Carthage staff conducted his study in the hinterland of Carthage between 1979 and 1983. His survey recorded 136 sites. Of the Punic settlements, a five-fold increase in the number of rural settlements was recorded after 300 B.C. he noted an abrupt drop in these immediately after the Roman destruction of Carthage in 146 B.C. In the Roman period up to the early fourth century A.D. settlement numbers peaked in the second and third centuries, but they were cut almost in half in the fourth. He speculates that a combination of environmental, social and political factors may have existed which were not recorded in contemporary sources.

Greene found a surge in site numbers during the fifth-century Vandal rule of Carthage. He observed a slight increase in settlements in the sixth-century decline until Carthage was captured by Arab invaders in A.D. 699.[94]

Conclusion

The story of North Africa with special focus on ancient Carthage can be written in her ethnic composition, her armies, her architecture and art, her harbors, acropolis, and her defensive walls. It is written also in the anguish of the cruel destruction of her city (as is evident nearly everywhere in the archaeological strata and their documentary sediments). The memory of the Punic experience soon died out, in their reconstruction activity which took place nearly everywhere in Africa, little was utilized by the Roman conquerors. The quarry sources discovered and exploited by the Phoenicians were opened once again and became the geological basis of some of the most beautiful designs and structures ever produced in the ancient world. This episode of history is brightly punctuated by that way in which the Romans portrayed themselves and the local environments they captured in their art and architecture. They expressed this in some of the world's most aesthetically inspiring mosaics and cut-stone pavements which have been revealed by archaeological research.

We are equally enriched by all this: the elegance of the sites, some of which are towns of nearly intact architecture, and the astonishing attractiveness of the art work of the mosaic floors and sculpture, which delight and captivate all who behold them and relate them to the culture of the sites of origin, especially as exhibited in the Bardo Palace Museum of Tunis.

Bibliography

Ben Khader, Aicha Ben Abed. "The African Mosaic in Antiquity," in *Carthage: A Mosaic of Ancient Tunisia*, A. Ben Khader and D. Soren, eds., 132–35. New York: The American Museum of Natural History in association with W. W. Norton, 1987.

Brett M. "The Spread of Islam in North Africa," in *The Cambridge Encyclopedia of Africa*, R. Oliver and M. Crowder, eds., 112–16. New York: Cambridge University, 1981.

Bullard, R. G. "The Environmental Geology of Roman Carthage," in *Excavation at Carthage, 1976, Conducted by the University of Michigan*, J. Humphrey, ed. Ann Arbor: University of Michigan Press, 1978.

———. "Sedimentary Environments and Lithologic Materials at Two Archaeological Sites," in *Archaeological Geology*, G. Rapp Jr. and J. A. Gifford, eds., 103–33. New Haven: Yale University Press, 1985.

Clark, J.D. "African Beginnings," in *The Horizon History of Africa*, A. M. Joesephy Jr., ed., 16–47. New York: American Heritage Pub., 1971.

Dunton, E. "Trek by Mule Among Morocco's Berbers." *National Geographic* 133, no. 6 (1968): 850–75.

Englebert, V. "I Joined a Sahara Salt Caravan." *National Geographic* 130, no. 10 (1965): 694–711.

Fantar, M. H. "Punic Civilization," in *Carthage: A Mosaic of Ancient Tunisia*, Ben Khader and Soren, eds., 88–109. New York: American Museum of Natural History in association with W. W. Norton, 1987.

Ghaki, Mansour. "The Berbers of the Pre-Roman Period," in *Carthage: A Mosaic of Ancient Tunisia*, Ben Khader and Soren, eds., 84–87. New York: American Museum of Natural History in association with W. W. Norton, 1987.

Hunt, C. and N. Wheeler. "Berber Brides' Fair." *National Geographic* 157, no. 1 (1980): 118–29.

Kittler, G. D. *Mediterranean Africa: Four Muslim Nations*. Camden, NJ: Thomas Nelson and Son, 1969.

Leutzion, N. *Ancient Ghana and Mali*. London: Methuen, 1972.

Murray, J. ed. *Cultural Atlas of Africa*. New York: Facts of File Publications, 1982.

Nyrop, R. et al. *Area Handbook for Algeria*. Washington, D.C.: U.S. Government Printing Office, 1972.

Pedicaris, I. "Morocco 'The Land of the Extreme West' and the Story of My Captivity." *Washington National Geographic* 17 no. 3 (1906): 117–57.

Schaar, S. "The Barbary Coast," in *The Horizon History of Africa*, A. M. Joesephy Jr., ed., 96–135. New York: American Heritage Publishing Co. Inc., 1971.

Slim, H. "From the Fall of Carthage to the Arrival of the Muslims," in *Carthage: A Mosaic of Ancient Tunisia*, Ben Khader and Soren, eds., 114–26. New York: American Museum of Natural History in association with W. W. Norton, 1987.

Soren, D. "Romanization" in *Carthage: A Mosaic of Ancient Tunisia*, Ben Khader and Soren, eds., 50–67. New York: American Museum of Natural History in association with W. W. Norton, 1987.

Thorp, M. B. "Geology and Geomorphology," in *The Cambridge Encyclopedia of Africa*, R. Oliver and M. Crowder, eds., 32–39. New York: Cambridge University, 1981.

Notes

1. Sebkhet er-Rianna, north of the Carthage tombolo is a contemporary example of this process.

2. J. L. Cloudsley-Thompson, "The Physical Environment" in *The Cambridge Encyclopedia of Africa*. R. Oliver and M. Crowder, eds. (Cambridge, England: Cambridge University Press, 1981), pp 32–37, *et passim*, and my own surface reconnaissance.

3. J. S. Oguntoyinbo, "Climate" in "The Physical Environment" in *The Cambridge Encyclopedia of Africa*, 40–44.

4. P. N. Bradley, "Vegetation" in "The Physical Environment." in *The Cambridge Encyclopedia of Africa*, 48–52; and personal observations.

5. Hedi Slim, "From the Fall of Carthage to the Arrival of the Muslims," *Carthage: A Mosaic of Ancient Tunisia*, Aicha Ben Abed Ben Khader and David Soren, eds. (New York: American Museum of Natural History, 1987).

6. A former near-shore island which has become attached to the mainland by one or more strands of sediment.

7. Reuben G. Bullard, "Sedimentary Environments and Lithologic Materials at Two Archaeological Sites," in *Archaeological Geology*, G. Rapp and J. Gifford, eds. (New Haven: Yale University Press, 1985), 121–25.

8. Mansour Ghaki says that an inscription at Karnak refers to a conquest by Pharaoh Merneptah defeating the Lebou (Libyans) in or about the year 1220 B.C. "The Berbers of the Pre-Roman Period," *Carthage: A Mosaic of Ancient Tunisia*, 85–87.

9. *Encyclopedia Britannica*, 9th ed., *s.v.* "Kables."

10. See also J. Gunther, *Inside Africa* (New York: Harper and Brothers, 1955), 67.

11. J. Desmond Clark, "African Beginnings," *The Horizon History of Africa*, A. M. Josephy, ed. (New York: American Heritage Publishing Co. Inc., 1971), 32.

12. S. Schaar, "The Barbary Coast," *The Horizon History of Africa*, A. M. Josephy, ed. (New York: American Heritage Publishing Co. Inc., 1971), 16–47.

13. Schaar, 99.

14. Ibid.

15. Ibid.

16. Elizabeth Dunstan, "Languages" in "The Peoples" in *The Cambridge Encyclopedia of Africa*, 75.

17. Gunther, 67.

18. Jocelyn Murray, ed., *Cultural Atlas of Africa* (New York: Facts on File and Co., Ltd., 1972), 124.

19. *Encyclopedia Britannica*, 9th. ed., *s.v.* "Africa".

20. Ion Perdicaris, "Morocco, 'The Land of the Extreme West' and the Story of My Captivity" *National Geographic* 17 no. 3 (March, 1906): 118–19.

21. Schaar, 100.

22. Nyrob, et al., *Area Handbook For Algeria* (Washington: United States Government Printing Office, 1972), 9.

23. Schaar, 130.

24. "The Peoples" in *The Cambridge Encyclopedia of Africa*, 79.

25. Ibid.

26. Strabo, *The Geography of Strabo,* Loeb Classical Library Series, trans. H. L. Jones (Cambridge, Massachusetts: Harvard University Press, 1967), 8:185

27. Soren, 26.

28. Schaar, 102.

29. Ibid., 100.

30. Robin Derricourt, "The Copper and Iron Ages" in "Before European Colonization" in *The Cambridge Encyclopedia of Africa,* 95.

31. Schaar, 104.

32. B. H. Warmington, *Carthage* (New York: Frederick A. Praeger, 1969), 23.

33. M'Hamed Hassine Fantar, "Punic Civilization," *Carthage: A Mosaic of Ancient Tunisia,* 103.

34. Ibid., 103, 104.

35. Schaar, 102.

36. The ever-changing shoreline of the western littoral of the Bay of Carthage is the result of geological processes.

37. Warmington, 26; Bullard, 126–32.

38. Warmington, 27.

39. Our excavations uncovered a bluish-gray clay deposit containing wood, nuts and other active port debris. Surprisingly, a tophet-style funerary stele was found in those early Punic harbor sediments. It was a Char el-Khebir sandstone already sculptured either at the quarries or at the harbor, and ready for removal to the Tophet cemetery. Unfortunately for the shippers, it fell into the harbor waters and was never retrieved.

40. Bullard, 127–29.

41. Appianus of Alexandria, *Appian's Roman History,* H. White, tr., The Loeb Classical Library VIII, 14.96 (Cambridge: Harvard University Press, 1912), 567.

42. Bullard, 123.

43. Several block fragments showing mortar and/or plaster attached to a remnant flat surface were encountered here by the Carthage harbor excavations, American Harvard/Chicago, ASOR team, 1975–81.

44. Terminology of Professor Robert L. Folk, Department of Geology, University of Texas at Austin.

45. There was, nonetheless, an attraction to this rather inaccessible lithic material which probably related to a Ferrous-Ferric Oxide pigmentation of the rock strata. This is a reflection of the environmental conditions of the carbonate sediment deposition.

46. A rough estimate of the quantity of burials, extrapolating the excavated area concentrations to the known tophet boundaries, is between 20,000 and 30,000 infant sacrificed burials (Dr. Larry Stager, personal communication).

47. Lawrence Stager and Samuel R. Wolf, "Child Sacrifice at Carthage–Religious Rite or Population Control?" *Biblical Archaeological Review* 10, no. 1 (1984): 40.

48. Schaar, 106.
49. Ibid.
50. Ibid.
51. Ibid.
52. Ibid.
53. Ibid.
54. Ibid.
55. Ibid., 107.
56. During the Third Punic War.
57. Schaar, 106.
58. Ibid.
59. Ibid.
60. Ibid.
61. Ibid.
62. Ibid., 108.
63. As noted in Schaar, 108–9.
64. Ibid.
65. Ibid., 108.
66. Ibid., 109.
67. Ibid.
68. Ibid.
69. Ibid.
70. Ibid., 110. Derricourt, Robin M., "The Copper and Iron Ages" in *The Cambridge Encyclopedia of Africa*, 95.
71. Schaar, 110.
72. Ibid., 110.
73. Ibid., 113–14.
74. Ibid., 118–19.
75. Ibid.
76. Ibid., 114.
77. Michael Brett, "Classical North Africa," in *The Cambridge Encyclopedia of Africa*, R. Oliver and M. Crowder, eds. (New York: Cambridge University Press, 1981) 104.
78. Schaar, 114.
79. Ibid., 123.
80. Brett, 104.
81. Schaar, 123.
82. Ibid., 121.
83. Aicha Ben Abed Ben Khader, "The African Mosaic in Antiquity," *Carthage: A Mosaic of Ancient Tunisia*, Ben Khader and Soren, eds. (New York: The American Museum of Natural History, 1987), 132.
84. Ibid., 132.
85. Ibid.

86. Ibid., 134.

87. Hedi Slim, "From The Fall of Carthage," 117.

88. Ibid., 118.

89. Ibid.

90. In 1975 a member of the family of the American ambassador escorted some of the Harvard excavation staff down a long trail on the precipitous headlands below the property of the ambassador's residence. We were shown cistern wall remnants adhering to the sandy cliffs face, constructed of tabular, small boulder–and large cobble–size quartz-pebble conglomerate members in a sand and calcined lime slurry mortar. This wall, approximately 20 centimeters thick, was surfaced on its interior with a water-proof plaster composed of a calcined limestone bonding. Environmentally, this is a silent witness to more than 2150 years of sea cliffs erosion on this Carthage headland.

91. Reuben G. Bullard, "The Environmental Geology of Roman Carthage," *Excavations at Carthage, 1976, Conducted by the University of Michigan,* vol. 4, John Humphrey, ed. (Ann Arbor: University of Michigan, 1978).

92. Ibid.

93. Reuben G. Bullard, "The Marbles of the Opus Sectile Floor," *Excavations at Carthage, 1976, Conducted by the University of Michigan,* vol. 4, John Humphrey, ed. (Ann Arbor: University of Michigan, 1978).

94. Joseph A. Green, "The Carthage Survey: Archaeological Reconnaissance in the Hinterland of Ancient Carthage, 1979–80." (unpublished Ph.D. diss., Semitic Museum: Harvard University, 1983).

7

An Archaeological Survey
of the Cyrenaican and Marmarican
Regions of Northeast Africa[1]

DONALD WHITE

❀

My intention is to outline the contributions to knowledge of both the classical world and of the history of the African continent recovered from the archaeological record of one of the currently least-familiar but potentially more rewarding areas for study along the southern Mediterranean littoral. I refer to the eastern half of the modern state of Libya ("Cyrenaica") and the western half of the northwest coast of Egypt ("Marmarica"), whose respective histories, although not identical, are nevertheless closely intertwined. (See fig. 7.1.) There is a long history of isolation in both regions, for political and geographic reasons, which continues yet today.

The Bedouin inhabitants of Cyrenaica, living under loose Ottoman control until the Turko-Italian war of 1910/11, early on acquired a possibly well-deserved reputation for xenophobia. This fear was indiscriminately directed toward all strangers, eventually including even "foreign" Moslems (meaning here any Arab not part of the Senussi or Sanusi order, a Sufic brotherhood established at the beginning of the 19th cent.) as well as all Christians and Jews.[2] Thus little in the way of written travel accounts survives before the year 1800. The first description of Cyrene by a European visitor is the 1706 report by the French consul, Claude Lemaire.[3] More than half a century was to pass before another attempted to retrace

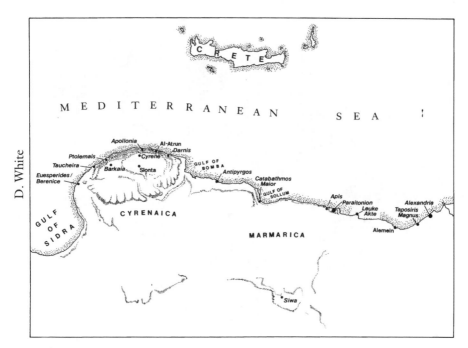

Figure 7.1 By the later third century A.D. "Upper Libya" or "Pentapolis" referred to the western half of Cyrenaica, while the western half of Marmarica was the equivalent of "Lower" or "Dry (Sicca) Libya."

his steps. While the Scottish adventurer, James Bruce, made his way along the Libyan coast as far east as Ptolemais in 1762 or shortly thereafter, he was diverted away from Cyrene at the last moment by rumors of tribal warfare, plague, and civil disturbances at Derna.[4] W. G. Browne, the earliest recorded European to travel out along the Marmarica coast from Alexandria, reached the oasis of Siwa in 1792 but also cut short his coastal journey in order to plunge directly into the desert just west of Abusir.[5] Because of the reputation for ferocity attached to the Sanusi tribesmen inhabiting both regions,[6] the nineteenth century produced only sporadic travel accounts. On the other hand, what survives by way of descriptive narratives, route and site maps, and graphic illustrations of the then preserved monuments, remains extremely useful from the scientific point of view. One thinks here of the accounts of several English travelers including the two Beechey brothers, Frederick and Henry (1825),[7] James Hamilton (1852),[8] and Capt. R. Murdoch Smith and Commander E. A. Porcher, sent out to collect for the British Museum (1860).[9] (See fig. 7.2.)

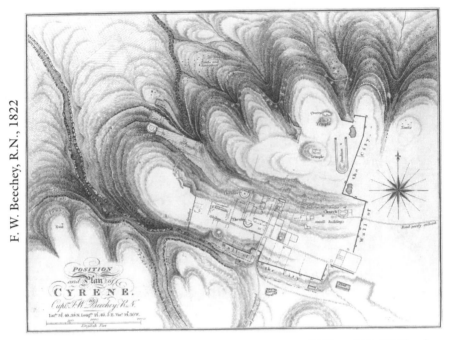

F. W. Beechey, R.N., 1822

Figure 7.2   Ancient Cyrene and its environs. From F. W. and H. W. Beechey, *Proceedings of the Expedition to Explore the Northern Coast of Africa* (London: J. Murray, 1828), 404.

There are as well the journals of the pioneer Italian explorers, Agostino Cervelli (1811–12)[10] and Paolo Della Cella (1816),[11] the French savant Jean-Raymond Pacho (1825)[12] and that country's acquisitive consul at Benghazi, Vattier de Bourville (1848),[13] and finally the two Germans, Baron von Minutoli (1825),[14] and the famous African explorer, Heinrich Barth (1846).[15] Of the two regions the Cyrenaica is today much the better served by its early travelers than is the Marmarica.

Geographical Setting

We shall, in a moment, take a look at the major historical episodes in the development of the two regions, but first a word about their geographic scope and characteristics.[16] The province of Cyrenaica today includes the whole of eastern Libya as far south as that country's border with Chad and Sudan. Most of this vast region is made up of desert, which, apart from its chain of oases, remains as barren of human occupation now as it did when the Roman poet Catullus compared the number of Lesbia's kisses he lusted after with "the Libyan sands of silphium-bearing Cyrene that lie between the oracle of torrid Jove and the holy sepulchre of ancient Battus."[17] In Roman times, "Cyrenaica" was joined with Crete into a single Senatorial province, the *Provincia Cretae et Cyrenarum*, until the reign of Diocletian (A.D. 284–305), when its African half was further split into two separate provinces, *Upper Libya* or *Pentapolis* and *Lower* or *Dry Libya*.[18] Pentapolis, which is to say the "Region of the Five Cities," eventually came to mean the western half of Cyrenaica, dominated by a 2000-foot high limestone plateau known as the Gebel Akhdar or the "Green Mountain" for its cover of coniferous scrub. The *gebel* (Arabic for "mountain") separates the rugged, rock-girt coast from the desert. Sufficient moisture falls along its crescent-shaped 175-mile length in the winter months to create a kind of mock northern Mediterranean climate that encourages a fairly intensive agricultural land use. The "five cities" includes the provincial capital, Cyrene, its port Apollonia, nearby Barcaia, Tauchira and Euesperides, all of which were functioning polities by the first quarter of the sixth century.[19] "Marmarica" refers to the territory stretching from ancient Darnis (modern Derna) to the eastern extremity of the Libyan plateau and thence along the barren Egyptian coastline as far as Paraetonium (modern Marsa Matruh).[20] To sow a final seed of confusion, "Lower" or "Dry Libya" was the same as the western half of "Marmarica." The oasis of Siwa, home to the celebrated oracle of Zeus Ammon consulted by Alexander in 331 B.C.,[21] lay at its southern limit. Thus, taken together, we are dealing with a very large expanse of nearly empty Sahara, a narrow strip of elevated, cultivable plateau, and an even narrower coastal plain, also cultivable and capable of inhabitation. Apart from the "five cities" just mentioned, the main population centers along this coast in antiquity were the previously-mentioned Paraetonium (modern Marsa Matruh), Catabathmos Maior (Salloum), Antipyrgos (Tobruk), Darnis (Derna), Ptolemais (Tolmeta), and Berenice (Benghazi), interspersed between a large number of lesser towns and villages, a fair number of which can be identified.[22]

The Libyans

It is accepted fact that the historical colonization of the Libyan Pentapolis by Greeks took place toward the end of the seventh century B.C., the conventional calendar date being 631 B.C. It is also commonplace knowledge that the Greeks were not the first to occupy this region. Herodotus, the fifth-century B.C. Greek historian, in his book IV account of the foundation of Cyrene makes it explicitly clear that the upland *gebel* as well as the vast "sea of sand" to its rear and east were under the shifting control of several large ethnic units of Berberized nomads, who were collectively and somewhat misleadingly labelled "Libyans" long before the arrival of the Greeks. Herodotus' description of the various Libyan tribes is perhaps the earliest and certainly one of the most entertaining stabs at cultural anthropology preserved in western literature. The Greeks must have been inspired early on to fashion some kind of symbiotic, cooperative relationship with the tribal Libyans,[23] since it was the Libyans who still controlled much of the upland countryside during the Archaic period. As well as providing traditional grazing space for the herds of native sheep, cattle, and horses, the *gebel* plateau produced most of the regions' exportable grains, legumes, and its principal cash crop, silphium, a widely sought-after medicinal and condiment. (See fig. 7.3.) For their own part, the Iron Age Libyans left a limited but still useful record of their presence in a small repertory of cultic reliefs,[24] funereal portraits,[25] onomastic inscriptions[26] and other miscellaneous artifacts, including the decorated gold sheet that perhaps depicts the early sixth-century B.C. clash between the Cyrenaican Greeks and the Libyans at Irasa.[27] (See fig. 7.4.)

Bronze Age Libyans and Egyptians

It is our good fortune to have Herodotus pick up the story of the eastern Libyans soon after the period where Egyptian sources leave off. Libyans figure with some frequency in New Kingdom accounts,[28] and although there are no explicit references to conflict between the Libyans and Egyptians in the 18th dynasty (1570–1320 B.C.), reports of clashes are commonplace during the 19th (1320–1200 B.C.) and 20th dynasties (1200–1085 B.C.). Both Merneptah, ca. 1220 B.C., and Ramesses III, ca. 1180 B.C., had to repel major Libyan invasions, spearheaded by the tribal Libu, who in time were to bequeath their name to the region to the west.[29] Already during Ramesses II's reign a series of coastal forts had been constructed along the northwest edge of the Delta and out along the coastal road as far as Um el-Rakham just west of Marsa Matruh to deal with Libyan attacks.[30] In the absence of direct site evidence, the principal non-literary evidence for Bronze Age Libyan culture has been heretofore the much commented-on bas-reliefs of idealized battle carved on the walls of

Figure 7.3 Silphium plant, displayed on a fifth-century B.C. silver hemidrachm struck by Cyrene and excavated in that city's Extramural Sanctuary of Dememter and Persephone. Courtesy of D. White.

the Mortuary Temple of Ramesses III at Medinet Habu, which may depict the defeat of the Libyan Meshwesh at the hands of the pharaoh during his fifth regnal year.[31] Since 1985 I have been investigating a fourteenth-century settlement on a small islet secreted at the end of a salt-water lagoon east of Marsa Matruh.[32] (See fig. 7.5.) The relevance of this site to African history lies in the fact that the island has provided, along with a sample of Egyptian and imported Cypriot, Canaanite, and Aegean artifacts, the first, albeit very restricted, assemblage of Libyan cultural objects—simple lithic tools, hand-made pottery, and ostrich eggshell fragments—to be recovered from an occupation site. (See fig. 7.6.) On the other hand, the island never functioned as a Libyan settlement *per se* but represents instead a "foreign" way-station maintained by Cypriot (?) mariners to facilitate their return by sea from Crete to the Delta and the Canaanite coast and thence back to Cyprus. (See fig. 7.7.) The Libyan objects found their way onto

Figure 7.4 Tiny archaic gold sheet (H. 2.3 cm) in the Cyrene Museum that perhaps depicts the ca. 570 B.C. battle at Irasa of Cyrenaican Greeks against an allied force of Egytians and native Libyans. Excavated during the 1920s by Luigi Pernier from Cyrene's Temple of Artemis. Courtesy of D. White.

the island as part of an exchange of goods between the Aegean islanders and the native pastoralists inhabiting the desert hinterland. We presume that fresh food and water were the principal commodities traded by the Libyans for finished imports and simple bronze artifacts manufactured by the mariners on the island. (See fig. 7.8.) In the thirteenth century the pharaoh Merneptah repelled a joint force of Libyans and "Sea-Peoples," who converged on the Western Delta.[33] Who the Sea-Peoples were is still actively debated, but they seem to have had connections with both Cyprus and Canaan, suggesting that their link with the Libyans in the Western Desert must have something to do with Marsa Matruh's harbor system and its way-station island facility developed during the previous century. The discovery of a genuine seasonal Libyan encampment, however, on both the Cyrenaican plateau and anywhere throughout the Marmaric region still eludes us, and all attempts to pin down the presence of Late Bronze Age Aegeans on the plateau have thus far proven fruitless.[34]

The Greek Colonization

The story of Cyrene's post-Bronze Age occupation by settlers from the island of Thera in the second half of the seventh century B.C. in Herodotos' Book IV is too familiar to bear repeating here.[35] It is enough to say that the historian's unusually complete literary account of the initial, tentative settlement by a small band of outcasts led by a certain Battus, strengthened fifty years later by a second larger wave of colonization

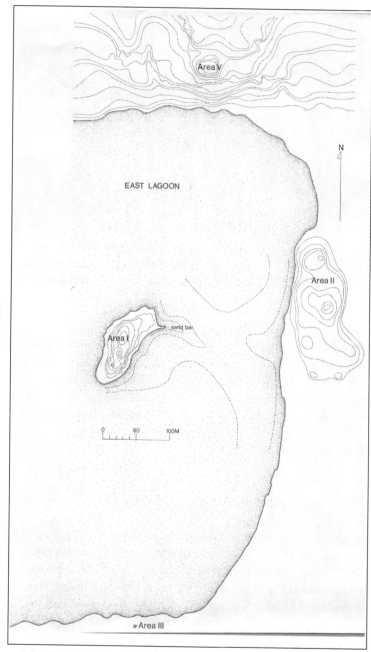

Figure 7.5   The eastern end of the first lagoon to the east of Marsa Matruh along the northwest coast of Egypt. The small island marked "area I" was utilized in the fourteenth and possibly the thirteenth century B.C. as a way-station by Cypriot mariners.

Figure 7.6   View from the northeast of the Late Bronze Age settlement named Bates's Island after its original discoverer, the American archaeologist Oric Bates, who explored Marsa Matruh during the winter of 1914. Courtesy of D. White.

drawn from the mainland as well as the islands, and the city's subsequent growth under the leadership of its brilliant but erratic monarchy is so faithfully mirrored in the archaeological site record that Cyrene's first hundred and thirty years can be treated as a kind of model for the entire Greek colonization movement. Since there is little archaeological record for the early histories of neighboring Bacaia, Apollonia, Tauchira and Euesperides, let us take a brief look at some of the principal monuments of the Archaic provincial metropolis, Cyrene.

Archaic Cyrene 631–500 B.C.

The first settlers were attracted to Cyrene because of its year-round availability of water in a dry land, and the first important monumental remains grew up at the foot of the perennially flowing fountain of Apollo that taps aquifers deep inside the massive limestone hill carrying the city's still unexcavated Archaic citadel. (See figure 7.9.) The two most striking monuments are here the Temple of Apollo[36] and smaller Temple of Artemis.[37] (See figure 7.10.)

The economic vitality of the sixth-century city, grown prosperous from agricultural exports, is attested by a cache of costly Archaic votive dedications thrown into a large pit just outside the eastern curtain of the Hellenistic city walls. Discovered in 1966 under bizarre circumstances, the

Figure 7.7   Selection of fourteenth-century B.C. Cypriot White Slip Ware II sherds excavated on Bates's Island, Marsa Matruh. Courtesy of D. White.

deposit included an imported marble votive column, topped by an Ionic capital and sphinx dated 560–50 B.C. (see fig. 7.11), a mutilated marble *kouros* torso of around 540 B.C., two nearly identical headless marble *korai* with strongly East Greek features (see fig. 7.12) dated again to between 560 and 550 B.C., a large number of undecorated bronze sheets pierced for nails, two bronze tondo figures of grimacing Medusas, and finally a bronze sheet depicting two wrestlers in typically Archaic juxtaposition (the Libyan earth giant Antaeus versus Heracles?).[38] (See fig. 7.13.) The bronze sheets evidently once belonged to a "brazen house" or

Figure 7.8   Late Bronze Age bronze weapon point (L. 8.4 cm; Inv. 851-M-1), probably cast on Bates's Island for trade with the native Libyans inhabiting the mainland. Courtesy of D. White.

Figure 7.9 The fountain of Apollo in the Sanctuary of Apollo at Cyrene. Courtesy of D. White.

Figure 7.10 The Temple of Apollo (left) and the much smaller Temple of Artemis (right) as they appear in their Roman development phases in the Sanctuary of Apollo at Cyrene. Courtesy of D. White.

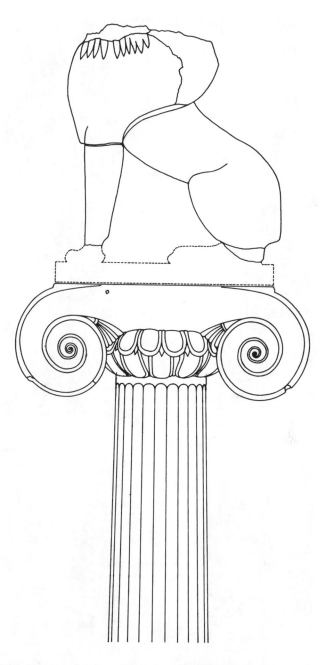

Figure 7.11 Drawing of the mid-sixth century B.C. dedicatory marble sphinx column buried in the Archaic pit deposit outside the walls of Cyrene. The sphinx's head was found after the drawing had been made and has been recently attached to its body. Courtesy of D. White.

Figure 7.12 Lifesize marble *Kore*, dating ca. 560–50 B.C. from Cyrene's extramural pit deposit. Courtesy of D. White.

Figure 7.13 A .50 by .55 m. bronze repoussé relief, depicting two wrestling figures (possibly Heracles and the Libyan giant Antaeus), recovered from Cyrene's extramural pit deposit. Courtesy of D. White.

chalkeios oikos, a sacred building sheathed in metal and decorated with bronze applied reliefs, including perhaps even bronze metopes. It, along with the expensive marble sculptures and even rarer votive column, were piously interred beneath the ground after a Persian expeditionary army on their way back to Egypt in the year 515 B.C. had wrecked an unidentified sanctuary or cult place that lay outside the protection of Cyrene's early walls.

Most of the excavation conducted at Cyrene before World War II concentrated on architectural monuments, sculptures, and inscriptions, to the exclusion of nearly everything else. More recent work during an Italian mission under Sandro Stucchi[39] in Cyrene's Agora and undertaken by me between 1969 and 1981 in the Extramural Sanctuary of Demeter and Persephone[40] has striven to bring about a more appropriate balance between the recovery and study of a wide range of humbler, more commonplace artifacts (including such obvious categories of evidence as pottery (see fig. 7.14), lamps, terracotta figurines, coins, personal jewelry, and faunal remains) and their larger and more glamorous counterparts. Thus, to cite just a couple of examples, the imported Archaic Greek ceramics excavated by us in the Demeter Sanctuary have provided pertinent data for refining our perceptions of the ethnic and commercial links between the Greek homeland and the distant African colony beyond what can be simply derived from our literary records.[41] The same kind of information has been made available by the careful study on the part of our British colleagues of the pottery deposits from another Demeter sanctuary, this time associated with Cyrene's Pentapolis neighbor, Tauchira.[42]

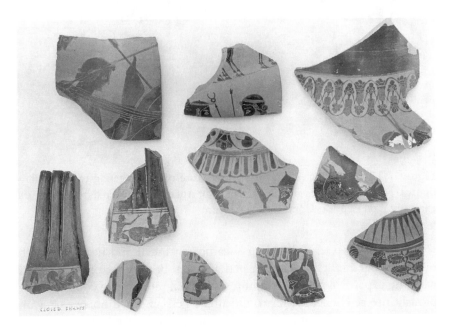

Figure 7.14 Miscellaneous sixth-century B.C. Attic black figure sherds from Cyrene's extramural Sanctuary of Demeter and Persephone. Courtesy of D. White.

Classical and Hellenistic Development 500–100 B.C.

Sculpture and architecture from Cyrene continue to highlight with brilliant effect the entire region's classical, fifth- and fourth-century development through such monuments as the bronze portrait head of her last king, Arcesilas IV, who himself suffered a literal decapitation at the hands of his domestic enemies around 440 B.C. [43] (See fig. 7.15.) These monu-

Figure 7.15 A 10.2 cm. high bronze portrait of a Libyan male, ca. 440 B.C., found in the Sanctuary of Apollo and now in the Cyrene museum. Perhaps King Arcesilas IV, the last of the Battiad monarchs. Courtesy of D. White.

ments also include the equally spectacular bronze head of a young Libyan man in the British Museum, done some time after 400 B.C. (see fig. 7.16),[44] and the enormous Temple of Zeus, seven and a half feet longer than the Parthenon, equipped in its latest Roman phase with a plaster and marble copy of Phidias' famous cult image of Zeus at Olympia.[45] (See fig. 7.17.) The only parts of the statue to survive the Christian iconoclasm of later antiquity are its marble fingers and toes. (See fig. 7.18.)

Following the death of Alexander the Great in 323 B.C. the archaeological record expands drastically throughout the province, allowing one to shift attention away from the metropolis to the province's two major port cities of Ptolemais, Barcaia's outlet to the sea, and Cyrene's own harbor town of Apollonia.

Apollonia, situated on the coast sixteen miles away from Cyrene, has today partially sunk beneath the sea, which covers its harbor-facing northern third with as much as eight feet of water. It was excavated by the Italians before World War II, by John Pedley and myself for the University of Michigan in the late 1960's, and since that time by a French team.[46] (See fig. 7.19.) With its three splendid intramural churches dating to the fifth and sixth centuries of this era and its important Ducal Palace, Apollonia is very much a Byzantine site, but its largely intact surrounding defensive walls belong to the late second, early first century B.C. The Apollonia wall system embodies nearly every advanced defensive measure under development at a time when counter-siege theory applied to urban architecture was at perhaps its most innovative and sophisticated peak. There is consistent application of an indented trace combined with projecting square towers and postern gates along the town's vulnerable land side facing the coastal plain and the use of twin massive round towers as firing-platforms for large-caliber ballistic machines on the east end facing its exposed beach frontage. (See fig. 7.20.) The use of a circular court complex recessed behind the main west city gate perhaps to establish a protected interior "killing ground," and finally the exploitation of outlying defensive forts or *phrouria* for an extensive early-warning system kept in communication with Cyrene through heliographic signal are the most prominent features of this model Hellenistic defensive system, which, appropriately enough, was never put to the test before the arrival of the Arabs.[47]

Ptolemais probably started off life as an independent settlement of unknown name soon after the founding of Cyrene, to judge from the recovery from its soil of a rim sherd from a pre-650 B.C. Attic SOS amphora as well as a later seventh century B.C. Rhodian bowl fragment.[48] It was then refounded by Ptolemy III some time between 246 and 221

Figure 7.16 Fourth-century B.C. lifesize (H. 30.5 cm.) bronze head of a native Libyan man, excavated by Smith and Porcher from under the mosaic floor of Cyrene's Apollo Temple and now in the British Museum. From R. Lullies and M. Hirmer, *Greek Sculpture,* New York: H. N. Abrams, 1957), pl, 198.

Figure 7.17 Cyrene's Temple of Zeus, first built in the sixth century B.C. and rebuilt on several later occasions, including the late second century A.D. For many years this great structure, seen here as it appeared in 1975, has been undergoing reconstruction under the supervision of the Italian Mission. Courtesy of D. White.

B.C. and named Ptolemais. A large city, squarish in plan, and laid out with an orderly street grid on the flat coastal plain, it has been only partially excavated, first by the pre-war Italians, then by the University of Chicago in the late 1950's, and most recently by the London-based Society for Libyan Studies.[49] (See fig. 7.21.) Five east-west avenues or *decumani* have been cleared, along with its two principal north-south *cardines*, producing standardized urban blocks that measure 180 by 36 m. A number of imposing individual monuments of Hellenistic date have been brought to light: the so-called Tauchira Gate on the city's west side, built with handsome drafted ashlars similar to the masonry of Apollonia's square towers.[50] The impressive *Gasr Faraoun* or "Pharaoh's Castle" that lies just west of the city's walls, a triple-leveled mausoleum whose design mimics the renowned Pharos at Alexandria.[51] And the familiar *Palazzo delle colonne*, a magnificent villa located to the southwest of the intersection of the East Cardo with the third decuman in from the sea. (See fig. 7.22.) The villa uses the width of an entire city block, and half as its north-south length.[52] It was built over rising ground and was forced to make extensive use of stone terracing to carry its northern half. The principal residential quarter of the palazzo, which lay to the south, was raised to an even greater elevation by the insertion of extra stories and raised colonnades, a tech-

Figure 7.18   Marble statue of a winged *Nike* or Victory perhaps once held in the outstretched hand of a colossal statue of Zeus erected in the Temple of Zeus at Cyrene during the later second century A.D. For many years on loan to the University Museum of Archaeology and Anthropology, University of Pennsylvania, the statue is today in the Glencairn Museum, Bryn Athyn, Pennsylvania. Courtesy of D. White.

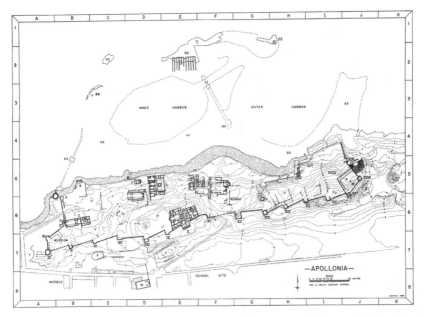

Figure 7.19   Plan of Apollonia, the Mediterranean port of ancient Cyrene. From
R. Goodchild, J. Pedley, and D. White, *Apollonia: The Port of Cyrene* (Tripoli:
Department of Antiquities, 1977), pl. lxxv).

nique described by the late John Ward-Perkins as "an echo presumably of
the vertical development imposed by the crowded urban conditions of
Alexandria."[53]

In the Marmarica, meanwhile, the old settlement at Marsa Matruh,
which, after some 600 years of dormancy, had begun to experience some
sporadic commercial contact with Greece as early as the late eighth century B.C.,[54] entered into its first real urban phase with the arrival of Alexander in 331 on his way to the famous oracle at Ammon. Greek tradition
says that it was Alexander who gave Matruh, which possesses the only
usable natural harbor between Alexandria and the Cyrenaican plateau, its
ancient name of Paraetonium.[55] It can be further assumed that the royal
visit stimulated its rapid expansion under Alexander's successors, the
Ptolemies. Unfortunately most of Paraetonium's Ptolemaic center has
been swept into oblivion as the result of the recent indiscriminate and
hasty development of the modern resort town. Excavation of the coastal
dune ridge west of the modern harbor could, however, still expose much
of interest, and consideration is being given to its clearance after the Late
Bronze Age island's final publication has gone to press.

Figure 7.20 Tower I of the third century b.c. Apollonia defensive walls as seen from the north. From its circular artillery platform, this massive installation was used to guard the coastal approach to the city from the west where more dry land was available for ground attack than today. Courtesy of D. White.

Roman Times 100 B.C.–A.D. 330

Despite the absorption of the Pentapolis by the Romans in 96 B.C.,[56] it and the Marmarican region to its east remained culturally Greek. Apart from the odd bilingual official inscription, the language of epigraphy, both in the private and public domain, literature, philosophy, and science was Greek, while in terms of religion and art, the main inspiration continued to flow mainly from the eastern Mediterranean. This is not to say that the two regions were not affected by Roman administration. Substantial grants-in-aid were distributed to Cyrene, for example, during the reign of Augustus when the city's walls were extensively repaired[57] and its chief sanctuaries refurbished, as in the case of the great Temple of Zeus, which received at the same time a new cult image.[58] As tokens of their gratitude the citizens of Cyrene erected statues honoring Octavia, the sister of Augustus, in the Demeter Sanctuary,[59] and a full-blown *Augusteum* for the worship of the Imperial family in the Agora.[60] (See fig. 7.23.) After the province was shocked by a major revolt of its Jewish citizens during the reign of Trajan (A.D. 115), which led to the physical destruction of much of the urban infrastructure throughout the entire Pentapolis as well as a massive loss of life, the emperor Hadrian (A.D. 117–138) brought in fresh settlers, including 3,000 veterans, and founded a new city between

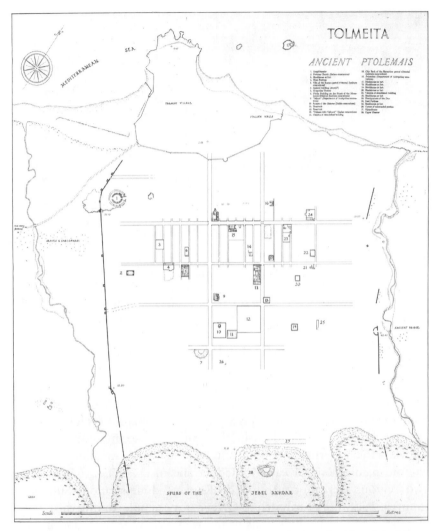

Figure 7.21 Plan of Ptolemais. From C. Kraeling, *Ptolemais: City of the Libya Pentapolis* (Chicago, Ill.: University of Chicago Press, 1962), fig. 3.

Berenice and Tauchira called Hadrianopolis.[61] At Cyrene his assistance in reconstructing roads and public buildings led to his being hailed in contemporary inscriptions as the new "Founder" of the city.[62]

Cyrene, Apollonia, Ptolemais and Tauchira all shared in the general prosperity of the second century A.D., while the old city of Euesperides, refounded in 247 B.C. as Berenice, took on special prominence as a Roman city, whose remains were the target of an important rescue excavation sponsored by the Society of Libyan Studies during the 1970's.[63] It is dur-

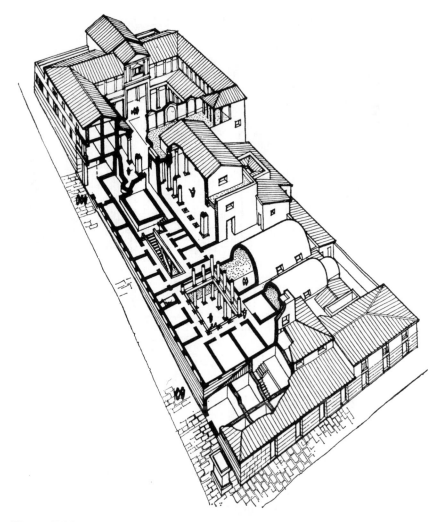

Figure 7.22 Axonometric view of the first century A.D. "Palazzo delle Colonne" at Ptolemais. From A. Boëthius and J. Ward-Perkins, *Etruscan and Roman Architecture* (Harmondsworth: Penguin, 1970), fig. 172.

ing the Roman period that life in the countryside begins to come into focus. Remains of isolated farms have been found by the hundreds, scattered over the *gebel* and coastal plain, some in the later period heavily fortified and surrounded by a water-filled moat that makes their function difficult to distinguish from military forts.[64] (See fig. 7.24.) Land barrages spanning the wadi beds for collecting rain water, sprawling semi-underground communal cisterns, and rural aqueducts all provide additional valuable evidence for the application of "dry farming" techniques to the

Figure 7.23   Reconstruction of Cyrene's *Augusteum*. From S. Stucchi, *L'agora di Cirene I: I lati nord ed est della platea inferiore* (Rome: "L'Erma" di Bretscheider, 1965), 206.

gebel region[65] as well as the coastal plain as far east as Marsa Matruh.[66] Research by the British at Berenice (Benghazi) has led to the recovery of a rich harvest of zoological and botanical data documenting the types of animals and plants normally either consumed or exported by city-dwellers but presumably produced in the rural countryside.[67]

The indigenous Libyan element must have achieved a significant degree of assimilation into mainstream society by Roman times, to judge from the relative ubiquity of funereal and honorific portraits honoring native subjects as well as the offspring of intermarriage.[68] (See fig. 7.25.) But the deliberate sabotaging of the valuable silphium crop, which depended on the Libyans preventing their sheep and goats from eating the plants which grew wild across the *gebel*, was begun by the Libyans themselves as early as the third century B.C. to protest excessive taxation and the restriction of their traditional grazing lands.[69] By the first century A.D. the plant's rarity made it an extremely expensive commodity to acquire on the foreign market and by the beginning of the fifth century

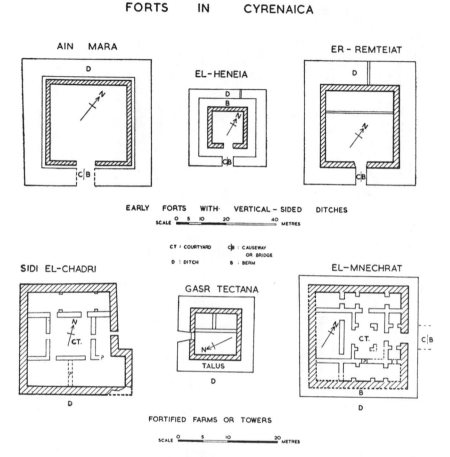

FORTS   IN   CYRENAICA

Figure 7.24   Plans of six rural fortified farms in Cyrenaica. From R. Goodchild, "The Roman and Byzantine Limes in Cyrenaica," *JRS*, xliii (1953): fig. 65.

silphium was virtually extinct. Perhaps the most haunting document of the later Libyans is the enigmatic third or fourth century A.D. remains of a sculpted open-air rock sanctuary at Slonta. Its necromantic and oracular functions indicate it was apparently used in the worship of the traditional forces of nature.[70] (See fig. 7.26.)

Byzantine Times

The final chapter in the development of the region before the seventh century invasions of the Arabs led by Amr ibn al-Aasi is characterized by a drastic curtailment in urban population, continuous armed resistance

Figure 7.25   Native limestone statue (H. 65 cm.) depicting a Libyan female deity with Isiac attributes, Cyrene Museum, Inv. 408. Courtesy of D. White.

Figure 7.26 Native Libyan sculpted bedrock reliefs from the third century A.D. (?) cave sanctuary at Slonta located south of Cyrene. The cave roof of the fertility shrine has collapsed. Courtesy of D. White.

against the incursions of tribal people onto the *gebel*, a still vigorous but increasingly isolated rural life, and above all, the rapid and often strife-ridden Christianization of the ethnic Greeks. If our concept of the province during Archaic and Classical times is largely shaped by Herodotus' *History*, our understanding of its later years is no less dependent on the writings of Synesios. Synesios, born in Cyrene to aristocratic parents, was named Bishop of Ptolemais around A.D. 410. His remarkable *Letters* provide a vivid picture of how the people of this corner of the Roman world adjusted to life marked by increasing privation and insecurity half a century after a cataclysmic earthquake had laid to waste most of the southeastern Mediterranean littoral.[71]

Although less diverse, the archaeological record is replete with examples of individual monuments during this twilight period,[72] which makes it hard to know what to select as representative. The picturesque basilica by the edge of the sea at Al-Atrun[73] a short distance east of Apollonia can suffice as one example drawn from the many paleo-Christian churches recorded for the two Libyas,[74] while it should be at least mentioned in passing that Paraitonion possessed two more churches during the time it served as capital of Marmarica as well as the seat of a bishopric.[75] (See fig. 7.27.) Many of the excavated churches have revealed traces of splendid

Figure 7.27   Al-Atrun's east church dating ca. A.D. 500, located on the coast east of Apollonia. Courtesy of D. White.

mosaics; none are more arresting than the fifty panels that decorated the floor of the nave of the east church at Gasr el-Lebia. Its iconographic, thematic content is still being digested by scholars.[76] (See fig. 7.28.)

When in the 630s the Arab invasions finally occurred, the urban populous had largely fled the upland *gebel* centers like Cyrene to take up safer residence by the sea in Apollonia and Ptolemais.[77] At the eleventh hour Apollonia attempted to drag its decaying fortifications back into some kind of hasty order by a number of means, including the desperate step of permanently shutting the city's main west gate with discarded building materials.[78] But soon after, the archaeological record suggests that the town's wealthier class of officials fled by ship to the safety of Greece and abandoned the demos they had left behind to the mercies of Amr ibn al-Aasi who took the town without striking a blow. What happened next is, as they say, another story.

Bibliography

Alfoldi-Rosenbaum, E. *A Catalogue of Cyrenaican Portrait Sculpture*. London: Oxford University Press, 1960.

Applebaum, S. *Jews and Greeks in Ancient Cyrene*. Leiden: Brill, 1979.

Figure 7.28   Mosaic dating to the first half of the sixth century A.D. from the East Church at Gasr el-Lebia west of Cyrene. One of fifty panels, this depicts a pagan satyr, transmuted into something close to the devil. Courtesy of D. White.

Barker, G., J. Lloyd, and J. Reynolds, eds. *Cyrenaica in Antiquity.* Society for Libyan Studies Occasional Paper 1; BAR International Series 236. Oxford: BAR, 1985.

Bates, O. *The Eastern Libyans.* London: MacMillan, 1914.

Chamoux, F. *Cyrène sous la monarchie des Battidaes.* Paris: E. de Boccard, 1953.

Goodchild, R. *Kyrene und Apollonia.* Zurich: Raggi, 1971.

Laronde, A. *Cyrène et la Libye hellénistique: Libykai Historiai.* Paris: Editions du Centre National de la Recherche Scientifique, 1987.

———. "La Cyrénaïque romaine, des origines à la fin des Sévères," *ANRW* 2.10.1 (1988), 1006–64.

Paribeni, F. *Catologo della scultura di cirene.* Rome: "L'Erma" di Bretschneider, 1959

Quaderni di archeologia della Libia 8 (1976): *Cirene e la Grecia.*

Quaderni di archeologia della Libia 12 (1987): *Cirene e i Libyi.*

Reynolds, J., ed. *Libyan Studies: Select Papers of the Late R. G. Goodchild.* London: Paul Elek, 1976.

Stucchi, S. *Architettura cirenaica.* Rome: "L'Erma" di Bretschneider, 1975.

Notes

1. In memory of Sandro Stucchi, the foremost authority of his generation on Libyan archaeology, who died in the summer of 1991.

2. E. Evans-Pritchard, *The Sanusi of Cyrenaica* (Oxford: Clarendon Press 1949).

3. For Lemaire see *Voyage du Sieur Paul Lucas, fait par orde du Roy, dans la Grèce, l'Asie Mineure, la Macedoine, et l'Afrique* (Paris: Chez Nicolas Simart . . . , 1712). See also R. Goodchild, "A Hole in the Heavens," in *Libyan Studies, Select Papers of the Late R. G. Goodchild* (ed. J. Reynolds; London: Paul Elek, 1976) 273–74, referred to hereafter as "A Hole in the Heavens."

4. J. Bruce, *Travels to Discover the Source of the Nile* (2nd. ed.; Edinburgh: A. Constable 1804), 7:46–52.

5. W. G. Browne, *Travels in Africa, Egypt and Syria, from the Year 1792 to 1798* (London: T. Cadell and W. Davies, 1799), 14–29.

6. See, for example, the characterizations of the dangers of travel, not untypical for their period, by A. Silva White, *From Sphinx to Oracle* (London: Hurst and Blackett, 1899), 6–11.

7. F. W. and H. W. Beechey, *Proceedings of the Expedition to Explore the Northern Coast of Africa* (London: J. Murray, 1828). Also "A Hole in the Heavens" 276–78; D. M. Bailey, "Some Beechey Plans of Buildings at Apollonia," *SLS* 12 (1980–81), 61–74.

8. J. Hamilton, *Wanderings in North Africa* (London: J. Murray, 1856); "A Hole in the Heavens" 279–81.

9. R. M. Smith and E. A. Porcher, *History of the Recent Discoveries at Cyrene* (London: Day and Son, 1864); "A Hole in the Heavens," 283–89.

10. For Cervelli see M. Delaporte, *Recueille des Voyages et des Mémoires* (Paris: Société de Géographie de Paris, 1825), 20 ff.; "A Hole in the Heavens," 274–75.

11. P. Della Cella, *Viaggio da Tripoli di Barberia alle frontiere occidentali del-l'Egitto* (Genoa: A. Ponthenier, 1819); "A Hole in the Heavens," 275.

12. J. R. Pacho, *Relation d'un voyage dans la Marmarique et la Cyrénaïque* (Paris: Firmin Didot, 1827–29); "A Hole in the Heavens," 277–78.

13. "A Hole in the Heavens" 278, 282 for bibliography.

14. J. H. von Minutoli, *Reise zum Tempel des Jupiter Ammon in der Libyschen Wüste* (Berlin: A. Rucker 1824).

15. H. Barth, *Wanderungen durch die Küstenländer des Mittelmeeres* (Berlin: W. Hertz 1849).

16. O. Bates, *The Eastern Libyans* (London: MacMillan 1914), 1–38. O. Bates, "Excavations at Marsa Matruh," *HAS* 8 (1927), 125–28; Evans-Pritchard, 29–46; A. Desio, "History of Geologic Exploration in Cyrenaica," in F. T. Barr, ed., *Geology and Archaeology of Northern Cyrenaica, Libya* (Amsterdam: Petroleum Exploration Society of Libya 1968), 79–113; R. Goodchild, *Kyrene und Apollonia* (Zurich 1971), 11–16.

17. Catullus, *Carmina* 7:3 (my translation).

18. P. Romanelli, *La Cirenaica romana* (Verbania: A. Airoldi 1943), 135–37.

19. Goodchild (supra n. 15) 17–25, 192; J. Boardman, "Evidence for the Dating of Greek Settlements in Cyrenaica," *BSA* 61 (1966) 149–66; M. Vickers and D. Gill, "Archaic Greek Pottery from Euesperides, Cyrenaica," *SLS* 17 (1986) 97–108.

20. D. White, "1985 Excavations on Bates' Island, Marsa Matruh," *JARCE* 23 (1986), 51, nn. 1, 2.

21. A. Fakhry, *The Oases of Egypt I: Siwa* (Cairo: American University in Cairo Press, 1973), 84–88.

22. S. Stucchi, *L'architettura cirenaica: Monografie di archeologia libica 9*; Rome: "L'Erma" di Bretschneider, 1975), 357–60, referred to hereafter as *Architettura cirenaica*.

23. Relations between the Iron Age Libyans and the Greeks have been the subject of an international congress at Rome and Urbino. For its proceedings see *QAL* 12 (1987): *Cirene e i Libyi*. See as well S. Applebaum, *Jews and Greeks* (Leiden: Brill, 1979), 361 *s.v.* "Libyans;" F. Chamoux, "Le Cyrénaïque, des origines a 321 a.c., d'après les fouilles et les travaux récents," *SLS* 20 (1989), 64–65.

24. E. Fabbricotti, "Divinità greche e divinità libie in rilievi di età ellenistica," *QAL* 12 (1987) 221–44.

25. E. Alfoldi-Rosenbaum, *A Catalogue of Cyrenaican Portrait Sculpture* (London: Oxford University Press, 1960), 13–28, 101–23; L. Bacchielli, "La contatto culturale greco-romano" and J. Reynolds and L. Bacchielli, "Catalogo delle stele funerarie antropomorfe," *QAL* (1987) 459–522.

26. O. Masson, "Remarques d'onomatistique cyrénéenne: quelques noms masculins en -is," *QAL* (1987), 245–48.

27. Discovered in the Archaic Artemisium in Cyrene's Apollo Sanctuary. See L. Pernier, "L'Artemision di Cirene," *AfrIt* 4 (1931), 193–95, fig. 20.

28. D. O'Connor, "New Kingdom and Third Intermediate Period, 1552–664 B.C.," in B. Trigger et al., *Ancient Egypt, A Social History* (Cambridge: Cambridge University Press, 1983), 183–278, henceforth referred to as *Egypt Social History*. A. Leahy, "The Libyan Period in Egypt: an Essay in Interpretation," *Libyan Studies* 16 (1985): 56–65. For the results of the SOAS-sponsored international conference on relations between the Libyans and the pharaonic Egyptians, see A. Leahy, ed. *Libya and Egypt, c. 1300–750* B.C. (London: SOAS Centre of Near and Middle Eastern Studies, 1990), henceforth referred to as *Libya and Egypt*.

29. A. Rowe, "A Contribution to the Archaeology of the Western Desert: II," *Bulletin of the John Rylands Library, Manchester* 36.2 (1954), 484–89; O'Connor (supra n. 28), 272; K. Kitchen, "The Arrival of the Libyans in Late New Kingdom Egypt," in *Libya and Egypt*, 17 ff.; D. O'Connor, "The Nature of Tjemhu (Libyan) Society in the Later New Kingdom" in *Libya and Egypt*, passim.

30. A . Rowe (supra n. 29) 485–86; L. Habachi, "The Military Posts of Ramesses II on the Coastal Road and the Western Part of the Delta," *BIFAO* 80 (1980), 13–30; *Egypt Social History*, 272, 274–75; Kitchen (supra n. 29), 18.

31. See Kitchen (supra n. 29), 16–17, 24, nn. 5–8 for references.

32. D. White (supra n. 20) 51–84; D. White, "Provisional Evidence for the Seasonal Occupation of the Marsa Matruh Area by Late Bronze Age Libyans," in *Libya and Egypt* 1–14; D. Conwell, "On Ostrich Eggs and Libyans. Traces of a Bronze Age People from Bates' Island, Egypt," *Expedition* 29.3 (1987), 25–34; D. White, "1987 Excavations on Bates' Island, Marsa Matruh: Second Preliminary Report," *JARCE* 26 (1989), 87–114; L. Hulin, "Marsa Matruh 1987, Preliminary Ceramic Report," *JARCE* 26 (1989), 115–26; D. White, "The Third Season at Marsa Matruh, the Site of a Late Bronze Age Trading Center on the Northeast Coast of Africa," *AJA* 94 (1990), 330.

33. Rowe (supra n. 29) 486; N. Sandars, *The Sea Peoples: Warriors of the Ancient Mediterranean* (London: Thames and Hudson, 1978); *Egypt Social History* 276–77; V. Stadelmann, "Seevölker," *Lexicon der Ägyptologie* (Wiesbaden: Harrassowitz 1984), 814–22.

34. B. Knapp, "The Thera Frescoes and the Question of Aegean contact with Libya during the Late Bronze Age," *JMA* 1 (1981), 249–79.

35. F. Chamoux, *Cyrène sous la monarchie des Battiades* (Paris: E. de Boccard, 1953); Applebaum (supra n. 21) 1–73.

36. S. Stucchi, "Le fasi construttive dell'Apollonion di Cirene," *QAL* 4 (1961), 57 ff. *Architettura cirenaica, 688, s.v.* "Tempio di Apollo." See also Goodchild (supra n. 16), 116–21, figs. 12a-c, pls. 58–60.

37. Pernier (supra n. 27); Stucchi, *Architettura cirenaica, s.v.* "Tempio do Artemide," 688.

38. R. Goodchild, J. Pedley and D. White, "Some Recent Discoveries of Archaic Sculpture at Cyrene," *LA* 3–4 (1966–67), 179–98; J. Pedley, "The Archaic Favissa at Cyrene," *AJA* 75 (1971), 39–46; D. White, "The Cyrene Sphinx, Its Capital and Its Column," *ibid.*, 47–55.

39. To attempt a full bibliography of this work would fall outside the scope of this brief report, but see J. Humphrey, "North African News Letter 2," *AJA* (1980), 75–87, especially pp. 75, 78–79. For additional bibliography see J. Lloyd, "Urban Archaeology in Cyrenaica," *SLS* 20 (1989), 79–81, 87.

40. D. White, "Cyrene's Sanctuary of Demeter and Persephone. A Summary of a Decade of Excavation," *AJA* 85 (1981) 13–30; D. White, "The Pennsylvania University Museum's Demeter and Persephone Sanctuary Project at Cyrene: A Final Progress Report?," *SLS* 20 (1989) 71–75; see especially pp. 74–75 for bibliographic references to the four final report volumes. Since then three more

DONALD WHITE**243**

final reports have appeared: D. White, *The Site's Architecture, Its First Six Hundred Years of Development* (Philadelphia: The University Museum, 1993); T. V. Buttrey, *The Coins,* and I. McPhee, *Attic Pottery* (Philadelphia: The University Museum, 1997); A. Kocybala, *The Corinthian Pottery* (The University Museum, 1999).

41. See G. Schaus, "Greek Trade Along the North African Coast in the Sixth Century B.C.," *Scripta Mediterranea* 1 (1980), 21–27; G. Schaus, *The Extramural Sanctuary of Demeter and Persephone at Cyrene, Libya. Final Reports II. The East Greek, Island and Laconian Pottery* (Philadelphia: University Museum, 1985), 2–4, 93–107.

42. J. Boardman and J. Hayes, *Excavations at Tocra 1963–1965. The Archaic Deposits* I (London: British School of Archaeology at Athens, 1966); J. Boardman and J. Hayes, *Excavations at Tocra 1963–1965. The Archaic Deposits II and the Later Deposits* (London: British School of Archaeology at Athens, 1973).

43. J. Charbonneaux, R. Martin, F. Villard, *Classical Greek Art* (New York: G. Braziller, 1972), 170, pl. 183.

44. Alfoldi-Rösenbaum, 35–36, pl. V.

45. R. Goodchild, J. Reynolds and C. Herington, "The Temple of Zeus at Cyrene," *BSR* 26 (1958), 30–62; *Architettura cirenaica,* 23–29.

46. R. Goodchild, J. Pedley and D. White, *Apollonia, the Port of Cyrene. Excavations by the University of Michigan 1965–1967* (Tripoli: Dept. of Antiquities, 1977). For work by the French see Humphrey (supra n. 39), 78; A Laronde, "Apollonia de Cyrénaïque et son histoire. Neuf ans de recherches," *CRAI* (1985), 93–115; J. Lloyd (supra n. 39), *passim.*

47. Goodchild, Pedley and White (supra n. 46), 85–156; D. White, "Static versus Reactive Defense: an In-Progress Case Study of the Apollonia and Cyrene Fortifications," *Atti del Convegno Internazionale di Studi. Macerata, 18-20 Maggio 1995* (Macerata 1998) 579-612.

48. E. Fabbricotti, "Tolemaide: una testimonianza arcaica," *QAL* 11 (1980), 5–9.

49. C. Kraeling, *Ptolemais, City of the Libyan Pentapolis* (Chicago: University of Chicago Press, 1962); O. Brogan, "Ptolemais," *Princeton Encyclopedia of Classical Sites* (Princeton: Princeton University Press, 1976), 742; J. Ward-Perkins, D. Little, and D. Mattingly, "Town Houses at Ptolemais: A Summary Report of Survey and Excavation Work in 1971, 1978–79," *SLS* 17 (1986), 109–53; D. White, "Ptolemais," *The Oxford Encyclopedia of Archaeology in the Near East 4* (Oxford University Press, 1997) 355-56.

50. Kraeling (supra n. 49) 58–60, plan IV, pls. vi-viii.

51. Ibid., 9–10, 113–15, figs. 39–40; S. Stucchi "L'architettura funeraria suburbana cirenaica," *QAL* 12 (1987), 284–94, 358–64, figs. 70–82, 190–98.

52. *Architettura cireniaca,* 682, s.v. "Palazzo delle Colonne."

53. A. Boethius and J. Ward-Perkins, *Etruscan and Roman Architecture* (Harmondsworth: Penguin 1970), 462.

54. D. White (supra n. 20), 74–75. This date is based on a single as yet

unpublished SOS amphora sherd identified by D. Bailey. For additional seventh- and sixth-century ceramic material see D. Bailey, "A preliminary Note on the Greek, Hellenistic and Roman Pottery," *Jounal of Roman Archaeology Supplement No. 10: Archaeological Research in Roman Egypt* (1996), 79.

55. Bates, *HAS* (supra n. 16), 128, 132–33.

56. For the province's Roman period see A. Laronde, "La Cyrénaïque romaine, de origines a la fin de Sévères," *ANRW* 2:10.1 (1987), 1001–64.

57. R. Goodchild, *Cyrene and Apollonia, an Historical Guide* (3rd. ed., Tripoli: Dept. of Antiquities, Libyan Arab Republic, 1970), 25.

58. Goodchild (supra n. 55), 99; Goodchild, Reynolds and Herington (supra n. 45) 38–39; E. Paribeni, *Catalogo delle sculture di Cirene* (Rome: "L'Erma" di Bretschneider, 1959), 77, pls. 104–5.

59. D. White, "Excavations in the Demeter Sanctuary at Cyrene 1971," *LA* 9-10 (1972–1973), 185, pl. lxxix, a.

60. S. Stucchi, *L'agorà di Cirene I: I lati nord ed est della platea inferiore* (Rome: "L'Erma" di Bretschneider, 1965), 207–20.

61. Applebaum (supra n. 23), 242 ff.

62. P. Fraser, "Hadrian and Cyrene," *JRS* 40 (1950), 84.

63. Lloyd (supra n. 39), 87 *c.v.* "Berenice" for citations of the first four volumes of the Society for Libyan Studies' final publication of its work at Sidi Khrebish, Benghazi.

64. *Architettura cirenaica*, 358–60.

65. R. Goodchild, "Roman Farming in Libya," *Geographical Magazine* 25 (1952–53), 70–80.

66. G. Walpole, "An Ancient Aqueduct West of Marsa Matruh," *Ministry of Finance, Survey of Egypt,* Paper No. 42 (1932).

67. G. Barker, "Agricultural Organization in Classical Cyrenaica: the Potential of Subsistence and Survey Data," in G. Barker, J. Lloyd, and J. Reynolds, eds., *Cyrenaica in Antiquity* (BAR International Series 236; Oxford: BAR, 1985), 122.

68. L. Bacchielli, "La scultura *Libya* in Cirenaica e la variabilità delle risposte al contatto culturale greco-romano," *QAL* 12 (1987), 459–527.

69. Applebaum (supra n. 23), 20–21, 23, 84, 111, 122–24, 206–7. F. Chamoux, "Le silphion," *BAR International Series 236: Cyrenaica in Antiquity* (1985), 165-72.

70. M. Luni, "Il santuario rupestre *Libyo* delle 'Immagini' a Slonta (Cirenaica)," *QAL* 12 (1987), 415–58.

71. R. Goodchild, "Synesius of Cyrene: Bishop of Ptolemais," in J. Reynolds, ed., *Libyan Studies: Select Papers of the Late R. G. Goodchild* (London: Paul Elek, 1976), 239–54; D. Roques, *Synésios de Cyrène et la Cyrénaïque du Bas-Empire* (Paris: Editions du Centre National de la Recherche Scientifique, 1987); D. Roques, "Études sur la Correspondance de Synésios de Cyrène," *Latomus* 205 (1989).

72. The easiest way to gauge the accuracy of this statement is to look through *Architettura cirenaica*, 358 ff.

73. Architettura cirenaica, 377–81, figs. 378–79.

74. R. Goodchild, "Chiese e battisteri bizantine della Cirenaica," *Corsi di cultura sull'arte ravennate e bizantina* (1966) 205–23; *Architettura cirenaica* 362–415.

75. D. White, "1987 Excavations on Bates's Island, Marsa Matruh: Second Preliminary Report," *JARCE* 26 (1989) 88–93; R. Goodchild, "A Byzantine Chapel at Marsa Matruh (Paraetonium)," *JARCE* 28 (1991) 201–11.

76. E. Alföldi-Rosenbaum and J. Ward-Perkins, *Justinianic Mosaic Pavements in Cyrenaican Churches* (Rome 1980) 121–33.

77. R. Goodchild, "Byzantines, Berbers and Arabs in Seventh Century Libya," *Antiquity* 41 (1967).

78. Goodchild, Pedley and White (supra n. 46) 111–12, 141–43.

8

Attitudes toward Blacks
in the Greek and Roman World:
Misinterpretations of the Evidence

F R A N K   M.   S N O W D E N ,   J R.

✺

Terminology: "Ethiopians," "Blacks," "Negroes," "Mulattoes"

Before turning to the subject of this paper, I should explain my choice of the word "black" to designate the dark- and black-skinned Africans of classical texts. Ethiopian (*Aithiops, Aethiops*), literally a burnt-faced person, was the most common generic word used by Greeks and Romans when referring to dark- and black-skinned people who lived south of Egypt and on the southern fringes of northwest Africa. The Ethiopians, most often mentioned in classical records, populated the Nile Valley south of Egypt (Kush, Ethiopia, Nubia), while others are reported to have lived in northwest Africa, roughly from present-day Fezzan in southwest Libya and the oases of Tunisia to the Atlantic coast of southern Morocco.

Scholars differ in their views as to the proper anthropological classification of the African blacks known to the classical world. The Greeks and Romans, however, in detailed descriptions and strikingly realistic portraits, have provided a very accurate and precise picture of the African peoples whom they described as Ethiopians. As early as the second millennium

B.C., artists on the islands of Crete and Cyprus, and in mainland Greece from the sixth century onward, depicted many individuals with variations of dark or black skin, woolly or tightly coiled hair, broad or flat noses, and thick lips—features of Ethiopians also portrayed realistically later in various parts of the Roman world (see figure 8.1–2). Written records were equally precise as to the physical characteristics of African blacks.[1] Ethiopians were black and flat-nosed in Xenophanes;[2] black with the wooliest hair of all mankind in Herodotus;[3] black, flat-nosed, and woolly-haired in Diodorus;[4] and in the *Moretum*[5] described with the detail and accuracy of later anthropological classifications of the so-called Negroid type. Regardless of modern opinion as to the precise racial identity or the proper anthropological classifications of ancient Ethiopians or Nubians, the Ethiopians of classical records as well as the many black- or dark-skinned persons depicted by ancient artists bear a close resemblance to physical types designated in the modern world as "colored," "black," or "Negro"—terms avoided by some scholars in discussion of African blacks of the ancient world.[6]

Following classical usage, I use a color word, "black," considered by Greeks and Romans as the most characteristic and unusual feature of Ethiopians—the blackest and most woolly-haired people on earth—as a general designation for the dark- and black-skinned African Ethiopians of this paper. Like the word "Ethiopian," "black" in my usage emphasizes color. At times I use "Negro" or "Negroid" when I have in mind some modern anthropological classifications of persons having variations of the physical characteristics included in such descriptions. And I designate as mulatto or mixed, individuals whose features, in my judgment or that of others, suggest black-white mixture.

Review of the Literature

More than twenty years ago W. R. Connor referred to the modern treatment of Ethiopians in the Greek and Roman world as a "shoddy chapter in the history of classical scholarship," and observed that "the signs of bigotry which we find in studying the history of classical antiquity are almost always among the modern scholars, not among their ancient subjects."[7] R. Lonis attributes the diversity in interpretations of Graeco-Roman attitudes toward Ethiopians to the existence of prejudices and ideological suppositions.[8] J. Desanges has noted the often dismaying prejudice of modern scholarship which projects its own complexes into antiquity.[9]

Figure 8.1   Herm with the head of a Negro (front) from the Baths of Antoninus Pius, Carthage. Mid-second century A.D., black limestone. Courtesy of the Musée National du Bardo, Tunis.

Figure 8.2 Herm with the head of a Negro (profile). Courtesy of the Musée National du Bardo, Tunis.

Figure 8.3 Head of a Negro youth. Second to first century B.C. Courtesy of the Charles Edwin Wilbour Fund, The Brooklyn Museum.

Observations such as these raise serious questions about some modern interpretations of the Ethiopians of classical texts and of the blacks depicted by Greek and Roman artists. It is for this reason that I have chosen as the topic for this paper, "Attitudes toward Blacks in the Greek and Roman World: Misinterpretations of the Evidence."

The first somewhat detailed examination of Negroid types in classical art was published in 1929. This study, *The Negro in Greek and Roman Civilization: A Study of the Ethiopian Type,*[10] was devoted primarily to blacks in the Greek world, confining its treatment of blacks in Roman literature to nineteen pages. Furthermore, even in her interpretation of Greek art, G. H. Beardsley made only scant use of the many references to Ethiopians in Greek literature. Her study revealed other serious shortcomings found also in some more recent treatments of blacks: (1) a failure to relate the blacks in the Graeco-Roman world to their African background; (2) insufficient appreciation of the import of the combined documentary and iconographical evidence; (3) a practice of making broad, general statements about blacks on the basis of a few lines from a single author or, at most, from a few classical texts without considering the total image of blacks in the ancient world; (4) a tendency to read modern racial concepts into ancient documents, and to see color prejudice where none existed; (5) and a failure to make use of relevant research in the social sciences on the origin and nature of color prejudice.

It was not until 1970 and later that the copious scattered sources relating to blacks in the Greek and Roman world were assembled and interpreted.[11] Even before the basic evidence was collected, however, scholars in various contexts expressed opinions on Greek and Roman attitudes toward blacks. Some of these opinions were clearly influenced by later conceptions of blacks. M. Bieber, for example, described a black woman dancer depicted on a fourth-century B.C. vase as an "old woman with grotesque features."[12] The woman, however, has been described by scholars acquainted with present-day Africa as an authentic portrayal of an African dancer and as a genuine ethnographic document.[13] C. T. Seltman observed that the ugliness of the Negro seems to have appealed alike to sculptor, engraver, and painter.[14] W. N. Bates noted that as a rule the Negro is most absurdly drawn in Greek vases.[15] M. Robertson observed that Memnon is represented as white because of the Greek aversion to Negroid features.[16] G. H. Beardsley wrote that "Memnon because of his great beauty was evidently white;" that "the average white man is inclined to view humorously a serious portrayal of an African negro"; and that "the negro perhaps unfortunately has always appealed to the comic side of the Caucasian" (a comment on a group of fifth-century B.C. vases depicting a Negro seized by a crocodile).[17] D. K. Hill, in describing a Hellenistic bronze of a Negro, considered the pose of the Negro one "no white person would think of assuming."[18]

Prior to 1970 there were also scholars, however, who commented on what they considered differences between ancient and modern views of blacks. J. Bryce observed that in the Roman Empire we hear little of any repugnance to dark-skinned Africans;[19] E. Baring, that color antipathy considered by itself, formed no bar to social intercourse in antiquity;[20] E. E. Sikes, that the ancients were quite free from the antipathy of the color bar;[21] A. E. Zimmern, that the Greeks showed no trace of color prejudice;[22] W. L. Westermann, that Greek society had no color line;[23] T. J. Haarhoff, that there never has been any color prejudice in Italy;[24] C. Kluckhohn, that the Greeks did not fall into the error of biological racism, that color was no stigma, and that men were not classified as black and white, but as free or servile;[25] and H. C. Baldry, that the Greeks were spared the modern curse of color prejudice.[26]

Opinions on classical attitudes toward blacks which have appeared in the last twenty years have been expressed in reviews of the earlier detailed studies of blacks in the Greek and Roman world,[27] in a few specialized articles,[28] and in monographs on blacks in classical antiquity.[29] B. H. Warmington in his review of *Before Color Prejudice: The Ancient View of Blacks* wrote that the author's demonstration of the lack of color prejudice" expressed in both his books is certainly correct (though a few scholars have doubted it)."[30] Very persuasive arguments on the question of the absence of color prejudice in the classical world, according to L. Cracco Ruggini, have been made in *Blacks in Antiquity: Ethiopians in the Greco-Roman Experience*.[31] In R. S. W. Hawtrey's opinion the view that there were no traces of the color bar in antiquity is not a new one but until the publication of *Blacks in Antiquity* the evidence had not been assembled with such completeness.[32] W. R. Connor observed that *Blacks in Antiquity* made "it possible to correct errors and omissions that have passed for the truth and let us glimpse a society which for all its faults and failures never made color the basis for judging a man."[33] And L. Castiglione remarked that classical antiquity did not know discrimination on the basis of the color of the skin, or the concept of apartheid, and added that the truth of these facts is indisputable and clearly demonstrated in *Blacks in Antiquity*.[34]

Misreadings of Classical and Early Christian
Attitudes toward Blacks

I now turn to an examination of the views of the few scholars who have seen what they consider evidence of color prejudice in the Greek and Roman world. In the first place, it should be emphasized that in the entire corpus of classical literature, with its countless references to Ethiopians, and in other relevant ancient sources, often confirmed by repeated events of history, there are only a few ancient concepts or notions that have been interpreted by some scholars as evidence of antiblack sentiment. And they are primarily these: the so-called ugliness of the Negroes of classical artists, the somatic norm image, black-white symbolism, and certain physiognomonical beliefs.

Some scholars strangely regard simple realistic portrayals of blacks as revealing a "degree of antipathy . . . [and] a sensory aversion to the physiognomy of blacks."[35] As early as 1879, however, E. de Chanot foresaw the importance of the classical representations of Negroes in his comments on the anthropological accuracy of south Italian lamps depicting Negroes and the value of these for Graeco-Roman relations with black Africans.[36] E. Mveng of the Federal University of Cameroon and others acquainted with contemporary Africans have seen in the vast tableau of Graeco-Roman art a profusion of exact physical detail in the depiction of blacks.[37] In addition, a wide range of mixed black-white types did not escape the eye of ancient artists. The emergence of mulattoes in Greek vase-painting about the middle of the fifth century B.C., and later, shows that the blacks depicted by artists, even in mythological scenes, often reflected anthropological reality. The mulattoes, often youthful, who served as models for fifth-century Greek artists, were in all likelihood the children of Greek women by Xerxes' Ethiopian soldiers.[38] Apparently such mulatto types attracted the attention of artists before Aristotle, in the next century, illustrated the transmission of physical characteristics in the descendants of black-white racial mixture by citing the families of a woman from Elis and another from Sicily.[39] As J. Boardman has observed, "art historians have perhaps been slow to recognize mixed black-white types, while the pure Negroid has, of course, always been readily observed."[40] Only the anthropologically naive or those unacquainted with black-white racial mixture in the modern world would deny the obvious Negroid admixture in many of the portraits of blacks from ancient workshops.

To see caricature and mockery in an artist's use of thick lips, flat nose, and exaggerated prognathism,[41] or to consider most of the Graeco-Roman portrayals of black as "hideous and implicitly racist in perspective,"[42] shows a complete misunderstanding of the artists' interest in Negroid types. Whites of many races, as well as gods and heroes, appeared in comic or satirical scenes. If Negroes had been depicted only as caricatures, had that been the rule and not the exception, there might be some justification for a negative view of blacks. By far the majority of scholars, see an astonishing variety and vitality in the blacks of ancient art, and penetrating depictions of types which appealed to the craftsmen for several reasons. Negro models presented the artists with a challenge to their skill to represent by texture and paint the distinctive features of blacks and with an opportunity, by contrasting blacks with white Mediterranean types, to express the infinite variety of a common human nature. The obvious aesthetic attractiveness of Negro models to many artists, some the finest from ancient workshops, and numerous sympathetic portrayals have given rise to a common view that ancient artists were free from prejudice in their depictions of blacks.[43]

Some scholars have seen color prejudice in certain references to the Ethiopian's color and evidence of a "child-psychological theory" which regarded black skin as unpleasant. Though obviously aware of the black man's color, classical authors attached no basic significance to the color of the skin. Ethiopians do not astonish Greeks because of their blackness and their physical appearance: such a reaction, Agatharchides wrote, ceases at childhood.[44] This statement was not only an accurate assessment of Greek reaction to the Ethiopian's color, but a sound observation on an aspect of child behavior noted by modern psychologists, according to whom "four-year-olds are normally interested, curious, and appreciative of differences in racial[45] groups." Children do not *necessarily* attach value judgments to racial differences, "especially those leading to the formation of racial stereotypes, *unless* they are exposed to socializing forces characterized by overt racial consciousness and/or hostility."[46] In other words, Agatharchides was merely recording the normal reaction of young children to observed differences in skin color, and he was not setting forth, as A. Dihle has suggested, a theory of aversion to the black man's color rooted in childhood.[47] It is not unlikely that a Greek or Roman parent, in response to a child's curiosity about an Ethiopian's color, gave either a mythological or a "scientific" explanation, perhaps both: either the story of Phaëthon who lost control of his father's chariot and blackened the skin and curled the hair of Ethiopians by coming too close to earth;[48] or some version of the environment theory setting forth the effect of environment on the physical characteristics of peoples and their manner of life. The anthropological explanation of the origin of racial differences was applied in a uniform manner to all peoples, black and white alike. The basic human substance—the same in all people—was tempered differently in different climates. The black, woolly-haired Ethiopians of the deep south and the fair, straight-haired Scythians of the far north came to be cited as the favorite illustrations of this theory. These geographical and anthropological contrasts, reflected in art as early as the Janiform black-white heads of the sixth century B.C. in Greece[49] and spelled out in the Hippocratic corpus,[50] were amplified and illustrated again and again by Greek and Roman authors.[51] Pliny the Elder, for example, wrote that Ethiopians are clearly burnt by the sun and have at birth a scorched appearance, curly beards and hair, whereas inhabitants of the opposite region of the earth have white frosty skin, and straight yellow hair. Ethiopians are wise, Pliny adds, because of the mobility of the climate, while northerners are fierce because of the rigidity of theirs.[52] And in view of the vast climate differences, as Diodorus observed, there was nothing unusual in the fact that Scythians and Ethiopians differed in so many respects from Greeks and Romans.[53]

According to the environment theory, people, regardless of color, who lived at the outer regions of the earth were reported to follow a primitive way of life. Wild habits of both Ethiopians and Scythians, for example, were attributed by the geographer Ptolemy to climate—excessive cold in one instance and torrid heat in the other.[54] In fact, according to Strabo, it was white people, not black, who were said to be the most "savage" in the world—more savage than the Britons were the inhabitants of ancient Ireland who considered it honorable to devour their fathers when they died and to have intercourse with their mothers and sisters.[55] Likewise, those who have interpreted physiognomonical observations as evidence of color prejudice have overlooked the fact that such beliefs, like many comments on "primitive" peoples, applied to whites as well as to blacks. The author of the *Physiognomonica*, for example, wrote that swarthy Egyptians and Ethiopians, as well as the woolly-haired, were cowardly, but he also stated that the excessively fair were likewise cowardly.[56] In short, blacks were not stereotyped as either "wild" or sole possessors of physiognomonical flaws.

Those who have seen color prejudice in various Scythian-Ethiopian and similar contrasts have failed to recognize the relevance of the environment theory and have overlooked the fact that such contrasts were purposely used later in important classical statements of conviction that race is of no consequence in evaluating men and in early Christian versions of the view that all whom God created He created equal and alike. Menander, for example, stated that it makes no difference whether one is as different from a Greek as an Ethiopian or a Scythian: it is merit, not race that counts.[57] In this statement Menander was attacking the validity of birth as a criterion for judging an individual, but he was not suggesting, as some have argued, the existence of a special belief concerning the inferiority of the Ethiopian qua Ethiopian.[58] And in his rejection Menander chose the familiar Ethiopian-Scythian contrasts which evoked the well known opposites of the environment theory and made it clear that all mankind was included. These northern and southern people, first used in geographical and anthropological contrasts, now appeared in a social and moral context in Menander, and, later, were to figure prominently in a highly spiritual Christian imagery.

In light of the fact that the Greeks and Romans regarded black and white skin as mere geographical accidents, with no stigma attached to the color of the skin, it is strange that some scholars have interpreted references to ethnocentric aesthetic preferences as evidence of color prejudice. Like other peoples before and after them, Greeks and Romans had narcissistic canons of physical beauty—what H. Hoetink has called a "somatic norm image."[59] Classical authors, while recognizing the subjectivity of their ethnocentric criteria, frequently stated a preference for "Mediterranean" complexion and features—a middle point between the extremes of blond, blue-eyed northerners, and black, wooly-haired southerners.[60] In view of widespread narcissistic standards, there is nothing odd or pejorative about preferences for a "white" type in a predominantly white society, or for dark-or black-skinned beauties in a predominantly black society. What was unusual, however, in the Graeco-Roman world was the spirit of those who observed that classical standards of beauty were relative and perhaps most surprising from the point of view of some twentieth-century commentators is the number of those who openly expressed a preference for dark- or black-skinned women.

Dio Chrysostom raised the question as to whether or not there was a foreign as well as a Hellenic type of beauty.[61] Men differed in their definitions of beauty, according to Sextus Empiricus, Ethiopians preferring the blackest and most flat-nosed; Persians, the whitest and most hooked-nosed; and others considering those intermediate in color and features as the most beautiful.[62] Herodotus, the first European writer to express an opinion about the physical appearance of blacks described Macrobian Ethiopians as the most handsome of all men.[63] Asclepiades praised the beauty of a certain Didyme in these words: "Gazing at her beauty, I melt like wax before the fire. And if she is black, what difference to me? So are coals, but when we light them, they shine like rose buds."[64] Ovid's Sappho tells Phaon that she is not fair but reminds him that Andromeda, dark with the hue of her native Ethiopia, captivated Perseus by her beauty.[65] Martial writes that, though he was sought by a girl whiter than a washed swan, than silver, snow, lily, or privet, he preferred a girl blacker than an ant, pitch, jackdaw, or cicada.[66]

"White," then, was for many in the ancient world a basic element in the somatic norm image, as it has always been in predominantly white societies, but it is often overlooked that there were "white" types which did not measure up to the "Mediterranean" image of Greeks and Romans. Furthermore, it is because of a failure to recognize the full import of the classical somatic norm image that adaptations of this image have been misinterpreted. For example, in the interpretation of an inscription from Antinoë in Egypt in which a master in the third-century addresses a black slave in these words: "Among the living I was very black, darkened by the rays of the sun, but my soul, ever blooming with white flowers, won my master's good will, for beauty is second to a noble soul, and it is this that covered my black body."[67] J. Desanges considers the contrast between soul and physical appearance in this epitaph—later a commonplace in the ecumenical black-white imagery of early Christian writings—evidence of a prejudice imbedded in whites, and an expression of a view that recognized blacks as fully human in spite of their blackness.[68] D. Wiesen writes that the emphasis on the slave's essential whiteness would have been unnecessary "if there had existed no tendency to regard Negro features as pejorative."[69] L. Cracco Ruggini modifies her agreement with such a view by pointing out that the prejudice expressed in the epitaph in biological and environmental terms is far removed from the sociological racism of the United States.[70] W. L. Westermann, however, in referring to the epitaph as "a remarkable example of the lack of racial feeling based upon distinctions of color,"[71] was apparently influenced in part by the overall favorable view of blacks in the ancient world. Remarkable though the sentiment may be from a modern point of view, it was what should be expected in light of the initial environmental approach to racial differences, and various views of the community of man conceived by sophists, Hellenic theorists, and early Christian writers.

Like those scholars who have maintained that ancient artists highlighted the Negro's ugliness, there are also some who, in the interpretation of several classical texts, have apparently been influenced by similar views of the Negro's physical features. G. Highet observed that it is not possible to tell whether Terence was a Negro or a Berber, but that since the poet was freed *ob ingenium et formam*[72] and since "Romans did not think Negro features handsome, we might infer that he was one of the fine-boned, sensitive, frail Berber types."[73] The description of Scybale, the black slave woman in the *Moretum* has been incorrectly cited as an example of a Roman aversion to the physical features of blacks. Arguments for this interpretation have been reduced to absurdity by L. A. Thompson in his *Romans and Blacks,* who regards the anonymous description of the black woman as an example of mockery and "open distaste . . . for . . . the somatic appearance of the 'typical' *Aethiops.*"[74] The description, however, is merely a detailed delineation of the physical characteristics of a black woman, not unlike that of some anthropological descriptions of Negroes: "African in race, her whole figure proof of her country, hair tightly curled, lips thick, color dark, chest broad, breasts pendulous, belly somewhat pinched, feet broad and ample."[75] She appears as the sole companion of a humble farmer who, even Thompson admits, is "fully comfortable in, and satisfied with, the familiar company of a black slave woman as his sole house-companion."[76] In spite of the realistically and sympathetically described life of the farmer, J. Desanges, followed by Thompson, suggests that the slave's name Scybale was derived from *skubalon* which has been translated as "shit."[77] A simple and more plausible explanation, however, in the context of a poem highlighting salad would be the herb *skuba—skouba.*[78] Similarly, Thompson's excremental suggestion that the lines "*corvus carbo cinis concordant cuncta colori. /Quod legeris nomen, convenit: Aethiopis,*" may be intended to evoke an imagery of *caca*—(excrement) is more than just dubious.[79]

Another illustration of an interpretation that has given inadequate attention to the full import of Greek and Roman ethnocentric aesthetic preferences is a tribute by the sixth-century poet Luxorius to a black athlete, Olympius, an idol of the amphitheater in Carthage.[80] The tribute was not, as Thompson argues, an exaltation of the white man's whiteness illustrating Roman worship of the somatic norm image[81] but was in the tradition of many before him who either emphasized the inconsequence of color in judging individual worth, rejected the traditional somatic norm image, or commented on the relativity of classical standards of beauty. Luxorius was not only describing black physical beauty but was expressing another important idea: excellence is found among all men, whatever their race. Menander had said that natural bent, not whether one is Ethiopian or Scythian, determines nobility;[82] Agatharchides, that success in battle depends not upon color but upon courage and knowledge of warfare.[83] Similarly, for Luxorius, it was Olympius' strength and skill in the arena that mattered. In the sixth century, Luxorius, in spirit of earlier Greeks, Romans, and Christians who wished to emphasize fundamental beliefs, deliberately chose and adapted a familiar symbolism—black in a white society with a somatic norm image of white—to highlight the inconsequence of color in evaluating men. Olympius' glory, Luxorius concluded, would live ever after him, and Carthage, a predominantly white community would always remember him.

The misinterpretation of a passage in Juvenal's second satire provides another illustration of a failure to comprehend the significance of Greek and Roman somatic black-white contrasts. Three words in this satire— *derideat Aethiopem albus*[84]—in the opinion of G. H. Beardsley, sum up Roman racial feeling.[85] The passage in which the words appear is one of those D. Wiesen cited as evidence that Juvenal despises the physical being of blacks and that the satirist "attached a special stigma to the physical attributes of blacks and finds in them faults which are neither of their own making, nor capable of being corrected."[86] The three words *derideat Aethiopem albus,* however, appear in a satire of one hundred and seventy lines in which Juvenal is not writing about blacks, much less a diatribe against blacks. In a passage concerning the practice of criticizing flaws in others resembling one's own, the satirist writes "a straight-legged man may laugh at a crooked-legged man, a white man at a black man" but, he continues by asking who will not confound heaven with earth and sky with sea if Verres denounces a thief; Milo, a cut-throat; if Clodius condemns adulterers; if Catiline upbraids Cethegus. In other words, straight and crooked, black and white are opposites, but the other combinations are not. But much more important, the *Aethiopem albus* contrast is largely a reflection of the familiar Roman ethnocentric criteria, and has no broader significance. Juvenal himself has the somatic norm image in mind when he writes that women in Meroë with large breasts (bigger than their babes) and Germans with blue eyes and yellow hair (greasy curls twisted into a horn) evoke no astonishment in their own countries because their physical traits are common, and that no one laughs at African pygmies because the whole population is no taller than one foot.[87]

Seneca also selected Ethiopians and Germans to illustrate his observations on the somatic norm image. Unlike Juvenal, however, Seneca found no reason for astonishment or laughter in somatic differences,[88] for like Diodorus who saw nothing surprising in such obvious differences, he observed that neither the color of Ethiopians nor the red hair of Germans is notable among their own people, and nothing in a man is to be considered odd that is characteristic of a nation.[89] In short, the total evidence relating to Roman ethnocentric standards of physical beauty does not warrant L. A. Thompson's conclusions that among the educated there was an "unashamed and open 'worship' of the somatic norm image"[90] or that "crinkly *Aethiops* hair, blond and greased German locks"[91] particularly aroused sensory aversion and offended the aesthetic sensibilities of Romans of the upper classes.

I now turn to misinterpretations of black-white symbolism in classical and Christian authors. Among Greeks and Romans, white was generally associated with light, the day, Olympus, victims sacrificed to the higher gods, with good character, and good omens; black with darkness and night, the Underworld, death, chthonian deities, with bad character and ill omens. Recent studies, however, point out that there seems to be a "widespread communality in feelings about black and white," that among both Negroes and whites the color white tends to evoke a positive and black a negative reaction, and that both colors figure prominently in the areas of human experience concerned with religion and the supernatural.[92] Furthermore, research in the social sciences has raised the question of whether individuals who react negatively to the color black also develop an antipathy toward dark-skinned people, and that, though such a reaction is in theory plausible, the evidence is far from conclusive.[93]

In view of the widespread association of white with good and black with evil, interpretations of the Greek and Roman application of a black-white imagery to Ethiopians as evidence of antiblack sentiment are questionable. The introduction of dark-skinned peoples—Ethiopian, Egyptian, Garamantian—in ill-omened contexts was obviously related to classical associations of the color black and darkness with death and the Underworld, and was in many respects a natural development. At the time of Caligula's death, for example, according to Suetonius, a nocturnal performance was in rehearsal in which scenes from the lower world were enacted by Egyptians and Ethiopians.[94] Homer's and Vergil's nether regions were dark and murky; the god of the Underworld himself was often described as black; and the ferryman Charon, son of Erebus and Night, was gloomy, grim, and terrible in his squalor. Why not add a bit of realism by casting blacks as actors in an Underworld scene since blacks were available and since the ancient world, unlike some post-classical societies, did not discriminate against black actors?

A metrical inscription from Hadrumetum (Sousse in present-day Tunisia) should be cited in full because, in the opinion of some commentators, it epitomizes antiblack sentiment: "The dregs of the Garamantes have come up into our region and the black slave rejoices in his pitch-black body. If the voice issuing from his lips did not make him sound human, the grim ghost would be frightening upon sight. Hadrumetum, may ill-omened Tartarus carry off your monster for itself. The abode of Dis should have him as a guardian."[95] Although the reference to the Garamantian is obviously pejorative and probably reflects hostility toward the Garamantes, "an indomitable tribe and one always engaged in brigandage on their neighbors,"[96] *faex Garamantarum* should probably be translated as "Garamantian dregs," like Juvenal's dregs from Greece (*faecis Achaei*),[97] and not as "shit," as it has been sometimes rendered. In fact, the inscription seems to be largely a poetic *jeu d' esprit* on the common theme of death and the Underworld, not an antiblack diatribe. The pitch-black Garamantian reminds the poet of Vergil's grim warden Charon (*portitor . . . horrendus*), guardian of black Tartarus (*nigra Tartara*); and the door of black Dis (*atri ianua Ditis*) in Vergil's Underworld is echoed in the grim ghost (*horrida larva*), whom the inscription would have as guardian of the abode of Dis.[98]

In view of the overall favorable attitude toward blacks in the Greek and Roman world, it is unlikely that the association of dark-skinned people with evil had an adverse impact on day-to-day reactions to blacks. The association of the Ethiopian's color with evil did not arise until long after the favorable image of blacks had been firmly established. It was the period after the mid-third century, according to L. Gracco Ruggini, that saw the development of concepts linking the color of the skin with ill omens, evil, wickedness, and sin. These notions, Cracco Ruggini further suggests, were associated with the image of Ethiopians as a dangerous military force and as a threat both to the Egyptian frontier and to the north African provinces.[99] The military threats in Egypt and North Africa, in the opinion of R. Lonis, were a principal factor in generating negative Roman opinions of blacks, and Roman hostility to the Garamantes was transferred to Ethiopians. And, in this connection, Lonis cites the inscription from Hadrumetum, already referred to, as an expression of the Roman fear, scorn, and hatred toward the Garamantes and their brothers who lived in Africa.[100] B. H. Warmington, however, contrasting the Roman experiences with the Germans and Ethiopians, rules out fear as a cause of color prejudice in antiquity and adds that neither Greeks nor Romans had any reason to fear Ethiopians either south of Egypt or in northwest Africa.[101] L. A. Thompson states that in any case there is no reason to believe that Roman difficulties in Africa, even though responsible for some pejorative images of blacks, gave rise to a fixed image of a black threat in other parts of the Empire unaffected by the anti-Roman activity of African blacks.[102] Furthermore, there is nothing in the art of northwest Africa (the source of the Garamantian inscription and the tribute to Olympius) which suggests that artists of the third century and later viewed blacks with hostility or attached importance to the color of the skin. The art of this late period, especially the mosaics, and written sources as well, point to no obstacles that blacks encountered because of their color.[103] Like other north Africans, blacks earned a livelihood in seaports, town, and country, participated in native uprisings against the Romans,[104] and won the plaudits of the populace for their skill in the amphitheater.[105] Blacks in northwest Africa intermarried with the predominantly white population[106] and left the influence of their native rituals on others.[107] They figured prominently in St. Augustine's Ethiopian exegesis, and the correspondence between a bishop and a deacon concerning the spiritual welfare of a young Ethiopian slave from inner northwest Africa records an interesting application of the principle enunciated by St. Augustine that Christianity, as the glory of God demanded, was to embrace Ethiopians who lived at the ends of the earth.[108]

And finally on this point, it should be emphasized that at the same time that the notion linking dark-skinned peoples and omens of disaster and death appeared proponents of the deeply rooted environment theory continued to set forth unprejudiced explanations of physical differences; the ancient image of just Ethiopians was being reinforced; and Christian writers were purposely using a rich black-white imagery to emphasize the black man's membership in the Christian brotherhood.

Those who have considered certain aspects of black-white symbolism in early Christian writings as antiblack in sentiment have given insufficient attention to the Christian black-white imagery in its entirety. In early Christian writings black-white symbolism figured prominently in two contexts, demonological and exegetical. In the visions of saints and monks, demons at times assumed the shape of "Ethiopians." Whether these Ethiopians, incarnations of evil and temptation, some repulsive and unsightly, appeared as women, little boys, or giants, the emphasis was on the color black—a contrast between the blackness of evil and light of God. A key to the emphasis on color appears especially in the description of a female demon in the *Acts of Peter* as "most Ethiopian (*Ethiopissimam*), not Egyptian but altogether black,"[109] phraseology reminiscent of the gradations of color found in classical descriptions of Ethiopians, Indians, Egyptians, and other dark peoples.[110] As J. M. Courtès has pointed out, "The concept of the black hardly goes beyond that of skin coloration, which seems to be the only racial characteristic taken into consideration by Christian writers . . . blackness [is regarded] simply as the darkest of various shades of color found among the peoples of the Mediterranean Basin and the East."[111] Also related perhaps to the emphasis on color and the absence of any similarity to real Ethiopians in these contexts is the fact that later iconography, in spite of the black and Ethiopian apparitions of apocryphal and patristic literature, portrayed so few demons with Negroid features.[112] The demonological use of black was obviously related to earlier classical notions about the color black, and a similar origin perhaps explains the contrast of the blackness of evil with the light of God. The Devil is black, according to Didymus the Blind, because he fell from the splendor and virtue of spiritual whiteness that only those who have been "whitened" by God can possess.[113] In the demonological context, however, there was no stereotypical image of Ethiopians as personifications of demons or the Devil. Nor does the symbolism of black demons seem to have had a negative effect on the generally favorable view of blacks dating back to Homer's "blameless" Ethiopians, favorites of the gods, and to Herodotus' Macrobian Ethiopians, the tallest and most handsome men on earth, whose just ruler upbraided the Persian King Cambyses for his injustice in coveting land not his own.

Much more important, however, is the fact that in spite of the demonological "Ethiopians," the exegetical interpretations of scriptural Ethiopians, much broader in scope and import than the limited demonological references, left no doubt as to the fundamental Christian attitude toward blacks and set forth a coherent body of doctrine in which Ethiopians in fact became an important symbol of Christianity's ecumenical mission. Building on classical usages, the Christian writers developed an exegesis and a black-white imagery in which Ethiopians illustrated the meaning of the scriptures for *all* men. In short, antiquity as a whole was able to overcome whatever potential for serious antiblack sentiment there may be in black-white symbolism.[114]

The pioneer in the use of an Ethiopian symbolism was Origen, who became the model for later patristic treatment of "Ethiopian" themes. Origen's choice of black-white contrasts may have been inspired in part by his firsthand acquaintance with blacks in the motley population of Alexandria, a daily reminder of the many Ethiopians on the southern fringes of the world who had figured prominently in classical imagery. By deliberately choosing and adapting these contrasts, and by relying on familiar patterns of classical thought, Origen and others after him realized that they could interpret scriptural references more meaningfully and could explicate their message more convincingly. In other words, in their exegesis of biblical references to Ethiopians the early church fathers assumed the positive view of classical tradition and merely imbued it with Christian interpretations.

The essential spirit of Origen's "Ethiopian" interpretations appears in his commentaries on the Song of Songs, which also includes observations on other important scriptural references to Ethiopians. In his commentary on the "black and beautiful maiden," Origen was not, as L. A. Thompson claims, apologizing "in deference to the dictates of the traditional and dominant values,"[115] but was illustrating the applicability of black-white imagery to all peoples: "We ask in what way is she black and what way fair without whiteness. She has repented of her sins; conversion has bestowed beauty upon her and she is sung as 'beautiful' . . . If you repent, your soul will be 'black' because of your former sins but because of your penitence your soul will have something of what I may call an Ethiopian beauty."[116] The mystery of the church arising from the Gentiles and calling itself black and beautiful, Origen points out, is adumbrated in the marriage of Moses to a black Ethiopian woman, which he interprets as a symbolic union of the spiritual law (Moses) and the church (the Ethiopian woman)— a foreshadowing of the universal church.[117] Origen expressed a basic Christian tenet when, by extending the traditional Ethiopian-Scythian formula and by making it more inclusive, he declared that it made no difference whether one was born among Hebrews, Greeks, Ethiopians, Scythians, or Taurians, all whom God created He created equal and alike.[118] In a similar spirit St. Augustine stated that under the name "Ethiopian" all nations are signified, a part representing the whole, and "properly by black men, for Ethiopians are black. Those are called to the faith who were black, just they, so that it may be said to them 'Ye were sometimes darkness but now are ye light in the Lord.'"[119] When Augustine declared that the catholic church was not to be limited to a particular region of the earth, but would reach even the Ethiopians, the remotest of men, he was not only recalling Homer's distant Ethiopians but he also had in mind those Ethiopians on the southernmost fringes of his own native northwest Africa.[120]

In a coherent body of exegesis during the first six centuries of Christianity blacks were summoned to salvation and welcomed in the Christian brotherhood on the same terms as others. All men were regarded as black who had not been illuminated by God's light and all men, regardless of the color of the skin, were considered potentially Christians. The baptism of the minister of the Ethiopian queen by Philip the Evangelist was a landmark in proclaiming that considerations of race were to be of no significance in determining membership in the Christian church.[121] All believers in Christ were eligible. Blacks were not only humble converts like the young Ethiopian slave, "not yet whitened by the shining grace of Christ," the object of concern in a correspondence between Fulgentius, Bishop of Ruspe, and a deacon Ferrandus.[122] St. Menas, sometimes portrayed as a Negro, was a national saint of Egypt, and pilgrims from Asia and Europe as well as from Africa came to his shrine west of Alexandria.[123] One of the most outstanding Fathers of the Desert of Scete was a tall, black Ethiopian, Moses, who, once a brigand, reached the height of perfection, left seventy disciples at his death, and was a model of humility and the monastic life, an excellent teacher and a Father's Father. Those who see evidence of color prejudice in certain references to the color of Abba Moses fail to comprehend the reasons for the application of the black-white symbolism to the monk, which are clearly stated by J. Devisse: "The person of Abba Moses seems to epitomize the *Aethiops*-sinner's symbolic road from the darkness of sin to the light of grace as the Greek, and especially the Western European Christian, would have thought of it."[124] In short, the Ethiopian imagery dramatically emphasized the ecumenical character of Christianity, and adumbrated the symbolism of the black wise man in the Adoration of the Magi. There is no evidence that Ethiopians of the first centuries after Christ suffered in their day-to-day contacts with whites as a result of metaphorical associations of this symbolism. Nor did the early Christians alter the classical symbolism or the teachings of the church to fit a preconceived notion of blacks as inferior, to rationalize the enslavement of blacks, or to sanction segregated worship. In the early church blacks found equality in both theory and practice.

To summarize, in the entire corpus of ancient evidence, we have seen, there are only a few notions or concepts which have sometimes been interpreted as evincing antiblack sentiment. There is no doubt that some of these have negative associations, but there is no evidence that these beliefs gave rise to reactions creating serious obstacles to blacks in their daily contact with whites. The association of black with evil, ill omens and sin, L. Cracco Ruggini has noted, was late in emerging and was to a large extent Egyptian and north African. J. Desanges, one of the scholars who have interpreted certain contexts as antiblack in sentiment, has emphasized, however, that to insist inordinately on such points would be to distort perspective, because Mediterranean antiquity was as a whole able to overcome the tendency among whites to associate black with evil.[125] D. L. Noel observed that the arguments for an overall absence of color prejudice in antiquity are sound and complement Stephen Gould's assessment of "latter-day scientists who perceive and interpret racial differences through lenses severely distorted by prevailing racism."[126]

"White" Perceptions of "Blacks"—Ancient and Modern

Misinterpretations of the ancient attitudes toward blacks have apparently been influenced, consciously or unconsciously, by projecting into antiquity views that have developed in later societies in which great importance has been attached to the color of the skin and in which blacks have suffered from virulent color prejudice. The pattern of black-white relations in the ancient world, however, differed from that in the modern world, and these differences are important for the proper assessment of classical images of blacks. In the ancient world there were prolonged black-white contacts from an early date. First encounters with blacks frequently involved soldiers or mercenaries, not slaves or so-called savages. Yet, a view of blacks as the equivalent of slave or savage has given rise to a frequent unwillingness to accept the full import of the ancient evidence. In spite of a widespread respect in antiquity for the military capabilities of peoples from south of Egypt and of their famous archers, Xerxes' Ethiopian contingent has been described as a "humble and almost grotesque auxiliary."[127] A similar view of blacks also explains the incredulity in the following observation on the Twenty-fifth Ethiopian Dynasty: "In the place of a native pharaoh or of the usurping Libyans the throne of Egypt was occupied by a Negro king from Ethiopia! But his dominion was not for long."[128] It was this Dynasty, however, that captured and ruled Egypt from about 751–663 B.C. and that founded a state which, with its later capital at Meroë, lasted for more than a thousand years—a span longer than any single period of Egyptian unification. It was the glory of this Dynasty that the book of Nahum recalled long after its fall at the hands of the Assyrians. And it was a pharaoh of this Dynasty, Taharqa, whose military power Strabo mentioned more than six hundred years after his death.[129]

Ancient slavery was color-blind and the majority of slaves were white, not black; hence, the antiblack sentiment which developed after slave and black became synonymous was absent. Nor were there theories that blacks were especially or more suited to slavery than whites. The black slave or freedman, therefore, was in a no more disadvantageous position than anyone else unfortunate enough to be captured as a prisoner of war or to be enslaved for any other reason.

Initial favorable impressions of blacks were explained and amplified, generation after generation, by poets, historians, and philosophers, and both Greece and Rome developed a positive image of Ethiopia (Nubia) as an independent state of considerable military, political, and cultural importance. In science, philosophy, and religion, color was not the basis of a theory concerning the innate inferiority of blacks. There were no hierarchical notions of human races, with whites occupying the highest and blacks the lowest positions. On the contrary, ethnic differences were explained in the same way for all peoples. Blacks were not stereotyped as "savages," but blacks and whites alike living at the outer extremities of the world were described as following a primitive way of life. Writers who referred to black-white racial unions, either as illustrations of the transmission of inherited physical characteristics or as evidence of adultery, included no strictures on black-white racial mixture, though some condemned adultery. Black gods, or heroes and their interracial amours presented no embarrassment and evoked no apologies from poets. Juba II, king of Mauretania, whose features in some likenesses suggest Negroid admixture,[130] was married first to Cleopatra Selene, daughter of Antony and Cleopatra, and later to the daughter of a king of Cappadocia. Blacks were physically assimilated into the predominantly white population of the ancient world as attested by the portrayal of mixed black-white types in classical art and by textual references to black-white racial mixture.

There is no evidence that blacks were excluded from avenues—occupational, economic, cultural, social, or religious—open to other newcomers. Like many others from alien lands, black slaves and freedmen found employment in occupations at the lower end of the economic scale. But blacks with special qualifications found a place for their talent. Blacks, like those who served in the army of Septimius Severus in Britain, had the same advantages upon discharge as other auxiliary soldiers in the *numeri*, and at least one black was apparently a member of Septimius Severus' elite corps.[131] Evidence from northwest Africa illustrates the great popularity and fame of black athletes, and the financial success of a black landowner like C. Julius Serenus in Thaenae.[132] There were blacks who were at home in the culture of the Mediterranean world. The dark- or black-skinned Terence, who might have been of Negroid extraction,[133] arrived in Rome as a slave from Carthage. He received a liberal education and his freedom from his owner, a Roman senator. Achieving fame as a playwright, Terence became a member of the learned Scipionic circle, and his daughter is said to have married a Roman knight. It was an Ethiopian, mentioned in the New Testament, who figured prominently in Christian exegetical texts as the first Gentile to be baptized by Philip. This official of the Ethiopian queen who was reading a roll of Isaiah when he met Philip apparently read Greek, and perhaps, Hebrew.[134] Juba II was a man of great learning who strove to introduce Greek and Roman culture into his African kingdom. Among Juba's many works (now lost) were a history of Rome, books on Libya and Assyria, and treatises on drama, painting, and plants. Memnon, the black protégé of Herodes Atticus, was one of the celebrated sophist's most talented disciples.[135] Blacks were welcomed on the same terms as whites in both Isiac worship and Christianity as converts and as priests or monks.[136]

Both the Greeks and Romans, in spite of ideas and concepts which a few scholars have described as negative and detrimental to blacks, had the ability to see and to comment on the obviously different physical characteristics of blacks without developing an elaborate and rigid system of discrimination against blacks based only on the color of the skin. Color, in spite of the existence of black-white symbolism, the somatic norm image, and the like did not acquire in the Graeco-Roman world the great importance it has assumed in some post-classical societies either in the self-image of many peoples, or in the denial of equality to blacks in theory and practice. The Greeks, Romans, and early Christians were free of what Keith Irvine has described as the "curse of acute color-consciousness, attended by all the raw passion and social problems that cluster around it."[137] Scholars may disagree as to the precise stage in the history of race relations at which color acquired the importance it has assumed in the modern world. One point, however, is certain: the onus of intense color prejudice cannot be placed upon the shoulders of the Greeks and Romans.

Notes

1. F. M. Snowden, Jr., *Blacks in Antiquity: Ethiopians in the Greco-Roman Experience* (Cambridge: Harvard University Press, 1970), 1–99, illustrations 1–78, 80–82, 84–100, hereafter cited as *Blacks in Antiquity; Before Color Prejudice: The Ancient View of Blacks* (Cambridge: Harvard University Press, 1983), 3–17, illustrations 14–33, 40–62, hereafter cited as *Before Color Prejudice;* J. Vercoutter, et al., *The Image of the Black in Western Art I: From the Pharaohs to the Fall of the Roman Empire* (New York: William Morrow, 1976), now distributed by Harvard University Press, hereafter cited as *Image of the Black,* 133–268.

2. Xenophanes, *Fragment* 16 (Diels).

3. Herodotus, 7.70.

4. Diodorus, 3.8.2.

5. *Moretum,* 31–35.

6. J. Desanges (Desanges, *Image of the Black,* 247.) states that prisoners, perhaps Garamantes, depicted in a first-century mosaic are "particularly dark and show Negroid features, although they are not Negroes." B. G. Trigger (Trigger, "Nubian, Negro, Black, Nilotic?" *Africa in Antiquity I. The Arts of Ancient Nubia and the Sudan* [Brooklyn: Brooklyn Museum, 1978], 27, hereafter cited as *Africa in Antiquity.*), considers the division of peoples of the Nile Valley into Caucasoid and Negroid stock "an act that is arbitrary and wholly devoid of historical or biological significance." Nubians, in the opinion of W. Y. Adams (Adams, *Nubia: Corridor to Africa* [London: A. Lane 1977], 8) may be described as black or white according to the prejudice of one's time and temperament.

7. W. R. Connor, Review of *Books Recommended by the Princeton Faculty* 21 (1970), 4.

8. R. Lonis, "Les trois approches de l'Éthiopien par l'opinion gréco-romaine," *Ktema* 6 (1981): 74, hereafter cited as R. Lonis, "Les trois approches."

9. J. Desanges, "L'Antiquité gréco-romaine et l'homme noir," *Revue des Études Latines* 48 (1970), 93, hereafter cited as J. Desanges, "L'Antiquité gréco-romaine."

10. G. H. Beardsley, *The Negro in Greek and Roman Civilization: A Study of the Ethiopian Type* (Baltimore: Johns Hopkins University Press, 1927; New York: Arno Press, 1967), hereafter cited as G. H. Beardsley, *The Ethiopian Type.*

11. F. M. Snowden, Jr., "Blacks, Early Christianity," in *The Interpreter's Dictionary of the Bible: Supplementary Volume,* ed. V. Furnish (Nashville: Abingdon Press, 1976), 111–14; "Aethiopes," in *Lexicon Iconographicum Mythologiae Classicae I,* 1: *AARA-APHLAD* (Zurich: Artemis, 1981), 413–19; 2:321 pl. 1, 2; 321–26; "*Melas-leukos* and *Niger-candidus* Contrasts in Classical Literature," *The Ancient History Bulletin* 2, no. 3 (1988): 60–64; "Bernal's 'Blacks,' Herodotus and Other Classical Evidence," *Arethusa* (Special Fall Issue 1989): 83–95; "Romans and Blacks: A Review Essay," *AJP* 111 (1990): 543–57. See also review of *Blacks in Ancient Cypriot Art* by Vassos Karageorghis in *AJA* 94 (1990): 72–74.

12. M. Bieber, *The History of the Greek and Roman Theater,* 2nd ed., rev. (Princeton: Princeton University Press, 1961), 296.

13. R. Lonis, "Les trois approches," 79.

14. C. T. Seltman, "Two Heads of Negresses," *AJA* 24 (1920): 14.

15. W. N. Bates, "Scenes from the Aethiopis on a Black-figured Amphora from Orvieto," *Transactions of the Department of Archaeology,* (Philadelphia: University of Pennsylvania, 1904), pts. 1 and 2, 50.

16. M. Robertson, *Greek Painting* (Geneva: Skira, 1959), 67.

17. G. H. Beardsley, *The Ethiopian Type,* 8, 21, 79.

18. D. K. Hill, *AJA* 57 (1953): 266.

19. J. Bryce, *The Relations of the Advanced and the Backward Races of Mankind* (Oxford: Clarendon Press, 1902): 18.

20. E. Baring, *Ancient and Modern Imperialism* (London: J. Murray, 1910), 139–40.

21. E. E. Sikes, *The Anthropology of the Greeks* (London: D. Nutt, 1914), 88.

22. A. E. Zimmern, *The Greek Commonwealth,* 5th ed. (Oxford: Oxford University Press, 1931), 323.

23. W. L. Westermann, "Slavery and the Elements of Freedom," *Quarterly Bulletin of the Polish Institute of Arts and Sciences* 1 (1943): 346.

24. T. J. Haarhoff, *The Stranger at the Gate* (Oxford: Blackwell, 1948), 299.

25. C. Kluckhohn, *Anthropology and the Classics* (Providence: Brown University Press, 1961), 34, 42.

26. H. C. Baldry, *The Unity of Mankind in Greek Thought* (Cambridge: Cambridge University Press, 1965), 4.

27. Some of the numerous reviews of my publications have used my studies as a point of departure to look at various aspects of the attitude toward blacks in the ancient world, e.g. J. Desanges, "L'Antiquité gréco-romaine;" E. Lepore, *La Parola del Passato: Rivista di Studi Antichi* 117 (1984): 310–20.

28. Examples of specialized articles are the following: J. Desanges, "L'Afrique noire et le monde méditerranéen dans l'Antiquité (Éthiopiens et Gréco-Romains)' *Revue française d'histoire d'outre-mer* 62 (1975): 391–414, hereafter cited as "L'Afrique Noire"; the detailed studies of L. Cracco Ruggini, especially valuable for the Roman imperial period: "Pregiudizi razziali, ostilità politica e culturale, intolleranza religiosa nell' impero romano," *Athenaeum* 46 (1948): 139–52; "Leggenda e realtà degli Etiopi nella cultura tardoimperiale, in *Atti del IV Congresso Internazionale di Studi Etiopici, Accademia dei Lincei* 1 (Rome: Accademia dei Lincei, 1974), 104–93; "Il negro buono e il negro malvagio nel mondo classico," *Conoscenze etniche e rapporti di convivenza nell' antichità*, M. Sardi, ed. (Milan: Vita e Pensiero, 1979), 108–35, hereafter cited as "Il negro buono," cf. "Intolerance: Equal and Less Equal in the Roman World," *CP* 82 (1987): 187–205, R. Lonis, "Les trois approches," 69–87; cf. *Afrique Noire et Monde Méditerranéen dans l'Antiquité: Colloque de Dakar: 19–24 Janvier 1976* (Dakar: Nouvelles editions africaines, 1978).

29. A. Bourgeois, *La Grèce antique devant la négritude* (Paris: Presence Africaine, 1971); E. Mveng, *Les Sources grecques de l'histoire négro-africaine depuis Homère jusqu'à Strabon* (Paris: Presence Africaine, 1972); L. A. Thompson, *Romans and Blacks* (Norman: University of Oklahoma Press, 1989).

30. B. H. Warmington, *IJAHS* 17 (1983): 520.

31. L. Cracco Ruggini, "Il negro buono" 118.

32. R. S. W. Hawtrey, Review of *Blacks in Antiquity*, by F. M. Snowden, Jr., *Prudentia* 4 (1972): 58.

33. W. R. Connor, Review of *Blacks in Antiquity* cited in note 7.

34. L. Castiglione, *Acta Archaeologica Academiae Scientiarum Hungaricae* 24 (1972): 441.

35. L. A. Thompson, *Romans and Blacks,* 160.

36. E. de Chanot, "Bronzes antiques," *Gazette Archéologique* 5 (1879): 209–10.

37. E. Mveng, *Les Sources grecques de l'histoire négro-africaine depuis Homère jusqu'à Strabon* (Paris: Presence Africaine, 1972), 67–68.

38. F. M. Snowden, Jr., *Image of the Black,* 167, illustrations nos. 169, 176, 197; *Before Color Prejudice,* 15.

39. Aristotle, *De generatione animalium* 1.18.722a; *Historia animalium* 7.6.585b.

40. J. Boardman, Review of *Image of the Black, CR,* n.s. 30 (1980) 308.

41. L. A. Thompson, *Romans and Blacks,* 25.

42. O. Patterson, *Slavery and Social Death: A Comparative Study* (Cambridge: Harvard University Press, 1982), 421, n. 16.

43. For examples of such views, see A. J. Evans, "Recent Discoveries of Tar-

entine Terra-Cottas," *JHS* 7 (1886): 37–38 and plate LXIV for the description of a third-century B.C. askos in the shape of an emaciated Negro boy sleeping beside an amphora as "probably without a rival amongst Greek terra-cottas" for its realism and true pathos; J. D. Beazley, "Charinos: Attic Vases in the Form of Human heads," *JHS* 49 (1929): 39, for the aesthetic attractiveness of Negroes as models; H. Read, *A Coat of Many Colours: Occasional Studies* (London: G. Routledge and Sons, 1945), 2, 5 for the description of a tiny Hellenistic bronze head as "a great work of art, even the greatest work of art in the world"; H. Deschamps, Review of *Blacks in Antiquity in Africa, Journal of the International Institute* 41 (1971): 68 for the view that classical art has an astonishing diversity and vividness, and a grace that bespeaks an absence of prejudice; D. M. Buitron, "Greek Encounters with Africans," *Walters Art Gallery Bulletin* 32 (Nov. 5, 1980), 1, for the high quality of the representations of Ethiopians in Greek art; and R. A. Higgins, *Greek Terracottas* (London: Methuen 1967), 120 for the view that a first-century B.C. terracotta of a Negro Spinario is a "creation of unusual charm," and "a human document, a sympathetic study of a racial type."

44. Agatharchides, *De Mari Erythraeo,* 16 GGM1, 118.

45. G. W. Allport, *The Nature of Prejudice* (Boston: Beacon Press, 1954), 304.

46. A. Marsh, "Awareness of Racial Differences in West African and British Children," *Race* 113 (1970): 301.

47. A. Dihle, "Zur hellenistischen Ethnographie," in *Grecs et barbares: six exposés et discussions,* H. Schwabl et al., eds., Entretiens sur l'antiquité classique t. 8; (Genève: Fondation Hardt, 1962), 214–15.

48. Ovid, *Metamorphoses,* 2.235–36.

49. F. M. Snowden, Jr. *Image of the Black,* 146 and plates 159–60.

50. Hippocrates, *Aër.,* xii, xvii-xxiv; Vict. 2.37.

51. F. M. Snowden, Jr., *Blacks in Antiquity,* 171–76; *Before Color Prejudice,* 85–87.

52. Pliny, *Naturalis historia,* 2.80. 189.

53. Diodorus, 3.34.7–8.

54. Ptolemy, *Tetrabiblos,* 2.2.56.

55. Strabo, 4.5.4.

56. Aristotle, *Physiognomonica,* 6.812a.

57. Menander, *Fragment* 612 in A. Koerte, 2nd ed (Leipzig: B. G. Teubner, 1959); Kock, *Fragment* 533.

58. M. Smith, Review of *Blacks in Antiquity,* by F. M. Snowden, Jr., *AHR* 76 (1971): 140; D. S. Wiesen, "Juvenal and the Blacks," *Classica et Mediaevalia* 31 (1970): 136, hereafter cited as "Juvenal and the Blacks." H. C. Baldry, *The Unity of Mankind,* 138, however, refers to the sentiment as one which "most strikingly transcends kinship ties and racial barriers."

59. H. Hoetink, *The Two Variants in Caribbean Race Relations: A Contribution to the Sociology of Segmented Societies,* trans. E. M. Hookyaas (New York: Institute of Race Relations, 1967), 120 and 126 where Hoetink cites as an example of

the somatic norm image a central African creation myth in which the Negro regards himself as perfectly cooked but the white man as undone because of a defect in the Creator's oven.

60. F. M. Snowden, Jr., *Before Color Prejudice*, 75–82.

61. Dio Chrysostom, *Orationes*, 21.16–17.

62. Sextus Empiricus, *Adversus mathematicos*, xi. 43.

63. Herodotus, 3.20.

64. Asclepiades, *Anthologia Palatina*, 5.210.

65. Ovid, *Heroides*, 15.35–38.

66. Martial, 1.115.

67. W. Peek, *Griechische Vers-Inschriften* (Berlin: Akademie-Verlag, 1955), n. 1167.

68. J. Desanges, "L'Afrique Noire," 411.

69. D. S. Wiesen, "Juvenal and the Blacks," 136; cf. L. A. Thompson, *Roman and Blacks*, 41–43.

70. L. Cracco Ruggini, "Il negro buono," 111–13, and "Leggenda e realtà degli Etiopi nella cultura tardoimperiale, *Atti del IV Congresso Internazionale di Studi Etiopici, Accademia dei Lincei* 1 (Rome: Accademia dei Lincei, 1974), 147, n. 32.

71. W. L. Westermann, *The Slave Systems of Greek and Roman Antiquity* (Philadelphia: American Philosophical Society, 1955), 104.

72. Suetonius, *Vita Terenti*, 1.

73. G. Highet, *Juvenal the Satirist: A Study* (Oxford: Clarendon Press, 1954), 255, n. 17.

74. L. A. Thompson, *Romans and Blacks*, 30–31, 119.

75. *Moretum*, 31–35.

76. L. A. Thompson, *Romans and Blacks*, 136.

77. J. Desanges, *Image of the Black*, 257, and L. A. Thompson, *Romans and Blacks*, 31.

78. Perhaps the herb charlock, cf. Hesychius, s.v. *skuba*.

79. *Anthologia Latina*, no. 182 (ed. 1, 1, F. Buecheler and A. Riese; Leipzig: B. Teubner, 1894); L. A. Thompson, *Romans and Blacks*, 37.

80. *Anthologia Latina*, no. 353. For a translation of this poem and that of a companion piece (*Anthologia Latina*, no. 354) in which Luxorius extols Olympius' skill in fighting wild beasts and his popularity with the spectators, see F. M. Snowden, Jr., *Before Color Prejudice*, 77–78.

81. L. A. Thompson, *Romans and Blacks*, 31–32. For a discussion of this poem and its relation to the classical somatic norm image, see F. M. Snowden, Jr., *Before Color Prejudice*, 77–79. For interpretations of the poem as evidence of antiblack sentiment, see J. Desanges, "L'Afrique Noire," 410–11; and L. Cracco Ruggini, "Il negro buono," 112.

82. Menander, frag. 612 A. Koerte.

83. Agatharchides, *De Mari Erythraeo*, 16.

84. Juvenal, 2.23–27.

85. G. H. Beardsley, *The Ethiopian Type,* 120.

86. D. Wiesen, "Juvenal and the Blacks," 149.

87. Juvenal, 13. 163–73.

88. Diodorus, 3.34.8.

89. Seneca, *De ira,* 3.26.3.

90. L. A. Thompson, *Romans and Blacks,* 48.

91. Ibid, 135.

92. K. J. Gergen, "The Significance of Skin Color in Human Relations," in J. H. Franklin, ed., *Color and Race,* (Boston: Houghton Mifflin, 1968), 120, 112–25.

93. K. J. Gergen, 121.

94. Suetonius, *Caligula,* 57.4.

95. *Anthologia Latina,* no. 183.

96. Tacitus, *Historiae,* 4.50.

97. Juvenal, 3.61.

98. For interpretations of this inscription as a disparaging reference to the black man's physical features, see J. Desanges, *Image of the Black,* 257; L. Cracco Ruggini, "Il negro buono," 112; R. Lonis, "Les trois approches," 86; and L. A. Thompson, *Romans and Blacks,* 36–37. For my discussion of the inscription, see *Before Color Prejudice,* 83–85.

99. L. Cracco Ruggini, "Il negro buono," 105–35 and "Intolerance: Equal and Less Equal in the Roman World," *Classical Philology* 82 (1987): 181–95, esp. 194–95.

100. R. Lonis, "Les trois approches," 86–87. Lonis' schema of three approaches—mythological, anthropological, and political—to the Greek and Roman view of blacks is too rigid and simplistic and, for example, underestimates the mythological and anthropological elements in the Roman view of blacks.

101. B. H. Warmington, Review of *Blacks in Antiquity, African Historical Studies* 4 (1971): 385–86.

102. L. A. Thompson, *Romans and Blacks,* 99–100.

103. J. Desanges, *Image of the Black,* 246–68; F. M. Snowden, Jr., *Before Color Prejudice,* 90–92, illustrations nos. 26 and 51–56.

104. E. g. Ammianus Marcellinus 29.5.37 for Ethiopians recruited by Firmus for a revolt in 372 A.D.

105. Olympius, the idol of Carthage, was not the only black North African animal-fighter as attested by a third-century mosaic from Thysdrus (El Djem) Tunis, Musée Nationale du Bardo, 3361, cf. F. M. Snowden, Jr., *Before Color Prejudice,* no. 26. For a black wrestler, see a third-century mosaic from Thaenae (Henchir Thina) and for black grooms, see a sixth-or-seventh-century mosaic from Capsa, *Before Color Prejudice,* illustrations, nos. 54–55; J. Desanges, *Image of the Black,* nos. 349 and 362.

106. The financial success of C. Julius Serenus, of unmistakable black-white extraction, is suggested by the scenes depicted on a third- or fourth-century funerary mosaic showing in separate panels Serenus and Numitoria Saturnina, apparently

his white spouse, each in semi-reclining positions, holding a golden goblet in the right hand, with three Cupids in each panel—one filling a basket with flowers, a second carrying flowers to the reclining spouse, and the third playing a cithara. See R. Massigli, *Musée de Sfax, Musées de l'Algérie et de la Tunisie*, no. 17 (Paris: Ernest Leroux, 1912), 9, no. 24 and plate V, no. 3; M. Yacoub, *Guide du Musée de Sfax* (Tunis: Secretariat d'État aux affaires culturelles, 1966), 44 and plate XIV, figs. 2–3; and F. M. Snowden, Jr., *Before Color Prejudice*, no. 56.

107. A fourth-century mosaic from Carthage from the House of the Seasons depicts a Negro performing an occult ceremony designed to invoke the powers of fertility—a ceremony, according to G. Charles-Picard, part of a religious triptych in which the Negro adds the virtues of his magic to the classic powers of Aion and Venus. J. Desanges, *Image of the Black*, illustration no. 360; F. M. Snowden, Jr., *Blacks in Antiquity*, 192; G. Charles-Picard, *La Carthage de Saint Augustin* (Paris: Fayard, 1965), 71–77.

108. *Infra*, n. 119–20, and 122.

109. *Actus Petri cum Simone*, 22.

110. See, for example, Manilius 4.722–30; Pliny *Naturalis historia* 6.22.70; Arrian *Anabasis* 5.4.4 and *Indica* 6.6.9.

111. J. M. Courtès, "The Theme of 'Ethiopia' and 'Ethiopians' in Patristic Literature," in J. Devisse, *The Image of the Black in Western Art II: From the Early Christian Era to the 'Age of Discovery,'* Part 1 *From the Demonic Threat to the Incarnation of Sainthood* (New York: William Morrow, 1979), 9, 19, now distributed by Harvard University Press, hereafter cited as *Image of the Black II.*

112. *Image of the Black*, 14 [L. Bugner].

113. Didymus the Blind, *Sur Zacharie*, 4.312.

114. Attention has been called to the potentiality of black-white imagery for vastly different uses. J. Desanges, "L'Antiquité gréco-romaine," 53, states that the association of blackness with death, the Underworld, and evil contains the germs of uneasy developments that antiquity was able to overcome. B. M. Warmington, Review of *Blacks in Antiquity*, by F. M. Snowden, Jr., *AHS* 4 (1971): 385, writes that even if the black-bad, white-good equation had nothing to do with the color of the skin, "one cannot altogether avoid a *frisson* of unease at the constant harping on the distinction between physical blackness and spiritual whiteness, innocent though it was in early Christian writing."

115. L. A. Thompson, *Romans and Blacks*, 134.

116. Origen, *Homilia in Canticum Canticorum* 1.6 (Die griechischen christlichen Schriftsteller, [GCS] Origen 8.36).

117. Origen, *Commentarium in Canticum Canticorum* 2.362 and 366–67 (GCS, Origen 8.115 and 117–18).

118. Origen, *De principiis* 2.9.5–6 (GCS, Origen 5.164–70).

119. Augustine, *Enarrationes in Psalmos*, 73.16, Corpus Christianorum, Series Latina [CCL] 39.1014.

120. Ibid., 71.12 (CCL 39.980).

121. *Acts* 8:26–39.

122. Fulgentius, *Epistulae* 11–12, Migne, Patrologiae Cursus Completus, Series Latina [PL] 65.378–392.

123. J. Devisse, *Image of the Black II*, 38–43. For *ampullae* depicting a Negroid Menas, see, for example, Oxford, Ashmolean Museum 1933.717: Paris, Musée du Louvre, MNC 140. Cf. *Romans and Barbarians*, (Boston: Museum of Fine Arts, 1976), nos. 237–38.

124. J. Devisse, *Image of the Black II* 62. For interpretations of the references to Abba Moses' blackness, see F. M. Snowden, Jr., *Blacks in Antiquity*, 209–11; P. Mayerson, "Anti-black Sentiment in the *Vitae Patrum*," *HTR* 71 (1978): 304–11; L. Cracco Ruggini, "II negro buono," 115–18; *Image of the Black II*, 25, 62, 113–14; L. A. Thompson, *Blacks and Romans*, 41–42, 47, 100, 123–24, 139.

125. J. Desanges, "L'Afrique Noire," 411.

126. D. L. Noel, Review of *Before Color Prejudice*, *American Journal of Sociology* 90 (1984): 227.

127. G. H. Beardsley, *The Ethiopian Type*, 53.

128. G. Steindorff and K. C. Seele, *When Egypt Ruled the East*, rev. by K. C. Seele (Chicago: University of Chicago Press, 1957), 271.

129. Nahum, 3:8; Strabo, 1.3.21; 15.1.6.

130. *Image of the Black*, figs. 363–64, and p. 265. E. Boucher-Colozier, "Quelques marbres de Cherchel au Musée du Louvre," *Libyca: Archéologie-Épigraphie* 1 (1953): 23–28, calls attention to the thick lips and curly hair of a head of Juba II in the Louvre and a skull of Negroid type in the Cherchel Museum.

131. For an Ethiopian reported among the auxiliaries of Septimius Severus in Britain, perhaps part of a *numerus Maurorum* billeted at one of the forts astride Hadrian's wall, see *Scriptores Historiae Augustae, Septimius Severus* 22.4–5 and R. G. Collingwood and R. P. Wright, *The Roman Inscriptions of Britain* (Oxford: Clarendon Press, 1965), 1.626, no. 2042; cf. A. Birley, *Septimius Severus: The African Emperor* (London: Eyre and Spottiswoode, 1971), 265–66; and for a scene on an early third-century marble sarcophagus showing, to the right of a general whose features resemble those of Septimius Severus, three soldiers—one a Negro—receiving suppliant captives, see L. Salerno, *Palazzo Rondinini* (Rome: DeLuca, 1965), 259, no. 85 and fig. 139.

132. See note 106, above.

133. F. M. Snowden, Jr., *Blacks in Antiquity*, 270, n. 3.

134. *Acts* 8:26–39.

135. Philostratus, *Vita Apollonii*, 3.11; and *Vitae Sophistarum*, 2.588; *Image of the Black*, 238 and illustrations 336–38.

136. F. M. Snowden, Jr., *Blacks in Antiquity*, 189–92, 196–215; *Before Color Prejudice*, 97–108.

137. K. Irvine, *The Rise of the Colored Races* (New York: Norton, 1970), 19.

9

Some Remarks on the Processes of State Formation in Egypt and Ethiopia

KATHRYN A. BARD
AND RODOLFO FATTOVICH

❀

In this study we would like to summarize the results of our research on state formation in Egypt and Ethiopia and to suggest a tentative comparison. Since the 1970s our research has been involved with state formation in Egypt[1] and Ethiopia; it is only in a preliminary stage.[2] At present, we are both involved with studying the processes of state formation in Ethiopia, and in 1993 we began conducting joint fieldwork, in northern Ethiopia at Aksum, which is focused on the problem of the rise of the early Aksumite state.[3] Although there are many lacunae in the data for state formation in Ethiopia, we suggest that comparisons with early Egypt may offer potential insights.

The processes of state formation in Egypt and Ethiopia occurred in regions with different environmental constraints. Ancient Egypt was located in the lower Nile Valley, a long oasis formed by the Nile cutting across the eastern Sahara. In ancient Egypt the Nile greatly facilitated centralized control and communication, whereas the mountainous terrain of northern Ethiopia greatly hindered these. Agriculture in Egypt was practiced in a large river valley, where crops were sown annually on the floodplain after the summer inundation. Fallow periods were not necessary, and the fertile silts of the floodplain were annually replenished. Basin irrigation technology was very simple, and did not require intensive labor to be effective.[4] Fish and waterfowl were a plentiful source of protein.

In contrast, the Aksumite state was located in the highlands of northern Ethiopia. The Tigrean plateau in northern Ethiopia is a high altitude region (2–2.5 km above sea level) broken by deep valleys. The mountainous terrain greatly hindered centralized control and communication. The major rivers of northern Ethiopia (Takeze, Mareb-Gash, Barka, and Anseba) are 500 m lower than the cultivated regions of the plateau. Cultivation is dependent on summer rains, which average 600–800 mm annually.[5] Rains on the Tigrean plateau are less reliable than farther south in central Ethiopia, and failure of rainfall in the north is frequent. Because of the mountainous terrain, many areas are much better suited for pastoralism of cattle, and sheep and goats. Farming is only possible on level ground in the valleys or on plateaus and piedmonts. Terracing of piedmont areas is labor intensive, and soil erosion can be severe. Irrigation is small-scale, and consists of channeling water to fields from mountains and rain-fed cisterns.[6]

State formation occurred at different times in Egypt and in Ethiopia: in the fourth millennium B.C. in Egypt, and in the first millennium B.C. in Ethiopia. Unique indigenous civilizations arose in both regions. In the methods of control and its symbolic expression, the Egyptian and Ethiopian states were particularized and emerged as a consequence of specific "historical processes."[7]

Despite the different times and environments in which early states arose in Egypt and Ethiopia, we can suggest some parallels in the processes of state formation in both regions. Although the environmental adaptations of subsistence strategies were very different in Egypt and northern Ethiopia/Eritrea, farming was the most important subsistence base in both regions. The rise of complex societies in Egypt and Ethiopia occurred only *after* the introduction of domesticated cereals and agricultural technology. In Egypt this occurred much earlier: in the late sixth and fifth millennia B.C. In northern Ethiopia there is no evidence at present for the introduction of cereals and plow agriculture, but it has been suggested that this occurred by the early first millennium B.C., possibly as a result of contact with South Arabia.[8] A subsistence base that produced surpluses, which could be used to support full-time specialists, was a prerequisite for complex societies in northeast Africa, and much more needs to be known about the origins of cereal agriculture in the Horn of Africa.[9]

Both the Early Dynastic Egyptian state and the Aksumite state did not evolve in isolation, but were (specific) sociopolitical adaptations to processes and interactions occurring on a much larger scale in the ancient Near East, northeast Africa, and (for Aksum) the Mediterranean and south Asia. As states formed in Predynastic Upper Egypt (late fourth millennium B.C.) and on the Tigrean plateau (first millennium B.C. and first millennium A.D.), there is evidence of fairly complex economic interaction and long-distance trade with other hierarchical polities, and concomitant with this was the probable spread of ideas/models of hierarchical control and organization.

Finally, both processes culminated in the formation of unitarian states with strongly institutionalized kingships which occupied the whole territory in the two regions: the pharaonic state (third millennium B.C.) in Egypt up to the first cataract at Aswan, and the kingdom of Aksum (first millennium A.D.) on the Tigrean plateau in northern Ethiopia and Eritrea.

State Formation in Egypt

The process of state formation in Egypt has been carefully investigated in the last twenty years.[10] Scholars presently agree that an early state arose in Upper Egypt in the late fourth millennium B.C., and quickly expanded its dominion over the whole valley north of Aswan to the Delta.[11]

In our opinion, this process can be outlined as follows:

Farming communities in mutual contact appeared along the lower Nile in the late sixth and fifth millennia B.C., in the Fayyum and southwestern Delta (Fayyum A; Merimde), and by the middle of the fifth millennium B.C. in Middle Egypt (Badari). Both the Lower Egyptian and Badarian populations apparently practiced some long-distance trade with Palestine: sea shells from the Red Sea have been found in Badarian graves. No inferences about hierarchical society can be made from the mortuary evidence, although some Badarian graves are richer in grave goods than others.[12]

By the fourth millennium B.C. populations with different cultural traditions were settled in Upper Egypt (Nagada culture), Lower Egypt and the northern Nile Delta (el-Omari/Maadi/Buto cultural complex), and the eastern Nile Delta (Eastern Delta Predynastic culture).[13]

The archaeological evidence points to a progressive commercial expansion and increasing social complexity in Upper Egypt at this time. In early Nagada times (Nagada I, c. 3800–3600 B.C.) long-distance trade was still limited to Palestine and the Red Sea coast, but the internal exchange network probably intensified. No highly differentiated society is evident in the cemeteries, except for a few richer graves.[14]

In middle Nagada times (Nagada II, c. 3600–3300 B.C.) long-distance trade and/or contact with Nubia, Syria-Palestine, and Mesopotamia intensified in Upper Egypt.[15] The presence of obsidian from highland Ethiopia in Predynastic graves in Upper Egypt suggests further complexity of the Egyptian trade network in the fourth millennium B.C.[16] Northward expansion of Upper Egyptian culture, perhaps through commercial contact and colonization, occurred during Nagada II times, and eventually the material culture of Lower Egypt was replaced by one originating in Upper Egypt.[17] Such trade probably represents greater control of the economy by elites in Upper Egypt, and incipient bureaucracies of some sort directing or controlling the trade network. This is supported by the discovery of a clay sealing in a Nagada II provincial site at Halfiah Gibli, near Nag Hammadi.[18] Increasing social differentiation is evident in Nagada II cemeteries.[19] Most likely, differentiation in the major Predynastic cemeteries of Upper Egypt, such as Nagada, is symbolic of status display and status rivalry,[20] which probably represent the earliest processes of competition and the aggrandizement of local polities in Egypt. An ideology that stressed the importance of participation in a mortuary cult emerged as well. Institutions of control became symbolically associated with a mortuary cult, the origins of which were in the Nagada culture of Upper Egypt.[21] At this time, highly organized polities probably appeared in Upper Egypt, with possible major centers at Nagada and Hierakonpolis.[22]

In late Nagada times (Nagada III, c. 3300–3100 B.C.), Egyptian commercial expansion increased, stretching from Mesopotamia and Syria-Palestine to Nubia.[23] The eastern Nile Delta was progressively inhabited by peoples whose cultural origins were in Upper Egypt.[24] Social differentiation was accentuated and an early state, with an elaborate royal ideology, appeared in Upper Egypt at the end of the Nagada III period (Dyn. O).

In Lower Egypt, Maadi, near modern Cairo, was an important intermediary in the trade network between Egypt and Syria-Palestine in the mid-fourth millennium B.C.[25] In the northern Delta, the German excavations at Tell el-Fara'in/Buto provide possible evidence for contacts with the Uruk culture of southwest Asia.[26] Social organization and the nature of external contacts of the culture found in the eastern Nile Delta in Predynastic times, however, are still completely unknown.[27]

At the end of the fourth millennium B.C., Upper and Lower Egypt were unified by southern kings. Unification may have been achieved in part through conquest in the north, but an earlier unification of southern polities may have been achieved by a series of alliances,[28] as centers such as Abydos and Hierakonpolis gained political ascendancy.

State Formation in Northern Ethiopia

The process of state formation in northern Ethiopia has been investigated mainly by historians and linguists.[29] To date, archaeologists have only contributed marginally to outline this process.[30] Archaeological evidence suggests, however, that the earliest complex societies arose in the western Ethio-Sudanese lowlands (Kassala in eastern Sudan) and possibly in Eritrea because of inclusion of these regions in a long-distance trade network between Egypt and the Horn.[31]

Complex society arose at Kassala ca. 2500–1500 B.C. (Gash Group). The Gash Group was contemporary with the Kerma culture in Upper Nubia, and was the intermediary between Kerma, the Red Sea, and the Ethiopian plateau. There is evidence of hierarchical settlement patterns in the Gash Group. A Gash Group cemetery at Kassala (ca. 2300–1800 B.C.), of burials associated with stelae, and a mud-brick building (ca. 1800–1500 B.C.) with magazines containing large storage jars have also been found. "Administrative devices" were also excavated there: clay stamp seals with geometrical patterns, tokens in various shapes, and clay sealings.[32]

The Kerma culture disappeared with the expansion into Nubia of the Egyptian 18th Dynasty (beginning ca. 1550 B.C.), and the Gash Group became marginalized from the trading circuit. During the New Kingdom an important trade route via the Red Sea was established by the Egyptians, who were interested in products of the land of Punt.[33] The site of Adulis on the coast in northern Ethiopia was probably one of the harbors of Punt. At Adulis are 10 m of stratified deposits, the upper 4 m of which are Aksumite (first millennium A.D.). Earlier levels possibly go back to the second millennium B.C.[34]

Most likely contemporary with Punt in the Asmara region of Eritrea is the Ona Group A culture.[35] Sherds of large storage jars of late Gash Group type from Kassala have been excavated at an Ona Group A site, suggesting that for the first time peoples on the Ethiopian plateau became involved as an intermediary between Kassala, where ivory and incense were obtained, and the Red Sea coast. Textual and representational evidence in Egypt concerning Punt may suggest that a hierarchical society arose in this region in the mid-second millennium B.C.[36]

With the end of the New Kingdom in Egypt, the Egyptian Red Sea trade collapsed. This opened up an opportunity for South Arabian commercial expansion along the Red Sea and in the Horn. Epigraphic and archaeological evidence points to strong contacts between southern Arabia and the Tigrean plateau in the early first millennium B.C.[37] From these contacts the kingdom of Daamat arose on the Tigrean plateau. This was the earliest state in Ethiopia, and this period is known archaeologically as the Pre-Aksumite Period.[38] It is possible that plow agriculture and simple irrigation were introduced into the highlands at this time.

A major center of the Daamat state was located at Yeha, east of Aksum in western Tigray. The site of Yeha is located on a wide agricultural plain, and during the middle of the first millennium B.C. it covered an area of about 50 ha.[39] Sherds of South Arabian wares have been found in the early levels at Yeha. Contemporary to them at Kassala are early Pre-Aksumite sherds. (Commercial) links were thus established between eastern Sudan, northern Ethiopia, and the west coast of the Arabian peninsula in the early first millennium B.C.[40]

The Daamat kingdom was a power c. 700–300 B.C. Although it had commercial relations with Saba in South Arabia, Daamat was politically independent.[41] There is evidence in northern Ethiopia and Eritrea at this time of South Arabian inscriptions, as well as art and monumental architecture of South Arabian style. The inscriptions of the Daamat kingdom were in South Arabian script. Also introduced from South Arabia was the cult of the sun and moon gods housed in temples built of finely dressed stone, along with the royal title of *mukarib*.[42] All of the South Arabian elements in northern Ethiopia/Eritrea are connected with elite centers; the rest of the material culture is thought to be indigenous.[43]

The seventy-three-year-old hypothesis of Conti Rossini proposes that the formation of the state of Daamat was the result of the migration of South Arabian elites to the Tigrean plateau where they subjugated local peoples and impressed their culture on indigenous ones. It is presently thought more probable that local chiefs adopted the South Arabian model of a state, as most of the material culture of the Daamat kingdom can be ascribed to an African tradition. A contrary hypothesis is that the South Arabian elements are a minor but impressive component of this culture, which might suggest that South Arabian influence affected only the upper stratum of the population.[44]

After the third century B.C. there are no more inscriptions from the kingdom of Daamat. Yeha remained an important ceremonial center, however, and a South Arabian style "palace" there continued to be occupied up to the second century B.C.[45]

A complex society characterized by a different material culture than that of Daamat arose in western Tigray in the late first millennium B.C. A stele field we are excavating on a hill northwest of Aksum, where, according to local tradition, the earliest occupation of Aksum occurred, has yielded ceramics which we are calling "Proto-Aksumite." Although of the same wares, these ceramics are typologically earlier than those associated with Early Aksumite burials in Aksum. Such evidence may push back the beginning of Aksum by one to two centuries into the late first millennium B.C.[46]

Aksumite power increased in the first–second centuries A.D., when a monumental stele field appeared at this site.[47] Finally, Aksum consolidated its control through military conquest on the Tigrean plateau in the second–third centuries A.D., as we can infer from a Greek inscription recorded by Cosmas Indicopleustes at Adulis. This inscription, usually dated to the third century A.D., reports the progressive incorporation of different tribes settled on the Tigrean plateau into the Aksumite state.[48] In the third century A.D., Aksum expanded its influence as far as Meroe and South Arabia.[49] As Aksum expanded its power and control, it must also have gained a monopoly on the lucrative trade in luxury materials with the Mediterranean.

The rise of the kingdom of Aksum was connected in part to trade with Ptolemaic and later Roman Egypt. Aksum was a trading partner of Rome, but never a part of the Roman Empire. Aksum provided Rome with ivory, incense, gold dust, hides, civet cat musk, rhinoceros horn, and slaves, via its port at Adulis.[50]

Aksumite culture is very different from the Pre-Aksumite culture of the state of Daamat, and the origins of the Aksumite state are probably indigenous. The ceramics are different wares from those associated with Daamat's ceremonial centers, and the monumental architecture of Aksum is also very different. There is no evidence of Aksumite stone temples such as were built by the Daamat state. Early Aksumite monuments consist of huge monolithic stelae associated with stone platforms, tombs, and burials. These differences suggest a change in state ideology, from one where public works were the cult temples of gods, to the state of Aksum where monumental works commemorated (elite) human burials. Perhaps this change also implies a shift in legitimation of rule, from a state which erected cult temples to demonstrate its connections with (foreign) gods, to the state of Aksum which derived its legitimacy from descent from indigenous elite and royal ancestors.

The Aksumite state, then, represents a break in the material culture of the Pre-Aksumite Period, especially in architecture and ceramics. The Aksumites also transformed the Sabean script in order to write their spoken language, Ge'ez. New mortuary practices are seen at Aksum, too, which may be related to cultural groups to the west in the eastern Sudanese lowlands (Gash Group). This form of mortuary symbolism also seems to represent a break with South Arabian culture.[51]

A major reason for Aksum's rise to power was the wealth that trade with the Mediterranean brought. The location of a polity centered at Aksum on the western Tigrean plateau may also be explained by sources of ivory, gold, and incense located in the lowlands to the west of Aksum. Aksum is located at a strategic point along a road from the lowlands to the plateau to the Red Sea.[52]

The location of the state's center in western Tigray probably depended on environmental and political factors. Aksum, like Yeha, is located in a region with highly fertile land that is optimal for plow cultivation and requires no "fertility intervention" other than crop rotation.[53] Thus Aksum had the agricultural potential to support a concentrated population of rulers, elites, and specialists. Butzer suggests that in the early first millennium A.D. there was a climatic shift which greatly augmented the spring rains, so that two crops annually would have been possible.[54]

State Formation: A Cross-cultural Comparison

Comparing the processes of state formation in Egypt and northern Ethiopia, we suggest that several factors were important in the rise of complex society and the state in both regions:

1) Regional economic interaction and economic expansion.
2) Long-distance trade in sumptuary (high status) craft goods and raw materials.
3) Greater control of the economy by elites and the establishment of a bureaucracy for procurement, manufacturing/processing, and distribution of goods and materials exchanged in regional and long-distance trade networks.
4) An ideology that reinforced economic control by elites, whose power was symbolized in mortuary cults.
5) Ascendancy in power and control and the successful expansion of particular polities.
6) Some warfare (though evidence for this is conjectural).

Population pressure as a factor in the rise of the early Egyptian and Ethiopian states is unknown and unquantifiable from present data.

Processes of state formation in Egypt and Ethiopia were *internal,* but *external* forces, such as long-distance trading relationships, migration, and warfare, then modified or transformed the internal processes. Internal demand for goods and materials that reinforced the status of elites, which led to external trade and exchange, was a factor in state formation in Predynastic Egypt. In contrast, external demand for materials for elite goods by a more complex society (Egypt and later the Roman Empire), was a factor in the rise of the state in Ethiopia, and probably accelerated the processes of social differentiation on the Tigrean plateau.

The rise of complex society and the state in northern Ethiopia/Eritrea is also indisputably related to earlier cultural developments in the Nile Valley, but a unique indigenous civilization developed there in the highlands. The progressive inclusion of the western Ethio-Sudanese lowlands and the plateau in the Egyptian interchange circuit along the Nile Valley and the Red Sea in the third-second millennia B.C. stimulated the rise of complex society in Nubia and an early state first at Kerma,[55] then the rise of complex society in the Gash Delta (Kassala) and possibly the Hamasien plateau (Asmara).[56] The commercial and political expansion of the South Arabs, that replaced Egypt along the Red Sea trade route, stimulated the transformation of a local hierarchical society into the Sabean-like kingdom of Daamat.[57] Roman commercial expansion by the first century A.D. again stimulated the formation of a powerful state centered at Aksum by the second-third centuries A.D. The Ethiopian peoples involved in these transformations, however, always maintained their cultural identity, which is well reflected in their material culture.

We know from later inscriptions that a powerful kingship developed at Aksum, which expanded its dominion possibly as far as Meroe and South Arabia. As Aksum expanded its power and control, it must also have gained a monopoly on the lucrative trade in luxury materials with the Mediterranean. How this trade was organized, and how the procurement and processing of materials were controlled are unknown at present. But we hope to know more about these factors, as well as to gain more information about the agricultural base, as investigations which were interrupted after 1974 resume once again in Tigray and Eritrea. Our fieldwork at Aksum in 1993–1998 certainly suggests that there is excellent preservation of archaeological sites, and the discovery of new evidence will hopefully illuminate issues presented in this study.

Notes

1. Kathryn A. Bard, "The Geography of Excavated Predynastic Sites and the Rise of Complex Society," *JARCE* 24 (1987): 81–93; idem, "The Evolution of

Social Complexity in Predynastic Egypt: An Analysis of the Naqada Cemeteries," *JMA* 2 (1989): 223–48; idem, "Predynastic Settlement Patterns in the Hu-Semaineh Region, Egypt," *JFA* 16 (1989): 475–78; idem, "Ideology and the Evolution of Complex Society in Predynastic Egypt," in *Ancient Thought: The Archaeology of Ideology*, Proceedings of the 23rd Annual Chacmool Conference, S. Goldsmith et al., eds. (Calgary: University of Calgary Press, 1992), 279–81; idem, "Toward an Interpretation of the Role of Ideology in the Evolution of Complex Society in Egypt," *JAA* 11 (1992): 1–24; idem, "Origins of Egyptian Writing," in *The Followers of Horus: Studies Dedicated to Michael Allen Hoffman*, Oxbow Monograph 20, R. Friedman and B. Adams, eds. (Oxford: Oxbow Books, 1992); idem, "Preliminary Report: The 1991 Boston University Excavations at Halfiah Gibli and Semaineh, Upper Egypt," *Newsletter of the American Research Center in Egypt* 158/159 (1992): 11–15; idem, *From Farmers to Pharaohs: Mortuary Evidence for the Rise of Complex Society in Egypt* (Sheffield: Sheffield Academic Press, 1994); idem, "The Egyptian Predynastic: A Review of the Evidence," *JFA* 21 (1994): 265–88; Kathryn A. Bard and Robert L. Carneiro, "Patterns of Predynastic Settlement Location, Social Evolution, and the Circumscription Theory," *Cahiers de Recherches de l'Institut de Papyrologie et d'Égyptologie de Lille* 11 (1989): 15–23; Rodolfo Fattovich, "Elementi per una ricerca sulle origini della monarchia sacra egiziana," RSO 45 (1970): 133–49; idem, "Trends in the Study of Predynastic Social Structures," in *Acts of the 1st International Congress of Egyptology*, W. F. Reineke, ed. (Berlin: Akademie Verlag, 1979): 215–20; idem, "Le sepolture predinastiche egiziane: un contributo allo studio delle ideologie funerarie," in *La mort, les morts dans les societés anciennes*, G. Gnoli and J. P. Vernant, eds. (Paris: Maison des sciences de l'homme, 1982), 419–27; idem, "Remarks on the Dynamics of State Formation in Ancient Egypt," in *On Social Evolution: Contributions to Anthropological Concepts*, W. Dostal, ed. (Vienna: Verlag Ferdinand Berger, 1984), 29–78; idem, "La dimensione sociale delle pratiche funerarie predinastiche nell'altro Egitto," in *Physical Anthropology and Prehistoric Archaeology*, Rivista di Antropologia 66, suppl.; (Rome: Istituto Italiano di Antropolgia, 1988), 395–410; Claudio Barocas, Rodolfo Fattovich, and Maurizio Tosi, "The Oriental Institute of Naples Expedition to Petrie's South Town (Upper Egypt), 1977–1983: An Interim Report," in *The Late Prehistory of the Nile Basin and the Sahara*, L. Krzyzaniak, ed. (Poznan: Muzeum Archeologiczne W. Poznaniu, 1989), 295–301; M. Chlodnick, Rodolfo Fattovich, and Sandro Salvatori, "Italian Excavations in the Nile Delta: Fresh Data and New Hypotheses on the 4th Millennium Cultural Development of Egyptian Prehistory," *Rivista di Archeologia* 15 (1991): 5–33; idem, "The Italian Archaeological Mission of the C.S.R.L.–Venice to the Eastern Nile Delta: A Preliminary Report of the 1987–1988 Field Sessions," *Cahier de Recherches de l'Institut de Papryologie et d'Égyptologie de Lille* 14 (1992): 45–62; idem, "The Nile Delta in Transition: A View from Tell el-Farkha," in *The Nile Delta in Transition: 4th-3rd Millennium B.C.*, E. C. M. van den Brink, ed. (Jerusalem: Israel Exploration Society, 1992), 171–90;

2. Rodolfo Fattovich, "Some Data for the Study of the Cultural History in Ancient Northern Ethiopia," *Nyame Akuma* 10 (1977): 6–18; idem, "Pre-Aksumite Civilization of Ethiopia: A Provisional Review," *Proceedings of the Seminar for Arabian Studies* 7 (1977): 73–78; idem, "Remarks on the Late Prehistory and Early History of Northern Ethiopia," in *Proceedings of the Eighth International Conference of Ethiopian Studies* I, T. Beyene, ed. (Addis Ababa: Institute of Ethiopian Studies, 1988), 85–104; idem, "Remarks on the Pre-Aksumite Period in Northern Ethiopia," *Journal of Ethiopian Studies* 23 (1990): 1–33; idem, "Ricerche archeologiche nel delta del Gash (Kassala): 1980–1989; un bilancio preliminare," *Rassegna di Studi Etiopici* 33 (1991): 89–130; idem, "At the Periphery of the Empire: The Gash Delta (Eastern Sudan)," in *Egypt and Africa: Nubia from Prehistory to Islam,* W. V. Davies, ed. (London: British Museum Press, 1991), 40–47; idem, "Evidence of Possible Administrative Devices in the Gash Delta (Kassala), 3rd-2nd Millennia B.C.," *Archéologie du Nil Moyen* 5 (1991): 65–78; idem, "Urban Developments in the Northern Horn of Africa in Ancient and Medieval Times," paper presented at the WAC Inter-Congress: *Urban Origins in Eastern Africa* (Mombasa, Kenya, January 1993).

3. R. Fattovich and K. A. Bard, "Scavi Archeologici nella Zona di Aksum. c. Ona Enda Aboi Zague (Bieta Giyorgis)," *Rassegna di Studi Etiopici* 35 (1993): 41–71; K. A. Bard and R. Fattovich, "The 1993 Excavations at Ona Enda Aboi Zague (Aksum, Tigray)," *Nyame Akuma* 40 (1993): 14–17.

4. Karl W. Butzer, *Early Hydraulic Civilization in Egypt* (Chicago: University of Chicago Press, 1976).

5. Karl W. Butzer, "Rise and Fall of Axum, Ethiopia: A Geo-Archaeological Interpretation," *American Antiquity* 46 (1981): 472–95.

6. Mariam M. Wolde, *An Introductory Geography of Ethiopia* (Addis Ababa: Berhanena Selam H.S.I. Printing Press, 1972).

7. R. Fattovich, "Processi storici e microrevoluzione umana: riflessioni sulla possibile integrazione tra le discipline storiche ed antropologiche," *Rivista di Antropologia* 68 (1990): 5–35.

8. Butzer, "Rise and Fall of Axum," 472; Steven A. Brandt, "New Perspectives on the Origins of Food Production in Ethiopia," in *From Hunters to Farmers; The Causes and Consequences of Food Production in Africa,* J. D. Clark and S. A. Brandt, eds. (Berkeley: University of California Press, 1984): 173–90; Fattovich, "Remarks on the Late Prehistory;" David W. Phillipson, "The Antiquity of Cultivation and Herding in Ethiopia," in *The Archaeology of Africa: Food, Metals and Towns,* T. Shaw et al., eds. (London: Routledge & Kegan Paul, 1993), 344–57.

9. Brandt, "New Perspectives."

10. Michael A. Hoffman, *Egypt Before the Pharaohs* (New York: Knopf, 1979); Bruce G. Trigger, "The Rise of Egyptian Civilization," in *Ancient Egypt: A Social History,* B. G. Trigger, B. J. Kemp, D. O'Connor, and A. B. Lloyd, eds. (Cambridge: Cambridge University Press, 1983), 1–70; Fekri A. Hassan, "The Predynastic of Egypt," *Journal of World Prehistory* 2 (1988): 135–85; Barry

J. Kemp, *Ancient Egypt: Anatomy of a Civilization* (London: Routledge & Kegan Paul, 1989); Robert J. Wenke, "The Evolution of Early Egyptian Civilization: Issues and Evidence," *Journal of World Prehistory* 5 (1991): 279–329.

11. Bard, *From Farmers to Pharaohs*, 1–27; idem, "The Egyptian Predynastic"; Werner Kaiser, "Eine Bemerkungen," *ZÄS* 91 (1964): 86–125; idem, "Zur Sudausdehnung der vorgeschichtlichen Deltakulturen und zur frühen Entwicklung Oberägyptens," *Mitteilungen des Deutschen Archäologischen Instituts Abteilung Kairo* 41 (1985): 61–87; idem, "Zur Enstehung des gesamtägyptischen Staates," *Mitteilungen des Deutschen Archäologischen Instituts Abteilung Kairo* 46 (1990): 287–99.

12. Wendy Anderson, "Badarian Burials: Evidence of Social Inequality in Middle Egypt During the Early Predynastic Era," *JARCE* 29 (1992): 51–66; Bard, *From Farmers to Pharaohs;* idem, "The Egyptian Predynastic;" Rodolfo Fattovich, "Definizione dei complessi culturali dell'Egitto Predinastico e loro rapporti reciproci," *Africa* 28 (1973): 257–89; idem, "Le sepolture predinastiche egiziane;" idem, "Remarks on the Dynamics of State Formation;" idem, "La dimensione sociale delle pratiche funerarie predinastiche nell'alto Egitto;" Hassan, "The Predynastic of Egypt"; Helene J. Kantor, "The Relative Chronology of Egypt and Its Foreign Correlations Before the First Intermediate Period," in *Chronologies in Old World Archaeology*, R. W. Ehrich, ed. (Chicago: University of Chicago Press, 1992), 3–21; Lech Krzyzaniak, *Early Farming Cultures on the Lower Nile: The Predynastic Period in Egypt* (Warsaw: Editions Scientifiques de Pologne, 1977).

13. Bard, *From Farmers to Pharaohs*, 280–81; idem, "The Egyptian Predynastic," 24.

14. Bard, "The Evolution of Social Complexity in Predynastic Egypt;" idem, *From Farmers to Pharaohs;* Fattovich, "Le sepolture predinastiche egiziane"; idem, "Remarks on the Dynamics of State Formation in Ancient Egypt"; idem, "La dimensione sociale delle pratiche funerarie predinastiche nell'alto Egitto"; Krzyzaniak, *Early Farming Cultures.*

15. Bard, *From Farmers to Pharaohs;* Fattovich, "Definizione dei complessi culturali dell'Egitto Predinastico;" Krzyzaniak, *Early Farming Cultures on the Lower Nile;* Trigger, "The Rise of Egyptian Civilization."

16. Juris Zarins, "Ancient Egypt and the Red Sea Trade: The Case for Obsidian in the Predynastic and Archaic Periods," in *Essays in Ancient Civilization Presented to Helene J. Kantor*, Al Leonard, Jr. and B. B. Williams, eds. (Chicago: Oriental Institute of the University of Chicago, 1989), 339–68.

17. Bard, "The Egyptian Predynastic;" Bruce G. Trigger, "Egypt: A Fledgling Nation," *Journal of the Society for the Study of Egyptian Antiquities* 17 (1987): 58–62.

18. Bard, "Preliminary Report: The 1991 Boston University Excavations at Halfiah Gibli and Semaineh, Upper Egypt."

19. Kathryn A. Bard, "A Quantitative Analysis of the Predynastic Burials in Armant Cemetery 1400–1500," *JEA* 74 (1988): 39–55; idem, "The Egyptian

Predynastic;" Fattovich, "Trends in the Study of Predynastic Social Structures;" idem, "Le sepolture predinastiche egiziane;" idem, "La dimensione sociale delle pratiche funerarie predinastiche."

20. Trigger, "Egypt: A Fledgling Nation," 60.

21. Bard, "Ideology and the Evolution of Complex Society;" idem, "Toward an Interpretation of the Role of Ideology;" idem, "The Egyptian Predynastic."

22. Bard, "The Egyptian Predynastic;" Fattovich, "Remarks on the Dynamics of State Formation;" see also Michael A. Hoffman, *The Predynastic of Hierakonpolis: An Interim Report* Egyptian Studies Association Publication no. 1 (Giza, Egypt: Cairo University Herbarium, Faculty of Science; Macomb, Illinois: Department of Sociology and Anthropology, Western Illinois University, 1982).

23. Fattovich, "Remarks on the Dynamics of State Formation."

24. M. Chlodnicki, Rodolfo Fattovich and Sandro Salvatori, "The Italian Archaeological Mission of the C.S.R.L.-Venice to the Eastern Nile Delta: A Preliminary Report of the 1987–1988 Field Seasons,"*Cahier de Recherches de l'Institut de Papyrologie et d'Égyptologie de Lille* 14 (1992): 45–62; idem, "The Nile Delta in Transition: A View from Tell el-Farkha," in *The Nile Delta in Transition: 4th-3rd Millennium B.C.*, E. C. M. van den Brink, ed. (Jerusalem: Israel Exploration Society, 1992), 171–90; Karla Kroeper, "The Excavations of the Munich East-Delta Expedition in Minshat Abur Omar," in *The Archaeology of the Nile Delta, Problems and Priorities,* E. C. M. van den Brink, ed. (Amsterdam: Netherlands Foundation for Archaeological Research in Egypt, 1988), 11–46.

25. William C. Hayes, *Most Ancient Egypt* (Chicago: University of Chicago Press, 1965).

26. Thomas von der Way, "Excavations at Tell el-Fara'in-Buto in 1987–1989," in *The Nile Delta in Transition: 4th.–3rd. Millennium B.C.*, E. C. M. van den Brink, ed. (Jerusalem: Israel Exploration Society, 1992), 1–10.

27. Chlodnicki, Fattovich and Salvatori, "Italian Excavations in the Nile Delta;" idem, "The Italian Archaeological Mission . . . to the Eastern Nile Delta;" E. C. M. van den Brink, "Report on the Excavations at Tell Ibrahim Awad, Season 1988–1990," in *The Nile Delta in Transition,* 43–68.

28. Trigger, "Egypt: A Fledgling Nation," 61; Kemp, *Ancient Egypt,* 45.

29. Carlo Conti Rossini, *Storia d'Etiopia* (Bergamo: Istituto di Arti Grafiche, 1928); A. J. Drewes, *Inscriptions de l'Éthiopie Antique* (Leiden: Brill, 1962); Roger Schneider, "Les debuts de l'histoire éthiopienne," *Documents pour servir à l'histoire de la civilisation éthiopienne* (Paris: Centre de la Recherche Scientifique, 1976), 7:47–54.

30. Francis Anfray, "Aspect de l'archéologie éthiopienne," *Journal of African History* 9 (1968): 345–66; idem, *Les anciens Éthiopiens* (Paris: Colin, 1990); Joseph W. Michels, "The Aksumite Kingdom: A Settlement Archaeological Perspective," in *Proceedings of the Ninth International Conference of Ethiopian Studies* (Moscow: Nauka Publishers, 1988), 5:173–83; idem, "Regional Political Organization in the Axum-Yeha Area During the Pre-Axumite and Axumite Eras," paper presented at the 10th International Conference on Ethiopian Stud-

ies, Paris, 1988; Fattovich, "Some Data for the Study of the Cultural History;" idem, "Remarks on the Late Prehistory;" idem, "Urban Developments in the Northern Horn of Africa."

31. R. Fattovich, "The Problem of Punt in the Light of the Recent Field Work in the Eastern Sudan," in *Akten des Vierten Internationalen Ägyptologen Kongresses,* S. Schoske, ed. (Hamburg: Helmut Buske Verlag, 1990), 4:257–72; idem, "Urban Developments in the Northern Horn of Africa."

32. Fattovich, "Ricerche archeologiche nel delta del Gash (Kassala), 1980–1989;" idem, "At the Periphery of the Empire;" idem, "Evidence of Possible Administrative Devices;" R. Fattovich, K. Sadr, and S. Vitagliano, "Society and Territory in the Gash Delta (Kassala, Eastern Sudan), 3000 B.C.–A.D. 300/400," *Origini* 14 (1988–89): 329–57; K. Sadr, *The Development of Nomadism in Ancient Northeast Africa* (Philadelphia: University of Pennsylvania Press, 1991).

33. R. Fattovich, "Punt: The Archaeological Evidence," *Beiträge zur Sudanforschung* 6 (1996): 15–29.

34. R. Paribeni, "Scavi sul luogo dell'antica Adulis," *Monumenti Antichi* 18 (1907): 437–52.

35. Fattovich, "Remarks on the Late Prehistory;" S. Munro-Hay and Giuseppe Tringali, "The Ona Sites of Asmara and Hamasien," *Rassegna di Studi Etiopici* 35 (1993): 135–70; G. Tringali, "Necropoli di Cascase e oggetti sudarabici (?) della regione di Asmara (Eritrea)," *Rassegna di Studi Etiopici* 26 (1979): 47–66.

36. Fattovich, "Punt: The Archaeological Evidence."

37. Conti Rossini, *Storia d'Etiopia;* Anfray, *Les anciens Éthiopiens.*

38. Fattovich, "Remarks on the Pre-Aksumite Period."

39. Anfray, *Les anciens Éthiopiens;* Fattovich, "Urban Developments in the Northern Horn of Africa," 29.

40. Fattovich, "Remarks on the Pre-Aksumite Period."

41. Drewes, *Inscriptions de l'Éthiopie Antique.*

42. Fattovich, "Remarks on the Pre-Aksumite Period."

43. Fattovich, "Pre-Aksumite Civilization of Ethiopia;" idem, "Remarks on the Pre-Aksumite Period."

44. Fattovich, "Remarks on the Pre-Aksumite Period."

45. Michels, "Regional Political Organization in the Axum-Yeha Area;" Fattovich, "Remarks on the Pre-Aksumite Period."

46. Bard and Fattovich, "The 1993 Excavations at Ona Enda Aboi Zague;" Fattovich and Bard, "Scavi Archeologici nella Zona di Aksum."

47. Stuart Munro-Hay, *Excavations at Aksum* (London: British Institute in Eastern Africa, 1989).

48. Conti Rossini, *Storia d'Etiopia;* Stuart Munro-Hay, *Aksum: An African Civilisation of Late Antiquity* (Edinburgh: Edinburgh University Press, 1991).

49. Conti Rossini, *Storia d'Etiopia.*

50. Butzer, "Rise and Fall of Axum,"473; Yuri M. Kobishchanov, *Axum*

(University Park, PA: Pennsylvania State University Press, 1979); Munro-Hay, *Aksum*.

51. R. Fattovich, "Some Remarks on the Origins of the Aksumite Stelae," *Annales d'Éthiopie* 14 (1987): 43–69.

52. Butzer, "Rise and Fall of Axum," 472–73.

53. Michels, "Regional Political Organization," 3.

54. Butzer, "Rise and Fall of Axum," 491.

55. Charles Bonnet, *Kerma, royaume de Nubie* (Geneva: Musée d'art et histoire, 1990).

56. See Fattovich, "Urban Developments in the Northern Horn of Africa;" Fattovich, Sadr and Vitagliano, "Society and Territory in the Gash Delta."

57. Fattovich, "The Problem of Punt."

10

Colonizing the Past: Origin Myths of the Great Zimbabwe Ruins

Maynard W. Swanson

❋

The Great Zimbabwe Ruins

Zimbabwe is the independent African republic just north of South Africa that was formerly the British settler colony of Rhodesia, its name connotes the spectacular and famous stone ruins of Great Zimbabwe, bearing witness to extraordinary endeavors and achievements of past times. More precisely the word *zimbabwe,* "house of stone" or "venerated house" in the Shona language,[1] refers to the ancient hilltop residences or citadels of chiefs and rulers. These were scattered across the high plateau of southern Africa, between the Zambesi and Limpopo Rivers, that has been the home of the Shona people for a thousand years or more. There are hundreds of stone ruins, but the remarkable character and imposing aspect of the Great Zimbabwe overshadows them all, causing Western popular interest and scholarly attention to focus upon it since the arrival of the Europeans about 1870.

Set on the southwestern edge of the plateau about two hundred miles inland, Great Zimbabwe commands a natural line of communication between the mineral-rich interior and the sea. Two large structures dominate the scene. On a high granite hill is the zimbabwe proper, overlooking a broad valley where a larger group of buildings forms an immense, roughly oval, enclosure. The zimbabwe on the hill is a complex of dry stone walls built among huge boulders to form a complex arrangement of

passages and enclosures. Some authorities emphasize its appearance as a
fort. Others see it as a place of ritual. The first European visitors in the late
nineteenth century labelled it "The Acropolis" with all the classical con-
notations that implies. From the outset this characterization came to dominate their interpretations of its functions. Let us call it the Hill Ruin.

A monumental enclosure in the valley below dominates a large cluster of smaller broken walls and enclosures. It is a very big building by any
standard: eight hundred feet in circumference, two hundred twenty feet
in diameter, with tapering walls up to thirty feet high and fourteen feet
thick at their base. Within this great wall are smaller ruined walls, platforms and enclosures giving the impression of a kind of labyrinth, with a
few narrow entrances. Inside it are several solid conical towers or remains
of towers, with one monumental tower measuring thirty feet high and
fifty-six feet in circumference at its base. This complex, called "The Temple" by the earliest European visitors, was imagined to be the center of
"Semitic" phallic religious ritual. Let us call it the Great Enclosure. (See
figs. 10.1 and 10.2.)

Constructed of brick-like granite stones laid without mortar in more or
less regular courses, the character of this architecture and the atmosphere
engendered by it have always had a strong and evocative effect on visitors

Figure 10.1   The Great Enclosure of the Great Zimbabwe ruins. Photo by
Robert Harbison, ©*The Christian Science Monitor.*

Figure 10.2   The Courtyard of the Great Enclosure. Photo by Robert
Harbison, ©*The Christian Science Monitor.*

and investigators. "Zimbabwe is one of those remarkable instances of man's
handiwork from which a glamour is distilled, which emanates an atmosphere elusive alike to reason and to definition," said the archaeologist
Gertrude Caton-Thompson in 1931,[2] even as she proceeded to demystify
it with her science to the irritation of antiquarian romantics and colonial
racists. Indeed, there is no geometry or regularity apparent in its physical
plan or construction. The architect Wilfrid Mallows noted this in 1984:

> Not one straight wall, not one rectangular space, no true right angles or
> circles or true arcs of circles in any portion of the plan. Great Zimbabwe
> . . . is devoid of geometrical control. All . . . shapes are curving, sinuous,
> infinitely flexible, . . . a purely instinctive feeling for shape. . . . This char-
> acteristic non-rectangularity alone makes the Great Zimbabwe ruins
> unique in the world. . . . It is another world of form altogether . . . , a
> kind of warm treacle of hand-made, sculpted shapes."[3]

Who inspired and who built Great Zimbabwe, when, how, and why?
And why did it and all its lesser namesakes go to ruin? The question of
Great Zimbabwe's origin and history was entangled from the very begin-
ning of modern European knowledge about it, and of white settlement in
Mashonaland, with the politics of colonial domination and the mythology

of race-thinking. This chapter is about these myths and politics, and the way they have bedeviled our understanding of this remarkable place. They involve as well the larger question of the relationship between African and Mediterranean, Near Eastern and Indian civilizations.

Diffusionist or Indigenist Origins?

Foreign or African builders? "Diffusionist" or "indigenist"[4] in inspiration? The question of origins and the modes of explanation have turned on these terms. The first European explorer to publicize the ruins was the German geologist Karl Mauch, who saw the Great Zimbabwe on 5 September 1871. Scrambling and picking his way through the trees and tangled vegetation that clothed the ruins, Mauch saw enough to launch the speculation that instigated the myth of Semitic origins. He thought in the notional terms of his time. His imagination was fixed upon the Biblical account of Solomon, Sheba and Ophir, and he concluded that here, or nearby, were the legendary mines of Solomon. Here, Mauch imagined, Sheba, on returning from her sojourn in Israel, had imitated Solomon's temple and introduced the religion of the Israelites.[5]

The Semitic myth of the Great Zimbabwe was emerging. Mauch's report fell upon fertile ground. Gold fever was everywhere. Popular knowledge was widely rooted in Biblical learning and traditions. There was awareness as well of the early Portuguese reports on southeastern Africa, of a gold trade at Sofala and the Kingdom of the Monomotapa in the Zambezi valley to the north. The Portuguese had dreamed of discovering the Eldorado of the ancients. More importantly, their Arab-Swahili informants may have invented the legend identifying Great Zimbabwe with Solomon and Ophir. Recent scholarship suggests that this was probably with the purpose of maintaining their own claim to primacy in the trade of Mashonaland against the Portuguese interlopers, who then picked up the idea.[6]

With Cecil Rhodes's seizure of Mashonaland in 1890, the colonialist ethos in southern Africa took hold in full force. Rhodes sought to replicate further north, under his own aegis, the bonanza of the Transvaal gold fields. He was a romantic and he was as fascinated with the ruins as he was with the lure of gold and the pursuit of power. Moreover, he understood the legitimating value of the myth of an alien precursor for his enterprise of domination and exploitation. Having seized Mashonaland from its presumably unworthy African inhabitants, Rhodes next sponsored investigations to prove that myth true. As Prime Minister of the Cape Colony he sent the Colonial Historiographer, George Macaulay Theal, to Europe to collect and publish archives on the subject. Theal's multivolume *Records of South Eastern Africa* became a bible of the diffusionists.[7]

The first official investigator of Great Zimbabwe itself was a classical antiquarian named James Theodore Bent, chosen for the task by the Royal Geographical Society at Rhodes' invitation. Rhodes knew exactly what he wanted his experienced antiquarian to find for him, and he kept a close eye on Bent's activity. The zimbabwes and ancient mineworkings of Rhodesia had enormous political and psychological as well as hoped-for economic value to Rhodes, his British South Africa Company, and the white settlers he had sent there. To the Europeans, the Rhodesian past was a history of conquest and exploitation by people rather like themselves. As it had been, so it now would be. The fundamental attitude and assumptions in this view were racist and supremacist in the Social Darwinist mode of the day: the Africans as a degraded and inferior branch of humanity could not have accomplished the material achievement evident in the ancient ruins of Mashonaland. Rhodes and his settlers saw themselves mirrored, as it were, in the presumed evidence of their imagined predecessors.

With these views fixed firmly in his mind, Bent proceeded to knock and dig at the ancient ruins for the remains of a "Semitic" master race. An unsystematic investigator, he selected what he could find to prove the diffusionist assumptions and desires he shared with his powerful sponsor. In an unguarded moment he confessed that he was discouraged by the lack of any unambiguous evidence and privately wondered if Great Zimbabwe really was "the place" of those ancient colonizers. Nevertheless, imagination ruled science. As he said: "We were able to repeople this country with a race highly civilized in far distant ages, a race far advanced in the art of building and decorating, a gold-seeking race who occupied it like a garrison in the midst of an enemy's country."[8] Bent did obey his inner doubts to the extent of rejecting Solomon and Sheba in favor of Arabs and Phoenicians as the colonizers of this garrison-post in an enemy's country. Although there was no true evidence of this hypothesis, either at Great Zimbabwe or in the records of it that Theal was dredging up copiously in the archives of Europe, to the true believer the lack of proof simply proved the case. As Bent argued, it was well known that "the Semitic nations . . . concealed from other countries the whereabouts of their commercial relations."[9]

These early ransackings did tremendous damage to the real evidence of the past which the ruins did contain, and thus to all future scientific study. What was called archaeology was in fact a treasure hunt. After all,

Rhodes and company were adventurers, and their great and costly speculation was expected to pay—and pay handsomely. This is exemplified by
the formation in 1894 of The Ancient Ruins Company which had a
monopoly from the British South Africa Company to extract gold from
the zimbabwes. Structures were pulled down and artifacts destroyed or
appropriated with little or no record kept of findings. Everything but
"treasure" was treated as debris. About fifty of the smaller zimbabwes were
ravaged in this way. For six years the devastation continued, until a public outcry and personal remonstrances with Rhodes brought an end to
these operations. A director of the company, William Neal, later gave Bent
some of his loot. He gave the company records to Bent's successor
Richard Hall, with whom he authored a report that became a major popular source for promoting the myth of the Great Zimbabwe. Rhodes himself was a great collector. He gathered nuggets, ornaments, bracelets,
beads, chains, even the famous and mysterious carved soapstone birds of
Zimbabwe, and gloated over their barbaric splendor, displaying them
prominently at his houses. But most was lost from the finds, sold off or
melted down. The extent of the loss will never be known.[10]

Finally, however, Rhodes appointed another gifted amateur, Richard
Nicklin Hall, a colonial journalist, to put a better face on things, especially
at Great Zimbabwe. Hall was as dedicated to the Semitic myth as Bent, his
acknowledged mentor, and vastly exceeded his charge with extensive excavations by way of "cleaning up". His method was appallingly simple, shov-
elling out the Great Enclosure to depths of five feet, in some places twelve
feet, to get at the bottom layers of "pure Semitic culture" on the assumption that the overlying material was just "the filth and decadence of the
Kafir [Mashona] occupation." But the bottom layers exhibited nothing significantly different from the Kafir filth and decadence in which, as later
investigators pointed out, the gold and other artifacts had been found. In
fact the gold did not occur at all in the lowest levels. Not deterred, Hall
simply gathered up the valuables and in his reports and book arranged them
schematically according to his pre-conceived chronological and racial
typology: the "fine" things earlier, the "crude" things later. Thus he
"proved" the myth he believed, despite what he actually found.[11]

David Chanaiwa, a historian of the Zimbabwe controversy, has
emphasized Hall's expression of the settler ethos. It was essential to
entrench the notion that Africans could accomplish no civilized art or construction without the inspiration and constant control of superior races
and colonizers, ancient or modern. Great Zimbabwe could not possibly
have been created by such a backward and inferior people as the blacks of

Mashonaland. Therefore a superior race had done so. Here was the Semitic myth of Great Zimbabwe in full bloom. Its outline ran thus: The Semites (Sabeans or Phoenicians) settled in Rhodesia between 2000 to 1000 B.C., mining and building in stone. They developed and controlled an empire there to the end of the first millennium A.D. Then the Bantu Africans moved in, swamping and absorbing the Semitic race and smothering their culture through "kafirization." The Bantu crudely copied the Semites, but the civilization degenerated into oblivion with the race who built it. Further evidence of this process supposedly remained in the so-called "Semitic" physical and cultural traits—in racial theory the two were assumed to run together—of individuals representing the African elite, such as the Shona ruling class or clan known as the "Makalanga." Hall described them thus: "well-shaped head, arched and decidedly Jewish nose, thin lips, high and intelligent forehead, rounded jaws and chin, . . . light skin and refined features. . . ." So-called "Semitic" African customs, such as a form of "monotheism" (the Mwari cult), veneration of ancestors, divination, millet beer-brewing, bride-wealth, musical instruments and certain games were taken as evidence of Semitic racial infusions.[12]

David Randall-MacIver

Criticisms of the Rhodesian adventurers and publicists, however, were mounting by the turn of the century. Into this broth of greed and prejudice there plunged in 1905, at the invitation of the British Association for the Advancement of Science, a young classically-trained archaeologist named David Randall-MacIver, a protégé of the famous Egyptologist and pioneer of modern scientific archaeology, Flinders Petrie. Randall-MacIver's report in 1905 transformed the discussion on the origins and nature of Zimbabwe civilization, triggering the diffusionist-indigenist controversy that has raged ever since. Its very title, *Medieval Rhodesia*, conveyed its message. Proceeding *de novo* without reference to previous speculations, Randall-MacIver concluded that there was not only no need, but no evidence, to explain Zimbabwe by a Semitic origin. His investigation was not exhaustive but it seemed sufficient to explode the work of Hall and the others. All the available evidence, he argued, including Hall's, stripped of its load of preconceptions, undermined the assumptions of alien provenance and great antiquity. Arguing from the principle that the ordinary occupation contents in and *under* the ruins must represent its builders and inhabitants, he showed that Hall's lower-level "pure Semitic" artifacts were identical with those in the so-called "Kafir" levels, and that they were essentially the same as modern Shona material culture. Nothing in the architecture necessitated or demonstrated the work of Eastern or Mediterranean builders, and no inscriptions or skeletal remains existed to indicate their presence. The buildings, he concluded, were "African in every detail and belong to a period which is fixed by foreign imports [Chinese, Arab and Persian] as . . . medieval."[13] All subsequent indigenist arguments have followed in this direction.

Randall-MacIver was scorned and resented by those of colonial opinion as an uninformed and mischievous interloper. Hall's indignant and highly defensive rebuttal restated the dogma of African inferiority and dismissed Randall-MacIver's assertion of Bantu initiative as a "faulty" hypothesis, an attack of "archaeological measles" born of youthful inexperience and ignorance of local conditions, for "The Bantu are not a progressive people. Nor is it possible that the primitive Bantu of medieval times had the capacity to suddenly evolve without the slightest influence from outside, the *renaissance* which resulted . . . in the Zimbabwe Temple."[14] A bitter controversy was underway. It would persist for more than seventy-five years. Other critics of the Semitic myth began to come forward as time went along, among them colonial residents, whose investigations of pottery or remains of dwellings and patterns of building as well as of African oral traditions began to establish a body of evidence for the zimbabwes that supported MacIver's indigenist argument.[15]

Gertrude Caton-Thompson

The next major effort to achieve conclusive evidence of Zimbabwe's builders took place in 1929 with another invitation from the British Association to a second Petrie-trained archaeologist, Gertrude Caton-Thompson. She extended and researched MacIver's work in the lowest levels, to establish unquestionably the earliest possible dating. Under the floors of the ruins outside the "Temple," in long trenches dug to bedrock beside it, in the hilltop "Acropolis" and further afield in other ruin sites she found the same evidence he had found, both over and *under* the floors within the Temple. Her findings confirmed MacIver's, except that new studies of imports, especially Asian beads, set his dating for the probable earliest building back by five centuries to about the seventh to ninth centuries. For Gertrude Caton-Thompson "It is inconceivable, as it was to Dr. MacIver, how a theory of Semitic origin could ever have been started. Every detail in plan, building, and contents seems African Bantu. . . .

Instead of a degenerate offshoot of a higher Oriental civilization, we have a vigorous native culture showing high organization, originality, and industry."[16] Randall-MacIver and Caton-Thompson had laid the foundations of the indigenist interpretation. All subsequent archaeology has not greatly altered these conclusions.

In 1929–30 Caton-Thompson's expedition invoked an end to "King Solomon's ghost" and urged respect for the African achievement instead of clinging to "a cherished but outworn romance." To the settler ideology, this was a problem. Such findings would contradict the belief that there was a gulf of superiority between alien achievers and African inferiors. It would detract from the equation of Rhodesia with mythical civilizers of the past. And so the myth lived vigorously on, despite the evidence of scientific archaeology. For one thing, and most importantly, it rested not merely upon the disputed interpretation of physical evidence, but upon a vision of cultural history and societal evolution which could even incorporate the contrary arguments for an indigenous African creation by modifying them and still asserting a distinction between the colonized inhabitants of Rhodesia and other presumed originators of their past.

The Hamitic Myth

Here we must step back a moment to the emerging Semitic myth at the turn of the century, to see a second racial myth shaping European ideas about Africa. We noted that interpreters of the Zimbabwe ruins had postulated Semitic racial infusions in the Bantu African population to account for their association with the ruins and to explain physical attributes that seemed to distinguish some Africans, presumed superior, from the negroid racial "type." In this distinction were echoed the conceptual ingredients of another, similar, collateral or parallel belief, also rooted in Biblical tradition, that had emerged by this time and would in the future perpetuate racial stereotypes to explain civilization in Africa generally. In the nineteenth and early twentieth centuries it had seemed necessary to account for both the presumed inferiority of the blacks *and* the achievements then revealed in Egyptian civilization and its derivative or associated African cultures. What could be the elusive agency of such influence? Another race, neither "Negroid" nor "White"? Ah! "Hamites"—and hence the "Hamitic myth." In her trenchant article on "The Hamitic Hypothesis,"[17] Edith Sanders has shown how in the nineteenth-century theological speculations, seeking to reconcile the imputed inferiority of blacks with the manifest achievements of civilization on the Nile, had altered the Biblical tradition of Noah's curse of Ham, the traditional progenitor of the blacks, by which Ham's descendants were to be forever "hewers of wood and drawers of water"—that is, natural inferiors and slaves. The new version assigned the ancient Egyptians, and their modern counterparts, to a branch of Ham's descendants *not* included in Noah's famous curse. In this line of thinking, only Canaan-son-of-Ham had been cursed, while the Egyptians as descendants of Mizraim, another son of Ham, were the creators of higher culture and civilization in Africa, and by that token, closer in race and nature to the whites. By the later nineteenth century, racial theory, bolstered by newly developing anatomical and linguistic studies, had appropriated these specially favored "Hamites" to a subordinate branch of the "Caucasian races." In wondrous variety they were supposed to include peoples in northern and northeastern Africa, from the blue-eyed Berbers to the darker Ethiopians and "Cushites" as well as the black Nilotics. They had "degenerated" or lagged behind the European vanguard of the "Caucasoids," but were presumed to carry the genius or potentiality of "civilization" and could be described with appropriate European-like features. In the terms of the Hamitic myth, every cultural step in Africa beyond hunting, gathering, and possibly the peasant subsistence agriculture of "the dark agricultural Negroes" (C. G. Seligman's phrase, 1930) was brought by the Hamites through their pastoral expansion and conquest, racial mixture, and influence. By the 1930s anthropologists and others were deeply influenced by this race-culture-diffusion paradigm. In 1930, the year before Caton-Thompson's book on *The Zimbabwe Culture: Ruins and Reactions,* one of the most prominent Hamitic exponents, C. G. Seligman, published *Races of Africa* with the message that "Apart from relatively late Semitic influence . . . the civilizations of Africa are the civilizations of the Hamites."[18] This conception had a long life and his book went to six editions, the last in 1966.

Diffusion From The East?

Still another diffusionist hypothesis was published in 1931. The German anthropologist Leo Frobenius, a devotee of the Vienna *Kulturkreis* or "culture sphere" school prominent in the 1920s, believed that much of Africa had been developed by influences from across the Indian Ocean which had created an "Erythraean" culture over much of the continent. Two streams had entered: one through Abyssinia westward into the sub-Saharan savannas; the other, thrusting onto the Rhodesian plateau from the Mozambican coast and as far as the southern rim of the Congo forests, supposedly accounting for outstanding features of cultural evolution there, including the Zimbabwean civilization. Although Frobenius' interpretation has been largely discounted, here it seems was the beginning of an Indo-African diffusionist thesis which has had a marginal but persistent effect on interpretations stressing Eastern origins and inspiration in African history.[19]

Caton-Thompson herself seems to have been influenced in some way by this notion, for though she was a convinced "evolutionist," she speculated on an external inspiration for the African builders of Great Zimbabwe. For her the real mystery still was *what* had started it, as distinct from *who?* Like most speculators who followed the slowly growing evidence for Iron Age expansion of the Bantu-speaking people, she postulated a migration from the far north within Africa of a group who were the progenitors of the Shona. But still the particular stimulus for the Zimbabwe culture must be explained, for it seemed apparent to her that in its Africanness, Great Zimbabwe was imitative in key aspects, "essentially the product of an infantile mind, a pre-logical mind." She turned to the East African coastal trading settlements, from which, "with quick imitative instinct," towers, walls and decorative motifs might have been replicated at the courts of Bantu rulers.[20] Others would in future follow this direction in search of the economic, if not the cultural, stimulus of Zimbabwe. The interest for us lies in her readiness to look for a source than a strictly autochthonous, or local inspiration. With this approach, the rejection of romantic antiquarianism and the settler ethos need not mean that Zimbabwe was *sui generis*.

Intra-African Diffusion?

Future debate among scholarly Africanists would focus on differences between champions of a purely autochthonous Shona creation, and those who saw a third dimension of larger movements of peoples and ideas within Africa on a continental scale—in other words, intra-African diffusionism. Here the Hamitic hypothesis, though not specifically its racial formula, would resonate into the future. An influential and respectable thesis of African history continues to postulate a southward and westward movement of peoples or cultural influences from the regions of the upper Nile. In this construction of history the Nilotic peoples were sometimes given a key connecting role in the creation of a pan-African, or at least a

Bantu, civilization that was held to display the same fundamental characteristics everywhere, deriving from the common base of an agricultural
revolution, iron age technology, pastoralism, and religio-political ideas
first seen in the Nile Valley—for example the "sacred kingship." As most
recently (1991) propounded by Roland Oliver, who explicitly rejects
Seligman's racialist stereotype,[21] this interpretation helps to account for
the broad outline of Late Iron Age development in the southward lobe of
the sub-Saharan "Sudanic" African civilization that comprised the great
Bantu expansion since the beginning of the Christian era. In this respect,
Oliver speaks of "a fairly massive injection" of Nilotic cultural influences
throughout eastern and southern Africa, of which the inception of Zimbabwe would be a part.[22]

Still, however, the older diffusionist themes persisted in the popular
mind, and the myths of alien racial intrusions and non-African origins
would be rejuvenated in the future struggles between white settler
domination and African nationalist resistance during the Rhodesian-
Zimbabwe independence war of the 1960s and 1970s. We will now turn
to these later episodes in the story.

Roger Summers

Over the next two generations archaeology, in the main, confirmed the
outlines propounded by Randall-MacIver and Caton-Thompson, with
significant changes in periodization, the character of the builders and their
purpose. Radiocarbon dating placed the dates of building between the
tenth and fifteenth centuries. Study of the patterns of walling established
a more detailed chronology that reversed the first-finest, last-worst
assumption of the diffusionists. Economic, historical, and ecological
analyses have placed Great Zimbabwe's decline and abandonment at the
end of the fifteenth century and set it clearly within a more complex history of Iron Age state-building and economic development on the central
African plateau. Finally, anthropology, ethnology, and study of oral tradition have identified the functions of Great Zimbabwe with Shona culture,
its social norms and its religio-political institutions.

The leading post-World War II Rhodesian authority was Roger Summers, an Englishman trained at the University of London, who held
important positions in the National Museum of Southern Rhodesia and
the Rhodesian Historical Monuments Commission in the 1950s and
1960s. He was a dedicated and successful popularizer, publishing, in addition to technical material, two major popular works in 1963 and 1971,

making the "Rhodesian mystery" accessible to general readers.[23] In 1963 he summarized "the modern answer," as follows: "Zimbabwe was an ancient sacred site, connected with an autochthonous religion [the Mwari cult] which even today has very many devotees." The local subclimate made it "a green island throughout the dry Rhodesian winter." The surrounding geology provided foliating granite stone for building the roughly coursed walls, the technique of which was probably invented there and the architecture almost certainly so, developing from the traditional mud-walled houses and open living spaces greatly enlarged in scale to enhance the rulers' prestige as wealth and population grew. This sacred place became the center of powerful rulers exhibiting the characteristics of the African sacred kingship, including seclusion—hence the labyrinthine complex of walls and passages—whose functions were focussed on the rituals of ancestral intercession with the Shona god Mwari. Great Zimbabwe thus became the seat of a powerful state, the center of a confederacy of the Rhodesian plateau adding economic to religious power through the rise and control of a luxury trade in gold and ivory for cloth, beads, and ceramics with the coastal settlements of mainly Arab traders. Summers pointed out that Zimbabwe was not a mining center, but rather the trading center. The identity of its occupants as determined from the archaeological evidence, cultural-anthropological study, and oral traditions, confirmed MacIver's thesis and was clearly of the African Iron Age, both early and late.[24]

Summers believed that Great Zimbabwe had flourished into the nineteenth century until about 1830, when all was destroyed by the invasion of warrior groups from South Africa. This, he felt, explained the findings of Hall's excavation, which had uncovered a mass of debris suggestive of a violent incursion. It also had the added appeal of connecting Great Zimbabwe directly with the recent history of the Shona. In this he was wrong. Subsequent radiocarbon dating and other analyses by his younger colleagues Thomas Huffman and Peter Garlake required a revision of the sequence, so that its rise, decline and collapse occurred within at most four hundred years from 1100 to about 1500, the Later Iron Age. But there was general agreement that the ruins remained a center of Shona religion long into the nineteenth century.[25]

Summers made a major effort to conciliate the politically charged diffusionist-indigenist controversy and put the most generous interpretation possible on both sides. He credited Hall with at least accurate observation and reporting of facts despite his lack of scientific excavation and his uncritical acceptance of his predecessors' views. He thought Randall-MacIver had been "quite unfair" and "brash" in his treatment of Hall. To Summers it was important to understand that their conflict had been the difference between two conceptual worlds: nineteenth-century romantic antiquarianism preoccupied with artifacts valued especially as corroboration of literary sources in the quest for the past; the other, thoroughly modern in its systematic attention to the residues of ordinary life as the true "text" of archaeology. "A whole scientific and technological revolution separated the protagonists."[26] He gave no credence to the colonialist mythology, but in his 1971 book, *Ancient Ruins and Vanished Civilizations of Southern Africa*, he urged readers to consider how the settlers' experience of the relatively backward and downtrodden Shona people they encountered in their day could have disposed them neither to understand nor to accept the latters' identification with the Zimbabwean past. But he was also willing, like Caton-Thompson, to consider an alien coastal inspiration for the buildings, much to the impatience of his younger indigenist colleagues.[27]

Independence and the Zimbabwe Controversy

It is clear that Summers wished to defuse the racial-political bombshell in the Great Zimbabwe controversy as Great Britain moved to force a multiracial decolonization on the settler society. But his moderation was overwhelmed in the rebellious Unilateral Declaration of Independence (UDI) by the white government in 1965. In the independence war that followed for the next fifteen years, the old Zimbabwe controversy gained new life. Scientific and scholarly inquiry were taken hostage as the diffusionist myths and hypotheses were mobilized in the ideological and psychological armory of white supremacy. Archaeologists, curators, even tourist guides in government service were pressured to suppress findings that credited the ruins to African origins. The curator of archaeology at Great Zimbabwe recalled:

> Censorship of guidebooks, museum displays, school textbooks, radio programmes, newspapers and films was a daily occurrence. Once a member of the Museum Board threatened me with losing my job if I said publicly that blacks had built Zimbabwe. . . . I wasn't allowed to mention radio carbon dates . . . (which) . . . show . . . that the Zimbabwean state flourished after 1000 A.D. . . . It was the first time since Germany in the thirties that archaeology has been so directly censored.

The prominent archaeologist Thomas N. Huffman, then senior curator at Queen Victoria Museum, Salisbury, put the issue succinctly:

We wanted to indicate to the average man in the street . . . what the evidence was, . . . and that's where we met opposition. . . . They wanted us to omit any mention of radio carbon dates . . . which would give the lie to other stories. Their thinking went like this: 'If we accept blacks could do something like that then, we must give them majority rule now.' [28]

The recrudescence of diffusionist mythology gained full force with a sustained polemic against the "pro-Bantu School" in the 1972, *The Origin of the Zimbabwe Civilization,* by Lord Robert Gayre of Gayre and Nigg. Honorary President of the Aberdeenshire-Banffshire Friends of Rhodesia, member of the Scottish Rhodesian Society and author of works on heraldry, genealogy and ethnography, Gayre brought a certain talent as well as prejudice to the cause he represented. He asserted that Great Zimbabwe, and the stone ruins throughout southern Africa, were a manifestation of megalithic antiquity transplanted at the beginning of the Christian era by "Judaized" Sabaean gold seekers, including "their Semitic relations based on Axum." They ruled in Rhodesia as overlords of a pre-Bantu Khoisan (Hottentot/Bushman) population in the mines. The Indian Ocean trade also introduced Indians and other Asian peoples, all subsumed in a "Caucasoid-Semito-Hamitic" cultural complex which, unlike Africans, built in stone, mined gold and developed large-scale agriculture and pastoralism to support the "cities" of Zimbabwe. For Gayre "blood," genes, and culture were conjoined and carried with them the inspiration of civilization. Here the spirit and method of Bent and Hall echo unmistakably. All the ingredients of the "antiquarian pastiche," as Mortimer Wheeler called it, the same evidence, the inferences and analogies, the ancient authorities, sixteenth, seventeenth and nineteenth century reports and speculations, philological excursions and linguistic equations, and loose comparisons of architecture and motifs—all were resurrected and reified as irrefutable. The massive walls, "phallic" tower, herringbone and chevron wall decorations, circular or oval ground plans, all were now designated megalithic, expressing one cultural complex from India to Stonehenge. "Such similarities cannot be fortuitous even if two thousand years were to separate them."[29]

Gayre returned as well to the "swamping" thesis of Bent and Hall, implicitly applying it to the contemporary independence struggle. The advent of the Bantu had brought about the decline and fall of Zimbabwe, not its rise—"the genetic or racial collapse of the Semitic strain and the accompanying economic and industrial decline, with all the weakness which from that ensues." Even if the Bantu had successfully adapted mining methods from outsiders, "why suppose that the direction throughout was other than that of former 'colonialists', whether Arabs, Abyssinians or Indians?. . . . If the Bantu learnt anything from these sources, it was as slaves."[30] Nor was there any oral tradition, said Gayre, to support the "pro-Bantuists." If the Bantu had really built Zimbabwe with its "mighty works," he demanded, why were they living in thatched huts ignorant of greatness when the European founders of Rhodesia arrived? Ethnologist Gayre relied for his answer upon the popular works of one Credo Vusamazulu Mutwa in South Africa, whom he claimed had definitively summarized "all the Bantu stories, legends and myths," categorically demonstrating that Zimbabwe was built "by white men who arrived before the Arabs."[31] Mutwa's academic reviewer, however, characterized his book as "neither a primary source of traditional history nor a piece of historical scholarship," but "a mixture of ethnic lore, . . . racist beliefs, and a political manifesto for 'Bantu' cultural revivalism" bearing the stamp of South African apartheid.[32]

Finally Gayre dismissed the "pro-Bantu School outright," relentlessly attacking both Summers and Garlake, as the victims of an obsession who "like amateurs with theories to justify" followed "with awe, the colossal errors of the foragers from abroad [here read Randall-MacIver and Caton-Thompson]."

"The obsession to prove a theory can become so great that, unconsciously, all evidence is twisted to justify the thesis."[33] Gayre's opponents could have applied this view equally to Gayre himself. Exotica flourished in the hothouse atmosphere of the beleaguered settler societies. The most interesting successor to Gayre came at the very end of the UDI period with the publication in South Africa of Cyril Hromnik's *Indo-Africa* (1981). Here the Erythrean ghost of Leo Frobenius seemed to rise anew, with his racial theme of African culture and civilization originating from Indian and Indonesian peoples. Hromnik's argument rested heavily upon linguistic claims asserting linguistic derivations of Indian words for mining, metallurgy and animal husbandry in Bantu and other African languages. For example, he gave the origin of *Mashona* as the ancient Pali Indian word for gold, *sona;* thus the country was *Sonabar* and Great Zimbabwe was *Sonakota*. Words for iron tools, stone buildings, musical instruments, food plants, and the humped Zebu-type cattle widespread from the Sudan to South Africa were supposed to illustrate this link. He claimed that the physical appearance of the Bantu, and Khoi as well, gave credence to Eastern genetic endowment, and the mining technology was that of south India in the first millennium B.C.[34]

Hromnik sought to demolish "Africanist" archaeology and history by pointing out that the assumption on which it was based, an equation of pottery sequences with the spread of Iron Age technology, was quite unproven. The whole Africanist argument, claimed Hromnik, was actually inspired by contemporary political ideology. At its heart was a convergence with African Nationalist liberation politics. "The African Iron Age theory does not rest on iron-evidence, and it ignores the abundance of historical and linguistic evidence" which proves that "iron technology was there before the arrival of the Negroids. . . . This Iron Age should be called . . . the Indian Iron Age in Africa."[35] To seal his thesis, Hromnik repeated and emphasized the prejudicial observations on African characteristics that had featured in the settler ethos and diffusionist argument since the founding of Rhodesia. These were "Negroid" conservativism and lack of "creativity," and the presumed meaninglessness to them of the ruins and artifacts. Thus the role of the Bantu after their arrival south of the Zambezi about the tenth century A.D., like the Khoi before them, had been to labor for colonial masters, as it was also in modern times. Echoing Gayre, Hromnick said that although they had learned to use copper and iron tools from their foreign employers they made no improvements and once left on their own had allowed the technology to deteriorate and vanish.[36]

Although it received considerable public notice, academic reviewers condemned Hromnik's reconstruction of the Zimbabwean mythology as at best methodologically naive, at worst "a racist tract." The *Journal of African History* accused him of "a reckless ignorance of what linguistic evidence is," perpetuating the essential premises, argument and logic of the old Bentian methodology: "there may have been a place for this kind of work in the nineteenth century. There is no place for it now." Christopher Ehret, whose own work on Bantu linguistics and historical anthropology Hromnik had sought to demolish, accused him of "racial determinism, pure and simple." "Hromnik's language evidence is bald-faced nonsense." It had demonstrated "not one plausible linkage between a word used in Africa and a word used in India." Ehret turned Hromnik's own imputations of ideological bias against him, concluding that "because it is politically useful in some quarters," *Indo-Africa* is "a dangerous travesty of scholarship."[37]

A Fresh Approach

Meanwhile a new generation of archaeologists and historians was developing a fresh approach. Criticizing their predecessors for preoccupation with who built the stone settlements to the neglect of why and how, they called for attention to questions of *social* change, rather than *population* change, thinking of cultural evolution as taking place within populations rather than postulating more or less dramatic migrations and invasions for every transition. Randall-MacIver and Caton-Thompson had thought of invasions by other Africans, or of penetration and influence by coastal aliens, to account for the rise and fall of Zimbabwe. Even Roger Summers and his colleagues had speculated on exotic inspiration and engineering techniques for the monumental buildings, and to violent invasions to explain their ruin. Indeed, as one surveys this history of contending interpretations, it becomes surprisingly apparent that both the diffusionists and the indigenists had hitherto assumed similar kinds of historical agents and dynamics of change. That is to say, both sides relied on the idea that culture change depended upon the movements of peoples defined by ethnic endowments of a racial-cultural character.

Perhaps we should rename the diffusionists "exotic-diffusionists," as their vision was fixed on agents of change exotic to Africa. The older "indigenists" we might now call "African-diffusionists," or "Intra-Africanists," because, as we have seen, their explanations rested mainly on a belief in African migrations of peoples and ideas, generally from the north. The protagonists of the new approach, however, (whom we shall continue to call "indigenists") argued that their ideas accorded more simply and directly with the evidence and accommodated more efficient explanations than the African-diffusionist one did. They disputed the idea that stylistic sequences in pottery or stone buildings, or the rise and fall of states, or even of the universally acknowledged major shift from the Early to the Later Iron Age in the eleventh century, were necessarily caused or governed by the appearance of new peoples. These considerations gave rise to a new view of Zimbabwe and its history: that the entire complex of stone ruins could and should be explained best in terms of its socio-economic context and cultural purposes. Ecology too, "the interplay of the community with its environment," was important to this view.[38] Thus an ecological collapse, the exhaustion of resources essential to its Iron Age subsistence economy and locally dense population, rather than the older notion of a "barbarian" invasion, came to be seen as the key to explaining Great Zimbabwe's abandonment just after its flourishing height in the mid-fifteenth century. This interpretation has been widely accepted in the historical literature.[39] Among historians, David N. Beach published in 1980 the most scholarly synthesis to date of these emerging revisionist views, *The Shona and Zimbabwe 900–1850*. In it he also incorporated Thomas Huffman's challenging if inconclusive suggestion of a southern origin for Shona society and culture in the Natal-Transvaal-Limpopo Valley region, attempting to balance it with the more conventional African-diffusionist model of migration from the north propounded most persuasively, as we have seen above, by Roland Oliver. In this respect, parenthetically, it is curious to observe both Beach and Hromnik, publishing at nearly the same time, employing to quite opposite ends the tantalizing, but still inconclusive, evidence of very early trade and metallurgy along the Limpopo River, the one indigenist, the other Indo-diffusionist.

The new view of Zimbabwe was spearheaded by Thomas Huffman and Peter Garlake, both, at first, archaeologists in the Rhodesian Government service. Garlake, scorned by Gayre as a "Bantuist" promoter of "insulting propaganda," had left his post in resistance to the official line. In a series of publications between 1970 and 1982, Garlake established the strongest argument for a thoroughly indigenist or, as he emphasized, "autochthonous" interpretation.[40] His major book, *Great Zimbabwe* in 1973, was tantamount to a rebuttal of Gayre. He also objected to Caton-Thompson's and Summers' ambivalence concerning the creative inspiration for the building of Great Zimbabwe and their shared attitude that it probably had lain beyond the capacity of the Shona to initiate or execute it unaided. Garlake's conclusion was uncompromising. "No," he wrote,

> Great Zimbabwe must be recognized for what it is . . . the product of two or three centuries of an indigenous stone-building technique, itself rooted in long traditions of using stone for field walls, building platforms and terraces. The structure reflects the economic dominance and prestige of a small oligarchy that had arisen within an Iron Age subsistence economy.

Thus, there could be no attribution of an alien hand in the conception or construction of Zimbabwe, nor in its functional purposes. Its founding elite had grown "out of the peasant stock."[41]

By the early 1980s Garlake had fully articulated his thesis of an autochthonous Zimbabwe civilization. The conventional findings of archaeology and linguistics, and the attempts of historians to synthesize diffusionist conclusions from them concerning its origins and evolution, were a rope of sand. The idea of distant African immigrants as the source of technological, economic, and societal change rested on evidence that did not support it. This uncertainty extended to the Early Iron Age, and even before that to the Late Stone Age. For example, the linguistic concept of a single proto-Bantu language as a phase in the development of Bantu peoples had been judged "a misleading oversimplification." Moreover, it "was no longer certain" from skeletal studies that Late Stone Age hunters and Early Iron Age farmers were racially different. And the analyses of Early Iron Age ceramics revealed "no coherent system of stylistic [or stratigraphic] relationships" that would demonstrate a convincing link between pottery change and new populations. There was no doubt that a great societal transformation took place at the beginning of the present millennium, but those changes, he believed, were far better explained by "economic rather than ethnic changes." To Garlake the external origin thesis was not needed.[42]

Garlake's point was that "All the differences between the Early and Later Iron Ages can be explained by changes in social organization, in particular a change from a matrilineal to a patrilineal system." This reflected a shift from an egalitarian subsistence agricultural society in which women, as cultivators, had held the dominant role, to one in which male occupations—"[m]etalworking, trading, war and herding"—grew dominant. With increasing inequalities of wealth and power, a stratified patrilineal society emerged. As for the problem of pottery changes, men had been the potters of the Early Iron Age, but in the new social conditions women had assumed this role, serving the needs of their households and therefore producing the simpler but more diverse ceramics of the Later Iron Age. He explicitly rejected the African-diffusionist view: it was "a situation so different from any existing north of the Zambezi that it is perverse to regard the Zimbabwe states as evidence of the diffusion of political institutions from the north."[43]

The new forms of society featured a shift of political focus from the farming villages to hilltop settlements, of which Great Zimbabwe was the first and largest, the prototype. All were dwellings of the Shona ruling class, "symbols of its power: political statements." The traditions of the Shona emphasized the religious role of founders and rulers, with Great Zimbabwe in the central position. Trade, too, had also made Great Zimbabwe's elite "a small but strong centralized authority" at the hub of a spreading network of subordinate zimbabwes contributing to its wealth by trade and tribute. Monumental building—the Great Enclosure complex begun in the fourteenth century—attested to the prestige, power and religious importance of the rulers who redistributed the wealth through the labor to build and maintain it. The social forces that explained these changes were, first, an increase in cattle herding, a "sign of status" and a "source of patronage" including bride wealth, which could be used as a powerful instrument of social control by the elite who distributed them to clients and allies. The second vital economic base was the trade in gold and other metals exchanged for prestige goods symbolic of rank and power for this small elite. Gold mining was "probably a communal and seasonal affair conducted by . . . agricultural villagers" induced by "exchange of state cattle for gold."[44]

Garlake estimated a surprisingly small population at Great Zimbabwe at its height, numbering 1,000–2,500 all told, with 100–200 forming the elite in the stone enclosures of hill and valley. Similarly small numbers, 750 in all, occupied the fifty or so subordinate or "provincial" centers active at any one time across the plateau. The labor to build the Great Enclosure wall was likewise modest: only 400 laborers, he calculated, working fifty days a year during off-time in the agricultural cycle, could have completed the edifice in four years! But this was, he said, a large population for an Iron Age settlement concentrated in one place for a century or more at its height between 1300 and 1450. By then its growth under such limitations made it "unwieldy" and vulnerable to environmental, economic or political crisis.[45] Later excavations revealed a far greater settlement of up to 18,000 people, which makes this point, especially its environmental implications, even more compelling.[46] Ecologically vulnerable, Great Zimbabwe must eventually have exhausted its available soil, grazing, game and timber. Food shortages coupled with economic or political disruption would precipitate a social crisis. By the mid to late fifteenth century these conditions appeared. "Dispersal" ensued, including a political breakup, and Great Zimbabwe swiftly lost its fragile eminence, reverting to "a place of great religious significance particularly favored by Mwari and the ancestors,"[47] as indeed it still was a generation before Karl Mauch came upon it in 1870.

Garlake was convinced that his interpretation offered an alternative "in at least as good agreement with the existing archaeological evidence as any migration theory and a great deal simpler and more economic." Most importantly, it presented the distant past in terms of historical and social analysis, so that the Iron Age and Great Zimbabwe could be seen as "an integral part of Zimbabwean history, part of a continuous process."[48] He saw its greatest value in this historical dimension; he wished to lay the ghosts of mythical Zimbabwe, of Sheba and Solomon, of Semites and Hamites, of alien inspiration and origin to rest. His purpose was to link the African present validly with the African past, especially for the Shona people, and to reclaim the reality of Great Zimbabwe for an African historical consciousness that would serve the new Zimbabwe, then emerging to independence with the end of the UDI war.

A New Stage

The end of the nationalist struggle for Rhodesia/Zimbabwe ushered in a new stage in the Great Zimbabwe "Question." Subsequent scholarship tended toward convergence and a blending of perspectives as the myth of alien origin or control lost its most powerful advocacy and political sustenance. Who built Great Zimbabwe was no longer the issue, but the questions of the stimulus to build, of why and to what purpose, and the nature of its society, continued to exercise the imagination of speculators and the ingenuity of researchers. External influence remained an issue, of course, but in terms of African initiatives within the context of their own history and cultural tradition. One might have expected that the "battle of the myths" would swiftly end, but this was not quite so, for new versions of the older traditions persisted.

A diffusionist reprise came with a "New Solution" for *The Mystery of the Great Zimbabwe* by Wilfred Mallows in 1984. It was, however, a reprise with a difference. He rejected the question, "African or foreign," as "too simple . . . to reflect reality." "We have streams of theory but very few facts," he averred, and proceeded to contribute his own speculation to the stream. Mallows considered Garlake's description of the ruins "definitive," but rejected "the canonical exclusion of any foreign influence whatever." Africans had built them all right, and controlled them, but had done so—and also mined the gold—with technical skills derived from India and in response to economic stimulus from the Persian gulf.[49]

An architect by profession, Mallows sought to deduce the origin and purpose of Zimbabwe from the logic, the "code" or "signature" of its design. He saw "a straightforward piece of military planning" in the "Hill Fort," although he had to admit that this fort was in fact indefensible because its highest point, on the easily approached northwest side, had no defensive walling! But the real "mystery" was the Great Enclosure in the valley below. Why so different, bigger, better than any others anywhere else? Its sheer size was its mystery. To Mallows it had been built without "the great religious compulsions" of ancient monumental structures elsewhere. Rather, it gave the unmistakable impression of a stronghold, but one to keep people *in*, not out. It was a prison. Here was Mallows' contribution: Great Zimbabwe was both a treasure house and the assembly point for a massive slave trade. Carriers of gold, iron and ivory to Sofala, these slaves were then sent to the east.[50]

Mallows followed the familiar lines of the Indian Ocean diffusionist tradition, despite the Later Iron Age dating for Zimbabwe: With the end of Meroë and the decline of their own mines at home, Indians had opened the Sofala trade. The "Islamic explosion" of the seventh century enormously stimulated this gold trade. Then the eighth century rise of Abassid power at Baghdad caused a vast need for labor in the plantations of the Mesopotamian delta, where some 300,000 "Zanj" (East African) slaves were sent in the ninth century. In Mallows' scheme, the Great Enclosure had been built for this trade by its African overlords, 400 years before the date allowed by the archaeologists.[51] It was an intriguing, but essentially specious, interpretation.

Meanwhile, Thomas Huffman carried to its logical conclusion his and Garlake's emphasis on Shona cultural tradition as the central thesis for explaining Great Zimbabwe. His persuasive essay, *Symbols in Stone: Unravelling the Mystery of Great Zimbabwe* (1987), elucidated the wholly indigenous nature of the buildings whose purposes and functions could be entirely explained by Shona cultural themes and were in keeping with the behavior of their ruling class. As his title indicated, Zimbabwe architecture and the objects within it were symbolic representations. Thus, the hilltop structure was the royal residence of a "sacred king," whose rituals of seclusion, fertility and the agricultural cycle, protection, and sustenance of the people, and communication with God and ancestors were identifiable in the various spaces and enclosures of the hill complex. For example, the stone monoliths found there were "the horns of Mambo," the spears and army with which, like a bull, he protected his people. The round stone towers on the walls were symbolic grain bins. The famed soapstone birds represented the royal ancestors and their role as messengers of God since, to the Shona, birds, especially the eagle, are messengers or symbols of the spirits as they mount to the heavens. The crocodiles and diamond patterns inscribed on beams and monoliths symbolized the Shona rulers themselves, fearless, dangerous, wise, connected with water and rainmaking.[52] The Great Enclosure and the complex of associated structures in the valley below housed the royal wives and their families. More monoliths, carved birds, and crocodiles found near the Great Enclosure indicated the need for the king to go there to invoke the ancestors of the *vahosi*, his "great" wife, who had control of the complex including the royal farms and grain stores, treasure-keeping, and procreation. In this last respect, Huffman interpreted the Great Enclosure as a premarital initiation school, "the domain of women." Again, for Huffman the symbolism of the Shona explains its design and decorative features as, for example, representations of young men's virility (the double chevron "snake of fertility" on the great outer wall), of the king's or senior male's functions (the great conical tower or grainbin symbol, decorated with the dentelle pattern meaning "crocodile"), of the king's senior sister who kept ritual charms in a special grain bin (the small conical tower), and of the young married women (the zebra pattern of dark stone bands on inner walls).[53] These and other symbolic representations suggested by Huffman formed a compelling interpretation that contrasted persuasively with the far-fetched fancies of the exotic-diffusionists.

Nearly every speculation on Great Zimbabwe had invoked the value of oral traditions, though few had employed them or even identified them objectively. Exotic-diffusionists from Hall to Gayre had scoffed at the thought that African tradition would support the claims of the indigenists. Few of the earlier disputants on either side had seemed to pay serious attention to the memory of the Shona themselves. In view of this, one is all the more struck by the prescience of one early investigator who did pay attention, the Reverend Samuel Dornan, whose conclusions reported in 1915 prefigured the general outline of later arguments for African origin. Skeptical of Bent and Hall, he had examined the ruins for himself and judged them, in style and method of construction, to be consistent with other buildings done within living memory and observed by others such as the hunter Frederick Courtney Selous before Rhodes's colonization. Their purpose as centers for residence, defense and the religious rituals of Shona chiefs was confirmed by "native tradition" explained to him by African informants. "The foreign influence theory must be given up," said Dornan, "Zimbabwe was built by natives, and recently abandoned, probably not more than 300 years ago . . . I cannot see what is to be gained by refusing to the forefathers of the present Makaranga tribes . . . the very moderate degree of skill and patience needed to erect them."[54] In its particulars, Dornan's findings differed from recent ones, but in spirit his report rings true to current interpretation and anticipated the major arguments of nearly every subsequent critic of the "Bentian" tradition. What a pity that such down-to-earth judgment and restrained reportage from direct experience and local familiarity was to be obscured in popular discourse by two generations and more of exotic preoccupations. We have seen, of course, what was to be gained in the political and ideological interest that underlay this obscurantism.

With Zimbabwean independence, as we have seen, this picture was changing. Huffman, Garlake and others deployed the traditions of the Shona with salutary effect. But the absence of the contemporary African voice had been noteworthy in almost all of these transactions. Garlake had called for that voice to be heard against the colonialist "cultural aggression" obscuring the Zimbabwean heritage. He also feared, however, that a "new emphasis on ethnic origins" and history as "a succession of migrations" would make Africans' new image of Great Zimbabwe simply "a mirror image of the settlers' own distortions."[55] This was vividly illustrated by controversy surrounding the first African Director of Museums and Monuments, Ken Mufuka. Mufuka seemed to impart a reverse racism to the Zimbabwe question by announcing as he took office that white scholars had no place in its interpretation and only blacks would have the final say. He went on to publish his own final say, defining "the bulk of European scholarship" as a conspiracy to accept Bent and Hall and reject Randall-MacIver and Caton-Thompson. Garlake quite rightly protested that this was "simply untrue" and could only be asserted in ignorance or calculated denial of the last 50 years of research and reputable publication. Mufuka dismissed Garlake as a promoter of European theories of social stratification and class conflict inappropriate to Africa, and depicted the classical Great Zimbabwe as a "golden age" of "outrageous delight" and carefree indulgence marked by the African genius for happiness and enlightened by classless unity under a king who embodied "socialistic spirit at its best" by providing food "for all the hangers-on at his court." An outraged Garlake condemned "this nonsense" as "another example of the racist cult history which Great Zimbabwe has always inspired."[56] What a bitter irony it seemed, as political, personal, and scholarly confrontation at the extremes bedeviled the popular understanding of Zimbabwe even beyond the time of settler history.

In conclusion, the view of Martin Hall, a widely respected South African archaeologist and prehistorian at the University of Cape Town, offers a generous perspective on this contretemps. Surveying Iron Age studies in southern Africa, he points out that the political-ideological dominance of the white settler ethos, its economy and the segregationist system that served it, had shaped and controlled access to knowledge of the past to its own advantage. Except for a recent few, professional archaeologists generally had been reluctant or unable publicly to challenge this domination. Thus the new Iron Age synthesis emerging since the 1970s remained esoteric, while "fringe" writing such as Mallows' and Hromnik's "continued to resurrect the old nineteenth century myths," which found their way into school curricula with official blessing. The result was that the true precolonial past remained a "Hidden History" to the new generation of Africans and their leaders. Although well aware of Great Zimbabwe as a symbol of past achievement and present aspiration, African nationalists and Black Consciousness leaders promoted uninformed "utopian" visions of the past. With archaeology aligned in the popular view with white domination, Mufuka's attitude was an understandable if unfortunate one.[57] Thus may history be hostage to interest, error and ideology in each generation.

In this account we have seen how the legacy of plundering and destruction at the hands of the first Rhodesian colonizers, together with the partial views of prejudiced investigators, impoverished the evidence that might have resolved the "mystery" of Great Zimbabwe. But in the absence of the kinds of evidence that characterize the subjects of classical archeology such as inscriptions and other remains of literate civilization, Zimbabwe might well have remained significantly enigmatic in any case.

Nonetheless, as we have also seen, the ingenuity and cumulative efforts at recovery and interpretation by generations of scientific diggers and scholars have produced a picture of the Great Zimbabwe's history which at present appears to be a broadly reliable and persuasive one. Recently, new investigations as well as planning for accurate restoration of Great Zimbabwe have been underway, intended to make more accessible to the public a better understanding of its past.[58]

Notes

1. Peter Garlake, *Great Zimbabwe* (London: Thames and Hudson 1973), 11; cf. David Chanaiwa, *The Zimbabwe Controversy: A Case of Colonial Historiography* (Syracuse, NY: Program of Eastern African Studies, Syracuse University, 1973, mimeograph), 2, n. 2, and Roger Summers, *Ancient Ruins and Vanished Civilzations of Southern Africa* (Capetown: T.V. Bulpin, 1971), 2–3.

2. Gertrude Caton-Thompson, *The Zimbabwe Culture; Ruins and Reactions,* 2nd ed. (London: Cass, 1971), 86. Quoted in Chanaiwa, *Controversy,* 49.

3. Edwin Wilfrid Nassau Mallows, *The Mystery of The Great Zimbabwe: A New Solution* (New York: Norton, 1984), 39, 41, 56.

4. Chanaiwa's term, to distinguish a local African origin of Zimbabwe from "evolutionary historical development" in Africa generally, *Controversy,* 3, n. 4.

5. Carl Mauch, *The Journals of Carl Mauch: His Travels in the Transvaal and Rhodesia 1869–1872,* F. O. Bernhard, E. E. Burke, ed. (Salisbury: National Archives at Rhodesia, 1969), 140–42, 184, 190–91, 215–16, 265–69; F. O. Bernard, *Karl Mauch, African Explorer* (Capetown: C. Struik, 1971), 26, 113, 116–19, 123–27, 237–39. cf. Roger Summers, *Zimbabwe: A Rhodesian Mystery* (Johannesburg & London: Nelson, 1963), 6–12, 17–19.

6. Scott T. Carroll, "Solomonic Legend: The Muslims and the Great Zimbabwe," *The International Journal of African Historical Studies* 21 no. 2 (1988): 233–47.

7. George Macaulay Theal, ed. & comp., *Records of South Eastern Africa* 9 vols. (Cape Town: C. Struik, 1898–1903); Chanaiwa, 86–87; Garlake, 65–66.

8. James Theodore Bent, *The Ruined Cities of Mashonaland, Being a Record of Excavation and Exploration in 1891* (London: Longmans, Green, 1893), 42; quoted in Chanaiwa, 108. Bent summarized his findings in a paper at the Anthropological Institute of Great Britain, "On the Finds at the Great Zimbabwe Ruins (with a View to Elucidating the Origin of the Race that Built Them)," *Journal of the Anthropological Institute* (1892–93): 124–36; cf. Summers, *Mystery,* 19–23; Garlake, *Great Zimbabwe,* 66–68.

9. Quoted in Chanaiwa, 109.

10. John E. Schofield, "Zimbawe: 'The Ancient Ruins Company, Limited,'"

Man 22 (February 1935): 19–20. Chanaiwa, 98–100; Summers, *Mystery,* 24–25; Garlake, *Great Zimbabwe,* 65–71.

11. Chanaiwa, 80–81, 110–14; Summers, *Mystery,* 25–28; Garlake, *Great Zimbabwe,* 71–75; cf. Richard N. Hall, "The Great Zimbabwe and Other Ancient Ruins in Rhodesia," *GJ* 25 (Jan.–June 1905): 405–14; and review of R. N. Hall and W. G. Neal, *The Ancient Ruins of Rhodesia, GJ* 19 (Jan.–June 1902): 495–98.

12. Chanaiwa, 3–6, 81–97. R. N. Hall, *Prehistoric Rhodesia* (London: T. F. Unwin, 1909), 400, quoted in Chanaiwa, 5.

13. David Randall-MacIver, *Medieval Rhodesia* (London: Macmillan, 1906), quoted in Summers, *Mystery,* 37, and Chanaiwa, 117; cf. David Randall-MacIver, "The Rhodesia Ruins: Their Probable Origin and Significance," *GJ* 27 no. 4 (April 1906): 325–36, and discussion, including Hall's remarks, 336–47. In general, see Garlake, *Great Zimbabwe,* 76–78; Summers, *Mystery,* 32–37.

14. Chanaiwa, 79, 113; Garlake, *Great Zimbabwe,* 78–80.

15. E. G. John Schofield, "Zimbabwe, A Cultural Examination of the Building Methods Employed," *South African Journal of Science* 23 (Dec. 1926): 971–86; The Rev. Samuel Dornan, "Rhodesian Ruins and Native Tradition," *South African Journal of Science* 12 (1915): 502–16; Summers, *Mystery,* 41–45; Chanaiwa, 118–20.

16. Gertrude Caton-Thompson, "The Southern Rhodesian Ruins. Recent Archaeological Investigations," *Nature* 124 (Oct. 1929): 619–21 (her preliminary report), and *The Zimbabwe Culture: Ruins and Reactions* (Oxford: Clarendon Press, 1931). See also Summers, *Mystery,* 45–48; Chanaiwa, 120–23; Garlake, *Great Zimbabwe,* 80–83; and review of Caton-Thompson's *Zimbabwe Culture* by H. J. Braunholz, *GJ* 79 (Jan.–June 1939): 323–25.

17. Edith Sanders, "The Hamitic Hypothesis: Its Origin and Functions in Time Perspective," *JAH* 10 no. 4 (1969): 521–32.

18. C. G. Seligman, *Races of Africa,* 3rd ed. (London: Oxford University Press, 1957), 85–141; see also *Pagan Tribes of the Nilotic Sudan* (London: G. Routledge & Sons, 1932), 3–5; cf. Chanaiwa, 76–77.

19. Leo Frobenius, *Erythräa, Länder und Zeiten des Heiligen Königsmordes* (Berlin: Atlantis Verlag, 1931); unpublished English tr. by Karsten & Eleanor Staplefeldt, "Erythrea, Land and Times of the Sacred Regicide, or, the Moon King Civilization." H. A. Wieschoff, an associate of Frobenius, later concluded that the sacred kingships common all over East Africa, and Zimbabwe itself, were of purely African origin; Summers, *Mystery,* 67–70, *Vanished Civilizations,* 221–22.

20. Mallows, 77.

21. Roland Oliver, *The African Experience* (London: Pimlico; New York: Icon Editions, 1991), 41–42; cf. Roland Oliver and J. D. Fage, *A Short History of Africa,* 6th ed. (London: Penguin Books, 1988), chap. 4.

22. Roland Oliver, "The Nilotic Contribution to Bantu Africa," *JAH* 23 (1982): 433–34, 439, 440–42; *African Experience,* 111–13, 115. Some scholars saw common stone-building techniques and patterned walling throughout Africa

from the Maghreb and Mauretania (Tichitt) through Nigeria to southern Africa. James Walton, "Patterned Walling in African Folk Building," *JAH* 1 (1960): 19–30, attributed it to the Berbers.

23. *Zimbabwe, A Rhodesian Mystery* (Johannesburg & London: Nelson, 1963), *Ancient Ruins and Vanished Civilizations of Southern Africa* (Cape Town: T. V. Bulpin, 1971).

24. Summers, *Mystery* passim; quotes from 107.

25. Roger Summers, Keith R. Robinson and Anthony Whitty, "Zimbabwe Excavations, 1958," *Occasional Papers of the National Museums of Southern Rhodesia* 3 (1961): 159–92; and review by Frank Willet, *JAH* 5 no. 2 (1964): 312–14; Summers, *Mystery,* chap. 8 passim. See summary in T. N. Huffman, "The Rise and Fall of Zimbabwe," *JAH* 13 no. 3 (1972): 353–66; cf. Garlake, *Great Zimbabwe,* 84–110.

26. Summers, *Mystery,* 35, 39; *Vanished Civilizations,* xix, 221–23.

27. Summers, *Vanished Civilizations,* xix; *Mystery,* 54, 75, 83, 90, 104–6; Garlake, *Great Zimbabwe,* 201–2. See also reviews of Summers, *Ancient Mining in Rhodesia* (Salisbury: Trustees of the National Museums of Rhodesia 1969) by Brian Fagan, *JAH* 2 (1970): 449–50, and Andrew Roberts, *African Social Research* 10 (1970): 791. Caton-Thompson's 1931 *Ruins and Reactions* also reappeared in a second edition in 1971.

28. Julie Frederickse, *None But Ourselves: Masses vs. Media in The Making of Zimbabwe* (Harmondsworth: Penguin Books, 1982), 10–12; cf. Garlake, *Great Zimbabwe,* 209–10.

29. R. Gayre, *The Origin of the Zimbabwean Civilization* (Salisbury: Galaxie Press 1972), 72, chaps. 5, 11. For Mortimer Wheeler: "General Editor's Preface," see Garlake, *Great Zimbabwe,* 7.

30. Gayre, 202, 215 and chap. 18 passim.

31. Gayre, 214.

32. Pierre Van Den Berghe, review of *My People, My Africa,* by Credo Vusamazulu Mutwa, *Journal of Asian and African Studies* 7 (1972): 140–41.

33. Gayre, 220–21 and chap. 20 passim.

34. Cyril A. Hromnik, *Indo-Africa. Towards a New Understanding of the History of Sub-Saharan Africa* (Cape Town: Juta, 1981), chaps. 4, 5, 6, 9, passim.

35. Hromnik, xiii-xiv, chap. 1 passim, 58–60, 81–83, 108–11.

36. Hromnik, 130–34.

37. C. A. Ownby, "The Indian Rope Trick," review, *JAH* 23 (1981): 415–16. Christopher Ehret, review, *IJAHS* 15 no. 3 (1982): 548–50.

38. Peter Garlake, "Prehistory and Ideology in Zimbabwe," *Africa* 52 no. 3 (1982): 1–19 (quotation from p. 11).

39. E.g. D. N. Beach, *The Shona and Zimbabwe 900–1850, An Outline of Shona History* (New York: African Pub. Co., 1980), 19–21, 46–47, 50–51; Graham Connah, *African Civilizations: Precolonial Cities and States in Tropical Africa: An Archaeological Perspective* (Cambridge: Cambridge University Press,

1987), chap. 8: "A Question of Economic Basis: Great Zimbabwe and Related Sites," 185–88, 207–9, 213; Ralph Austen, *African Economic History* (London: J. Currey; Portsmouth, NH: Heinemann, 1987), 73–74.

40. Peter Garlake, "Rhodesian Ruins—Preliminary Assessment of Their Styles and Chronology," *JAH* 9 no. 4 (1970): 495–513; *Great Zimbabwe* (London: Thames and Hudson, 1973); "Early States in Africa," Andrew Sherratt, ed., *The Cambridge Encyclopedia of Archaeology* (New York: Cambridge University Press, 1980), chap. 53, 348–54; "Prehistory and Ideology in Zimbabwe," *Africa* 52.3 (1982), 1–19. This was the most important statement of his argument.

41. Garlake, *Great Zimbabwe*, 183, 201–2.

42. Garlake, "Prehistory and Ideology," 5–9; "Early States," 352. See also his review of *The Later Prehistory of Eastern and Southern Africa*, by D. W. Phillipson, *JAH* 20 no. 3 (1979): 457–62.

43. Garlake, "Prehistory and Ideology," 13; "Early States," 353.

44. Garlake, "Early States," 353; *Great Zimbabwe*, 193. See also R. D. Penhallurick, *Tin in Antiquity* (London: Institute of Metals, 1986), 10–11, for work on metallurgy in Transvaal and Zimbabwe supportive of the indigenist position, but relating it to Nigerian origins of the Sub-Saharan Iron Age. I am obliged to Professor Yamauchi for this reference.

45. Garlake, *Great Zimbabwe*, 195–96.

46. T. N. Huffman, *Symbols in Stone: Unravelling the Mystery of Great Zimbabwe* (Johannesburg: Witwatersrand University Press, 1987), 1; Beach, *Shona and Zimbabwe*, 50–51.

47. Garlake, *Great Zimbabwe*, 200.

48. Garlake, "Prehistory and Ideology," 14.

49. Wilfrid Mallows, *The Mystery of the Great Zimbabwe. A New Solution* (New York: Norton; London: Hale, 1984), xv, 78–79.

50. Mallows, xv, 17–29, 31, 39, 44, 56, 84–88, 92–96.

51. Mallows, 104–18, 132–33.

52. Huffman, *Symbols*, 6–11, 14–18; cf. "Expressive Space in the Zimbabwe Culture," *MAN*, n.s., 19, no. 4 (Dec. 1984), 593–612.

53. Huffman, *Symbols*, 27–29, 37, 40–41; "Expressive Space," passim.

54. Rev. Samuel S. Dornan, "Rhodesian Ruins and Native Tradition," *South African Journal of Science* 12 (1915): 502–16, esp. 503–4, 507, 516.

55. Garlake, "Prehistory and Ideology," 14–15.

56. Garlake, "Ken Mufuka and Great Zimbabwe," *Antiquity* 58 (1984): 121–23.

57. Martin Hall, "'Hidden History': Iron Age Archaeology in Southern Africa," in *A History of African Archaeology*, Peter Robertshaw, ed. (London: J. Currey; Portsmouth, NH: Heinemann, 1990), chap. 4, 59–77. For an evaluation of Hall's thesis in the context of the "New Archaeology" generally, see Bruce G. Trigger's conclusion to this volume, chap. 18. See also Martin Hall's fine

popular pre-and early history of southern Africa, *Farmers, Kings and Traders: The People of Southern Africa, 200–1860* (Chicago: University of Chicago Press, 1990). Chaps. 8 and 9 focus on Zimbabwe and Great Zimbabwe.

58. Webber Ndoro, "Great Zimbabwe," *Scientific American* 277, no. 5 (Nov. 1997): 94–99.

List of Contributors

William Y. Adams is Professor of Anthropology at the University of Kentucky, and former chair of the department. He directed excavations for the Sudan Government Antiquities Service, and coordinated the activities of 14 other expeditions. He was the director of the excavations at Kulubnarti and at Qasr Ibrim. He is on the boards of the American Research Center in Egypt, the Sudan Studies Association, and the International Society for Nubian Studies. He is the author of *Nubia: Corridor to Africa*, recipient of the Melvill J. Herskovits Award of the African Studies Association. He has also authored *Ceramic Industries of Medieval Nubia* and *Meroitic of North and South*. He has contributed chapters to *The Archaeological Map of the Sudan*, *Ägypten und Kusch*, and *Africa in Antiquity* and articles to *Archaeology*, *Journal of Egyptian Archaeology*, *Orientalia*, and *World Archaeology*.

Kathryn A. Bard is Associate Professor in the Department of Archaeology, Boston University. She is co-director with Rodolfo Fattovich of the I.U.O./B.U. excavations at Bieta Giyorgis (Aksum, Ethiopia), where they have been conducting fieldwork since 1993. Her research interests include the orgin of complex society and the state in northeast Africa. She has published *From Farmer to Pharaohs: Mortuary Evidence for the Rise of Complex Society in Egypt*. With Fattovich she has published articles on their field work in *Nyame Akuma*, *Rassegna di Studi Etiopici*, *Annales d'Éthiopie*, and *Journal of Field Archaeology*. She is also the editor of *The Environmental and Cultural History of Aksum: Preliminary Report*.

Reuben G. Bullard is Professor of Geology & Archaeology at Cincinnati Bible College & Seminary and Lecturer in Biblical Archaeology & Environmental Geology in the College of Continuing Education, University of Cincinnati. He has served as a consultant in Archaeological Geology for excavations of the American Schools of Oriental Research in Israel, Jordan, and Cyprus, and as a staff geologist at the excavations at Carthage.

He has contributed chapters to the *University of Michigan (Carthage) Excavation Report* and a chapter on "Sedimentary Environments" in *Archaeological Geology*, as well as articles to the *Andrews University Seminary Studies*, *Biblical Archaeologist*, and *Seminary Review*.

Stanley M. Burstein is Professor of History at California State University at Los Angeles, and has been President of the Association of Ancient Historians. He is the author of *Outpost of Hellenism: The Emergence of Heraclea on the Black Sea* and of *The Babyloniaca of Berossus*. He has translated Agatharcides of Cnidus, *On the Erythrean Sea*, and has edited, *Panhellenica*, and *The Hellenistic Age from the Battle of Ipsos to the Death of Kleopatra VII*. He has contributed articles on Meroe in *Zeitschrift für ägyptische Sprache und Altertumskunde*, *Meroitica*, *Journal for the American Research Center*, and *Beiträge zur Sudanforschung*.

Rodolfo Fattovich is Professor of Ethiopian Archaeology and Egyptology at the Istituto Universitario Orientale, Naples. He was the director of the Gash Delta Archaeological Project (Kassala, Sudan) and of the expedition of the Centro Studi e Ricerche Ligabue in the East Nile Delta, and is co-director with Kathryn A. Bard of the I.U.O./B.U. Joint Expedition at Aksum, Ethiopia. He is the author of *Materiali per lo studio della ceramica preaksumita etiopica*, and *Lineamenti per la storia dell'archeologia dell'Etiopie e Somalia*. He has contributed to the *Rassegna di Studi Etiopici*, *Ethiopian Studies*, *Nubica*, *Archéologie du Nil Moyen*, *Egypt and Africa*, and *A History of African Archaeology*. He has received the Giorgio Maria Sangiorgi Award of the Accademia dei Lincei (Rome) for African Archaeology.

Carleton T. Hodge was Emeritus Professor of Linguistics and Anthropology at Indiana University, and the former director of its Intensive Language Training Center. He was the editor of the I.U. African Series and the associate editor of *African Languages Review*. He also served as Professor of Linguistics at the Foreign Service Institute and as the editor of its basic course series. He is the author of *An Outline of Hausa Grammar* and the editor of *Afroasiatic: A Survey*. He contributed chapters to: *Current Issues in Linguistic Theory*, *Discussions in Egyptology*, *Essays in Historical Linguistics*, *Genetic Classification of Languages Symposium*, *Papers in Linguistics*, *Rhetorica/Phonologica/Syntactica*, *Semitic and Egyptian Studies*, and *Trends in Limnguistics* and articles to: *Anthropological Linguistics*, *International Journal of American Linguistics*, *Jewish Quarterly*

Review, and *Language.* (Professor Hodge passed away on 8 September 1998.)

Edna R. Russmann is a Curator in the Department of Egyptian, Classical, and Ancient Middle Eastern Art, Brooklyn Museum of Art. She is the author of *The Representation of the King in the XXVth Dynasty* and of *Egyptian Sculpture: Cairo and Luxor,* as well as numerous articles about Egyptian art and the Kushite period. She is also the principal author of *Eternal Egypt: Masterworks of Art from the British Museum.*

Frank M. Snowden, Jr. is Professor of Classics & Department Chair Emeritus at Howard University, where he also served as the Dean of the College of Liberal Arts. He has served as a member of the U.S. delegation to UNESCO in Paris, and as a cultural attaché of the American Embassy in Rome. He is the author of *Blacks in Antiquity,* which received the Charles J. Goodwin Award of Merit from the American Philological Association and of *Before Color Prejudice: The Ancient View of Blacks,* and is the co-author of *The Image of the Black in Western Art I: From the Pharaohs to the Fall of the Roman Empire.* He has contributed a chapter to: *The African Diaspora,* and articles to: *American Anthropologist, American Journal of Philology, L'Antiquité Classique, Arethusa, Biblical Archaeology Review, The Numismatic Chronicle of the Royal Numismatic Society,* and *Traditio.*

Maynard W. Swanson was Professor of History at Miami University. He was formerly on the faculty at Yale University, and served as a visiting professor at the University of Natal. He is the author of *The Views of Mahlathi: Writings of a Black South African.* He contributed articles to: *African Studies, Journal of African History, Journal of Natal and Zulu History, International Journal of African Historical Studies,* and *Natalia.* (Professor Swanson passed away on 16 July 1995.)

Donald White is Curator of the Mediterranean Section of the University Museum of the University of Pennsylvania. He has served as the director of the Marsa Matruh Expedition, Egypt, and of the Expedition to Cyrene in Libya, as well as co-director of the Expedition to Apollonia, Libya. He has also excavated at Morgantina, Sicily. He is the author of *The Extramural Sancutary of Demeter and Persephone at Cyrene, Libya* and the co-author of *Apollonia, The Port of Cyrene.* He has contributed articles to the

American Journal of Archaeology, Antike Kunst, Expedition, Journal of the American Research Center in Egypt, Libya Antiqua, Libyan Studies, and *Quaderni di archeologia della Libia.*

Edwin M. Yamauchi is Professor of History at Miami University. He has authored *Foes from the Northern Frontier, Greece and Babylon, Persia and the Bible, Pre-Christian Gnosticism, The World of the First Christians,* and *New Testament Cities in Western Asia Minor.* He has contributed chapters to: *Orient and Occident, Études Mithriaques, The Bible World,* and *Studies in Gnosticism and Hellenistic Religions,* and articles to: *Berytus, Biblical Archaeologist, Church History, Journal of Near Eastern Studies, Journal of the American Academy of Religion, Journal of Biblical Literature, Journal of the American Oriental Society, Near East Archaeological Society Bulletin, Vetus Testamentum,* and *Zeitschrift für die alttestamentliche Wissenschaft.*

Frank Yurco is Consultant on Egyptology at the Field Museum of Natural History, Chicago, and an instructor for the Oriental Institute's Adult Education Program. He has served as an epigrapher of the Oriental Institute's survey in Luxor, Egypt. He is an authority on Pharaoh Merenptah of the late nineteenth Egyptian Dynasty. He has contributed to *Scenes and Inscriptions in . . . the Temple of Khonsu* and to *Battle Reliefs of King Sety I,* and written articles for *Biblical Archaeology Review, Dossiers Histoire et Archéologique, The Field Museum Bulletin, Journal of the American Research Center in Egypt, Metropolitan Museum of Art Journal, Serapis,* and *Society for the Study of Egyptian Antiquaries Journal.*